The Legacy
of the Goddess

The Legacy of the Goddess

*Heroines, Warriors and Witches
from World Mythology
to Folktales and Fairy Tales*

RACHEL S. MCCOPPIN

McFarland & Company, Inc., Publishers
Jefferson, North Carolina

ISBN (print) 978-1-4766-9095-7
ISBN (ebook) 978-1-4766-4934-4

LIBRARY OF CONGRESS AND BRITISH LIBRARY
CATALOGUING DATA ARE AVAILABLE

Library of Congress Control Number 2023006629

Front cover: Baba Yaga, the witch from Slavic folklore.
(Shutterstock/Natalia Mikhalchuk)

Printed in the United States of America

*McFarland & Company, Inc., Publishers
Box 611, Jefferson, North Carolina 28640
www.mcfarlandpub.com*

To
Season and Landon

Contents

Preface 1

Introduction 3

1. Mother Nature, Animal Brides, and Mistresses of Animals 11

2. Wise Old Women 39

3. Maidens and Otherworldly Women 69

4. Monstrous and Ghost Women 97

5. Defiant Women and Women Warriors 126

6. Heroines on Their Own Quests 155

7. Mothers and Stepmothers 183

8. Witches 211

Conclusion 243

Bibliography 247

Index 253

Preface

Most people within a culture know their own folktales and fairy tales. In fact, often folktales and fairy tales are known as well as, or better than, religious doctrine or political history. Books, films, plays, and even advertisements often portray the figures from folktales and fairy tales; therefore, people tend to intimately know the archetypes found within their culture's folktales and fairy tales: the brave hero, the wicked stepmother, the prized maiden, the witch, etc. Sometimes, people even classify the people they meet, value the lessons they learn, or hold their own lives accountable according to the standards set forth in folktales and fairy tales.

Many people acknowledge that a culture's myths are the sacred, religious stories of bygone eras, but feel that folktales and fairy tales are more for entertainment and amusement. Many also assume that the female characters found within folktales and fairy tales are mere stereotypes, who mostly serve as victims in need of rescue, boring one-dimensional princesses, or egotistical and conniving villains. However, this book will argue that folktales and fairy tales often carry elements that are similar to the sacred mythological narratives of many ancient societies, especially the tenets that are associated with the female characters within folktales and fairy tales. Goddesses were once worshipped in most cultures around the globe; they were revered as strong, formidable, benevolent or malevolent, and even at times as leaders of divine pantheons. If one looks more closely at the myriad female characters within global folktales and fairy tales, one can oftentimes see a connection between them and the goddesses of many mythic narratives, as many folktale and fairy tale women serve in powerful roles, such as brides who can transform into animals; wise old women who live alone in the deep wilderness; maidens who are also warriors; and witches who can command the elements of nature. In contemplating this revised analysis of many female characters within global folktales and fairy tales, audiences can see that the goddesses of mythology have never truly been forgotten.

It is important to understand that when some mythic elements

1

became modified within folktales and fairy tales, vital information regarding female characters often became altered or denigrated; however, this book argues that despite this, the many formidable females that remain in global folktales and fairy tales still hold elements related to traditional religious belief systems that revered goddesses and sacred women. While this book will attempt to connect folkloric and fairy tale females to mythic goddesses and sacred women, it will not argue toward a universal concept of goddess worship among diverse cultures, as argued by some archeologists and scholars, such as Marija Gimbutas or Merlin Stone; instead, this book openly acknowledges the similarities and differences of many goddesses in myriad cultures. This book merely suggests that existing archetypes regarding female characters in folktales and fairy tales hold similarities with the divine and sacred females of ancient mythic narratives. With this said, this book does not have the intention of definitively proving ancient connections in folktales and fairy tales, as such an endeavor would often be impossible. Instead, this book examines the female characters in folktales and fairy tales under the lens of mythological female divinities and sacred women in order to add more meaning to old interpretations of the folktales and fairy tales many people cherish today.

    I would like to offer thanks to all the people who helped make this book a reality. Without a doubt, I owe the utmost gratitude to Landon and Season for showing me on a daily basis what a hero and heroine look like. I would like to thank Mary for showing me the value of wise old women who live in the wilderness, as well as Joe for his unfailing support of my many large endeavors. I also would like to thank Thom and Aaron for their passion of classic tales. Finally, I would like to express gratitude to the administration of the University of Minnesota Crookston for their support of this endeavor.

Introduction

There has been a legacy passed down by our great grandmothers to our grandmothers, mothers, and us within the folktales and fairy tales we cherish today. This legacy preserves the fact that women once reigned as powerful goddesses, shamans, queens, priestesses, etc., in many world cultures. This legacy encourages women to remember this powerful past, so when they envision the height of who they are, and can become, they envision no less than the highest concepts.

This book argues that remnants of goddess worship found in ancient mythology were preserved in cultural folktales and fairy tales. Many scholars confirm that elements of myriad folktales and fairy tales come from ancient mythology. The mythology of a culture is much more than tales of entertainment, as a culture's mythological record captures the sacred, religious stories of a people. For millennia, many cultures around the globe told myths of powerful goddesses who held supreme positions of authority. However, in many regions of the ancient world, such as India, the Mediterranean, Europe, etc., Indo-European invasions, as well as other invasions and episodes of diffusion, caused traditional concepts regarding the worship of supremely powerful goddesses to be altered, so that goddesses were often demoted to inferior positions within male-dominated pantheons. For example, cultures that encountered Indo-European influence over centuries often shifted a supreme goddess's power into divided representations of goddesses who held subordinate positions and maintained traits in line with patriarchal belief systems. This perhaps most clearly was seen in Greece where the concept of a dominant Mother Goddess was replaced by separate female divinities who each held less power than the gods at the top of the pantheon: Zeus, Poseidon, and Hades. By separating a supreme, united Goddess into many less powerful, and often stereotypical, goddesses, such as Aphrodite, representing the goddess of love; Hera, being designated as the goddess of marriage and childbirth; and Demeter, as the goddess of the harvest, the role of the supremely powerful Goddess became demoted to suit patriarchal agendas. Additionally, in many regions throughout the world, Semitic, Islamic, Christian, Confucian, Buddhist, etc., influences also revised, and often obliterated, the religious/spiritual reverence people held for goddesses under ordinances that proclaimed that there was only one male divinity and/or proclamations that male spirituality superseded female spirituality. For instance, with the adoption of Semitic, Islamic, and Christian beliefs, many goddesses became identified as false, or even evil, folkloric figures. In Slavic mythology, for example, once sacred female divinities "became demoted to an identification of evil, demonic beings who existed as dwarves or spirits of the forest, and who should be feared and shunned for their malicious intent" (Phillips & Kerrigan 60). Likewise, the cultures affected by Christian influences during conquest and colonialism, such as those within Africa, Asia, the Americas, and Australia, were often pressured to replace indigenous goddesses with European models of male divine dominance.

However, it is often the case that the people of cultures that experienced an influx of new beliefs, through conquest, colonization, diffusion, etc., often maintained their traditional beliefs alongside new beliefs. Sometimes worshippers continued to openly revere traditional divine figures alongside new divinities; the Romans, for instance, were quite willing to allow this. But sometimes, if one culture was mostly called to eliminate traditional belief systems, the people often found ways to maintain their old beliefs in disguised format, such as folk festivals and celebrations or folktales and fairy tales. For instance, for the Celts and Slavs, Christian "scripture ... had no place for the old gods ... but there was still room in the hearts of the ordinary people" (Phillips & Kerrigan 60) for a continuation of their worship, as verified in the rituals and festivals that were still embraced long after Christianity dominated. In fact, to gain converts in Celtic and Slavic regions, as well as many other regions around the world, Christianity often merged pagan concepts into its ideology and practices, as many Christian holidays were commemorated around pagan holy days. For example, Easter and Christmas celebrations recall pagan festivals that directly honored powerful goddesses such as Eostre, Ostara, Frigg, and Freyja. Similarly, in Peru, ancient, well-preserved customs are also still alive and well in celebrations, such as Día de la Pachamama, which merges concepts of the Catholic Virgin Mary with the ancient Earth Mother Pachamama. In addition, around the world, many once divine beings became portrayed as folkloric figures, such as fairies, wizards, ghosts, witches, leprechauns, etc. This preservation of traditional religious divinities within the folklore of a culture is a common practice around the world, though the once divine figures often appear in global folklore as demoted, mysterious, or evil.

Folktales are "stories that have been transmitted orally, generation to generation, from as far back as antiquity" (Paradiž x). The act of telling stories in this manner allowed tales to be modified depending on the storyteller and audience. Interestingly, it was often the women of a community who created and preserved folktales that included female protagonists; "Within the shared esprit of ... late-night communes, women not only practiced their domestic crafts, they also fulfilled their role as transmitters of culture through the vehicle of 'old tales,' inherited from the oral tradition" (Rowe 404). However, "with the rise of literacy and the invention of the printing press in the fifteenth century," the tradition of passing on folktales orally became transformed into printed folktales and later fairy tales (Tatar 415). Because of the value presented in the collected folktales by such figures as Giambattista Basile, Charles Perrault, the Grimm brothers, etc., almost every European country created a folklore society intent on collecting and recording cultural folktales (Cole xix). In time, this effort spread to Asia, Africa, and the Americas, so that folktales began to be preserved and published "from almost everywhere" (Cole xix). Just as women storytellers often passed on oral folktales to each other for generations, many women storytellers were responsible for imparting their oral folktales to authors who would transmit them to print (Rowe 405; Warner 411). In fact, Warner states that many of the most popular fairy tales, which were based on cultural folktales passed on by the oral tradition, were relayed to the Grimm brothers, Perrault, etc., by female storytellers (Warner 407). Rowe reiterates this, stating that one should not "forget the matrilineal lineage, the 'mothers' who in the French *veillées* and English nurseries, in court salons and the German *Spinnstube*, in Paris and on the Yorkshire moors, passed on their wisdom" through the telling of oral folktales, so that they could be published (Rowe 405). However, many male authors in converting oral folktales to written form often revised the material to portray patriarchal representations of female characters, who differed greatly from the original folktale representations as told by women storytellers. Nevertheless, if one examines many published folktales and fairy tales closely, one can still often see striking examples of powerful women who impart important messages that may be connected to the goddesses and sacred women of ancient mythology.

Though folktales and fairy tales often get categorized as mere entertainment or simple tales meant to impart educational lessons, thus lacking spiritual content, many scholars argue that in fact folktales and fairy tales actually quite often involve story patterns that are reminiscent of ancient religious myths. In Russia, for example, it is widely accepted that the "'sacred text' through which the female divinity was revealed to her Russian worshippers was the folktale" (Hubbs 41). In fact, many folktales and fairy tales have elements and structural plots that have been proven to be thousands of years old, such as with the fairy tale "Jack and the Bean-stalk," which is believed to be over five thousand years old. Therefore, it is highly likely that many elements of folktales and fairy tales were transferred from religious myths, which were often well known and considered sacred by a great many people. Folktale and fairy tale expert Jack Zipes explains that folktales, and later fairy tales, because again many fairy tales were largely created from folktales, were "related to the belief systems, values, rites, and experiences of pagan peoples" (Zipes 21). Anderson concurs, stating that folktales and fairy tales hold content which has existed "since ancient times" (Anderson 2). Though there are usually many variations of a given folktale or fairy tale, depending on the storyteller or author, Anderson states that often a tale can still remain quite similar to its ancient counterpart, even though hundreds, or even thousands, of years have passed (Anderson 15). In fact, an Israeli trickster-tale that was recorded in the 1940s was found to be "virtually identical" to a Babylonian myth from two and a half millennia earlier that was deciphered after the tale was recorded in the 1940s (Anderson 15). Darnton also relates how many "oral traditions have enormous staying power," as plot structures can remain unchanged throughout diverse cultures for hundreds of years (Darnton 372). Darnton also discusses how many tales include similar plot structures throughout many cultures via, most likely, cultural diffusion, showing the lasting power of many folktales despite time and place (Darnton 373). Zipes explains that many folktales include elements that were once "part of initiation rituals in pagan times, and as the world changed, so did the sacred initiation tales that became myths and later 'degenerated' into secular wonder tales ... to fit new social and cultural conditions" (Zipes 68). This concept is important because it shows that many myths transformed, or as Zipes puts it "degenerated," into folktales and later fairy tales, which arguably makes folktales and fairy tales still full of elements left over from ancient mythology. Famous folklore scholar Vladimir Propp agrees that many of the themes within folktales and fairy tales are connected to sacred rituals found in ancient myths (Propp 499). For example, Propp states that folktales and fairy tales hold remnants of characters who served religious functions in sacred myths (Propp, *Morphology*, 503). Therefore, it is certainly plausible that many female characters within folktales and fairy tales present aspects of goddess worship found in myriad early religions. Birkhäuser-Oeri supports this, stating that folktales and fairy tales "come from a level relatively unaffected by the patriarchal tendencies of ... [many] culture[s]; there, for instance, the great universal goddess of the very early civilizations ... is still active. In fairy tale characters, as in those early goddesses, we find the suprapersonal image of a female who never dies, even if killed three times over" (Birkhäuser-Oeri

18). Zipes also declares that the ancient divinities of many cultures merged to eventually give birth to the female characters of folktales and fairy tales, stating that the folktale's and fairy tale's "evolution can only be understood if we study explicit and implicit references to goddesses ... of the pagan world, for their symbolic significance is still with us today" (Zipes 57). Thus, the intent of this book is to show how myriad global folktales and fairy tales maintain reverence once paid to the goddesses of many world cultures by displaying powerful folktale and fairy tale female characters who hold attributes in line with these mythic goddesses.

Sometimes in folktales and fairy tales, "the heroine is a good girl, one who knows her place in the patriarchal scheme of things and does well in the traditional female roles of passive maiden, self-sacrificing mother, or obedient and dutiful wife"; and though these women do occupy many folktales and fairy tales, this book will largely ignore these portrayals of women in favor of what Young calls the "female counter-hero [who] is indifferent to patriarchal values" (Young 5). Young states that the female counter-hero "harkens back to an earlier, non-patriarchal time and to non-patriarchal sources of knowledge" (Young 5). It is thus these formidable heroines that this book will identify. And in fact, when folktales and fairy tales are examined while searching for connections to ancient concepts of goddess worship, one sees that many female characters in folktales and fairy tales are not at all passive or obedient; instead, they often serve as the guiding force behind the whole story. Therefore, this book argues that the females of many folktales and fairy tales should be better identified as divinely inspired teachers and guides for the education they provide to the characters they interact with, and to the audiences they inspire.

Many scholars contend that the heroic journey is a decidedly male enterprise as portrayed throughout mythology, folktales, and fairy tales. It is true that famous mythologists such as Otto Rank, Lord Raglan, and Joseph Campbell mainly focused on male heroes. Weild states that perhaps the most famous mythologist, Joseph Campbell, claimed that a hero can be either a man or a woman, yet he "almost exclusively use[d] male exemplars of the 'monomyth' (departure, initiation, and return) of the 'adventure of the hero' in *The Hero with a Thousand Faces* (1949, 1968)" (Weild 198). This is certainly true, and it remains true in many of the examinations of heroic quests in myths, folktales, and fairy tales even today, as male characters are often identified as active, brave, and strong, while female characters are often identified as passive, weak, and in need of being saved. However, many world myths that do not showcase a female character as the heroine of the myth, still repeatedly portray powerful female goddesses or sacred women as helping, or guiding and teaching, male heroes every step of their journeys. This trend continues in folktales and fairy tales as countless female characters are presented as animal brides, wise old women, prized maidens, ferocious monsters, etc., in order to guide and educate male protagonists through their heroic journeys. Therefore, though many female characters in myths, folktales, and fairy tales may initially appear in inferior positions, as merely helpers to male heroes, one should reexamine the role of mythic, folkloric, and fairy tale females in order to see that they often hold a superior position to the male heroes, as teachers, guides, priestesses, or shamans seldom hold an inferior position to their pupil or initiate. For instance, when a folktale and fairy tale male hero is examined in relation to the female characters within the tale, "we find that his behavior is at odds with an apparently father-centered society.... In his quest ... he ... must be exposed to the animistic world of the forest and meet its mistress before he can fulfill his destiny.... In short, although the folktale uses the patriarchal social and political order as the context of the quest ... it is the [female characters within] the realm of nature ... which shapes the fate of the hero" (Hubbs 146). Once one realizes that the female characters in many folktales and fairy tales are often actually serving as guides and educators to male heroes, the legacy of mythic goddesses comes forth. Thus, the message that these goddess representatives teach arguably needs to be analyzed further because it might allow audiences a glimpse to a distant, yet vital, past of goddess worship.

Therefore, the first half of this book will examine how the female characters within folktales and fairy tales often serve as guides and teachers to the male protagonists they encounter. The messages these female folkloric and fairy tale teachers impart are often connected to similar messages relayed by goddesses within many ancient myths around the world. Chapter 1 of this book, "Mother Nature, Animal Brides, and Mistresses of Animals," examines how female characters in many global folktales and fairy tales appear in ways quite similar to mythic representations of Earth Mothers, who are portrayed as representations of the earth itself, such as the German Frau Holle who can transform the weather at will. This first chapter of this book also looks to the myriad animal bride tales from around the world that portray women in animalistic forms who marry men in order to teach them about the ways of the environment. Finally, this chapter examines other folktale and fairy tale women who appear similar to mythic portrayals of Mistresses of Animals, whose goddess-like command of the animal kingdom also serves to teach the males they encounter about the laws of the natural world. Chapter 2, "Wise Old Women," focuses on the many folktales and fairy tales from around the world that portray old women as wise helpers. These old women characters often live outside of the confines of the community; therefore, they serve as exemplars of female independence to the characters who encounter them. The wisdom held by these old women, which often reflects messages carried forth by goddesses in many ancient myths, plays a central role in educating the male folktale and fairy tale heroes who encounter them. Chapter 3, "Maidens and Otherworldly Women," portrays the archetypal maiden of many folktales and fairy tales who often appears as merely a prize for a male hero, but when these maidens are examined more closely, then one can see that their purpose in the narrative is to educate male heroes about tenets associated with mythic goddesses. This chapter also shows that using otherworldly women, who reside in fantastical realms full of vitality and abundance, is a common element found in mythology, and in folktales and fairy tales, to signal goddess qualities to male heroes. Chapter 4, "Monstrous Females and Ghost Women," traces the many female characters within folktales and fairy tales who appear as monstrous, materializing in the forms of giantesses, succubi, mermaids, rusalki, etc. Just as in many ancient myths, even though these monstrous women appear in folktales and fairy tales as hindrances to the quest of the hero, they ultimately serve to educate male heroes about the true meaning of their quest, which again often aligns with concepts associated with mythic goddesses. The many ghost women who appear in folktales and fairy tales around the world are also discussed in this chapter, as they often serve as agents to teach male heroes about how they, particularly as females, have been wronged by males or by patriarchal systems, and thus have been thwarted from completing their own heroic quests.

As stated, most myths around the world display male heroes partaking in heroic quests, and seldom focus on heroines who participate in their own heroic journeys. But this is not at all the case with folktales and fairy tales, as thousands of folktales and fairy tales portray formidable, independent female heroines who indeed partake in their own heroic quests. As Hubbs states, "the women of ... folktale[s] are active. As though in conscious opposition to the ... [patriarchal] vision of women, they ... are morally and spiritually superior to the male. Thus, the folktale sets the social order on its head" (Hubbs 147). Therefore, the second half of this book will focus on the formidable heroines found in many folktales and fairy tales from around the world. Chapter 5 of this book, "Defiant Women and Women Warriors," displays myriad folktale and fairy tale women who defy patriarchal social, political, and religious structures, and thus serve to become heroines within their tales. Like their male heroic counterparts, the heroines of folktales and fairy tales are also often guided by powerful female characters, who again resemble ancient goddesses. Thus, Chapter 6, "Heroines on their own Quest," Chapter 7, "Mothers and Stepmothers," and Chapter 8, "Witches," trace the quests of many folktale and fairy tale heroines who are guided upon their journeys by female teachers who appear in the roles of mother, stepmother, wise old woman/grandmother, or witch. Folktale and fairy tale female educators teach heroines tenets associated with goddesses of many ancient myths, such as skills associated with nature and mysticism. For instance, many heroines of folktales and fairy tales around the globe learn how to command natural elements or perform acts such as reanimation or resurrection; these mystical acts are directly connected to abilities of mythic goddesses. In this way, the folktale and fairy tale heroine realizes that she, like her female educator, comes from a long line of powerful mythic women. Therefore, the last three chapters of this book show that the heroines of folktales and fairy tales often learn elements associated with the quintessential heroic quest displayed by mostly male heroes, such as autonomy, the facts of mortality, and the wisdom of self-actualization, but they also move beyond these common elements of male heroic quests into a heightened apotheosis, which appears as a realization that they are representations of goddesses themselves.

1

Mother Nature, Animal Brides, and Mistresses of Animals

Mother Nature

The concept of women being connected to nature is as old as human existence. As early cultures witnessed the ability of women to create and birth new life, religious conceptions were created that envisioned nature as feminine. Therefore, myriad cultures around the world conceived of the earth itself as a Great Mother/Earth Mother. This Great Mother/Earth Mother allowed all beings to be born and supported their survival by providing a balance of environmental resources. This Great Mother/Earth Mother created and destroyed landscapes at will, enabled the seasons to change, and maintained fertility for all beings. She caused the life-giving rain to pour down upon crops, flowers of all colors to blanket the earth, sunsets to paint the sky, as well as hurricanes, tornadoes, and blizzards to halt all existence. The interior of the earth was the Great Mother's/Earth Mother's womb, whereupon all of earth's beings would both emerge from in birth and return to in death.

Starting as early 50,000 to 10,000 years ago, in the Upper Paleolithic period throughout Africa, the Middle East, and Europe, there is evidence of reverence for a Great Mother/Earth Mother in the form of artistic depictions on cave walls, as well as many bone and stone figurines that portray the female form. Leeming and Page explain that these artifacts provide "a portrait of the Goddess in her early stages.... She seems to have been absolute and parthenogenetic—born of herself—the foundation of all being. She was the All-Giving and the All-Taking, the source of life and death and regeneration. More than a mother goddess or a fertility goddess, she appears to have been earth and nature itself" (Leeming & Page 7). Many world cultures, such as those of the Amerindians, Chinese, Africans, Greeks, Romans, Indians, Celts, Slavs, etc., embraced the concept that the earth was a Great Mother/Earth Mother. For example, it is believed that the indigenous inhabitants of the Indus Valley worshipped an Earth Mother, who was a conception of the land itself, as their primary deity (Gupto 39). In addition, many Amerindian tribes revered, and often continue to revere, the earth as Mother; "From the Athapascans to the Zuni, Native American accounts of mother as creator, earth as mother ... emerge in a vast diversity of images and legends" (Stone 284). For instance, the Barasana people of southeastern Columbia believed that the earth was created directly from the body of a primordial mother, Romi Kumu (Leeming & Page, *Goddess*, 35), and the Anasazi-Pueblo and Inca believed that the first beings emerged directly from the womb of their Earth Mother. In addition, in Western Africa, the Igbo believed that the Earth Mother, Ala, both birthed all life from her natural form and welcomed the dead back into her womb; Ala was also responsible for producing the earth's resources, thus enabling the beings of earth to survive. For the Greeks, the Earth Mother was Gaia, and it was she who created the earth and many of its inhabitants.

In addition, many Celtic tribes revered Earth Mothers, such as Danu, sometimes Anu or Dana, Ernmas, and Mór Muman, whose names mean Great Mother. The Celts inhabited much of Europe beginning in about 1200 BCE. They were eventually overtaken in many regions by other cultures, such as the Romans, who modified their belief systems; however, in Celtic strongholds like Ireland, Scotland, and Wales, Celtic religious beliefs remained until the coming of Christianity in about the fourth and fifth centuries CE. The widespread adoption of Christianity in Ireland, Scotland, and Wales largely eradicated the Celtic religious beliefs that people held for centuries, causing once sacred gods and goddesses to become identified as false pagan deities. However, as is often the case, and was especially true for these regions, many of the people of Ireland, Scotland, and Wales maintained elements of their former religious beliefs in their customs and folklore. In Scotland, for example, folktales of the Cailleach Beira, the Queen of Winter, have explicitly preserved mythic conceptions of a Celtic Earth Mother. In Celtic mythology, the Cailleach was identified as an Earth Mother who was responsible for the transition of the months of growth and fecundity in spring and summer to the sterility of winter. Furthermore, the Cailleach Beira was often referred to as the Mother of all Scottish deities, as well as the one who shaped the landscape of Scotland.

In Scottish folklore, the Cailleach Beira appears almost identical to her mythic portrayals, despite the coming of Christianity, which labeled the Cailleach as pagan and thus suspect. Even today, the Cailleach is a beloved aspect of Scottish culture, as many folktales and celebrations still revere her, such as Samhain celebrations that mark the coming of winter. The most famous Scottish folktale of Beira (Mackenzie 22–32) shows her in clear Earth Mother imagery. The folktale states that Beira reigned supreme each winter, but each summer, the Summer King Angus and his wife Bride (or Brìghde) would partake in a battle to conquer Beira for dominance of the season. Some winters, Beira would attempt to prevent Angus and Bride from reinstating the period of growth, unleashing blizzards, ice storms, and frost that would delay the coming of spring. One particular winter, Beira refused to make way for spring. The winter fury that Beira unleashed caused the landscape of Scotland to become so frozen that the animals all perished; because of this, "Beira's efforts brought disaster to mankind, and the 'Weeks of Leanness' came," as food was scarce, and the people started to starve (Mackenzie 27). Finally, Angus and Bride were shown in the folktale to ultimately defeat Beira's efforts. Therefore, Bride was able to bestow to the land her gifts of growth; "Bride dipped her ... hands in the high rivers and lochs which still retained ice. When she did so, the grass grew quickly, and seeds were sown" (Mackenzie 31). Therefore, this folktale shows both Beira and Bride to be remnants of Celtic Earth Mothers in their ability to control the landscape and maintain the cycles of the seasons.

Similarly, the Cailleach in Ireland is often known as the Cailleach Bheur in Irish folklore. Like the Cailleach Beria, the folkloric Cailleach Bheur appears almost identical to her mythic portrayal as a Celtic Earth Mother, as in Irish folklore, the Cailleach Bheur was also able to modify the natural landscape, transform into any natural element, and change the weather at will. One Irish folktale (Stone 66–7) shows the Cailleach Bheur as an Earth Mother who can command the elements of nature to do her bidding, as well as a divine judge of humankind. In the folktale, the Cailleach Bheur is shown to test three brothers by appearing to them one night as they sat in the secluded forest by their fire. It is of course fitting that the Cailleach Bheur appeared to the brothers as they were in her natural realm of the deep wilderness. The Cailleach Bheur approached the young men in the disguised form of an old beggar woman who asked them for a bite to eat and a place to sit by their fire, as she was testing them to see if they adhered to her ideology, as an Earth Mother representative, of sharing the bounty of her natural resources. The two older brothers showed that they failed her test, as they attempted to keep her own resources for themselves, but the third and youngest brother graciously offered the disguised Cailleach Bheur his food and a place next to him by the fire, just as the earth as mother provides the resources needed for the survival of all living beings. As a reward, the Cailleach Bheur revealed herself in her mystical splendor, again showing her to have maintained her goddess qualities even within the format of a folktale, and bestowed the youngest brother gifts of natural prosperity for the rest of his life, as he went on to have many children and always produced a successful harvest. The fact that the Cailleach Bheur bestows elements of fertility and agricultural prosperity to the youngest brother explicitly proves her to be a preserved Earth Mother from Celtic mythology. In addition, as a remnant of a mythic Celtic Earth Mother, the folkloric Cailleach Bheur serves a role found in many religious texts that shows a divine being testing mortals to see if they are worthy of reward or punishment; this scenario shows the lasting power of the Cailleach Bheur as both a feared and revered divinity who maintained reverence even after the coming of Christianity to Celtic regions.

In a series of migrations, the Germanic tribes, which originated in Scandinavia, grew to dominate much of Europe during the Germanic Iron Age (550–800 CE). The Germanic people, like the Celts, also revered nature as sacred; therefore, many of their gods and goddesses were also directly connected to the environment. The Germanic tribes, like the Celts, also conceived of the earth as Mother and worshipped her under such names as Nerthus, Ertha, Freya, Frija, Frigg, etc. Reaves explains that in "Germanic sources, Mother Earth holds a prominent position," as she was worshipped in "seven northern European nations" as a supreme deity (Reaves 89). However, also like the Celts, Christianity eventually dominated Germanic belief systems, which began in about the fifth-century CE, and eradicated the worship of Germanic gods and goddesses. Despite this, there is evidence that many Germanic beliefs survived in the folk customs and beliefs of the common people. For instance, it appears that the Germanic Earth Mother at least partially survived in German folktales and fairy tales in figures such as Frau Holle, sometimes identified as Frau Holda, and Perchta, sometimes Berchta.

Frau Holle often appears in folklore as "a matronly figure ... [who] makes the snow and rain fall" (Reaves 299). Frau Holle also "dwells in ponds and wells" and is "closely associated with agriculture, spinning, and domestic affairs" (Reaves 299). Again, like the Scottish Cailleach Beira and the Irish Cailleach Bheur, Frau Holle's folkloric ability to alter the weather, as well as live within watery dwellings and produce successful harvests, connects her to Germanic Earth Mothers. Reaves supports this, stating that the folkloric Frau Holle is indeed "Mother Nature herself, the old heathen Earth Mother. In Christian times, her teaching remains" (Reaves 299). Further support of Frau Holle's ancient, divine associations appears in her watery abode within "lakes, wells, and ponds," as these sources of water often appear in folklore as the "entryway[s] to her hall" (Reaves 292). Likewise, the Germanic people believed that their goddesses, such as the Germanic Earth Mother Nerthus, also dwelt within watery abodes, and thus could be appeased by offerings left for her in bodies of water. Frau Holle also often appears in many of her folktales with a wagon, plow, and elements connected to spinning, which are also all traditional aspects of Germanic Earth Mothers.

The Grimm brothers' fairy tale of "Mother Holle" (J. Grimm & W. Grimm 81–3) explicitly connects the character of Mother Holle to Germanic Earth Mother imagery. In this fairy tale, a maiden went to get water from her well, but she ended up falling into the well. Instead of drowning though, the maiden found that she woke up "in a beautiful meadow, where the sun was shining and thousands of flowers were growing" (J. Grimm & W. Grimm 81). The natural imagery and abundant resources of this realm beneath the well immediately signals it as the mystical home of a divine Earth Mother. In this abundantly natural realm, the maiden came to an apple tree that spoke to her and told her to shake the apples from its branches, which she did and thus received sustenance unlike any she had ever experienced. Again, the fact that a tree is portrayed as able to speak to the maiden and its fruit fills her with mystical sustenance within this realm explicitly shows that she is immersed within the domain of an Earth Mother. This Earth Mother is revealed to the maiden when further upon her journey, she finally arrived at the home of Mother Holle, who was immediately portrayed in goddess-like terms, as she had mystically large teeth that frightened the maiden. However, Mother Holle told the maiden not to be afraid, but to stay and live with her, helping her do her housework, which again shows the Earth Mother figure of this tale, just like the previous tale of the Cailleach Bheur, as testing the maiden to see if she understands the importance of helping others as the earth helps its inhabitants. Mother Holle told the maiden to make her bed for her, specifically telling her to be sure to give the mattress a good shake, so that the feathers flew. Mother Holle explained that when the feathers flew, it would cause it to snow in the maiden's former realm. Showing Mother Holle as able to control the weather, like the Cailleach Beira and the Cailleach Bheur, again portrays her as a remnant of a Germanic Earth Mother. The Grimm text includes a note that confirms this, stating that "whenever it snowed in olden days, people in Hessia used to say Mother Holle is making her bed" (J. Grimm & W. Grimm 82). Once the maiden proved that she passed the tests of the goddess-like Mother Holle by doing all that was asked of her, Mother Holle delivered the maiden to the entryway of the well in which she came, so that she could go back home. At the entryway, the maiden found herself standing before a large gate, and when the gate opened, an enormous amount of gold showered down upon the maiden, ensuring her nature's bounty for the rest of her days, similar to the reward the Cailleach Bheur bestowed to the youngest brother within her Irish folktale.

This fairy tale makes it clear that Mother Holle is meant to serve as a figure who possesses skills that connect her to mythic Earth Mothers, such as her ability to live beneath the water in a realm full of fecundity, nurture trees that speak and provide mystical sustenance, and initiate snowstorms upon the earth. Furthermore, this fairy tale, like the one of the Irish Cailleach Bheur, shows the figure of Mother Holle also testing those who enter her natural domain. This tenet of testing characters, and then rewarding positive behavior with prosperity, is a common theme found in many myths of ancient goddesses, especially Earth Mothers, as goddesses who were believed to be representations of the earth were often seen as benevolently bestowing the bountiful resources of nature to those who treated them with respect. This presentation of a pagan Earth Mother, in only slightly altered folkloric form, shows that despite Christian efforts to eradicate traditional goddesses, the people often found a means to preserve the reverence for their ancestors' belief systems. In fact, even today the German people show their continued reverence for this Earth Mother by their celebration of Holle's Day in early January (Reaves 99).

In Switzerland, Bavaria, and Austria, Frau Holle appears modified as Frau Perchta or Berchta. In the folktales of these regions, Frau Perchta emerged "during the Twelve Nights from Christmas Eve to *Perchtentag* ('Perchta's Day'), the 6th of January" (Reaves 101). On these nights, Perchta was said to wander the streets as a beautiful woman wearing a shining blue robe and surrounded by children, bestowing gifts of natural prosperity. Sometimes, though, Perchta would appear as a frightening old woman with a band of demons who would serve to scare away winter weather (Reaves 101), showing her, like the Cailleach Beira, Cailleach Bheur, and Frau Holle as holding the ability to alter the weather, an ability that only mythic Earth Mothers possess. Likewise, Perchta's ability to choose the form she will appear in, as a maiden or an old woman, also solidifies her connection to Germanic Earth Mothers, as they too could alter their appearance at will. Even today, festivals in celebration of Perchta, that include partygoers dressing up as the former goddess figure in her many forms, are still held throughout Switzerland, Bavaria, and Austria (Hodges 34).

Perchta was also believed to come out on Walpurgis Night, the night before May Day, with "a train of followers" who would draw "men into danger with alluring sounds and spells, exposing and punishing their hidden sins" (Reaves 101). Perchta was also often envisioned as judging people on Perchtentag; on this night, she was said to punish those she deemed lazy by splitting their bellies open. Again, it is telling that many folkloric Earth Mothers are portrayed as judging the behavior of mortals. This passing of judgement directly connects the folkloric female characters to a high position of authority that is again usually assigned to divine beings. The fact that a folkloric woman can pass seemingly divine judgement upon humankind, as in the Irish tale of the Cailleach Bheur, the German tale of Frau Holle, and now Perchta, shows the lasting reverence given to such Earth Mother figures even in folklore. Though, it should be noted that the presentation of Perchta, or Berchta, as a judge of mortals is nebulous, as she is often presented in demonized terms with her overtly brutal punishments, similar to how the folkloric figure of Krampus, who steals naughty children on Krampusnacht, is portrayed in the same Alpine regions. This somewhat demonic portrayal of Perchta/Berchta, as well as Krampus, suggests the influence that Christianity played upon the once pagan figures over the centuries.

Many scholars contend that figures such as Frau Holle, Perchta/ Berchta, etc., may be specifically connected to the Germanic Earth Mother Frija (Norse Frigg) or Freya (Norse Freyja), or a combined form of the two as often Frija and Freya are thought to have once been one united goddess (Reaves 131). For instance, the folklore surrounding the Germanic and Scandinavian Wild Hunt presents Frau Holle and Perchta/Berchta as connected to Frija/Frigg and Freya/Freyja. The mythic Wild Hunt, which was often led by Frija/Frigg or Freya/Freyja, or sometimes the Germanic Woden (Norse Odin), was said to take place in midwinter during Yule festivities. Myths of the Wild Hunt presented it as a sacred means to make sacrifices to the earth, so that the earth could be renewed at the end of winter, similar to how Perchtentag celebrations held Perchta as capable of scaring away winter, so the season of growth could be initiated. However, as time went on and Christianity dominated, the Wild Hunt became a thing of folklore; therefore, it was no longer presented as a sacred hunt where the Earth Mother participated in the necessary activities to induce spring; instead, like tales of a demonized Perchta/Berchta, it became presented as a demonic hunt that involved bygone mythic divinities and folkloric figures who led supernatural beings on a hunt to punish evildoers by extravagantly brutal means. Therefore, Frau Holle or Perchta/Berchta were often portrayed as members of the folkloric Wild Hunt, replacing Frija/ Frigg or Freya/Freyja, and providing a sinister flair to the event, while at the same time preserving remnants of the role of the Germanic Earth Mother within the hunt.

The Grimm brothers' fairy tale of "Frau Gauden" (Reaves 199–200) portrays its female protagonist, Frau Gauden, as holding a name identifiable as explicitly connected to the divine Woden, and thus presents Frau Gauden as also connected to Woden's wife, the Earth Mother Frija and/ or Freya. Reaves concurs, stating that Frau Gauden is certainly connected to Woden, and through him to Frija and Freya, as well as their folkloric counterparts Frau Holle and Perchta/Berchta; "the further north one travels into Germany, the more Frau Holle's bynames identify her as Woden's wife. From the farthest southern regions of her range ... she is called Frau Holle, Berchta, Perchta," but as one travels north, she is called "Frau Herke, Harke, Frekka, Frau Gode [Gauden], and finally Frau Woden" (Reaves 132). This fairy tale also explicitly connects Frau Gauden to the Wild Hunt, again showing her as connected to traditional conceptions of a Germanic Earth Mother, as it presents Frau Gauden as a huntress with twenty-four daughters who all enjoyed hunting more than anything else. To solidify this point, Frau Gauden herself proclaimed, while out hunting, that "'hunting is better than heaven'" (Reaves 200). However, showing the transformation of values over the centuries of Christian indoctrination, the fairy tale presents Frau Gauden's words to be so blasphemous that Frau Gauden's "twenty-four daughters ... [were] turned into hunting dogs" as a punishment to her (Reaves 200). Frau Gauden then was forced to continue hunting, with her daughters as dogs, for all eternity. As evidenced in this fairy tale, and in tales of similar former goddess figures such as Perchta/Berchta, the Christian Church tried to portray such figures as suspect or even evil, because they "represented pagan elements that the Church wanted suppressed and demonization was the easiest way to ruin ... [their] reputation and kill ... [their] worship" (Hodges 36). This trend to define once powerful mythic goddesses as outdated or evil was a popular technique used in folktales and fairy tales to demote once divine beings into meeting the standards of new belief systems, such as in this case Christianity. Still, the German people maintained an embrace of Frau Gauden as connected to traditional conceptions of a Germanic Earth Mother by preserving folk traditions that portrayed Frau Gauden and her pack of dogs as a part of Christmas celebrations (Reaves 201). For instance, it was said that if Frau Gauden found an open door during the nights surrounding Christmas, she would send one of her daughters, in dog form, into the home, where the dog would begin to cry out, destroying the peace of those who lived inside, whimpering and whining "the whole year through" (Reaves 201). The fact that Frau Gauden's daughters, in the form of dogs, cry out for a whole year may be a folkloric attempt to remind people of the lost power of their once revered Germanic goddesses.

Animal Brides

Many global cultures once revered animals as sacred, even as far back as the Upper Paleolithic period. Animals within almost every mythology around the world appeared as protectors, symbolic sources of power and virility, and agents of sacred wisdom. Thus, many cultures revered animals as totemic figures, marking them as spiritual guides for the people.

Therefore, when an animal appears in a myth, folktale, or fairy tale, the animal often symbolizes an element of sacrality that might extend back to prehistoric times.

Furthermore, the presentation of a sacred woman who is linked with an animal also extends back to prehistoric times throughout many cultures. For instance, throughout Europe many depictions of anthropomorphic, female birdlike figurines have been discovered from the Upper Paleolithic period and later Neolithic period (9000–3000 BCE). One of the most well-known of these figurines is the Venus of Lespugue (ca. 25,000–18,000 BCE), which shows a female's upper arms as wings, "heavy and hunched forward where they attach to the body" and "thin and feathery ... below the bent elbow" (Johnson 16). In addition, in Europe the Upper Paleolithic symbol of the bear was also connected to portrayals of female divinity. In later periods, goddesses such as Artio, the Celtic bear goddess, and the Greek goddesses Calisto and Artemis maintained this Upper Paleolithic connection to bear imagery. When a divine female is connected to an animal in mythology, the woman is often identified as an earth goddess—one who is symbolic of the processes and/or elements of nature. Earth goddesses, as representatives of the natural environment, often teach the characters who interact with them the importance of respecting the interrelated sacrality of all of the elements of nature, and they often do this by transforming into the form of an animal or by having an animal as their guardian or companion. For instance, the Egyptian Hathor is symbolized by a cow and can transform into a cow at will; the Chinese Nu Wä appears in snake form; the Celtic the Morrígan's presence is signaled by ravens as she can also take on their form; the Greek Athena is associated with the owl, and the Phrygian Mother Goddess Cybele shows her command of all elements of nature by standing peacefully between ferocious animals of many species.

Many myths present males as marrying women who can transform from animal to human form at will. Because of their extraordinary ability of metamorphosis, these mythic women, identified as animal brides, were often considered sacred for their connection to totemic reverence or were presented as divine earth goddesses. Animal bride myths often document the union of a people with their totem animal, showing the animal/human marriage as evidence of their totemic ancestry, and thus the community's sacred bond with the elements of nature (Propp 143). For example, a myth thought to be connected to the indigenous Cambodian cultures before the arrival of the Khmer Empire shows the land being guarded by divine beings who were half snake and half human. The myth states that the snake king's daughter "married an Indian Brahmana named Kaundinya, and gave birth to the Cambodian people" (Frankel 69), which in turn enabled the people to revere the snake as their totemic figure.

Many myths, and later folktales and fairy tales, also present a male embarking upon a heroic quest. Often the male heroic quest involves a hero leaving behind his former selfhood, which has been shaped by societal influences, upon a journey, that can be physical as well as psychological, which ultimately teaches the hero how to find a revised selfhood. Oftentimes, the hero encounters a helper along his quest, and quite often this helper appears in the form of a female, who guides the hero toward realizing his psychological and/or spiritual transformation. These female helpers repeatedly appear in the form of divine or sacred agents who are directly aligned with the natural environment; furthermore, they often hold the ability to metamorphose from human to animal form. For example, in Amerindian mythology, male heroes often married women who were identified as sacred because of their dual identities as humans and animals; one such example can be found in a myth from the Yekuana of Venezuela and Brazil (Bierhorst 71–2). The Yekuana, like many Amerindian tribes, worshipped nature and all of its elements as sacred; therefore, it is common in Amerindian mythology for sacred or divine beings to test the worth of a mortal hero by appearing in the myth as connected to both animals and humans. In this Yekuana myth, a man named Maichak partook on a heroic quest to make contact with vultures, as he believed they possessed sacred wisdom. Maichak hid in a field all day next to a dead tapir to wait for vultures to arrive. Once the vultures came, Maichak chose the largest vulture to follow, believing it to be the chief, but to his amazement, the vulture metamorphosed into a beautiful woman. The vulture woman instructed Maichak to follow her to the domain of the vultures where they could be married, if her father, the vulture chief, agreed. Once in the vulture realm, the vulture chief stated that he would allow Maichak to marry his daughter on the condition that he pass a series of tests. The tests required Maichak to: "drain an enormous lake and bring in all its fish for the chief to eat[;] ... build a house on a certain ledge, which required that holes for house poles be dug into solid stone[; and] ... carve a shaman's bench in the likeness of the chief himself ... [which was] a seemingly impossible task as the chief always kept himself covered and no one but his daughter knew that he had two heads" (Bierhorst 71). As is common in Amerindian myths of heroic quests, Maichak found that the animals of the forest came to help him achieve his tests, so that he could finally unite in marriage with the vulture woman. Thus, Maichak's heroic quest, that was initiated and guided by his animal bride, enabled him to learn her sacred wisdom of nature and become a spiritually transformed shaman for his people.

When animal brides appear in folktales and fairy tales, the sacrality of the totemic or divine representative is not lessened as the tale moves from myth to folktale and fairy tale. For example, the husbands of animal brides within folktales and fairy tales are also often presented as partaking on a heroic journey when they marry an animalistic wife. Like Maichak, folktale or fairy tale heroes often learn the sacred wisdom of nature, and thus transform psychologically and/or spiritually because of their experiences with their animal brides; however, many folktale and fairy tale male protagonists end their tales as failed heroes because they try to force their animal brides to fit expectations shaped by their society and thus fail to grow beyond definitions of self that are shaped by patriarchal ideologies. When folktale and fairy tale husbands of animal brides fail their quests, the animal brides often leave their mortal husbands behind as their punishment. This failure on the part of many folktale and fairy tale husbands suggests that the lesson, of remembering the proper reverence owed to totemic or divine women, is truly meant for the audience of the tales.

Some of the most famous animal bride folktales involve swan maidens, such as a Scandinavian folktale entitled "The Swan Maiden" (Tatar 79–80). Scandinavian/Norse mythology holds similar tenets to its predecessor of Germanic mythology. Like Germanic religion, Scandinavian religion also worshipped nature. Scandinavians embraced a wide array of deities who held associations with the environment, such as Thor, the god of thunder, and all the members of the Vanir pantheon, the old Norse pantheon of fertility deities, such as Frey and Freyja, who were directly connected to the environment. In Norse mythology, the leading pantheon of the Aesir, with its father god Odin, was said to have taken over the power of the old Vanir pantheon. This mythic event may account for the historical shifting of Germanic beliefs after Indo-European contact, when the worship of fertility deities moved to more patriarchal deities who focused on kingship and warfare. This transition of beliefs is said to have lessened the power of many earth goddesses who may have once held superior positions within the Vanir pantheon, such as the Vanir goddess Freyja, discussed earlier in this chapter as the Germanic Earth Mother Freya. In Norse mythology, after the fall of the Vanir, Freyja is said to have agreed to live with the Aesir pantheon in order to maintain peace, and when she joined the Aesir, her demoted role became evident, as she mostly became portrayed in Norse myth as a sexualized, fickle, and untrustworthy plaything of the more powerful gods of the Aesir. However, coming from her heightened Germanic role as Earth Mother, Freyja is believed to have maintained in Norse religion some elements in connection with her traditional elevated status, such as her association with death, as Freyja was said to select fallen warriors to live with her in Folkvanger, just as warriors were chosen for Odin's Valhalla. Another tenet within Norse religion that suggests that Freyja's traditional role was once elevated beyond her common portrayal in Norse mythology, is her presentation as the goddess of prophecy and magic, as well as her connection to animal symbolism, as she was said to own a feathered cloak that allowed her to metamorphose into falcon form and fly. This connection of divine women being related to animals, especially birds, may extend back to prehistoric times in Scandinavia, and it remains a common tenet found within Norse mythology, such as is found with the mythic Valkyries who could shapeshift from divine female form to bird form in search of the worthy slain upon the battlefield. Thus, the animalistic swan maidens of Scandinavian folklore hold clear connections with the divine women of Norse religion.

The Scandinavian folktale, "The Swan Maiden," begins with a young man who was out hunting alone, a common start to a male heroic quest, when he saw three swans land near him. The man was astonished to see that the swans appeared to take off their feathers, as if they were a garment, and transformed into three beautiful maidens. The young man watched as the maidens bathed and played in the water, and then he saw them put their feathers back on and fly away. In the days to come, whenever the man thought about the youngest swan maiden, he began to feel that he must possess her; in fact, he could think of nothing else besides being with her. The young man's longing for the swan maiden had so transformed him that his mother noticed that he grew unwell. He told his mother what bothered him, and interestingly, the mother immediately knew how her son could possess the swan maiden. The mother told her son to go again to the pond in which he saw the swan maidens, and when they disrobed, he should steal the feathered attire of the youngest maiden. The young man did exactly as his mother instructed and saw that indeed the youngest swan maiden could not fly away with her sisters when he had stolen her feathered robe. The young man proceeded to tell the swan maiden that the only way she would get her feathers back was if she agreed to become his wife. The difference in portrayal of the mythic Maichak, who so revered the sacrality of the vulture woman that he underwent a dangerous quest to try and win her love, with the man of this folktale, who steals the animalistic element that makes the swan maiden sacred and tries to overpower her through marriage, shows that this folkloric man will not achieve the heightened spiritual transformation that Maichak achieved, and will thus be identified as a failed hero. The swan maiden sadly agreed to marry the man who stole her swan robe, and the couple lived together for seven years. However, one night the husband, reminiscing about the day he stole his bride, brought out her swan robe, and as soon as he placed the robe in her hands, his swan wife transformed into her swan form and flew forever away from him, indeed showing that the husband of the folktale failed his heroic quest by only maintaining his identity as a product of a patriarchal culture that oppressed divine, as well as human, women.

Many swan maiden tales, such as this one, display the historical demotion of goddesses, and subsequently the women who served them, that occurred in many civilizations throughout the world. Many civilizations within the regions of the Middle East, Asia, Africa, Europe, etc., once revered goddesses in supreme positions of authority, but in moments of conquest, diffusion, technological advancement, etc., systematic efforts on the part of developing patriarchal societies often undermined the power of these formidable goddesses. For instance, as was discussed with the mythic shift from the worship of the Norse Vanir pantheon to the Aesir patriarchal pantheon, many earth goddesses were demoted from their heightened positioning in this transferal, likely due to Indo-European influence that gained dominance in Scandinavian regions between 5000 to 2000 BCE. Furthermore, the Scandinavian adoption of Christianity by the eleventh-century CE eradicated existing goddess reverence with the worship of one supreme male deity; therefore, many once divine figures became presented as demoted figures within Scandinavian folklore. Therefore, animal bride tales, such as this Scandinavian folktale of a swan maiden, often display remnants of mythic goddesses of traditional religions as folkloric animal brides who, at least for a time, are forced to succumb to the life of a housewife.

A similar swan maiden folktale from Melanesia (Allan, Fleming, & Kerrigan 85) also shows the clear mistreatment of a "divine race of women who visited earth in the guise of swans" (Allan, Fleming, & Kerrigan 85). Melanesian mythology, like Amerindian and Norse mythology, displays a reverence for the natural world and its elements. Melanesian gods, goddesses, and culture heroes were therefore often presented as connected directly to nature. Therefore, animals often appear in Melanesian mythology as teachers of sacred wisdom to human characters, and often mystical beings appear in both animal and human form. However, European colonial powers in the nineteenth century brought Western religious, social, and political influences to Melanesia that decimated the existing traditional beliefs of the Melanesian people. For instance, Christian concepts greatly reduced, and in many cases eradicated, the worship of traditional Melanesian goddesses; this demotion of divine, and along with them human women, is conveyed within this Melanesian swan maiden folktale.

The folktale states that "divine" swan women came to earth one evening to fish (Allan, Fleming, & Kerrigan 85). It is significant that this folktale explicitly defines the swan women as divine, as this element is often only presented implicitly within folktales and fairy tales. A man who spied the swan maidens took the wings of one of the women and hid them under the main post of his house. In the morning, one of the swan women found that she could not return to her swan form in order to fly to her celestial home, so seizing his opportunity, the man captured the divine woman and forced her to be his wife. Again, the fact that the man in this folktale steals from the divine representation of the swan maiden in order to possess her signals that he will end up a failed hero instead of a spiritually transformed hero. And indeed, the folktale goes on to show that the man did not revere his divine, animalistic wife, but instead abused her, beating her every day. The swan woman grew so sad that she "wept bitter tears that washed away the earth floor of their home. The more she wept the more the soil ran away, until one day, she spotted the wings her husband had hidden" (Allan, Fleming, and Kerrigan 85). In a flash, like her Scandinavian counterpart, the swan woman put her wings back on, retained her divine and animalistic form, and left her husband forever, confirming that her husband did not complete his heroic quest.

Though the swan maiden of this Melanesian folktale, and the one in its Scandinavian variant, are shown to be demoted divine or totemic women in their portrayals of mere folkloric women who are forced to experience the degradation of being housewives to abusive husbands, they also reveal that they still hold a remnant of their former power when they eventually declare their independence, and thus proclaim their sacrality, in striking scenes that show them transform into their true wild self and leave behind failed husbands. The emotionally charged imagery of a woman escaping the confines of a husband who wishes to entrap her with domesticity, symbolic of patriarchal restrictions within a culture, certainly seems to send a strong message from the cultures that created and embraced these tales about their longing for the return of traditional ideologies.

A popular Chinese folktale (Larrington 238–9), recorded by Feng Menglong in 1645 CE, also shows a young man named Xüxan, who abuses his animal wife and thus becomes a failed hero; however, as implicitly portrayed in the swan maiden tales just discussed, this Chinese folktale explicitly reveals a cultural belief that Xüxan was wrong for his treatment of his sacred wife. This folktale shows Xüxan crossing West Lake in Hangzhou to visit a temple during the Festival of the Dead, and after doing so, he found his animal bride, who was not a swan woman, but a snake woman. In ancient China, supremely powerful goddesses were once quite prevalent. For instance, in Neolithic China (8000–2000 BCE), many "clay female figurines and fragments of life-sized female icons" have been found that suggest dominant goddess worship (Jiao 58). Later, Chinese mythology also portrayed many formidable goddesses, who were often connected to the natural environment, such as Nu Wä, who was conceived of as the Great Mother (Nelson 159). In the role of Great Mother, Nu Wä was attributed as creating the landscape of China and its inhabitants. In connection to this folktale of the snake woman, Nu Wä often appeared as having the upper body of a woman with the lower body of a snake, or as being able to transform into human or snake form at will. Therefore, this cultural remembrance of figures such as the goddess Nu Wä, certainly seems to be a part of this Chinese folktale of West Lake.

In the folktale, after visiting the temple, Xüxan shared a ferry with the woman who was to be snake wife. The woman, referred to as Madame White, was dressed in white, and the maid who was with her was dressed in blue. After some time passed, Xüxan and Madame White ended up married and lived together happily, until one day an abbot from a local temple warned Xüxan that his wife and her maid were demons. Believing the abbot, Xüxan now only felt distrust for his wife. While looking out one afternoon across West Lake, and thinking of his wife with only hatred now, Xüxan saw that she and her maid approached, but as if nature had responded to his hatred, Madame White's boat overturned, and it appeared that both Madame White and her maid drowned before Xüxan's eyes. However, when Xüxan returned home, he found his wife alive and well, but she was very angry with him "and treated him sternly, refusing to let him out of her sight…. He became scared of her now that he was convinced that she was not a human being" (Larrington 239). When he was able, Xüxan commissioned the help of the abbot who warned him about his wife's hidden nature. The abbot gave Xüxan a magic bowl, that if pressed on Madame White's head, would force her to be under his control. Xüxan took the bowl, and with the help of the abbot, did as instructed, and Madame White shrank in size and revealed that she was indeed a snake woman, as her true form was that of a white python that lived in West Lake. Madame White stated that she fell in love with Xüxan, and thus forfeited her snake form for that of a human woman, so that she could be with him. Madame White begged Xüxan and the abbot to show pity toward her, but the abbot captured her and her maid, who was now in the form of a small blue fish, and imprisoned them both under a pagoda. However, the tale makes it clear in its ending that Xüxan was wrong for giving in to the pressure of the abbot, as the tale ends with Xüxan being punished by the gods for the treatment of his snake wife, as the gods forced Xüxan to "run away" from his community forever (Larrington 239).

It is significant that the religious figure of the Buddhist abbot in this folktale is portrayed as an antagonist, as the tale directs blame upon the abbot for convincing Xüxan to go down the wrong path and mistreat his sacred animal bride. Buddhism, which came to China around the first century CE, along with Confucian values that had been in place since the sixth-century BCE, imparted philosophies that held male spirituality as superior to female spirituality, which lessened, and in some instances eliminated, the reverence of traditional Chinese goddesses. However, this folktale, admonishes Xüxan's treatment of his animal bride by portraying him as a failed hero, thus imparting to audiences a message that maintains the reverence for traditional goddess-oriented ideology over that of the philosophies of Confucianism and Buddhism.

Often animal brides who marry husbands who fail their heroic quests still end up imparting a lesson about what they represent as remnants of earth goddesses to the children they leave behind from the failed marriage. For example, another swan maiden folktale (Nauwald 20–2), this time from east Siberia among the Korin-Burjates, tells how a swan maiden's influence upon her children allowed them to spiritually transform. Similar to Amerindian and Melanesian culture, nature was revered as sacred in Siberia; therefore, animals in Siberian mythology often appeared as totemic teachers of spiritual wisdom to mythic characters. In addition, Siberian mythology often linked the reverence of nature with the worship of goddesses. For instance, a Great Mother, who was envisioned as the land itself, was revered in Siberia for thousands of years, and many natural elements were believed in Siberia to be divine females, such as Fire Mother, who was envisioned as fire itself (Hays-Gilpin 199). Likewise, Siberian goddesses were often merged with animals, appearing with animalistic, especially birdlike, properties. In fact, Siberian shamans, who were both men and women, were said to be descended from Mother Tomam, the goddess of birds. Thus, by way of wearing a feathered cloak, Siberian shamans were able to tap into the wisdom of the goddess Tomam. Therefore, one must assume that the swan maidens of Siberian folklore also carry elements of this totemic goddess worship.

The swan maiden in this particular Siberian folktale married a man named Tangkalsingh after he stole her feathered gown. As with other swan maiden tales, the swan wife in this tale is shown to be demoted when she was forced to take part in domestic affairs, such as becoming a housewife and birthing children, in her case five sons and five daughters. After many years, the swan wife convinced her husband, who was drunk one night, to return her feathered gown back to her, saying that she promised not to leave him. But, once she got her feathered gown back, she immediately metamorphosed into her swan form, signaling her totemic/divine form, and flew away, leaving her husband and children behind. However, this folktale shows that the swan woman called out to her children before she left them: "'My daughters, become shaman women! My sons, become shamans!'" (Nauwald 21). Thus, though this folktale presents an unworthy husband who fails to become a hero from the spiritual guidance of his sacred wife, it does portray the children of the swan woman as gaining their mother's sacred wisdom and becoming spiritual advisors to their communities.

Likewise, a Japanese folktale (Kobayashi 125) shows a man who marries a snake wife, who also passes on her sacred wisdom to her children rather than her human husband. In this folktale, the man rescued a snake that had been abused by local children. Because the man treated the snake with kindness, the tale signals that he was worthy of the spiritual union that comes with marrying a sacred nature representative. And this is exactly what happens in the folktale, as a woman appeared at the man's home that night and asked him to marry her. The man was stunned by this proposal, but he agreed. The couple lived happily for a time, until the woman became pregnant and was about to give birth. The woman told her husband that he was not to come into her room as she was giving birth; however, the man could not resist when he heard her cries, so he broke his promise. Looking into the birthing room, the man, instead of being kind as he had been when he saved the abused snake, was disgusted to see that his wife had metamorphosed into a massive snake. Because the husband failed to recognize his wife's transformation into an animal as sacred, the wife, after giving birth, stated that she must leave him forever. However, before she went, the snake wife gave her husband one of her eyeballs and asked him to give it to their son, so he could "lick the eyeball" throughout his life, and thus gain spiritual knowledge (Kobayashi 125). Furthermore, the snake wife told her husband to tell their son that if he was ever in need, he should come to his mother in the lake. Thus, like the previous tale of the swan mother, this tale ends with the snake woman's son becoming a spiritual leader for his people because of his mother's connection to sacrality.

Another folktale from Japan (Kobayashi 127) also shows a son gaining from his animal mother the wisdom his father could not from his animal bride. The man in this folktale left Japan to sail to China in the Tang dynasty (618–907 CE); however, the man never made it to his original destination, as his boat drifted off course and shipwrecked on a desert island. A she-bear found the man in distress, so she nursed him back to health. Because of the bear's kindness, the man married the she-bear and had a son with her. However, one day, worried about the social stigma of being married to a bear, the man took their son and left the island, "abandoning his bear wife" who died of a broken heart (Kobayashi 127). However, the tale concludes not with the behavior of the father, but with that of the son, as the son superseded the wrong act of his father by going back to the island himself and gathering his mother's bones, so that they could be honored by his people "as a deity" (Kobayashi 127). The fact that the father in this folktale is simply eradicated from the narrative sends a message that his act of not recognizing the sacrality of his animal bride was morally and spiritually wrong; thus, he too is presented as a failed hero. However, in showing the son remedy the fault of his father by teaching the people to worship the she-bear as their divine totem animal, the tale signals that the son gained spiritual, even shamanic wisdom, because of his sacred bear mother.

For centuries, the Japanese worshipped powerful female deities, such as Amaterasu, the goddess of the sun, who served as the head of the Shinto pantheon. In Japanese Shinto, nature was revered as sacred, and Shinto divine beings, like Amaterasu and Kaya-no-hime, the goddess of vegetation, were directly connected to nature. With the open worship of powerful goddesses, ancient Japanese culture also held women in prestigious positions. For example, Japan's first ruler was the shamaness-queen Himiko. Additionally, shamanesses were an integral part of Japanese culture for centuries. Chinese culture penetrated Japanese customs in the seventh and early eighth centuries CE, which led to the adoption of Confucian and eventually Buddhist beliefs, that, as happened in China, lessened the divine roles of Japanese goddesses and the social positioning of Japanese women. Also, in the Kamakura and Muromachi periods (1100–1600 CE), Japanese culture began to further value male dominance, which caused the role of women, divine and mortal, to become even more demoted. However, the popularity of animal bride folktales in Japan, that featured mystical female characters who taught males about the proper way to revere women, suggests the people's lasting embrace of traditional goddess worship as it once appeared in Japan. Kobayashi concurs, stating that the "Japanese people were (and still are) fond of telling, sharing, and retelling stories about gritty female characters who do not care much about the patriarchal norms of Japanese social codes…. An animal woman is never naïve, meek, and obedient; instead, she is assertive. Through Japanese Animal-Wife tales, the Japanese people have preserved" the power their goddesses once held (Kobayashi 101).

Not all animal bride tales show husbands as failed heroes upon heroic quests, as some animal bride folktales and fairy tales do show husbands learning from the guidance of their sacred animal brides, such as is shown in another folktale from Japan (Kobayashi 124) that portrays a man marrying a fish wife. In this folktale, a lonely fisherman, instead of killing and eating the fish he caught on his daily patrol, decided to save the fish and treat it kindly by keeping it and feeding it each day. After showing kindness to the fish, the man found an unknown woman in his kitchen one afternoon. The woman revealed to the fisherman that she came from the "sea-dragon god's undersea palace in order to help him" (Kobayashi 124). The two soon married and had children. However, in time, the townspeople made fun of the union of the fisherman and his fish wife, which led the fisherman to feel embarrassment and shame, so he turned his back on the woman he loved, thus turning his back on the goddess representative of the tale, which signals that he failed to revere nature as sacred. The fisherman ordered his fish wife to leave their house. His wife looked sadly at her husband, turned back into her fish form, and left him. However, unlike the husbands of the animal bride tales discussed thus far, the fisherman grew to regret his decision to mistreat his fish wife and furtively began searching for her. In being unable to find his fish wife, the fisherman, in an element that is rare in animal bride folktales, turned himself into a bat. The unique ending of this folktale shows that the fisherman experienced a spiritual transformation because of the time he spent married to an animal bride. Unlike the husbands of animal brides discussed so far, the fisherman in this tale did learn the sacred lessons of nature that were embodied in the goddess representative of his fish wife, as his ultimate decision to become an animal shows that he realized the interconnectivity of nature and learned not to value his human identity above that of the elements of the environment. In addition, it is telling that the fisherman did not choose to metamorphose into the form of a fish, but instead chose the form of a bat, because it reveals that the man did not simply choose his wife to love in fish form, but chose the greater message his fish wife represented—that the natural world is what must be worshipped, as this is the sacred wisdom that animal brides, as sacred totemic figures and earth goddess representatives, impart.

A Finnish fairy tale by Parker Fillmore entitled "The Forest Bride" (1922) (Cole 387–94) shows another male character who learns spiritual wisdom from his animal bride. In ancient Finland, as in many other regions already discussed, goddesses were often viewed as representations of the natural environment, such as Akka, who was envisioned as Mother Earth. All aspects of nature, including animals, were viewed as sacred. Thus, many Finnish myths show natural elements guiding mythic protagonists along their journeys. Both males and females could serve as shamans in ancient Finland. These shamans often worshipped the goddess Louhi, who was the ruler of Pohjola, the Finnish underworld, and adept at using magic, especially to shapeshift. In addition, Finnish shamans often envisioned that eagles guided them upon their shamanic journeys. Therefore, many Finnish folktales and fairy tales that feature animalistic women who serve as guides, such as is found in the "The Forest Bride," arguably carry remnants of traditional Finnish goddess worship.

In "The Forest Bride," a farmer instructed his three sons to each chop down a tree; the farmer went on to tell his sons that whatever direction their tree fell was the direction where they should find their future wives. The first two sons did as their father instructed and saw that their respective trees pointed toward farms where beautiful maidens lived, so they went happily to meet their new brides. However, the third son named Veikko chopped down his tree and found that it fell pointing to the forest where only animals lived. Still, Veikko was undeterred, so he went to see what was in store for him in the forest. Veikko soon came upon a small cottage in the woods, but when he went inside, he found that only a small mouse stood on a table. Veikko declared that "'there's nobody here,'" but the mouse reproached him saying, "'Why, Veikko, I'm here'" (Cole 388)! With that, Veikko laughed and told the mouse that she did not count; however, the mouse retorted "'Of course, I count!'" (Cole 388)! Thinking about the mouse's answer, Veikko decided to reveal the purpose of his quest to her. Once he told her, the little mouse declared that Veikko should marry her. At first, Veikko thought the idea absurd, but as he talked more with the mouse, the more he liked her, so he agreed to marry her.

When Veikko arrived back at his father's farm, he was greeted by his two older brothers, who were quite happy, having just come home from finding their beautiful, human brides. Veikko also related many nice details about his bride-to-be, but he left out the part about her being a mouse. The father, overjoyed that his three sons had all found their future brides, declared that they should undergo a series of tasks to make sure that the brides were worthy of his sons. The first test involved baking a loaf of bread. The first two sons saw no issue with this and went to ask their fiancés to accomplish the test, but Veikko felt only sadness and fear, as he knew that there was no way a mouse could bake a loaf of bread. Still, Veikko went back into the forest and told the mouse about his troubles. The mouse, however, only laughed and said that it was not a problem, as she was quite good at baking bread. And sure enough, the bread made by the mouse was the best that Veikko's father had ever tasted. Veikko's father next asked that the intended brides present him with a sample of their weaving, and again, the mouse bride provided the best sample. Finally, the father wished to meet his future daughters-in-law, and again the two older brothers cheerfully went to get their fiancés, but Veikko once more worried about the ridicule he would receive from his older brothers when they saw that his bride-to-be was a mouse. However, Veikko overcame these feelings and went to retrieve the mouse that he had grown to love. Veikko told his beloved mouse as he walked with her to his father's home "not to be frightened, that he would take good care of her. His father, he told her, was a gentle old man and would be kind to her" (Cole 392).

The tale continues to show Veikko and the mouse maiden making their way to Veikko's home with a procession of five mice servants for the mouse maiden. However, a man encountered the sight as they were all crossing a bridge, and finding it ridiculous, he pushed all the mice over the side of the bridge. Veikko, proving his true devotion, yelled at the man: "'What have you done! ... You've drowned my poor little sweetheart! ... You poor little mouse! ... How sorry I am that you drowned! You were a faithful, loving sweetheart, and now that you are gone, I know how much I loved you'" (Cole 393)! Once these words were spoken, Veikko looked up from the ravine and saw a coach coming toward him that held a beautiful human maiden. The maiden revealed to Veikko that she was the mouse maiden all along, and in fact, she was a princess who had been placed under a spell that forced her to appear in animal form. Now that the mouse maiden was free, both her and Veikko made their way to Veikko's home, where they were married. As an added bonus, Veikko and his princess bride went off to her kingdom to rule the land.

The format of this fairy tale shows that the male protagonist, Veikko, had to prove that he respected nature as portrayed by the representation of the mouse maiden. And indeed, Veikko repeatedly proved that he was able to overcome his feelings of shame at marrying an animal bride who he initially thought was insignificant. Therefore, because Veikko was finally able to love a mouse maiden, he, like the fisherman of the previous tale, proved that he fulfilled his hero's quest and was thus worthy of the spiritual rewards the natural goddess representative provided, portrayed symbolically in this tale by Veikko gaining the reward of royalty, which is a common folktale and fairy tale reward meant to convey the spiritual transformation of the hero.

Mistresses of Animals

Like tales of Earth Mothers and animal brides who serve as representations of traditional earth goddesses or totemic figures around the world, there are also myths, folktales, and fairy tales that present women as capable of taming or harnessing the elements of nature, thus, also signaling their connection to sacrality or even divinity. Mythic women often specifically showed their mastery of the environment by displaying the ability to tame ferocious beasts; thus, these women were often defined as divine Mistresses of Animals. For example, in artistic Neolithic goddess imagery from Crete and Anatolia, a Mistress of Animals is often shown standing or seated between ferocious animals, such as lions, tigers, or snakes, in full control of them. Likewise, the Phrygian goddess Cybele and the Greek goddess Artemis are often portrayed as Mistresses of Animals in mythology, and their myths also show them in command of the environment by their ability to tame wild animals. One of the most famous examples of a mythic woman who was able to harness the elements of nature and tame ferocious beasts appears in Homer's *Odyssey* (c. eighth-century BCE) in the character of Circe. Circe was shown to live alone on an isolated island filled with immense wilderness and surrounded by animals, many of which she transformed from human form into animal form, as she did to Odysseus's men by turning them into swine. Circe's ability to mystically transform humans into animals, as well as tame ferocious beasts, shows that she was in command of the forces of nature, and thus presents her as a divine Mistress of Animals. Similarly, in the Mesopotamian myth *The Epic of Gilgamesh* (c. 2100 BCE), the character of Shamhat was also shown to be a Mistress of Animals when she was the only one who was able to subdue the wild beast-like creature Enkidu because she was a priestess of the goddess Ishtar and thus possessed the sacred abilities of the goddess.

A Sicilian folktale, that was recorded by Laura Gonzenbach in 1868, entitled "The Snake Who Bore Witness for a Maiden" (Zipes 82–3) displays a maiden who is presented as similar to a mythic Mistress of Animals. The maiden in this tale lived in the deep wilderness with her mother. Immediately, the presentation that the maiden and mother live together in a secluded natural environment, outside of civilization, marks them as connected to pagan concepts of sacred women. In the tale, when the maiden's mother left to sell herbs in the city, a prince ventured into the forest, saw the maiden's small abode, and when he caught sight of the beauty of the maiden, he broke into her house and raped her. While the maiden was struggling with the prince, she saw a snake slither across the floor, and showing her ability to harness the powers of nature and command wild animals, she demanded that the snake bear witness to the unjust act against her. Once the prince left her alone, the maiden ordered the snake to follow the prince back to his kingdom to assure that he would be unable to marry anyone but her, which according to the customs of her era, was her right. And indeed, back at his kingdom, the prince found that the snake had coiled itself around his neck. When the prince tried to marry another woman, he was unable to, as the very thought only tightened the snake's grip. Showing the maiden as gaining the upper hand within the tale, she came to the prince's castle and enlightened the prince as to why a snake was wrapped around his neck. The prince tried to pretend that he did not know the maiden, but the maiden, showing herself to be a folkloric Mistress of Animals, commanded the snake's pressure to increase, soon jeopardizing the life of the prince. The prince, now fully at the mercy of the goddess-like maiden, had no choice but to agree to marry her. The tale thus ends assuring that the maiden will hold the superior position within her marriage and within the societal realm when she becomes queen. The fact that this tale explicitly presents a wronged maiden who uses mystical abilities in line with mythic Mistresses of Animals shows that the Sicilian people may have held onto Roman mythic remnants that venerated powerful goddesses who would assuredly punish any male who tried to assault the power of a goddess.

Some mythic women appear in the role of Mistress of Animals when they marry an animal husband. For instance, the Opayé of Brazil tell a myth (McCoppin, *Ecological Heroes*, 232–6) where a woman chose to marry a jaguar. The myth states that the woman's people were starving, as they did not possess the skills to properly hunt in their dense jungle environment, so the woman was presented as understanding that she must find a jaguar to marry if she was to save her people. Once the woman married the jaguar and brought it to live amongst her people, in order to teach them its ways of survival, they reacted only with fear and demanded that the jaguar and his wife leave. When the jaguar and the woman left the people, they began to starve once more, until they saw that the woman had chosen to become a jaguar herself. When they saw the example of this mythic Mistress of Animals, they adopted the jaguar as their sacred totem animal, and finally learned how to hunt like the jaguar, so that they never starved again.

Like mythic Mistresses of Animals who marry animal husbands, folktales and fairy tales also show women marrying animal grooms. In fact, many folktales and fairy tales that present women marrying animals, or beast-like creatures, portray the women in roles similar to mythic Mistresses of Animals precisely because they serve to guide their husbands upon heroic quests to embrace nature as sacred, just like animal brides attempted to do with their husbands.

For instance, in a folktale from Spain entitled "The Wounded Lion" (Lang), a maiden proved herself a Mistress of Animals when she healed and married a lion man. The maiden in this tale saw a lion one day as she was tending her cows. The sight of the lion initially scared her, and she wanted to flee, but the tale shows that the maiden overcame her fear, as she saw that the lion appeared injured. The maiden decided to approach the lion and saw that he had a large thorn sticking out of his paw, so the maiden pulled the thorn out. The lion thanked the maiden by licking her hand. The maiden's ability to tame and heal the lion immediately portrays her within this tale as a folkloric Mistress of Animals.

The folktale further shows the maiden in the mythic role of Mistress of Animals when she healed the lion two more times, before growing curious about where the lion lived. The maiden was shown as following the lion one night as he went to his cave. Once at the cave, the maiden bravely entered the domain of the beast, that would assuredly spell death for most, and spoke to the lion, who spoke back to her. The lion told the maiden that he was a prince who was transformed into lion form because of a spell cast upon him by an evil giant. The maiden learned that she could help the lion man by accomplishing a dangerous quest of taking a lock of hair from a local princess, spinning it into a cloak for the giant, and then presenting it to the giant at his fortress high upon a mountain. The maiden, showing herself to be a goddess representative, completed all the required tasks with ease and returned to the lion man, where she proceeded to induce the metamorphosis of the lion man back into his human form, which she did in clear goddess fashion—by killing him, cutting him up into many pieces, burning the pieces, and then resurrecting him. This almost identical pattern of death and resurrection at the hands of a mystical or divine woman is found in many mythic narratives. Many myths show goddesses, or women connected to goddesses, who take part in a process where a mythic male is killed, dismembered, and then resurrected to make him stronger upon his heroic journey. For example, the Greek Medea, who was a priestess of the goddess Hecate, killed, cut up, boiled, and then resurrected Jason before marrying him and helping him to achieve his heroic quest. Thus, this folktale certainly presents the maiden as a goddess-like Mistress of Animals, who served to guide her husband through a heroic quest, as his metamorphosis from lion to man, and his experience with death and rebirth, taught him about the laws of the natural world, which brought about his psychological, and perhaps spiritual, transformation. The tale ends with the metamorphosed and resurrected man asking the folkloric Mistress of Animals to marry him and become queen of his kingdom, assuring that she, like the maiden of the previous Sicilian folktale, would go on to reign supreme throughout her land.

Perhaps the most famous example of a woman marrying an animalistic man appears in Madame de Beaumont's fairy tale "Beauty and the Beast" (1756). Like the folktale from Spain just discussed, the character of Beauty in this fairy tale, as another remnant of a mythic Mistress of Animals, is shown to be the only one who can tame her animalistic husband, and is thus portrayed as the guide for the Beast upon his heroic quest. Some critics, such as Tatar, believe that "Beauty and the Beast," and other animal groom tales, point to cultural norms that strengthened patriarchy, as these types of tales made it acceptable for families to turn over their daughters to "beasts" if it increased their wealth and status (Tatar 34). To an extent this is true, as many animal groom tales do show young maidens, such as Beauty, being forced to marry abysmal husbands at the decree of their fathers. However, "Beauty and the Beast," and many other animal groom tales like it, may be imparting messages that portray the maidens who marry beasts, not as pawns of patriarchy, but as powerful Mistresses of Animals who are in full control of the beasts.

For example, "Beauty and the Beast" shows that an enchantress, a woman with explicit supernatural abilities, which signals her connection to traditional goddess-oriented ideologies, as the one who orchestrated many of the events within the tale, as she made an unworthy male turn into a beast, so that he could learn the ways of nature and the importance of sacred women. Therefore, the role of the enchantress is directly connected with Beauty in the fairy tale, as united, both women serve the same agenda. Beauty steps into the narrative as a defiant daughter who willingly marries the Beast to save her father's life. Her father attempted to refuse Beauty's offer of marriage to the Beast, but Beauty insisted on the marriage, stating to her father before he set out to the Beast's castle, "'you cannot hinder me from following you'" (Leprince de Beaumont). Beauty's insistence in this scene does not portray her as a victim, but instead as a woman in charge of her own decisions. Furthermore, when Beauty first interacted with the Beast, she was portrayed with more power than one might expect of a maiden in her situation, as she was fearful of the Beast for only a moment, but then proceeded to act as a divine Mistress of Animals might act when she almost instantaneously took over command of the Beast. This is conveyed in the narrative when the Beast, upon meeting Beauty alone for the first time, yielded his power to her when he stated, "'you alone are mistress here; you need only bid me gone, if my presence is troublesome, and I will immediately withdraw'" (Leprince de Beaumont). Furthermore, throughout the remainder of the fairy tale, Beauty continued to hold the upper hand in the relationship, as the Beast was repeatedly portrayed as entirely under her authority. Therefore, Beauty served, not as a victim who was forced into an inadequate marriage, but as the guide of the Beast upon his heroic quest, as it was the Beast's acceptance of his animalistic form, as well as his devotion to Beauty, as a remnant of a mythic Mistress of Animals, that finally allowed him to be psychologically transformed, portrayed when the enchantress allowed the Beast to metamorphose back into human form. With this interpretation of Beauty as powerfully in command of her own life, and of those around her, instead of at the command of patriarchy, the fairy tale reveals that it may have originated from older tales involving goddess ideologies.

Beauty's role within "Beauty and the Beast," of a remnant Mistress of Animals, appears in many similar folktales and fairy tales that also show female characters, not as young maidens forced to forfeit their happiness with unsuitable spouses, but as folkloric Mistresses of Animals who chose to marry "beasts" because they were the only ones who were able to tame them (Tatar 35).

For instance, a Chinese folktale entitled the "The Fairy Serpent" (Heiner 216–7) shows that a maiden's father became entrapped by a giant serpent, who coiled his massive body around the man, only letting him go if he agreed to have his daughter marry him. The tale, like "Beauty and the Beast," thus initially appears to show a father forcing his daughter to enter into a highly unsatisfactory marriage; however, the tale soon reveals that the power of the relationship between human wife and animalistic husband is really in the hands of the female, as the snake husband, like the Beast, is revealed to "dote" on his wife, meeting any command she asked of him (Heiner 216). Further portraying the wife in this tale as in command of her snake husband, as a remnant of a mythic Mistress of Animals, she one day picked up her husband, who was so big that he could coil around her father's body at the start of the tale, and thrust him into the water, which caused him, at her mystical command, to metamorphose into the form of a human. Thus, the wife's extraordinary abilities in this tale to command a beast, wield superhuman power, and initiate metamorphose certainly portrays her as a goddess representative who aids her animalistic husband upon his heroic quest.

Similarly, in the Russian folktale, the "Snotty Goat" (Afanas'ev 200–2), the maiden of the tale is described as defiant, formidable, and wise throughout her whole narrative. The maiden is portrayed in the folktale as longing to marry a goat, though her sisters wanted to marry human men. Once the sister indeed married a goat, all others viewed their union as ridiculous, but the maiden was shown to literally slap anyone who made fun of her, showing her not at all to be forced into an unsuitable marriage. When the maiden decided to turn her goat husband into a man, as she was portrayed as growing tired of his animalistic behavior, she merely took his goat skin and threw it into the fire, whereby her husband metamorphosed into a man. Again, the maiden's ability to metamorphose an animal into a human clearly connects her with portrayals of mythic Mistresses of Animals, portraying her not as a victim of a patriarchal culture that demands she accept a life that is unsuitable to her, but as the sacred instructor of a male hero who needs to transform psychologically and/or spiritually.

Also, in the Grimm brothers' tale of the "Frog King" (J. Grimm & W. Grimm 13–5), of which there are many variants around the world, the maiden of this tale also seems initially forced by her father to marry a frog, but her defiant actions throughout the narrative, best shown when she threw her frog husband against the wall when he asked to sleep in her bed, allows the maiden to be seen as similar to the other Mistresses of Animals who likewise refused to submit to patriarchal rules. Furthermore, the maiden within the "Frog King," like many other maidens within animal groom tales, mixes her defiance with profound mystical ability that appears initially harsh, as the frog is transformed into a man precisely because the maiden roughly threw him against the wall. Likewise, in

Scottish and Irish versions of this frog groom tale, the maidens behead the frogs to induce their metamorphosis (Tatar 35). A Korean variant, "A Frog for a Husband," shows the wife of the frog cutting his skin off with scissors in order to transform him into a man. And a Polish variant of the tale "replaces a frog with a snake and recounts in lavish detail the ... [maiden's] act of tearing the creature in two" before initiating his metamorphosis (Tatar 36). All of these acts show the maidens as Mistresses of Animals as they are portrayed in absolute command of their animal grooms, but specifically the harsh portrayal of the mystical act of transformation connects the maidens of these tales to mythic narratives of goddesses, or goddess representatives, who teach male heroes about the cycles of nature through death and rebirth, just as the maiden within the Spanish folktale did when she transformed the lion man into a hero by means of his death, dismemberment, and resurrection. Thus, folktales and fairy tales of animal grooms, such as the variants of the "Frog King," often present maidens as remnants of divine Mistresses of Animals, who take harsh measures to teach male heroes about the laws of nature, in order to help their husbands become heroes.

Finally, many mythic, folkloric, and fairy tale women are also portrayed as capable of birthing animalistic children, which again portrays them as connected to mythic examples of Mistresses of Animals. Many mythic women have been presented as sacred for their ability to birth children of a different species; for example, the Passamaquoddy of northeastern North America tell a myth (McCoppin, *Ecological Heroes*, 226–29) of a woman who fell in love with a snake man who appeared to her from the lake near her home. Despite the fact that her parents and community shunned her for her decision to unite with a snake man, the woman listened to her own desires and married the animal man. In marrying the snake man, the woman proved herself sacred by giving birth to hundreds of snake children and finally becoming a snake herself, which led to her people adopting the snake as their sacred totem. In addition, many creator goddesses also birthed animals as part of their role in creation, such as the Japanese Izanami, the Greek Gaia, and the Inuit Sedna.

Similarly, folktale and fairy tale women have also often birthed elements of the natural environment, such as portrayed in the Persian folktale "The Pumpkin Child," where a mother births a pumpkin, and in the French folktale "The Snow Child," where a mother births a child made of snow. In India's folkloric collection the *Pañćatantra* (c. 200 BCE) by Viṣṇu Śarma, a mother gives birth to a snake son, which proves her connection to sacrality. The snake son goes on to find a sacred wife who also aids in his transformation from snake to human, similar to the animal groom tales just discussed. Also, in the German Grimm brothers' fairy tale "Hans my

Hedgehog," a mother births a boy with the upper body of a hedgehog and the lower body of a human, who also marries a woman who helps him transform from an animal into a man, again signaling the women of the fairy tale as remnants of traditional goddesses.

In Francesco Straparola's Italian fairy tale "The Pig King" (1550–1555), a female character is shown to be a remnant of a mythic Mistress of Animals when she births an animalistic child in the form of a pig boy. The queen's representation as a Mistress of Animals is supported by the fact that she, by giving birth to an animalistic son, is shown in the tale to teach her husband, the king, as well as their subjects, the value of loving nature, through their ability to love the pig boy. The father of the pig boy initially wrestled with wanting to kill his own child in order to save himself the humiliation of having a pig for a son. As shown, often husbands of animal brides similarly wrestled with perceived humiliation because of their animalistic spouses, but in order to grow spiritually, they had to dispel societal prejudices and embrace the sacred value of their natural wives. Therefore, the father in choosing to love his pig son in this fairy tale, despite his animalistic appearance, becomes an actualized hero when he learns from his goddess-like wife what animal brides and Mistresses of Animals often teach their husbands within their respective tales—that one must respect all elements of the natural environment as sacred. Finally, the fairy tale states that the pig boy's curse would only be lifted by the wife he marries, which again portrays a fairy tale woman as in command of the goddess-like power of metamorphosis.

As this chapter has shown, for thousands of years people worshipped goddesses who were directly aligned to the natural environment and its elements. Even when goddess ideologies fell away in many cultures, the reverence for women in connection to nature remained an aspect of many folktales and fairy tales. Often, when a woman is deeply connected to nature within a folktale or fairy tale, holding such abilities as initiating seasonal change or altering the weather, metamorphosing between animal and human form, or marrying or birthing natural elements, it signals her as a traditional earth goddess representative who carries sacred, even transformational, wisdom for the other characters of the tale. The next chapter will explore folktale and fairy tale wise old women who likewise are connected to once revered goddesses.

2

Wise Old Women

Wise Old Shamanic Women

Because of women's perceived connection to nature, their ability to create life, and their shared form with revered goddesses, many societies worldwide envisioned women as holding especially close ties with the spiritual realm; thus, many women served in the revered role of shaman. Many global regions, such as Asia, Europe, Sub-Saharan Africa, North America, South America, Mesoamerica, etc., show evidence of cultures that revered female shamans since pre-recorded history (Dashú). For example, archeological excavations at the Dolní Věstonice site in the Czech Republic reveal that women served as shamans since the Upper Paleolithic period (Tedlock 3). Coastal Algonquian tribes believed that "women shamans were regarded as particularly powerful by virtue of their sex" (Grumet 54). Scandinavian communities also believed that women were especially in tune with spiritual affairs, so they held the respected shamanistic role of völva. The Siberian Chukchi embraced a proverb that stated that a "'Woman is by nature a ... shaman'" (qtd. in Dashú), indicating their widespread adoption of women within the role of shaman. The monumental skill, adeptness, bravery, and spiritual wisdom required of the female shaman meant that often the role was available for only the most experienced members of a community—the wise old women.

In various cultures, the role of the mature female shaman was one of healer for her community, as her extensive life experience was viewed as giving her the spiritual wisdom to heal the sick or cure the injured. Women shamans were also often believed to possess other spiritual and mystical skills, such as defeating supernatural adversaries, holding the power to shapeshift into various natural elements, or altering natural occurrences, as was presented as abilities of many nature goddesses and their representatives within Chapter 1 of this book. Some highly experienced female shamans were also believed to be able to journey to the underworld, the land of the dead, in order to retrieve the souls of the deceased and assist in their resurrection, which was also a skill of some of the goddess representatives discussed in Chapter 1. Because of the similarity in the skill sets of female shamans with those of mythic goddesses, and because shamans were often embraced by communities who worshipped goddesses, women shamans portrayed in mythology, who were in fact sometimes presented as divine, often imparted goddess-oriented lessons, such as the importance of embracing nature and its unending cycles, to audiences of the myths.

For example, the Yuchi of Tennessee present a myth about Grandmother Sun, who was portrayed as an old woman, a deity, and a shaman (Lankford 213–5). The myth begins with four brothers who killed their wives because their wives demanded they do it, so that they could prove to their husbands that there was no such thing as death in nature. Before ordering their husbands to kill them, the wives told their husbands that once they were dead, they should go on a quest to search for them within a sacred cave known only to shamans (Lankford 213). Once the brothers killed their wives in the myth, they made their way to the sacred cave of the shamans, where they endured tests of their spiritual resolve before finally making it to the inner realm of the cave where they found the divine, old shaman Grandmother Sun. Grandmother Sun, upon seeing the brothers, began teaching them about the processes of cyclical life in nature. Before the men's eyes, she planted corn, bean, and squash seeds, and immediately plants sprouted from each seed and began to grow at an elevated rate, so that in no time the brothers each had more than enough food to eat from the plants. Grandmother Sun then told the brothers that their wives were correct in stating that there was no such thing as death in nature, as the lives of humans advanced in similar ways to botanical agents through death and rebirth. To prove this to the brothers, Grandmother Sun placed giant gourds in front of them and stated that each gourd contained one of their wives. And indeed, when the brothers smashed open the gourds, they were instantly reunited with their resurrected wives.

As an old shaman and a goddess, Grandmother Sun guided the brothers upon a typical shamanic journey within this myth. The brothers, by entering her cave domain, were portrayed as submerging into the symbolic womb of the earth, which is, as discussed in Chapter 1, an image often used in the mythic presentation of divine Earth Mothers who are envisioned as the earth itself. Within the interior of the earth, many mythic narratives involving goddesses show that what enters the earth in death will one day emerge from the earth reborn. Similarly, many shamanic journeys require the shaman to go to the underworld, often portrayed as within the earth, in order to meet a goddess and learn that the lives of all living beings undergo a process of life, death, and rebirth according to the terms of nature's cycles. For example, the Arctic Inuit declare that all shamans must journey into the interior of the earth beneath the sea in order to learn from the goddess Sedna about cyclical life (McCoppin, *Hero's Quest*, 142). Once the shaman within many global cultures learns this goddess-oriented message by having experienced a symbolic death within the underworld, the shaman can leave the underworld, experiencing a symbolic resurrection, and move on to accomplish extraordinary feats, such as resurrecting others from death, which in mythology is often presented as an achievable act by shamans and goddesses alike. This is why the divine shaman Grandmother Sun taught the brothers about cyclical life only after they journeyed into her domain within the womb of the earth and underwent a symbolic death and rebirth. This Yuchi myth ends with the brothers becoming shamans themselves because Grandmother Sun taught them the means to serve their communities as representatives of her divine wisdom.

Like the shaman women of mythology, who are often presented as old and sometimes divine, many folktales and fairy tales portray wise old women characters in shamanistic roles in order to extend ideology associated with goddess worship.

For example, in Siberia, women shamans were considered to be an important part of the culture directly because of their widespread embrace of prominent goddesses, as discussed in Chapter 1. In fact, it is believed that in Siberia "the first shamans were women" (Davis-Kimball 84). However, when Christianity moved into Siberia in about the ninth-century CE, it identified goddess worship and the practice of shamanism as pagan. Though many converted outwardly to Christianity, many Siberian people maintained their traditional belief system through the means of folk customs and folklore. As with other regions that preserved traditional pagan beliefs through folklore, Siberian folktales became an outlet for "sources of information about Siberian shamanism.... The images and plots of magic tales and legends recount the whole course of a shaman's life and work, from the call and initiation, through relationships with helping spirits, through healing the sick through recovery of stolen souls, and accompanying the souls of the dead to the next world" (Van Deusen xii).

One Siberian folktale (Frankel 246–7) has preserved the role of the experienced Siberian shaman woman. The folktale presents an old woman who served her community as a shaman for many years. Her adult son was portrayed in the tale as dying, but the old shaman woman resolved to briefly pause her care of him, so she could tend to another young boy who was also dying in her village. Her husband tried to force her to stay and care for their son, but she retorted that the boy of the village was also someone's son. The old shaman went to the young boy and found that he had already died when she arrived. She asked the boy's parents for two reindeer teams if she was able to resurrect their son, of which they readily agreed. And indeed, beating her shaman drum, and chanting over the boy's body, the old shaman was able to bring the young boy back to life.

When the old shaman woman went back home, she found that her own son had also died. She tried again beating her shaman drum and chanting, but this technique did not work for her own child. So, though it was quite dangerous, the old shaman woman knew what she had to do. The old shaman woman told her husband that he must kill her and one of the reindeer teams she brought home, so that she may ride the reindeer through the underworld to find their son. Her husband, horrified, at first refused to do the gruesome task. But, trusting the skill of his wife, he did as she instructed and killed her, along with the team of reindeer. This folktale presents the old shaman woman as actually experiencing death herself in order to journey to the underworld, but often the death of the shaman is portrayed in myths, folktales, and fairy tales as symbolic. Again, the requirement for a shaman to physically or symbolically experience death shows that the shaman must embrace the goddess-oriented lesson of nature's ceaseless cycles in order to complete a successful shamanic journey, portrayed by the shaman's physical or symbolic resurrection, as well as the ability to resurrect others from death.

Once in the underworld, the old shaman woman's spirit rode a sleigh drawn by the spirits of the reindeer up to the sky where she met a raven and an eagle who admired her team of reindeer. Promising the reindeer team to the birds if they aided her in her task, she gained their help in finding out that a demoness had stolen the soul of her son. Unafraid of the horrible punishment that a demoness could unleash upon her if she tried to free her son, the old shaman woman went to the home of the demoness and stole her son's soul away. As the demoness chased her, the old shaman woman called upon the help of the eagle and raven, who halted the demoness and carried the two out of the underworld, which resurrected the shaman. The old shaman woman then beat her drum and chanted over the body of her son, until she was able to also resurrect him. Thus, by preserving the shamanistic practices of their once revered old shaman women by means of this folktale, Siberian audiences were able to continue their embrace of their goddess-oriented ideologies.

Like Siberia, as discussed in Chapter 1, China also held a long history of goddess worship. The widespread worship of powerful goddesses in Neolithic and Bronze Age China (10,000–1200 BCE) directly aided women in holding the respected role of shaman, known in China as shamanka. Shamankas were believed to be able to conduct "divination themselves" and interpret "the results of divination to others," as they possessed "the power to appeal directly to the ancestors in divination by asking questions about various concerns for the future" (Nelson 95). In the Bronze Age Shang dynasty (1600–1046 BCE), shamankas "were regularly employed in the interests of human and natural fertility, above all in bringing rain to parched farmlands" (Shafer 13). However, similar to the embrace of Christianity in Siberia, the popularity of Confucianism in the Zhou dynasty (1046–256 BCE) and the Han dynasty (206 BCE–220 CE) led to the embrace of widespread patriarchal values within China, which lessened long-standing traditions regarding goddess worship and women who held high religious and social positions, such as that of the shamanka.

A Confucian-influenced Chinese folktale entitled the "River God's Wife" (Chu 61–8) captures the historical attempt to supersede the powerful role of the shamanka by replacing the central religious role within the community with Confucian patriarchal leadership. The "River God's Wife" presents a village that periodically sacrificed one of their girls to a river god, a practice that was mandated and overseen in the folktale by the village shamankas. However, a male newcomer, Ximen Bao, arrived at the village and convinced the villagers not to sacrifice one of their youths, but to instead kill the leader of the shamankas, declaring her to be a witch. Ximen Bao then threw the "old witch in her seventies with a gaudily painted face" into the river, and then went on to throw the rest of the shamankas into the river to drown. This folktale preserves the attempt to define the traditional, goddess-oriented practice of female shamanism in China as outdated and even evil. As discussed in Chapter 1, many myths, folktales, and fairy tales around the world were created in an effort to try and replace existing goddess-oriented belief systems with new patriarchal ideologies. For instance, many European folktales in the Middle Ages often defined women who maintained pagan practices in communal roles, such as that of healer or spiritual advisor, as witches in an effort to secure male expertise in Christian religious affairs.

However, in China, the attempted eradication of the shamanka was not entirely successful, as reverence for female shamans picked up again during the Qing dynasty (1644–1912 CE) when the Manchus gained control of China in 1644. Unlike the predominant belief systems of China during this era, that had become heavily Confucian, Manchu belief systems still revered powerful goddesses, as well as female shamans who were believed to be able to directly converse with female deities and the ancestors of the Manchus. However, after overtaking authority in China, the Manchus eventually adopted Chinese Confucian values, which resulted in the demotion of the role of Manchu folk deities and the shaman women who served them. Though Confucian values convinced many to demote the role of Manchu folk deities and female shamans, many people continued to revere their traditional belief systems by maintaining folk customs and folklore that preserved this reverence.

For instance, a Manchu folktale from the Qing dynasty preserves the reverence of an old shaman woman identified as the Nišan shaman (Young 173–8). This folktale reveals that the old shaman woman was a widow, and thus possessed autonomy over her own life in an era when female autonomy was a rare social allowance in China under Confucian authority. The tale begins with a powerful Confucian official coming to seek out the Nišan shaman's help to save his young son. However, the Nišan shaman, instead of immediately helping the distressed father, treated the Confucian official with disdain, teasing him for seeking her out, as the act conflicted with his Confucian ideology. In fact, the Nišan shaman continued to tease the official, until he begged her for her help. Keller points out that this scene shows the tension between the traditionally patriarchal Confucian influence upon Manchu culture in China, as it shows the "Confucianized male Manchu (the official) and a traditional female Manchu (the shaman) … at odds with one another" (Keller 227). Thus, this folkloric scene preserves the historical strife felt by the Manchu people as their traditional values were being threatened by new belief systems. As stated, though Manchu culture largely adopted and maintained Confucian concepts, many people continued to embrace their traditional religious beliefs, which held female shamans as essential in spiritual affairs. The fact that the Confucian official in this folktale seeks out the assistance of the Nišan shaman shows that he too, in his time of need, turned to his people's traditional belief systems.

Once the Nišan shaman felt assured that the official had acknowledged the value of her role, she agreed to help his son. The Nišan shaman prepared "herself … by washing her face, thus cleansing herself of this world in preparation for entering another realm … the Land of the Dead" (Young 174). When the Nišan shaman entered the Land of the Dead, she immediately encountered her own dead husband who had died years ago. Seeing her, he began to "berate and threaten to kill her for not restoring him to life" (Young 175). However, the folktale makes it clear that the Nišan shaman chose not to bring her husband back from the dead. This choice presents her as desiring to maintain her powerful role as shaman instead of being forced to accept the role of an obedient wife, as Confucian values during the Qing dynasty ordained. Confucianism declared that "women were to be obedient" to their husbands (Keller 227), who maintained "almost unlimited control over" their wives (Kinney 31). The Nišan shaman further illustrated her intent to live independently in this folktale when she "easily" got rid of her husband's soul "by calling on her great bird-spirit and telling it to snatch him up and drop him in the city of the Lord of the Underworld" (Young 175). This scene, similar to the scene of consternation between the Nišan shaman and the Confucian official, presents again the historical strife between traditional Manchu goddess-centered ideologies that readily supported female shamans and the patriarchal Confucian system that oppressed women at the time of the tale's construction.

Next upon the Nišan shaman's journey within the underworld, she came to "the tower of the female spirit who distributes souls" (Young 176). There, she found "a woman who show[ed] her where children are taken in order to be reborn" (Young 176). The woman was the goddess Omosi-mama, "the Womb Goddess in the sky, who granted fertility, prosperity, health, and longevity" (Young 176). The fact that the Nišan shaman must learn from an explicitly referenced goddess, Omosi-mama, about death and rebirth, connects her to the brothers in the Yuchi myth who gained similar wisdom from Grandmother Sun within the interior of the earth, showing the Nišan shaman to directly gain the wisdom, and thus power, she does because of goddess-oriented ideology. Once visiting Omosi-mama, the Nišan shaman was finally able to leave the Land of the Dead and symbolically resurrect herself, delivering the soul of the boy back into his body, physically resurrecting him, as a traditional goddess would be able to do.

This folktale ends by showing the Nišan shaman as becoming famous for her shamanic abilities, but the tale concludes with one final remark that firmly places it within its patriarchal time period of the Qing dynasty. A Confucian message is added to the end of the folktale that shows the Nišan shaman being held accountable for not working to bring her husband back to life, as "the emperor of China decide[d] to punish her by having all her shamanic clothing and implements destroyed" (Young 176). Thus, in the end of the folktale, the "Confucian state ... [took] away her power" (Young 176). Again, following the Bronze Age, this practice of stripping the power of once revered shamankas was widespread in China as Confucianism gained dominance, and as the tale indicates, and as was discussed, the same demotion of the female shaman occurred after Manchu culture too eventually adopted Confucianism. However, the fact that the Chinese even today continue to embrace this folktale of the Nišan shaman shows their unyielding value of the cultural practice of shamanism held by once high-standing women, as well as the traditional reverence of goddesses who enabled such heightened spiritual power.

From as early as Japan's Jōmon period (14,000–300 BCE) female shamans, identified as miko, were also an important part of Japanese culture. As stated in Chapter 1, Japan had a vibrant and long-lasting history of worshipping goddesses, and as was the case in China, this reverence for divine females directly enabled women to serve in the role of miko. Japanese miko were believed to be "clairvoyant.... Hence, they often functioned as protectors of their people. When the men in their community were to go to sea ... [they] would predict the weather conditions and catches, and when the community went to war, they supplicated the deities for protection. As healers ... [they] were sought to cure injuries, illnesses, and even children's tantrums by their magic and prayers" (Aoki 68). Reverence for Japan's powerful goddesses and miko lasted undisturbed until about the eighth-century CE when Confucian concepts entered into Japan from China. As the centuries progressed, the revered role of the miko, as well as many Japanese goddesses, became demoted; however, as was seen in the Manchu folktale just discussed, the value of the miko was well preserved within Japanese folklore.

For example, one Japanese folktale (Mutén 19–26) implicitly presents an old wise woman in the role of a miko when she partakes on a journey into the underworld realm of the supernatural oni. Though this folktale does not explicitly identify the old wise woman as a shaman, as the Siberian and Manchu folktale did with their female protagonists, it still makes it clear that the woman of the tale is meant to be viewed in this traditional role because of the skills she obtained upon her shaman-like journey. This pattern of presenting old wise women characters as partaking on shaman-like quests to obtain supernatural skill sets is a part of many global folktales and fairy tales; thus, these wise old folkloric women helped to preserve traditional goddess-centered ideologies that once encouraged women to hold powerful positions of spiritual authority within their communities.

This Japanese folktale begins showing the old woman to be a peasant who lived alone in a small, poor village. The old woman was known by her community for cooking the best dumplings in the village. One day the old woman lost one of her dumplings when it fell to the ground, and an oni, a supernatural creature of Japanese folklore, snuck in and took it. Most people left the oni alone, fearing their supernatural abilities, but the old woman in this folktale was only overcome with anger when the oni stole her dinner, so she decided to chase it to try and retrieve her dumpling. In time, though, the old woman found that she was in the underworld realm of the oni, and as she looked about, she was shocked to find hundreds of oni all around her. The old woman found that the leader of the oni, having just eaten the dumpling the oni underling brought him, approached her and invited her to stay as his guest. The old woman felt that she had no choice but to stay and do what the oni leader wanted.

The oni leader requested that the old woman cook dumplings for all the oni, but she found that they only gave her one grain of rice to do this.

The old woman objected that the task was impossible, but she found that the oni leader just encouraged her to try. The old woman was astonished to see that when she stirred the rice pot with a giant spoon given to her by the oni leader, the one grain of rice turned into enough flour to make plenty of dumplings for everyone. This scene reveals that the old woman is being instructed upon her underworld journey by a supernatural agent, in this case the oni leader, in order to teach her the lessons of the underworld, similar to how the goddesses of the myths and folktales just discussed instructed the shamans who ventured into their underworlds. Day after day, the old woman made dumplings this way for the oni, but in time, she knew that she needed to think of a way to return back to her realm, so she devised a plan to escape her supernatural captors in order to leave the underworld, just as many shamans are mythically portrayed as defeating supernatural beings within the underworld in order to symbolically resurrect.

The old woman remembered hearing that the oni were unable to swim, so this became the crux of her plan. After the old woman fed the oni an unusually large portion of her dumplings, she began to sing a soft melody to them, which immediately put the supernatural creatures to sleep. Then the old woman climbed into her magic rice pot, used the giant spoon as a paddle, and pushed off into a nearby stream to make her escape. When the oni woke up, they saw the old woman trying to escape, so they began to control the natural environment, a common skill for the oni within Japanese folklore, suggesting their tie to traditional Japanese mythology, as many scholars believe that the oni were once Japanese deities who lost status by becoming folkloric figures when new ideologies gained dominance in Japan. The oni began to drink up the stream, so that in no time, there was hardly any water left for the old woman to paddle away. Fish began to flop into the old woman's makeshift boat, but having learned from her time in the underworld, the old woman had grown wise, so she countered the attack of the oni by throwing fish at them, telling them to eat their fill. Unable to resist an easy meal, the oni ate the fish and forgot about drinking the remaining water in the stream, so the old, now wise, woman was able to get away from the supernatural oni and their underworld realm, thus symbolically resurrecting. The old wise woman then returned to her village with the spoils of her quest: the supernatural rice pot and spoon that would cause ceaseless meals to be made for her poor community from a single grain of rice, making the old wise woman similar to the Japanese goddess Ogetsuno, who was believed to be able to provide endless food for the people by producing it from her own body. Thus, the old woman was able to become a goddess-like provider for her people directly because she underwent a quest that mimicked the shamanic journeys of the Japanese miko.

As stated in Chapter 1, Ireland also has a long history of revering goddesses, as well as women who were viewed as being especially adept at harnessing the power of goddesses. For instance, Celtic mythology includes many mortal and divine women who held shamanic abilities, such as Ceridwen, who mythically was portrayed either as a mortal woman or goddess who was able to shapeshift, foretell the future, cast magical spells, transgress otherworld and underworld realms, and accomplish feats of resurrection. For example, in the Irish myth of "Bran the Blessed," Ceridwen gave Bran her magical cauldron that was capable of resurrecting the dead, so that he gained an army that could not be defeated, as it was ceaselessly replenished. Centuries of revering spiritually powerful divine and mortal women in Ireland led to the popular embrace within folk beliefs of women known as Wise Women within local communities. The village Wise Woman was often an elder who excelled in the healing power of plants and other natural elements. She also was often believed to be able to aid villagers in mystical affairs and generally serve as a spiritual or shamanic leader within the community. Thus, myriad Irish folktales identify old female characters as Wise Women because of their ability to control supernatural elements as a shaman or goddess would.

One Irish folktale (Mutén 51–8) shows a widowed mother and her daughter receiving help from their old village Wise Woman. The folktale shows the mother and daughter being awakened one night when fairies entered their home. When Christianity gained a stronghold in Ireland, the divine pantheon of Celtic mythology, the Tuatha dé Danann, became demoted to characters within folklore, often appearing as the sidhe or fairies of Irish folktales. Thus, when fairies appear within Irish folktales, they often carry with them tenets that were once viewed as sacred. The mother and daughter of the folktale watched as ten small men carrying wool and ten women carrying spinning wheels began to set up their implements within their home. When the fairies began spinning their wool, the widow told her daughter to run and ask the village Wise Woman what to do about their magical, yet uninvited, guests.

Arriving at the home of the old Wise Woman, who lived separated from the community deep within the forest, which is often a quintessential place for old wise women within folktales and fairy tales to live, the young maiden begged for her help. Immediately, the old Wise Woman knew exactly what to do with the mystical fairies, as similar to many old wise women in folktales and fairy tales, she had ample knowledge of the supernatural. The old Wise Woman relayed to the young maiden mystical words that she must chant to get the fairies to leave her home. So, the maiden rushed home after perfectly memorizing the magic words. When the maiden uttered the mystical words to the fairies, they indeed picked up their belongings and left the mother and daughter in peace. However, once the fairies discovered that they were tricked into leaving, the folktale shows them returning and trying again to gain entrance into the home of the mother and daughter. However, because the maiden was instructed by the old Wise Woman, the fairies were no match against the mystical power that the daughter now held.

The old Wise Woman of this folktale is depicted in shamanic terms, as she is the only one who holds the correct supernatural wisdom to control the mystical fairies, who again are probable remnants of Celtic deities. Furthermore, this folktale presents a generational passing of the Wise Woman's shamanic wisdom from mother and crone to the maiden of the folktale. The mother in sending her daughter to seek the help of the old Wise Woman, instead of a Christian religious authority to rid their home of the supernatural fairies, shows her as guiding her daughter upon a journey to gain the shamanic, and thus goddess-oriented, insight that the old Wise Woman possesses, assuring that the young maiden will one day grow into the role of the old Wise Woman. The presentation of the three women: daughter, mother, and old Wise Woman within this folktale carries special importance in alignment to goddess ideology. Triads were often used in the presentations of Celtic goddesses, such as the triple goddesses of Irish sovereignty, Ériu, Fódla and Banba, to show the unification of the goddesses, even though they could appear individually. This concept of unity despite the presentation of separate identities sent a message in Celtic mythology that each individual woman was also connected to a united concept of goddess reverence. Therefore, this folkloric triad of women: maiden, mother, and crone shows the three women as united in their role to preserve the reverence of the traditional goddess ideologies of Ireland throughout the generations.

Similarly, a folktale from France (Barchers 309–11) also shows an old wise woman who holds connections with mythic goddesses and the shamans who served them. The old wise woman of this tale is sought after by her community, as she is the only one who possesses the wisdom to save them from a fearsome dragon. Again, the ability to control supernatural elements aligns the old woman in this folktale to traditional goddess worship and shamanic practices, which were prevalent in France, as the ancient Gauls were a Celtic people who worshipped myriad female deities and revered shamanic women. The dragon of this folktale lived deep in the forest, and it began to attack people who ventured into the depths of the wilderness. The people came together and decided that the best course of action for them was to avoid going into the forest, but this plan did not work, as when the people stopped going into nature, the dragon came into the village and ate a whole family within their own cottage. In retaliation, the villagers gathered sixteen of their best men to track the dragon down and try to defeat it. However, the brutal might of the men proved useless against the dragon, as the dragon killed half of the men, while the other half fled back to the village. The community, in a state of forlornness, wished for a magician to come and help them from their seemingly hopeless situation, but one community member mentioned that they did not have a male magician. Another villager spoke up and declared that they did have an old wise woman who lived nearby. Showing the villagers first wanting a male magician, but then remembering the old wise woman who still thrived in the forest near them suggests a time of cultural transition when male superiority took over roles once held by powerful females. The fact that the people must remember that they have an old wise woman suggests that the folktale is purposefully speaking toward a message of remembrance for a time when old wise women were central to the religious belief systems of the region.

When the people finally sought the help of their old wise woman, named Martha, she was presented as an expert in knowing exactly how to control unruly dragons, just as other old wise women in folktales and fairy tales often possess shamanic abilities to control supernatural elements. Martha devised a plan to go into the forest alone and defeat the dragon by herself, taking only holy water with her (Barchers 310). This inclusion of the Christian element of holy water into the folktale suggests a merging of traditional Gaulish/Celtic beliefs with Christian beliefs. Many global myths meant to eradicate goddesses from positions of authority portrayed dragons or serpent-like creatures as symbolic forms of traditional goddesses because these creatures were often associated with goddesses in mythic and artistic depictions around the world. Many myths showed male characters brutally killing these dragons and serpent-like creatures to assert their dominance over traditional belief systems and usher in new patriarchal ideologies. In Mesopotamian mythology, for example, Marduk killed his mother, the giant serpent-like creature Tiamet, so that he could reign over the new pantheon. In Christian ideology, Saint Patrick drove the serpents, meant to symbolize pagans, out of Ireland, and Saint Columba drove a massive serpent-like creature out of Loch Ness, which symbolized Christianity's domination in Scotland. Saint George also famously killed his own dragon to again assert Christian dominance over traditional pagan beliefs. Martha in this French folktale is presented as expertly traversing the place where she herself dwelled, the forest, finding the dragon, and precisely dealing with the mighty, supernatural creature by throwing her holy water into its mouth, causing it to become her pet. Martha then brought the tamed dragon back to the village with her. The people of the community were "awed when Martha and the dragon entered the town. She led it to the town square and ordered it to lie down" (Barchers 311). Thus, this scene, like the tales of Saint Patrick, Saint Columba, and Saint George, could signal the power of Christianity to dominate supernatural elements and thus pagan ideologies. However, most Christian storylines meant to carry messages about eradicating supernatural/ pagan elements present male religious officials as the only ones capable of such spiritual power, as women were not allowed to maintain the highest religious offices in Christianity. Therefore, Martha's ability, as an old wise woman, to control the supernaturally powerful dragon suggests that her shamanic abilities come from an older set of Gaulish/Celtic belief systems. For instance, Martha, who is not at all portrayed as a Christian religious official, tamed the dragon and paraded it through the community as her pet, much like a mythic Mistress of Animals would do, instead of brutally killing the dragon, as most male authorities are portrayed as doing to dragons in Christian narratives. In addition, the "holy water" Martha used to subdue the dragon may not have been defined as such according to Christian ideology, as water was often considered a sacred element associated with goddesses in Gaulish/Celtic belief, such as the Gaulish goddess Sirona, who reigned over the land's healing springs. Thus, Martha's authority of both the wilderness, where she resides, and the supernatural creatures who live within the wilderness, presents her as in command of a repertoire of pagan knowledge that ties her to goddess ideology. Therefore, this folktale suggests that Martha is meant to be a reminder to audiences of a time when women were revered as goddesses or believed to be especially capable of harnessing supernatural elements as shamanic servants of goddesses.

In pre–Conquest South America, many goddesses were also revered as part of sacred ideologies, and because of this, women often "served as curers, soothsayers, shamans, priests, sacrificers and sacrifices, divine ancestors, and innovators of and participants in domestic and community cults" (Bruhns & Stothert 167). In fact, female shamans were so respected in many regions throughout South America that Spanish colonizers, in an effort to gain converts to Christianity, especially "persecuted women shamans" in South America, calling them "devil-ridden old women ... and destroying their shrines and sacred objects" (Dashú). Still, as in many regions around the world, many folktales throughout South America preserved the reverence the people once held for shamanic women who officiated over goddess ideologies.

For instance, a folktale from Chile and Argentina (Martín 118–9) shows a shamanic old wise woman as the only one who can save the people from a water monster called Hueke Heukú. The tale starts with a family that was traveling in an unknown region. They stopped to rest at a lake for the night, but the father almost immediately felt supernaturally drawn to the lake. In fact, despite the lake being quite cold in this region of the mountains, the father began to walk into the water. Bewildered by this strange behavior, the man's family tried to stop him, especially when they saw that the water began to bubble on the surface. The family was horrified to see that out of the water appeared a stretched cowhide that started to wrap itself around the man; "the edges of this skin had appendages with sharp claws with hooks, except at one far end where instead it had huge eyes of an intense red color" (Martín 118). The family found that they could do nothing to stop the monster as it took the father into the lake. Distraught, the family ran to the nearest village and begged for help. Immediately, the people believed the family, as they knew well the capabilities of the monster Hueke Heukú. The people at once sought out the only person who could help them, their Machi, the old shaman woman. The fact that it is the Machi who is the only person who is capable of saving the man from the water monster shows the maintenance of a belief in the adept ability of women to combat supernatural agents within Chilean and Argentinian belief systems. The fearless old Machi ran right up to the mystical lake and began to assemble thorny branches into the shape of a human body. The Machi then threw the mass into the water. Immediately, this wisdom of how to conquer the Hueke Heukú proved worthwhile, as the Hueke Heukú attacked the thorny mass. The spikey branches of the mass wounded the body of the Hueke Heukú so much that it finally died. Thus, like the French folktale of Martha, this folktale preserves the respect the Chilean and Argentinian people held for their old wise women, whose knowledge, bravery, and mystical power allowed them to serve as spiritual leaders for their people despite the influence of new belief systems that strove to eradicate this reverence.

Finally, a folktale from the Malinke of West Africa (Barchers 207–9) also portrays an older shamanic woman as the only one who can save her people from a man who metamorphosed into a vicious lion. In this folktale, the people of the village appealed to their legendary male warrior Kambili to defeat the troublesome lion man. However, Kambili knew he would need the help of his wife Kumba, who possessed powerful shamanic abilities, in order to defeat the lion man. Many cultures throughout Africa, including that of the Malinke, revered powerful goddesses who "were regarded as ultimate supreme beings, and as mother and earth deities of creation, fertility, and agriculture" (Ogunleye 196). Because goddesses played such a key role in many religions throughout Africa, social and religious roles for women were often quite high (Ogunleye 198), as women were often viewed as especially connected to goddesses, and thus best able to communicate with them (T. Fernyhough & A. Fernyhough

200). Thus, women within many African cultures served in the role of shaman. For example, in South Africa, "Ethnography suggests that about 30 percent of women become shamans, including curers, game shamans, and rain shamans" (Hays-Gilpin 172), and in Ethiopia, "women often played a pre-eminent role in spirit beliefs ... interpreting personal fortune and misfortune, and major events, in terms of spirit intervention" (T. Fernyhough & A. Fernyhough 200). The introduction of Islam and Christianity into many regions throughout Africa strove to eradicate the reverence of indigenous goddesses and the shamanic women who served them; however, like other regions discussed in this chapter, many African cultures maintained aspects of their traditional belief systems through folk customs and folklore. Therefore, when the character of Kumba in this Malinke folktale is shown to be respected enough to be sought after to use her shamanic abilities to save the village, this shows the Malinke's lasting reverence for their female shamans.

In the folktale, the shamanic Kumba gained the assistance of the spirits and learned from them that because the lion man held great power, it would be very hard to kill him. The spirits told Kumba that to gain power over the lion man, she should take one hair from his head and one of his sandals and bury them both in the ground. So, Kumba, like Martha and the Machi of the previous folktales, went by herself to bravely defeat the community's menace. Once in the lion man's domain, Kumba pretended that she had fallen in love with him. Fully falling for Kumba's deceit, the lion man accepted Kumba into his home. Once inside, Kumba began to cook a meal for the lion man, but Kumba doused his meal with poison, so that the lion man fell into a deep sleep, enabling her to obtain the needed hair and sandal from him. Kumba then left the lion man's home and buried the items in the earth, as the spirits instructed her to do. Once she did this, the land itself gave Kumba the knowledge she needed to kill the lion man.

Kumba learned from the earth that she must lure the lion man to a grove of trees, using herself as sacrificial bait. Then, at the last moment, she would finally need her warrior husband Kambili to spring out of the bushes and slay the lion man. Intent on meeting the requirements of the vision presented to her by the earth, Kumba, just as a shaman would, sang "a magical song ... [that] drifted to where the beast prowled" (Barchers 208), and indeed the shamanic song led the lion man to Kumba. However, as the lion man was also supernaturally powerful, he forced Kambili to fall into a deep sleep. When the lion man approached, he caught sight of Kumba, but he slid right past her toward the sleeping Kambili. When Kumba saw that the lion man had outsmarted her and was about to kill her husband, she again mystically cast a spell that awakened her husband, whereupon he finally slayed the lion man. Thus, the Malinke forevermore held Kambili, but especially the old shaman woman Kumba, as renowned heroes of the community.

Wise Old Oracles

In addition to being portrayed as wise old women in shamanic roles, wise old women in folktales and fairy tales also closely resemble the women of mythology who served their communities as oracles, seeresses, and soothsayers.

As stated, many global regions, such as China, Greece, Rome, Scandinavia, South America, believed that women were especially adept at holding central religious and spiritual roles, like that of shaman, precisely because of their sex and thus close connection to goddesses. This same connection to goddesses enabled many women to also serve in prophetic roles as oracles and seeresses within their communities. For example, in steppe-nomadic cultures, the "religious leaders of the ancient nomads were almost always women … because that sex was credited with greater intuitive powers that would facilitate communion with" the divine (Davis-Kimball 69). In Germanic and Norse cultures, völvas were attributed as possessing the ability to foresee the future, just as the pythias of Greece and sybils of Rome were able to receive sacred messages from divine sources and thus guide inquisitors on advisable courses of action. Many myths from these cultures often portrayed these wise women offering their sacred counsel to most often male gods and mortals alike. For instance, in the "Völuspá" from the *Poetic Edda* (c. 1270 CE), a völva predicted the destruction of the world in Ragnarök for the leader of the Norse pantheon Odin. In the Roman *Aeneid*, the hero Aeneas was advised by the Cumaean Sybil for much of his heroic quest, and in the Greek myth of King Croesus, the Pythia of Delphi provided a prophecy that the king misconstrued to suit his own desires, which caused his downfall.

Many folktales and fairy tales present women who maintain a role that is similar to the mythic portrayal of female oracles, seeresses, and soothsayers, and often these women are portrayed as old and wise because of their ability to decipher elements, most commonly riddles, that often male protagonists cannot decode.

For example, a Japanese folktale entitled "The Wise Old Woman" (Uchida) shows an elderly woman saving her community because she is the only one who can solve riddles for the male leaders of her community. The tale begins with a cruel lord who ordered that all people over the age of seventy-one must be taken to the mountains to die. The villagers were appalled by the lord's decree, but fearing for their life, they followed the horrific demand. However, a young farmer found that when his own mother reached the age that spelled her doom, he could not follow the lord's decree, so the farmer hopelessly tried to think of ways to evade the ordinance, such as fleeing his village and trying to survive away from human habitation. The old mother interjected her son's fantasies though and instructed him to dig a hole beneath their kitchen, so she could hide there. The old mother hid this way for months, until a warlord threatened the safety of the village. To evade his wrath, the warlord demanded that the villagers solve a riddle by giving him "a thousand ropes of ash" (Uchida). The existing cruel lord of the village gathered his wise men, the village leaders, together to find a solution to the riddle and thus save the village from the warlord and his invaders, but the wise men were at a loss for a way to solve the warlord's impossible riddle. Things looked grim, until the old mother from her hiding spot "laughed softly and said, 'Why, that is not such an impossible task. All one has to do is soak ordinary rope in salt water and dry it well. When it is burned, it will hold its shape and there is your rope of ash! Tell the villagers to hurry and find one thousand pieces of rope'" (Uchida). The farmer told the solution to the riddle to the village lord, who was very impressed and ordered the villagers to comply at once. The same format continues in the folktale two more times, as the warlord returned and demanded the solutions to two more seemingly impossible riddles, of which the village wise men and cruel lord had no idea how to solve. But again, the wise old mother easily came up with the desired solutions to the riddles, and her son relayed them to the village lord. At this, the initially cruel lord demanded that the farmer reveal how he came up with the solutions that saved the village from the warlord's invasion, and the farmer revealed that because he disobeyed the lord's ordinance to abandon his elderly mother to death, his old wise mother saved everyone with her uncanny wisdom. At this, the village lord rescinded his unjust ordinance forevermore and learned to embrace the wisdom of his elders.

The old wise woman's ability to solve riddles that literally meant life or death for her people is portrayed as almost a mystical ability, as no one else in her community, even the male village leaders, are capable of achieving her seemingly supernatural insight. Because of this, the old wise woman is presented in this folktale as reminiscent of a mythic oracle, or more precisely an itako spirit medium who traditionally guided leaders of Japanese communities on the right course of action. It is also telling that the folktale makes a point of reminding its audience on not only the benefit of the wisdom of elders, but specifically on the wisdom of an old wise woman, as this tenet serves to preserve Japan's long held value of their sacred women, as adept spiritual advisors for their communities because of their direct connection to Shinto goddesses.

In a similar Arabic folktale entitled "The Old Woman, the Merchant, and the King" (Payne), another old wise woman helps a king by solving a riddle that no one could decipher. The folktale begins with a village king ordering an old woman to be ostracized from the village, as he believed her to be only a burden to the villagers. The old woman however, like the old mother of the previous Japanese folktale, defied the king's ordinance and hid away in nearby ruins. One day a merchant came into the village and saw the old woman trying to survive with no resources, so he gave her some money to help her situation. The old woman repaid the merchant's kindness by extending her wisdom to him. She told the merchant that newcomers to her village were often forced by the king and his vizier to solve seemingly impossible riddles or have their goods forfeited from them. To evade this, the old woman instructed the merchant to seek her counsel when the king's vizier presented a riddle to him. The merchant agreed, and went the next day to meet with the king's vizier, who indeed presented him with a riddle—"how does one find the weight of an elephant" (Payne)? The merchant did not attempt to solve the riddle, as he had no idea how to answer it, instead he asked the vizier for time to think of a solution and went to the old wise woman. The old wise woman instructed the merchant to tell the vizier to "'Make a ship and launch it on the sea and put in it an elephant, and when it sinketh in the water ... mark the place to which the water riseth. Then take out the elephant and cast in stones in its place, till [sic] the ship sinks to the mark aforesaid; whereupon do thou take out the stones and weigh them and thou wilt know the weight of the elephant'" (Payne). Impressed by the apparent wisdom of the merchant, the vizier next asked him to solve another riddle, whereupon the merchant again gained time to find his answer from the wise old woman. Hearing again the solution to another seemingly impossible riddle, the king's vizier was so impressed with the merchant that he asked him how he had gained such wisdom, and like the previous Japanese folktale, the merchant revealed to the vizier the truth of the wise old woman who, like an oracle, possessed almost mystical wisdom and had thus instructed him every step of the way. At this, the vizier imparted the lesson to the king, who, like the Japanese lord, learned that old wise women must be cherished for their wisdom instead of treated with disdain. Again, as with the Japanese folktale that served to preserve the ancient practice of female spiritual leaders in Japan, this tale also implicitly preserves the role of women who once served Arabic nations as prophetic guides for their people.

In a fairy tale by the Grimm brothers entitled "The Devil and his Grandmother" (J. Grimm & W. Grimm 405–8), male protagonists are again guided by the oracle-like abilities of an old wise woman who appears as the grandmother of the devil. The tale presents another unjust king, who barely paid his soldiers enough to survive. In retaliation, three soldiers decided to desert their offices by hiding in a wheat field near their camp until their regiment left them behind. However, their regiment did not leave in due time, so the soldiers began to starve. A dragon, who was really the devil in disguise, spotted the soldiers as they hid, and seeing their deplorable predicament, offered to save them if they agreed to serve him for seven years. The devil also added that at the end of their seven years of service, their souls would belong to him if they could not solve one of his riddles. Feeling like they had no other option, the soldiers agreed.

After seven years of serving the devil, the soldiers were greeted by an old woman who advised them to go into the forest and search for a small house to save themselves from the devil. The appearance of an old woman who serves as a savior to the soldiers at the moment when they need it most, as they are about to face the topmost Christian opponent—the devil himself—immediately suggests components of goddess ideology at work within the tale, as the men are not guided by a Christian religious official to fend off the devil, but a symbol of traditional pagan ideology—the wise old woman. This theme will be reiterated in the tale with the introduction of the devil's grandmother as another wise woman who serves to save the men. The fairy tale shows that the third soldier heeded the advice of the old wise woman, after his companions chose to disregard her, and journeyed into the forest, the precise place many folktale and fairy tale characters encounter goddess representatives. Once in the forest, the third solider found the small house the old wise woman told him about. Inside the home, he met "an ancient woman" (J. Grimm & W. Grimm 406), who told him that she was the devil's grandmother. The proclamation that the ancient woman is older than the Christian devil, as she is his grandmother, reminds audiences that the traditional goddess ideology the grandmother represents predates Christian belief systems. The soldier was forthright with the devil's grandmother, telling her everything that happened to him and his companions, and his honesty caused the ancient woman to want to help him. The devil's grandmother lifted a large rock upon her floor, revealing a place for the soldier to hide when the devil came home. When the devil arrived, his grandmother had dinner waiting for him, and sat with him talking. In time, the old grandmother asked about the devil's daily happenings; when the devil mentioned that he was about to gain the souls of three men if they could not solve one of his riddles, the ancient woman adeptly tricked the topmost adversary within Christianity by convincing him to reveal the solution to his riddle. The fact that the ancient woman could so easily trick the devil, who is presented in this tale like a child to his grandmother, suggests that her mystical skill sets are vastly superior to his, presenting her as a powerful representative of goddess ideology, an ideology that is thus shown in the tale to effortlessly conquer Christianity's most challenging adversary. The devil revealed the solution to his riddle: "There's a dead monkey lying in the great North Sea. That will be their roast. A whale's rib will be their silver spoon, and an old horse's hoof will be their wine glass" (J. Grimm & W. Grimm 407). At this, the devil went off to bed, and the old grandmother lifted the rock away and freed the solider with the knowledge he needed to answer the devil's riddle. And indeed, when the devil met the third soldier and asked his riddle, the third soldier had all the right answers, which saved all three men. Again, because the wise ancient woman of this fairy tale easily eradicated the threat of the devil by her mystical ability to outsmart his inexperienced riddles and thus saved his adversaries, the fairy tale solidifies that the ancient woman is an agent of a much older ideology that in the context of this tale supersedes Christianity.

The Arthurian tale "The Wedding of Sir Gawain and Dame Ragnelle," one version of which appears in Chaucer's "The Wife of Bath's Tale" in his *Canterbury Tales* (1387–1400 CE), also shows a male protagonist being educated by an old wise woman who, like a mythic oracle, excels at solving riddles. Furthermore, this tale explicitly connects its oracle-like, old woman to portrayals of mythic goddesses. Arthurian tales often portrayed female characters, such as the Lady of the Lake, Morgan le Fay, and Guinevere, as similar to portrayals of Celtic goddesses once revered throughout Europe, and this is certainly the case with the old wise woman of this tale. The plot unfolds to present the male protagonist Gawain, a Knight of the Round Table, encountering an old woman while he was alone in the wilderness outside of Camelot. Again, like the devil's grandmother of the previous tale, the fact that the old woman meets the male protagonist outside of civilization, within the wilderness, immediately connects her to traditional goddess ideology. Gawain appealed to the old woman about a problem he faced, stating that in order to save Camelot, he must help Arthur answer a riddle about what women really want. The wise old woman told Gawain that she would solve the riddle for him if he agreed to marry her. Gawain was horrified by the prospect of marrying an old woman, who is described in the text as a hag, but, being a Knight of the Round Table, Gawain had to protect the interests of King Arthur, so he agreed to the marriage. Once the couple was married and in the privacy of their wedding chamber, the old woman transformed into a beautiful young woman. Shapeshifting from old to young also immediately signals the old woman's connection to divinity, as this is a skill of many Celtic goddesses, as discussed in Chapter 1. The woman told Gawain that she could either be young and beautiful during the day and old at night, or vice versa. She then instructed Gawain to choose what option he would prefer for his wife. After Gawain thought about it, he answered with the appropriate response, which was the answer to the riddle King Arthur sought about what women really want—"'whatever you choose will make me happy, for it is your own life'" (Chaucer). Gawain was then rewarded according to the old wise woman's standards, as she would appear as young and beautiful both day and night. Again, like the other tales of this section, because of the old woman's ability to solve riddles that no one in Camelot, including King Arthur, could solve, she appears as similar to a mythic oracle. Yet, this tale, like the one of the devil's grandmother, also connects the old woman's ability to solve riddles with her holding traits of mythic goddesses, as she is presented as mystical not only for her impressive wisdom but also for her magical ability to shapeshift. Therefore, this tale, like the previous fairy tale of the devil's grandmother, helps to connect the oracular old women of folktales and fairy tales, who solve riddles that confound male leaders and help save communities, to mythic portrayals of goddesses who also are often portrayed as teaching spiritual wisdom to others and saving those in need.

Wise Old Women and Male Heroic Quests

Like the wise old women who were portrayed in the previous tales as solving riddles for male protagonists, many wise old women in myths, folktales, and fairy tales are presented as educators to male protagonists upon their heroic quests. Many wise old women also serve as educators to females upon heroic quests in myths, folktales, and fairy tales, like Mother Holle did with her maiden pupil in Chapter 1, but female guides upon the quests of heroines will be discussed in the second half of this book.

As briefly discussed in Chapter 1, the male heroic quest, as defined by many mythic scholars, including Campbell, is outlined by a basic format that shows the hero being first called to a quest that most often takes place outside of his familial and societal frame of reference, so that he can grow psychologically and spiritually. The hero often enters an otherworld stage that forces him to interact with elements that compel him to move beyond who he was at the start of the myth. Next, the hero usually must face the underworld stage of his heroic quest, which forces him to face the fact of mortality, so that he may reach a heightened state of psychological and/ or spiritual transformation, defined by Campbell and other mythologists as apotheosis. Apotheosis for the male mythic hero, according to Campbell, is attained when the hero finally learns to embrace goddess-oriented ideology, as Campbell literally defined apotheosis as "Meeting with the

Goddess"; the "meeting with the goddess is the final test of the talent of the hero" (Campbell, *Hero*, 94). As referenced in the introduction, Hubbs states that even in folktales and fairy tales, the culmination of the male heroic quest is the hero's alignment with goddess ideology; "although the folktale [and fairy tale] uses the patriarchal social and political order as the context of the quest ... it is the [goddess representative who] ... shapes the fate of the hero" (Hubbs 146). Therefore, though female characters often appear to be on the sideline of the plot of many male heroic quests within global mythology, folktales, and fairy tales, their roles should be analyzed more closely, as often the female characters within the male heroic quest serve as instrumental forces who orchestrate the components of the hero's journey in order to educate the hero about concepts that are in line with goddess ideologies. For instance, in mythology, the Greek *Odyssey* focuses primarily on the male hero Odysseus; however, when the text is examined more closely, one sees that Odysseus is really the student of the females within the narrative who led his quest, such as the goddess Athena, the enchantress Circe, the goddess Calypso, the princess Nausicaa, and his wife Penelope. Similarly, the male Celtic hero Cúchulainn in the *Táin Bo Cuailgne* is aided by the goddess the Morrígan and his old warrior teacher Scáthach, while he is forced into his role of sole fighter by queen Medb and the goddess Macha, showing him, like Odysseus, to be the pupil of the many women who guided his heroic quest.

Quite often, the mythic guide of the male hero appears as an older female who tests or instructs the hero toward goddess-oriented apotheosis, and often this old wise woman is used as a trope to signal to audiences that she is a representative of goddess worship, or that she is divine herself. For instance, in the Greek myth of Jason and the Argonauts, the goddess Hera tests the heroic worth of Jason by disguising herself as an old woman in need of assistance across a stream. Passing her test, the young Jason picks her up and carries her across the water, proving him a worthwhile hero who goes on to gain the continued guidance of Hera throughout much of his quest. Similarly, the culture hero Glooscap, or sometimes Gloscabi, who appears in many of the myths of the Abenaki of Canada and the northeastern portion of the United States, is consistently guided upon his quests by his sacred Grandmother Woodchuck.

An ideal example of a myth (Swanton 59–62) that identifies an old divine woman as a teacher to a male hero upon his quest is presented by the Tlingit of the Pacific Northwest Coast. The myth begins with the Tlingit people starving because of famine. A young boy found a dog in the wilderness, and because he was kind to the dog, the dog turned out to be a mystical helper to him and his people, as the dog easily caught prey each day for the people to consume. However, one day, the boy lost the dog, so he set out on a journey to find it, which became his heroic quest. On the boy's journey, he was stopped in the wilderness by an old divine woman by the name of Lūwat-uwadjīgĭ-cānak. Lūwat-uwadjīgĭ-cānak, who called the boy "grandchild" (Swanton 34) revealed to him that she would teach him to become a powerful shaman. To display her divine power, she first told the boy that his dog was not a dog but the son of a wolf chief; with this news, she then sent the boy out to retrieve his companion. To find his wolf companion, the old woman gave the boy a canoe the size of an acorn, but the boy only stared at the miniature canoe that he believed would not support him. Lūwat-uwadjīgĭ-cānak laughed delightedly at the perplexity of the boy and ushered him toward the tiny canoe that mystically grew before his eyes to accommodate his size. Lūwat-uwadjīgĭ-cānak then instructed the boy to think about where he wanted to go, telling him that the magical canoe would easily glide along the river, until he arrived at his destination. The boy again doubted Lūwat-uwadjīgĭ-cānak, but he decided to trust her, so he pushed off from shore and began his journey to find his companion. This scene in the myth presents the boy as experiencing otherworldly components, as he is clearly out of his element and must trust the supernatural guidance of the divine Lūwat-uwadjīgĭ-cānak. While on the water, the boy indeed found that just as the old woman had said, when he merely thought about his destination, the canoe did guide him directly to the wolf chief's community, where he was reunited with his companion. The wolf chief told the boy that his wolf son could not go back again to live with him, but the wolf chief sent the boy home with gifts that ensured that his people would never go hungry again. However, when the boy arrived home, he was thrust into the underworld stage of his heroic quest when he found that his people had all starved to death while he was away, including his own mother. But, because the boy had been taught by the old divine Lūwat-uwadjīgĭ-cānak upon his heroic quest, he had grown into a shaman, so he was able to use his newfound shamanic abilities to resurrect his mother and all the people of his tribe, thus showcasing his spiritual transformation and goddess-oriented apotheosis.

In a similar myth from Wales (Frankel 44–6), the mature Ceridwen appears as a goddess who also guides the male Gwion upon his heroic quest. The myth states that Ceridwen created a potion for her son from her magic and regenerative cauldron, again known to provide ceaseless resources and bring the dead back to life. However, Gwion, the boy she entrusted to stir the cauldron while the potion brewed for over a year, accidently tasted the potion when three drops splashed on his hand. Thus, Gwion obtained the powers meant for Ceridwen's son. Feigning anger, but really initiating Gwion's heroic quest, Ceridwen chased Gwion and forced him to partake of otherworldly experiences, as the heroic quest requires.

For instance, while Ceridwen chased Gwion, she made him realize that the potion enabled him to experience life in animal form, as he could transform into any animal he wished to evade the goddess. So, Gwion became a hare and swiftly fled from Ceridwen, but, as she was the goddess who bestowed him with his otherworldly powers, she simply metamorphosed into a greyhound and adeptly chased the hare. Gwion, almost entrapped by Ceridwen, then transformed into a fish, so Ceridwen, to continue Gwion's education upon his heroic quest, became an otter and chased him until Gwion became a sparrow, but again, showing her superiority, Ceridwen became a hawk. Finally thinking he had outwitted Ceridwen, Gwion became a grain in a pile of wheat, but Ceridwen simply became a hen and swallowed Gwion (Frankel 44), causing his death and thrusting him into the underworld stage of his heroic quest. However, Ceridwen revealed the epitome of her power as a goddess to Gwion when she used the seed of Gwion within her body to impregnate herself, so that she gave birth to Gwion, initiating his rebirth into the apotheotic Taliesin, who became, in some accounts, Merlin of Arthurian legend (Frankel 45). It is clear that Ceridwen in this myth is portrayed as the guide to Gwion/Taliesin/Merlin upon his heroic quest, as she instructed him about the quintessential message within Celtic goddess ideology, and goddess ideology within many world cultures—that all beings must follow nature's cycles.

Folktales and fairy tales also maintain the mythic trope of portraying older female characters as instructors to male heroes, and thus preserved elements of traditional goddess worship.

For instance, in another Arthurian tale featuring the knight Gawain, entitled "Sir Gawain and the Green Knight," Gawain goes on a heroic quest orchestrated by the mystical woman Morgan le Fay, who appears in this tale as an old woman. "Sir Gawain and the Green Knight" shows Arthur's court enjoying Christmas and New Year's celebrations, when a giant green knight came into the court and challenged the Knights of the Round Table to cut off his head, with the stipulation that in a year's time, the decapitator would have to visit the Green Knight's chapel and let the Green Knight chop off his head. As with his experience with the old wise woman who became his wife, Gawain again defended Arthur and accepted the Green Knight's challenge by cutting off the mystical man's head, whereupon the Green Knight picked his head back up and told Gawain to meet him in one year. In the tale, Gawain went upon a typical heroic quest, leaving the confines of Camelot to traverse the deep wilderness to search for the Green Knight's abode. While upon his heroic quest, Gawain faced many otherworldly elements, such as the harsh environment, Lord and Lady Bertilak, Morgan le Fay, who appeared at the Bertilak's court as an old woman, and finally the Green Knight's chapel. Gawain also faced the underworld stage of his quest when he awaited his own decapitation at the hands of the Green Knight. However, Gawain was shown to face the underworld stage of his quest with deception, as he wore a hidden green girdle, given to him by Lady Bercilak, that would not allow him to die, thus he was portrayed as not keeping up his side of the Green Knight's challenge, as well as not fully facing the underworld. At this deception, the Green Knight revealed to Gawain that the whole affair was actually a test presented to him, and to King Arthur's court, by the mystical woman Morgan le Fay. Having failed her challenge, the Green Knight nicked Gawain's neck as a reminder of his dishonesty. Gawain at the conclusion of his heroic quest returned to Camelot and always wore the green girdle, as did the other Knights of the Round Table, as a reminder of the lesson taught them by the mystical Morgan le Fay.

Christian and pagan messages are intertwined in this Arthurian tale. Though the whole situation takes place during Christmas celebrations, and though Gawain and all of Arthur's court are supposed to be Christian, the lessons of Morgan le Fay are decidedly pagan in nature. The Green Knight, revealed as being sent by Morgan le Fay, is a clear pagan symbol, as he is green, wears clothing embroidered with natural elements, carries a bough of holly, and can die and resurrect at will. This portrayal of the Green Knight is very similar to how members of the Tuatha de Danann of Celtic mythology are often presented. Also, instead of Gawain trusting that his death after a virtuous life would be rewarded in an afterlife of heaven, meeting Christian criteria, Gawain sided with the Celtic beliefs that the soul of a person resided in the head and only life in the present moment held meaning. Because Morgan le Fay concocted the whole affair, the lesson she wanted Gawain and Arthur's court to gain, which seemingly they did as they all vowed to forevermore wear a green girdle in remembrance of her orchestrated event, was therefore a Celtic lesson about trusting the cyclicity of life, as many scholars believe Morgan le Fay to be a representation of a Celtic goddess, perhaps the Morrígan (Matthews 11). In fact, Matthews states that Arthurian tales that feature Morgan le Fay portray "a compelling feminine power dimly remembered in Western culture as 'Mother Nature'" or the "Great Goddess" (Matthews 11). Therefore, Sir Gawain's education by Morgan le Fay's orchestrated quest means that he became "the champion of the Goddess" (Matthews 173) and was thus able to reach apotheosis at the conclusion of his quest.

In the Russian folktale "The Maiden Tsar" (Phillips & Kerrigan 105–7), a male hero is also instructed upon his quest by, in this case, many old wise women who hold connections to mythic goddesses. In the tale, a merchant's son fell in love with the tsar's daughter, but in order for the youth to win the maiden's hand in marriage, he would have to undertake a quest to reach her, "far away across the sea in the otherworld" (Phillips & Karrigan 105). The young man left at once on his heroic quest to prove his love for the Maiden Tsar. After traversing through the wilderness, the young man happened upon an old woman living within the forest; again going into the deep wilderness and encountering an old woman who lives there is often a quintessential stage for the male heroic quest. Some versions of this folktale identify the old woman as the witch Baba Yaga, who will be discussed in the last chapter of this book, though this tale highlights the woman for her wise woman attributes more than her witchlike attributes. However, it should be noted that there is often a fine line between portrayals of folktale and fairy tale old wise women and witches—which also will be discussed in the last chapter of this book. Upon seeing the old woman, the young male hero inquired if she knew the location of the otherworld, and though she certainly did as the youth was already in the otherworld environment of the solitary forest with its goddess representative who was orchestrating his quest, she lied to him in order to test him. The old woman stated that she did not know where to find the otherworld, but she said that the youth should continue his journey deeper into the wilderness to seek the help of her older sister. The young man eventually found the second, even older, woman and again inquired about the location of the otherworld. The second old woman also stated that she did not know its location and told the young man to go even deeper into the forest, and thus deeper into the otherworld, to seek help from her even older sister. The presentation of these old women who live alone within the otherworldly wilderness, as they hold mystical knowledge the hero seeks, immediately signals the women as connected to traditional conceptions of goddess worship, as the Slavs, as discussed in Chapter 1, worshipped goddesses in close connection to the environment for centuries. Furthermore, the triad presentation of the old women also connects them to Slavic portrayals of divinity, as the Slavs were also known to worship triple deities such as the god Triglav.

The tale goes on to show the young man continuing his quest, which is really a test by a series of old women to see if he is a hero worth the Maiden Tsar. After apparently successfully traversing the otherworld, the old women then forced the young man to journey to the underworld stage of his heroic quest, as when he found the third, and oldest, woman, instead of helping him, she captured him and threatened to eat him. However, just before he was eaten, an "immense flock of birds appeared, the lovely Firebird in the midst of them all"; the Firebird lifted the man upon its back and took him to the land of the Maiden Tsar (Phillips & Kerrigan 105). The tale ends with the Firebird bringing the youth to yet another old woman, who provided him with food and a place to rest. This fourth old woman told the young hero that he must find the Maiden Tsar's love for him, as it remained well hidden. With the fourth old woman's help, the young man learned that the Maiden Tsar's love was hidden in "an egg, within a duck which lay inside a hare. The hare in turn ... was concealed in a coffer which was buried beneath an oak tree" (Philips & Kerrigan 105–7). The fourth old woman, as confirmation that the hero successfully passed all of the old women's tests of him upon his heroic quest, helped the young man find the egg, whereupon she invited the Maiden Tsar to her home and served the egg to the maiden. With this, the young pair fell "into each other's arms, [and] resolved never ... to be parted" (Phillips & Kerrigan 107).

This fairy tale presents four united old wise women that orchestrated a heroic quest to see if the young man was worthy of the Maiden Tsar's hand in marriage. Many myths, folktales, and fairy tales likewise portray old women as overseeing the union of two youths; this portrayal aligns the old matchmakers to pagan goddesses who ordained over aspects of fertility, as was also a common concept in Slavic mythology. Therefore, tales such as this one show that when an old woman, or in this case a group of old women, tests a young male to see if he is worthy of being united with a maiden, the prize of gaining the maiden in marriage signals that the male protagonist has moved from childhood into the mature stage of heroic apotheosis directly because he attained the blessing of a goddess representative[s].

The English fairy tale "Jack and the Beanstalk" (1898), recorded by Joseph Jacobs, also shows an old wise woman who serves as a guide to a male hero, and who thus may be aligned to traditional goddess reverence. In fact, the origins of "Jack and the Beanstalk" may support the embrace of goddess ideology, as elements within this tale are believed to be thousands of years old. In the fairy tale, Jack was told by his mother to sell their cow for food, as they were starving, and the cow had stopped producing milk, but Jack made the seemingly poor deal of trading the cow for a few beans. When Jack's mother found out what he had done, she threw the beans out the window, which revealed them to be magic beans, as a giant beanstalk started to grow. It is significant that Jack's mother instigates the plot of the fairy tale, as she is the reason that Jack went to the market and was introduced to magical elements that would change his future. In addition, Jack's mother throwing the beans out into nature initiated a natural response that often only goddesses can achieve in myths, as overnight the beans grew into a massive beanstalk that reached up to the sky, similar to how the corn, beans, and squash grew before the eyes of Grandmother Sun's shaman initiates; these elements suggest remnants of divinity in Jack's mother, just as they also suggest that she may be instigating her son's heroic quest.

Jack began his heroic journey by climbing up the natural beanstalk, which revealed an entrance to an otherworldly realm within the sky. Once in the sky realm, Jack discovered that a giant old ogress lived there. Sensing the old ogress as a helper to him, Jack immediately appealed to her kindness, stating how hungry he was. The ogress instantaneously took pity on Jack and fed him. The fact that Jack upon seeing a giant woman within the sky immediately felt her to be a beneficent figure suggests that she may be intended as a traditional goddess figure. The ogress continued to serve as a helper to Jack when her husband, the old ogre, arrived home, as she hid Jack away and lied to her husband about smelling human blood, telling him that he was imagining things. Once the ogre fell asleep, the old ogress freed Jack from his hiding spot and told him that it was safe for him to return home. Before fleeing the sky realm, Jack stole a bag of gold possessed by the ogres, apparently showing the act as blessed by the ogress, as she did not try to stop him from stealing from her. This same pattern continues in the fairy tale two more times. Each time Jack transgressed the sky realm, his life was saved only because the old ogress allowed Jack within her home, and then hid him away until it was safe for him to come out and steal more of their possessions—a hen that laid golden eggs on his second visit and a golden harp on his third visit. The old ogre was shown to finally catch Jack in the act of stealing his golden harp, but when the ogre chased Jack down the beanstalk, Jack, after making it safely to the ground, quickly chopped down the beanstalk, severing once more the realms of earth and sky, and the ogre died by falling to the ground. The fairy tale ends with Jack going home to his mother, whereupon they both became incredibly wealthy. Jack's newfound wealth, that resulted from his heroic quest, is symbolic of his heroic apotheosis, as he certainly faced otherworldly and underworld components while in the sky realm. The end of the fairy tale shows Jack marrying a princess, which is a common tenet of many folktales and fairy tales that signifies the successful quest of an apotheotic male hero, as was displayed with the hero within "The Maiden Tsar." Thus, it is clear that, despite being married to the ogre, the old ogress served as a goddess-like guide for Jack upon his quest, which might connect the ogress to traditional goddess ideology found within Celtic mythology.

Jack's role within this fairy tale seems to resemble a Celtic king who must prove his connection with the land, which again in Celtic mythology is portrayed as a goddess. The tale begins by showing a time of communal need, as environmental conditions appear so bad that Jack and his mother are starving; this could represent the reign of a Celtic king who lost favor with the land, thus losing favor with the goddess of the land, as many Celtic myths portray kingship as directly aligned to goddesses of the environment. It is widely theorized that Celtic kings had to prove their tie to the goddess of the land in order for the goddess to honor the king's right to rule. For example, in Ireland the land itself, symbolized by a sacred stone called the Lia Fáil, was mythically said to reveal the decree of the divine Tuatha de Danaan when the stone cried out if the man who touched it was to be king. When a Celtic king was ineffective, the goddess of the land was said to reject his reign by causing the land to enter into a non-productive state; it was then that the old king had to be sacrificed to the goddess in order to help the land regenerate, so that a new, young, and vibrant king could step forth. Therefore, when Jack killed the old ogre, who kept too much wealth only for himself within the sky, Jack caused the wealth of the sky, perhaps symbolic of rain, to pour forth upon the earth in a promise of regeneration. With this interpretation, it makes sense that Jack must gain the favor of a female divine being, which in the context of the tale is the old ogress who lives in the sky realm, as again, Celtic goddesses were believed to be the only ones who could bestow the favor of the land to a worthwhile king. Therefore, when analyzing this fairy tale using Celtic concepts of goddess worship, Jack is viewed as worthy to serve the next generation as king, since he ends the tale marrying a princess, because he has shown, through the guidance of a goddess representative upon his heroic quest, that his reign will bring forth wealth, prosperity, and crops of enormous size to all the people.

Many times, it is assumed that female characters, especially elderly women within folktales and fairy tales are only portrayed in highly negative stereotypical fashion, such as weak and mostly useless grandmothers, wicked witches, or comical busybodies. However, as has been pointed out in this chapter, many cultures portrayed folktale and fairy tale elderly women in roles reminiscent of the highest offices once held by respected members of their communities, such as shamanic saviors to their communities, oracular wisdom holders, and teachers to male heroes. Again, because so many wise old women played such respected roles within folktales and fairy tales, they helped to preserve traditional components of goddess worship within their respective cultures.

What is interesting and worth noting, though, is that there appears to be more folktales and fairy tales that portray young maidens or monstrous women guiding males upon heroic quests than old wise women. As was discussed in Chapter 1 and within this chapter, many global cultures experienced a transition away from societies that worshipped powerful goddesses and revered formidable women to decidedly patriarchal social, political, and religious belief systems. Thus, patriarchal cultures often increasingly identified women in stereotypical ways within their mythologies, which resulted in less of a cultural focus on respected wise old women and more of a focus on female mythic, folkloric, and fairy tale characters being stereotypically portrayed as either sexually appealing or monstrous.

Thus, innumerable young and beautiful maidens abound within the male heroic quests of many myths, folktales, and fairy tales, as do countless monstrous females, both of which will be discussed in the next two chapters. What is telling, however, is that oftentimes the beautiful and young or monstrous and terrifying females of myths, folktales, and fairy tales end up imparting very similar messages to male heroes as those of their wise old women counterparts, proving that though patriarchal efforts strove to portray women as either sexual objects or monsters, women still found a way to teach male heroes about a time when goddesses reigned supreme.

3

Maidens and
Otherworldly Women

Maidens and otherworldly women within myths, folktales, and fairy tales, like their old wise women counterparts, often serve as representations of goddesses who impart wisdom to male heroes. There are numerous folktales and fairy tales, more than myths in fact, that show strong, brave, and adventurous maidens upon their own quests, rather than only aiding male heroes upon their journeys, but these maidens will be discussed in Chapters 5–8 of this book.

The maidens and otherworldly women of mythology, most of whom are portrayed as divine or as connected to goddesses in service to them, often teach goddess-oriented concepts associated with fertility, everlasting abundance, and vibrant life to male heroes. For example, many world cultures worshipped various young and beautiful goddesses who were associated with fertility, such as the Mesopotamian Ishtar, Egyptian Isis, Greek Aphrodite, Norse Freyja, Aztec Xochiquetzal, etc. Some of the best mythic examples displaying fertility goddesses come from the Neolithic period of many regions, such as the Middle East, the Mediterranean, Europe, and portions of Africa and Asia. In the Neolithic period, that produced the shift from hunter/gatherer to agricultural methods of subsistence, the Paleolithic belief in Great Mothers/Earth Mothers and animalistic mates gradually transformed into a belief in a Mother Goddess who represented the cycles of the harvest, but also commanded all aspects of life and regeneration for all living beings. Therefore, these Neolithic goddesses, and the goddesses who were inspired by Neolithic forms in later eras, often were connected to clear images of fertility. The Greek goddess Persephone, for instance, was regarded as a mythic maiden who aided in the coming of a fertile spring, just as her Roman counterpart Flora was imagined as doing. As representations of fertility, many Neolithic and other fertility goddesses have myths that describe them in highly sexual terms. For instance, many global cultures believed that sexual encounters between the Neolithic Mother Goddess and a male consort, marked both in many Neolithic myths and communal ritual rites, initiated the fertility of the land and the propagation of the crops. One prime example is found in the Sumerian myth that shows the fertility goddess Inanna as a maiden who marries a mortal man named Dumuzi. Their sexual union shows Inanna, as an earth goddess of fertility, being literally fertilized by copulation with Dumuzi; "Inanna spoke: 'Who will plow my vulva?/ Who will plow my high field?/ Who will plow my wet ground?'… Dumuzi replied: 'Great Lady … I, Dumuzi the King, will plow your vulva'" (qtd. in Wolkstein & Kramer). Copulation between a fertility goddess, or one of her representatives, and a young male, identified as the male consort, and in some instances future king, became a central religious ritual, identified as the Sacred Marriage, within many Neolithic civilizations.

Neolithic and other fertility goddesses who served as representations for the cycles of the harvest, and thus all life, were also envisioned as in control of death for earth's inhabitants. For instance, again the Greek divine maiden Persephone initiated the growth of spring, but she was also the goddess of the underworld along with her husband Hades. Because Neolithic and other fertility goddesses were so closely connected with the cycles of the harvest and nature, they were often envisioned as needing to be appeased through sacrifice. In many cultures, sacrifice could be offered by leaving foodstuff, libations of wine, figurines, etc., for the goddess, but sometimes animal sacrifices, or even the sacrifice of a mythic male consort or other humans, were envisioned as necessary. For instance, Neolithic myths throughout the Middle East, India, Africa, the Mediterranean, and Europe display mythic male consorts, such as "Dumuzi, Tammuz, Attis, Adonis, Osiris, … Baal," etc., being mythically sacrificed to honor fertility goddesses (Stone 20). Symbolically within myth, these male consorts underwent the same natural processes of the harvest; they were "all nearly torn apart, dismembered, brutally mutilated, and killed before they … [could] rise again, with the crops, to new life" (Armstrong 47–8). Therefore, myths of maidenly fertility goddesses, and later folktales and fairy tales of maidens who educate male heroes, often connect sacrifice and death to the fertility offered by the maiden.

However, as Neolithic and other fertility goddesses of mythology often showed that they required sacrifice and death to aid in the cycles of the harvest and greater nature, they, as representatives of the cycles of nature, also promised a ceaseless process of rebirth for all earth's inhabitants. For example, the myths that present male consorts dying to fertilize the earth in preparation of the harvest often also present them in myths as actually or symbolically resurrecting with the new harvest. For instance, again in the myth of Inanna and Dumuzi, Dumuzi died after copulating with Inanna, but he was portrayed as resurrecting annually each spring with the promise of a new harvest.

Folktales and fairy tales often portray maidens and otherworldly women in a similar fashion to the portrayal of mythic fertility goddesses. Maidens and otherworldly women within folktales and fairy tales often display vast fertility in the promise of male characters potentially winning and marrying them. Many folktales and fairy tales likewise connect death to the interaction of a male protagonist to a prized maiden or otherworldly woman. When a folktale or fairy tale male protagonist does meet the requirements of the maiden or otherworldly woman in the tale, which is often presented as a test or quest that the maiden has orchestrated, he is often rewarded with elements that symbolize the tenet of rebirth found in Neolithic and other fertility goddess myths, suggesting that the male protagonist has been deemed an apotheotic hero by the maiden of the tale. Therefore, like the folktales and fairy tales that featured old wise women who taught male protagonists lessons that were connected to traditional goddess ideologies, folktale and fairy tale maidens and otherworldly women also serve as guides and educators to male heroes upon quests to learn the lessons of goddesses.

Mystical Maiden Teachers

The Greek myth of Theseus, Ariadne, and the Minotaur provides a prime example of the role the maiden often serves for the male hero of mythology. In this myth, the hero Theseus of Athens goes to Crete, a stronghold of Neolithic goddess worship, in order to try and kill the monstrous Minotaur, who is half bull and half man. Theseus is immediately portrayed in the myth as a young, brave man who was willing to sacrifice himself to try and save the Athenians from having to provide their own youths to be sacrificed by the Minotaur in payment to Crete. However, upon arriving in Crete, the myth makes it clear that Theseus cannot be successful in achieving his quest of killing the Minotaur without the aid of the maiden Ariadne, the princess of Crete and half-sister of the Minotaur. Possessing mystical wisdom, Ariadne systematically taught Theseus how to accomplish his heroic quest. She taught him the secrets of the otherworldly labyrinth, which housed the Minotaur, and then instructed him how to endure his heroic underworld stage by facing and killing the Minotaur with a sword that she provided. This education proved beneficial, as Theseus was able to successfully complete his quest, and thus become an Athenian hero. After this task, Theseus and Ariadne left Crete and made their way to the island of Naxos, where Ariadne lost her virginity to

Theseus, who upon waking up the next morning, decided to flee, leaving Ariadne alone.

At first glance, Ariadne within this myth seems like little more than a foolish girl who gave up everything only to be taken advantage of by Theseus. However, there is more to this myth beneath the surface. Ariadne was once a Neolithic fertility goddess revered on Crete; "originally Ariadne was a vegetation goddess in Crete…. Sometimes Ariadne was associated with the surname "Very Holy Maid"; she was worshipped in this form on Crete as well as on the "islands of Naxos, Delos, Cyprus, Chios, Lemnos, … and the Peloponnese, especially Argos" (Trckova-Flamee). Viewing Ariadne as a goddess allows her role within the myth to be better understood not as the victim of Theseus, but as his educator. It is widely believed that Neolithic fertility goddesses, such as Ariadne, reigned supreme on Crete. In addition, bull representations, often interpreted as portrayals of mythic male consorts, have been found in many sites on the island, such as the palace of Knossos. With this knowledge, the Minotaur's sacrifice by Theseus, perhaps thrusts Theseus into the same role the Minotaur held—that of male consort. When Ariadne teaches Theseus how to kill the Minotaur, she may be preparing him to become her next sacrifice, showing that his true heroic quest was not complete after killing the Minotaur, but had only just begun. Ariadne's role as a deity, and her instruction of Theseus, instead of his abuse of her, is signaled when Ariadne is united in marriage with the fertility god Dionysus after Theseus left her on Naxos, an ending that certainly shows Ariadne as divine instead of as a mere victim. Later myths of Theseus's life show that he continued upon a quest to indeed meet a similar fate as the Minotaur, as he was shown to wander through otherworlds of defeat in his lifetime, first facing the death of his own father because of an error he made, and then when his own people grew to distrust him as king of Athens and forced him to abandon his throne to wander Greece alone. With his heroic deed of saving the people of Athens from the Minotaur forgotten, Theseus then was mythically shown to have to face the underworld when he was murdered by King Lycomedes of Skyros, who pushed him off a cliff, which was the same way his own father died. The sobering mythic life story of Theseus shows not a hero who is forever revered by his people for only completing a heroic deed of strength and bravery, typical traits of many male heroic myths, but instead shows a true hero of goddess ideology, as Theseus was eventually forced to learn the spiritual lesson that goddesses often teach within their mythic narratives—that all living beings must accept that they are merely natural beings who will have to succumb to the processes of nature. Thus, the mythic maiden Ariadne in her divine role as a fertility goddess was shown to have guided Theseus upon a long journey toward understanding that he, like all living beings, was no different than the Minotaur, whose death allowed for the continuation of all life.

Zipes contends that "in the hands of male tellers, writers, and collectors," folktale and fairy tale maidens, unlike many mythic maidens who are often portrayed in powerful divine roles, have often been "depicted as helpless, if not passive," as many folktales and fairy tales portray maidens in stereotypical ways "because of a general patriarchal view of women as domestics and breeders, born to serve the interests of men" (Zipes, *Irresistible Fairy Tale*, 80). This is certainly true in some folktales and fairy tales; however, many folktales and fairy tales display maidens in superior roles to the male protagonists of the narratives, as they hold the role of educator to male heroes in ways that are quite similar to the fertility goddesses of mythology.

For example, in a folktale from Scotland (Don 95–107), a maiden who resembles a mythic fertility goddess, clearly is portrayed as the educator to a young male hero. The folktale shows that a young man began his quest by venturing into the forest where he proceeded to treat the animals of the forest with kindness, immediately identifying him as worthy of a heroic quest in accordance to goddess ideology, as often mystical maidens, and other female folktale and fairy tale characters aligned with traditional goddess worship, will reward or punish protagonists based on their respect of nature. The young man in this folktale thus passed his test when he freed a wolf from a trap, a hawk from a bird line, and an otter from a net, and was rewarded with the immediate aid of a mystical maiden who appeared to him in the wilderness. The maiden appeared to the young man as being trapped like the animals he encountered, signaling her alignment with nature, as she appeared similar to the animals in the tale. The young man found out that the maiden was trapped by a giant, who was dragging her in chains. The entrapment of the animals and the mystical maiden suggests that this folktale may be imparting a message about embracing traditional elements of Celtic religion. In Celtic ideology, as discussed, nature was revered as sacred, and goddesses were often depicted as in command of the natural environment. Thus, the giant, who continually trapped Celtic sacred representations—animals and mystical women—certainly could represent cultural influences that strove to revise traditional sacred ideologies. The young man, then, could represent one who was on the cusp of embracing either traditional, goddess ideology or revised, patriarchal beliefs. Thus, the young man is portrayed in this tale as needing to learn from the maiden that patriarchal elements, like strength and force, often advertised in myths, folktales, and fairy tales to show the worth of a male hero, are not all that is needed to embrace traditional Celtic components. In order for the young man to become a true

Celtic hero, the mystical maiden must first educate him about the ways of Celtic fertility goddesses.

The tale shows the young man, as he did with the animals, wishing to free the maiden, but he found that unlike before, when he easily freed the animals, he now had to rely on the help of the maiden to free her. The young man went up to the cave where the giant held the maiden captive and chopped the giant's head off while he slept. Feeling triumphant, the young man went to the maiden and touted his success to her. However, the maiden is shown to know the intricacies of the natural and supernatural world, aligning her to Celtic goddess worship, so she, like Ariadne did with Theseus, taught the young man that true heroism is not obtained by force. The maiden told the young man that the giant could not be so easily killed, since he held the ability to heal all wounds. Therefore, the maiden stated to the young man that the giant could only be killed by the knowledge and skills that she possessed. The maiden then told the young man that the giant could not be killed by regular means because his heart was housed elsewhere. The young man tried to offer new plans to kill the giant, again involving stereotypical male skills like force, but the maiden simply repeated to the young man that patriarchal skills of strength and violence would not work with this giant. Finally, after many days, the young man had to fully immerse himself in what was an otherworld for him, as he had to accept that he must learn a new way of life from the maiden. Once he accepted this, he watched the maiden use her own mystical techniques to trick the giant into revealing where he hid his heart. Learning that the giant's heart was housed in a tree stump outside of his cave, and learning to wait for the instruction of the maiden, the young man was finally able to use the force he initially wanted to use to chop the tree stump in half. When he did this, a deer sprang forth from the stump and tried to run away with the giant's heart, but the young man called upon the wolf that he saved at the start of his quest, and the wolf killed the deer. However, when the deer died, a duck flew out of its mouth, so the boy called to the hawk he saved, which caught the duck and caused a salmon to flop out of the duck's beak and swim into a nearby river. The young man then called upon the otter he saved to catch the salmon, which the otter did, retrieving the egg. The fact that the young man is shown to be able to harness the power of nature at this stage of his heroic quest shows that he has successfully navigated the otherworld stage of his quest and has learned some of the lessons of his maiden teacher, lessons that are aligned with Celtic goddesses such as mysticism and concepts of natural rebirth. Further showing the psychological evolution of the hero, when the young man got the egg, instead of breaking it, he took it to the maiden for her guidance on what to do with it. Once the mystical maiden received the egg, which is a symbol of fertility goddesses throughout many cultures, as eggs often signal rebirth, she knew exactly what to do with it. The maiden waited for the giant to come home, and then she smashed the egg on his forehead. In the maiden's mystical hands, the egg broke easily and caused the giant to die. The maiden then took the hero's sword and freed herself. The fact that the tale ends with the maiden knowing full well how to free herself shows her in a superior role as educator to the young hero. When the maiden used the egg to kill the symbolic representation of patriarchy, the giant, she thus teaches the young hero that renewed life can come from a rejection of what the giant stands for if he embraces what the mystical maiden, as a remnant of a Celtic goddess, represents.

The Grimm brothers' fairy tale "Maiden without Hands" (J. Grimm & W. Grimm 99–103) presents another good example of a maiden who resembles a mythic fertility goddess who attempts to educate two males toward achieving heroism. In this fairy tale, a miller encountered the devil in the woods and mistakenly made a deal with him to trade his daughter for wealth. The miller thought that he had only traded the devil his apple tree, but in three years' time, the devil came to claim his daughter. However, when the devil appeared, the maiden "drew a circle around herself and purified herself [with water]. Consequently, the devil couldn't go near her" (J. Grimm & W. Grimm 100). This task performed by the maiden, that overpowers the leading adversary of Christian ideology, presents her as having mystical abilities that are similar to those of Celtic and Germanic goddesses. Thus, the maiden is immediately presented as a possible educator to her father on heroism according to goddess ideology. When the devil realized that he could not abduct the maiden, he ordered the maiden's father to take away all water from her, so that she could no longer purify herself. The father, proving that he was incapable of learning about heroism from his goddess-like daughter, merely did as he was ordered by the devil. The devil returned the next day, but he found that the maiden had again purified herself, this time with her own tears, so once more, the devil was thwarted from taking the maiden. The fact that the maiden could purify herself with her own tears, instead of with holy water sanctified by a priest for instance, suggests that she holds within herself innate goddess-like qualities that can supersede the power of Christianity's greatest opponent. It is also important that the text shows the Christian father at the mercy of the devil, as it suggests that the father, who is decidedly portrayed as unheroic, is not fully protected by his faith. However, the maiden is shown to be protected by her pagan mysticism against the Christian adversary; this fact again promotes the idea that the maiden serves as a preserved remnant of a traditional Celtic or Germanic goddess.

Enraged, the devil in the fairy tale next ordered the father to cut off his daughter's hands to stop her from protecting herself. The father refused to do this heinous task, but when the devil threatened to take him instead, the father, utterly proving himself a failed hero, relented to the devil's order, cut off his daughter's hands, and again gave the devil permission to abduct his maimed daughter. Both the father and devil represent strong patriarchal elements in this fairy tale. The father, in wholly adopting the patriarchy of his society and religion, that makes it acceptable to give one's daughter away without her permission, is portrayed as a shameful failure in this tale, which certainly holds important meaning about the message of this work. Similar world myths display fathers cutting off the hands or fingers of their daughters. For instance, the Inuit myth of Sedna, a sea goddess, shows her father cutting off her fingers to save his own life. Also, the Chinese myth of Guan Yin, sometimes identified as a goddess and sometimes as a bodhisattva, is shown to have her own hands cut off by her father when she refuses to follow his decree of getting married. Portraying fathers as cutting off the fingers or hands of their own daughters to save themselves, or protect their patriarchal principals, imparts a message about the injustice of harming the sacred female just to maintain a flawed patriarchal system. However, this fairy tale, like the myths of Sedna and Guan Yin, does not end with only a fatalistic message about patriarchy's power over goddess ideology; instead, the maiden of this tale is portrayed as highly capable of using her own means to survive, just as Sedna and Guan Yin were portrayed as doing in their own myths, as both Sedna and Guan Yin undergo the trauma of losing their fingers/hands, but move on to teach lessons to audiences about the superiority of goddess-oriented ideology over flawed patriarchal systems.

Therefore, the maiden in this fairy tale, though she had her hands brutally cut off, was shown to still be able to resist the devil when he came a third time, just as a goddess would be able to. Again, the maiden used her own mystical abilities to ward off the devil by crying so much that her tears purified her mutilated body, and the devil lost all claim to her. The tale shows that the father gained so much wealth as a result of his deal with the devil that he promised he would see to it that his daughter lived in opulence, but the maiden declared that she wished to leave her father forever and venture out into the world alone, showing the goddess-like maiden as discontinuing her attempt to educate her father toward heroism. Thus, the maiden had her maimed arms tied behind her back and set off into the wilderness, where she finally arrived at a king's compound. Once there, she saw an apple tree, in which she used the weight of her body to shake the tree, until apples fell to the ground. The maiden survived off of these apples for some time, until the king's guards spied her and sent her to prison. However, when the young prince of the kingdom saw the maiden in prison, he set her free, asking that she tend his chickens. The prince soon fell in love with the maiden, and the two were married and lived happily for many years. At this point in the narrative, it becomes clear that the mystical maiden will now attempt to educate her husband to become a hero in line with goddess ideology.

The tale moves on to present the prince's first challenge upon a heroic quest that is seemingly instigated by his mystical wife. When the prince became king and went off to fight a battle, his wife, now the queen, gave birth to a healthy baby; however, the devil, who begins to appear in the tale as an element created by the maiden to test the heroism of the men in her life, sent a message to the king that his child was a changeling, an infant who was believed to be switched at birth by fairies according to Celtic and European lore. The king, horrified, quelled his fear and sent news that nevertheless his wife and child should be protected until he returned, thus passing his first test of heroism. However, the devil, again a manifestation seemingly created by the maiden, intervened and interjected the king's message, sending instead a message back to the authorities of the kingdom that stated that the queen and her child should be exiled from the land. So, once more, the maiden asked that her arms, and now her infant, be bound to her back as she set out again into the wilderness. The tale at this point seems to project the injustice of the current position of women as powerless in a patriarchal world, as the maiden's lack of hands to manage her own life, even to adequately manage her child, is symbolic of women within patriarchal societies being forced to forfeit their own self-reliance. However, the tale immediately moves on to show that the maiden is not at all powerless in her current patriarchal world, as she is portrayed as connected to a much older ideological system of goddess worship, which the tale solidifies at its conclusion. Thus, the exile of the queen and her child again seems to be an orchestrated event that she designed to test the heroism of her husband, the king.

The fairy tale shows the maiden and her baby again going deep into the forest where she encountered a kind old man who helped her untie her infant from her back. In this forest, the maiden then went to a magic tree and placed her maimed arms around the tree, until her hands grew back. This scene finally solidifies the maiden's portrayal as a goddess remnant of traditional ideologies, as the presentation of mutilation and death being mystically restored, often within nature, is repeatedly a part of many mythic narratives of fertility goddesses. For example, again the Chinese myth of Guan Yin presents her as revealing her divinity/sacrality when she too was able to restore her maimed hands. The maiden in this tale is further portrayed as a remnant of a Celtic or Germanic fertility goddess when she is next portrayed as choosing to live with no man, but instead lived for some time in her magic tree. The education of her husband, the king, toward heroism is solidified when the text reveals that he went on a heroic quest, searching far and wide for his wife and child, until he finally found them. At their reunion, the goddess-like maiden presented her husband with his final test by demanding that he ask her for permission to come into her natural abode three times. The mystical maiden's demand that her husband ask to be let into her home shows that she, as a goddess representative, will always refuse to succumb to the demands of patriarchy, a lesson she attempted to teach her father when she did not allow him to give her away to the leading adversary of Christianity. The husband, unlike her father, is shown as fully accepting the mystical maiden's demand; thus, he becomes an actualized hero according to the standards of goddess ideology. The tale ends showing that together, as king and queen, the pair are foreshadowed to hold a balanced rulership, sending a message to audiences of the importance of preserving traditional, goddess-oriented belief systems in the midst of their current patriarchy.

Prized Maidens as Elements of Worship

Many myths, folktales, and fairy tales present maidens as elements of worship or as a prize that must be won by male characters. For example, Atalanta from Greek mythology was viewed as so highly prized that many eligible males willingly competed in a foot race to marry her, though any who failed to outrun her were killed. In India's *Mahabharata*, the princess Draupadi was viewed as so worthwhile that she was given as a prize to any male who could accomplish a seemingly impossible task, which consisted of lifting a tremendously heavy bow, striking an arrow through a fish's eye as it rotated on a plate on top of a roof, all while looking at the eye by way of a reflection in the water. The narrative element of extreme reverence for a prized maiden resembles one's worship of a fertility goddess; therefore, when this tenet appears in a myth, folktale, or fairy tale, it often signals the maiden as either divine or as a divine representative. When myths, folktales, and fairy tales portray a worthwhile male as marrying such a prized maiden, he is often presented as a hero who earned the maiden by embracing the lessons of goddess ideology. The final union of the male hero and the maiden in myths, folktales, and fairy tales, often reveals the maiden's lasting promise, as a fertility goddess or fertility goddess representative, of maintaining nature's ceaseless cycles.

For example, Charles Perrault's fairy tale "The Sleeping Beauty in the Wood" (1697) portrays the maiden of Sleeping Beauty as so highly venerated, though she remained comatose for most of her narrative, that males from far and wide willingly lost their lives trying to reach her; therefore, the extreme reverence for Sleeping Beauty directly connects her to concepts of goddess worship. Yet, many scholars "have targeted Sleeping Beauty as the most passive and repellent fairy-tale heroine of all" (Tatar 117). Scholars, like Tatar, specifically point to folktale and fairy tale maidens like Sleeping Beauty to discuss the injustice found in many tales that present male protagonists actively upon a quest, while female characters remain passive, stating that there are few maidens more passive than Sleeping Beauty (Tatar 117). However, in looking at Giambattisa Basile's "Sun, Moon, and Talia" (1634–36), the tale that inspired "Sleeping Beauty of the Wood," Sleeping Beauty's apparent passivity can be better understood as a narrative device meant to present her as deserving of the reverence of a goddess.

In the "Sun, Moon, and Talia," the plot shows a young, beautiful maiden who was poisoned by a splinter that went underneath her fingernail, which caused her to enter into a deep sleep. A married king saw Talia in this state and immediately was filled with lust for her. The king had sex with Talia while she was in a comatose state, which caused her to become pregnant and eventually give birth, still in a deep sleep, to twins named Sun and Moon. When Talia's infant daughter tried to nurse, she mistakenly sucked on Talia's finger, which caused the splinter to come out and Talia to awaken. The king's wife discovered the king's connection to Talia and the children, so she sought revenge upon her husband for his infidelity. The queen ordered the cook to kill the children and serve them to the king, but they were saved by the cook, who fed the king lamb instead. The queen also demanded that Talia be burned alive, but Talia was saved at the last minute by the king, and the queen herself was instead thrown into the fire, which resulted in Talia and the king getting married.

This tale, though clearly derogatory to women, holds connections to traditional mythic narratives involving the worship of fertility goddesses. For instance, the king's obsession over Talia, even though she remained in a deep sleep, resembles the concept of worship for a divine being. Many folktales and fairy tales present a high-standing male character, such as the king of this tale, falling completely at the mercy of a maiden just by her image, similar to how worshippers idolize icons of deities. Thus, this ability to cause the male character to do almost anything in order to obtain the maiden gives the maiden a position of power similar to that of a goddess. Throughout mythology, and history, males have sacrificed a great deal, sometimes even their lives, as was seen in Neolithic male consort myths, for concepts associated with female divinity. Likewise, the king of this fairy tale is described as rendered helpless upon viewing the still and silent Talia, who appears like an icon of a goddess, so he sacrificed his morality, and current marriage to his wife, to be with Talia. Furthermore, the repeated portrayal of beauty as connected to maidens within folktales and fairy tales initially seems to be tied to stereotypical presentations of women as simply objects for men to desire. However, the repeated portrayal of a folktale and fairy tale maiden's beauty, so that it renders a male protagonist helpless, presents the beautiful maiden, like Talia, as holding a heightened, seemingly mythic, status. For instance, many mythic accounts similarly classify maidens as beautiful, but often this is done to connect the beauty of the maiden with divinity. Often a mythic maiden will appear to men with such beauty that they immediately know that she is sacred, such as happened in the Lakota myth when mortal men met the sacred White Buffalo Calf Woman (McCoppin, *Lessons of Nature*, 105) and in the Celtic myth when Pwyll met the divine Rhiannon.

Also, the sexual act between Talia and the king, which is properly identified as rape to modern audiences since Talia was asleep, is reminiscent of the sexual acts described in mythic narratives of fertility goddesses. As discussed at the start of this chapter, Neolithic mythic male consorts, or future kings, often worshipped fertility goddesses, like the Sumerian Inanna/Akkadian Ishtar or Greek Aphrodite, by taking part in sexual intercourse with the goddess or her temple priestess in order to initiate the fertility of the land. Likewise, Talia, in clear goddess imagery, gives birth to twins with celestial names, Sun and Moon, after copulation with the king. Identifying the children as Sun and Moon suggests that the patterns of nature will remain intact because of the union between the fertility goddess representative of Talia and the king of this tale.

"The Sleeping Beauty in the Wood" draws upon elements found in the "Sun, Moon, and Talia," but also incorporates even more tenets that show the maiden, Sleeping Beauty, in concepts related to goddess worship. The fairy tale portrays Sleeping Beauty as pricking her finger on a spinning wheel and falling into a deep sleep for years, which draws mythic connections to the Fates in Greek mythology and the Norns in Norse mythology. In this tale, as well as the fairy tale of "Briar Rose" (J. Grimm & W. Grimm 162–5) by the Grimm brothers, Sleeping Beauty, as well as Briar Rose, received such a fate because their parents, the king and queen, did not invite one fairy to feast in the celebration of their christening. The inclusion of fairies, or perhaps more aptly Wise Women, as described by the Grimms' "Briar Rose," explicitly connects the stories to various traditional European mythologies, such as that of the Romans and Celts. Zipes explains that "clearly, pagan divinities were the predecessors of fairies" in many European folktales and fairy tales, and that "their roles and functions were transmitted mimetically in different cultures over thousands of years to form the modern concept of the fairy" (Zipes 30). In fact, Zipes points to the origin of fairies in the West as beginning with the "Moi-rai (Greek fates) and Parcae (Roman fates)," whose "basic function was to prophecy the destiny of a newborn. Eventually the Romans endowed Fauna with some of these qualities as the goddess of fertility and prophecy, and tales circulated about her as the Bona Dea, or the good goddess, who had her own cult and came to be associated with wild nature and eroticism because she was deemed to be the force of life" (Zipes 29). Zipes continues to state that Laurence Harf-Lancner in *Les Fées au Moyen Âge* identified two types of fairies in Europe during the Middle Ages: "the fates (parcae) … and the ladies of the forest" (qtd in Zipes 31). Harf-Lancner believed that the concept of the divine Fates from Greek and Roman mythology merged in the European Middle Ages with the fairy of the forest found in Celtic mythology, so that tales produced after the Middle Ages identified fairies as mystical beings who were still clearly aligned with their mythic, and thus sacred, past of goddess worship (Zipes 31–2). Maintaining their connection to mythic goddesses, often fairies in folktales and fairy tales hold a significant tie to fertility, which is also the symbolism of the fer-tile maiden within many folktales and fairy tales; this is perhaps why the fairies appear in "Sleeping Beauty in the Wood" and "Briar Rose" with the birth of the maidens. In both Perrault's and the Grimms' version of the tale, the fairies/Wise Women who were invited to Sleeping Beauty's/ Briar Rose's christening granted the maidens many blessings. However, one fairy, described in Perrault's story as being left out because she rarely left her house, and in the Grimm's version because the parents did not have a proper golden place setting for her, cursed the children to die in maid-enhood by pricking their fingers. In both tales, Sleeping Beauty and Briar Rose were saved by a remaining fairy yet to give her blessing, who less-ened the severity of the curse by stating that the maidens would merely fall asleep when they pricked their fingers on a spindle. Thus, Perrault's and the Grimm brothers' tales both present the fairies/Wise Women as setting up Sleeping Beauty and Briar Rose, with their blessings and curses, to be figures who will test the heroism of the men who encounter them, firmly connecting the maidens to the divinity associated with the fairies/Wise Women.

Sleeping Beauty and Briar Rose in their respective tales are shown to move from childhood into maidenhood, where they were indeed fate-fully pricked by a spindle, which caused them to sleep, along with the rest of their fathers' kingdoms, for one hundred years. The folkloric and fairy tale presentation of the death of a maiden, even if it is symbolic, also car-ries mythic connections, as many mythic maidens and fertility goddesses, such as the Greek Persephone, died in maidenhood, and because Perse-phone was a fertility goddess, her death directly affected the natural world, which was often the case when a mythic maiden died. Likewise, when Sleeping Beauty and Briar Rose fell into their death-like states, nature was also shown in the tales to react by enveloping and preserving the youth and beauty of the maidens, explicitly signaling their connection as fertility goddess representatives.

Because Sleeping Beauty and Briar Rose are silent figures in their own tales, one could assume that all individuality is stripped away from them, as it seemed to be for Talia who likewise remained silent in her fairy tale, yet there is a reason why the works are named after the three maidens and not the princes who won them. Hearing the legends of a beautiful, slumbering princess within a forgotten kingdom, deep within an overgrown wilderness, princes came from far and wide, in both the Perrault and Grimm versions of the tales, to try and awaken the maidens. However, most of the males failed their quests, dying in the effort. This challenge or competition to win a maiden is similar to the veneration of the maiden described in the tale of Talia, as again the willingness of the young men to sacrifice their lives for a silent maiden is reminiscent of male consorts sacrificing their lives for abstract notions of fertility goddesses. Thus, the dramatic willingness of the suitors within these tales to sacrifice everything for the maidens suggests that Sleeping Beauty and Briar Rose are not only silent and passive figures in their tales, but goddess-like maidens who serve as initiators for the male characters within the tales to go on their heroic quests.

As discussed in Chapter 2 and earlier within this chapter, many female characters orchestrate male heroic quests, as the goal of the male heroic journey, as stated by many scholars, most notably Campbell, is the hero's final union with a goddess representative, which signals his apotheosis. Both tales show princes who were able to finally overcome all challenges to win the slumbering princesses by way of strength and bravery, typical elements of a male heroic quest. Thus, Sleeping Beauty and Briar Rose awakened from their death-like sleep in symbolic resurrection before the heroes to reward them with the promise of a fruitful and fertile union in marriage, displaying what appears to be the culmination of the hero's quest, which is unification with a goddess representative. However, the apotheosis of the hero often takes place after the hero has faced the fact of mortality in the underworld stage of his quest, but the princes of these tales have not yet faced the reality of death, as they only fell in love with the concept of everlasting life promised by many fertility goddesses, that the maidens of both tales perfectly embody in their paused state of youth and beauty while preserved in sleep. Therefore, the tales suggest that the heroes have not yet fully attained apotheosis, as the worship of the fertility goddesses' concept of everlasting life cannot be realized without the full embrace of mortality. Though a fruitful marriage is assured to the successful heroes of these tales, a more somber future is also promised to them. The paused youth of Sleeping Beauty and Briar Rose as they slumber will fade with age once they have reawakened; this fact of mortality thus sends a message to the heroes of the tales that youth, vigor, vitality, and fertility are only momentary states of existence. Thus, the brave, strong, and adventurous folktale and fairy tale heroic males must learn, as their mythic male consorts had to learn with their experiences with fertility goddesses, that such youthful stages cannot last. In fact, this is often the ultimate lesson of many male heroic quests that are orchestrated by fertility goddesses. For instance, Gilgamesh in the Mesopotamian *Epic of Gilgamesh*, ventured upon a quest to find immortality, but finished it knowing, with the help of the fertility goddess Ishtar, that he could never attain this goal. The heroes of these fairy tales, likewise, will have to learn that their unification with Sleeping Beauty and Briar Rose will only perpetuate a ceaseless life cycle that will assure their own demise, as the heroes are destined to mate, produce the next generation, age, and one day die. Thus, the heroes' unification with the fertility goddess figures of Sleeping Beauty and Briar Rose will eventually, throughout the long course of their lives, teach them to become true apotheotic heroes in line with goddess ideology, as they are forced to accept the demands of nature.

Maidens and Death

As implied with the fairy tales of Sleeping Beauty and Briar Rose, maidens within myths, folktales, and fairy tales often show audiences that the life stage of vitality and fertility will fade into old age and death; thus, mythic, folkloric, and fairy tale maidens often serve as representations of death. However, the maidens of mythology, folklore, and fairy tales also serve as a promise of the renewal of life that comes after death within the natural environment. As discussed in this chapter, many mythic, folktale, and fairy tale maidens are portrayed as connected to fertility goddesses who embody the cycles of nature. Thus, many maidens in mythology, folktales, and fairy tales, serving as representations of fertility goddesses, often guide male protagonists upon heroic quests that teach them that their youth and vibrancy will not last forever, as all living beings must die, but the reward of a successful quest often also includes the maiden revealing to the hero spiritual concepts of everlasting life by his embrace of the cycles of the natural world.

For example, the Greek myth of Orpheus and Eurydice presents a young male protagonist, Orpheus, in the prime of his life, as he was a renowned lyre player, and he had just married the beautiful maiden Eury-dice. However, before the marriage could be consummated, Eurydice was bitten by a snake, which killed her and sent her to the underworld. At the start of the myth, Orpheus was portrayed as too egotistical, believing that he could conquer the cycles of nature by going to the underworld and demanding that Eurydice be returned to him. He went directly to Hades and Persephone, the divine rulers of the underworld, and played his lyre with the belief that his musical ability would force them to forfeit Eury-dice. Persephone was moved by Orpheus's music, perhaps because she related to the maiden Eurydice since she too was thrust into the under-world in maidenhood, so Persephone told Hades to let Eurydice go back to the land of the living with Orpheus. Hades agreed, but he stated that Orpheus could only have his wife back if he did not ever look back for proof that she followed him out of the underworld. However, Orpheus fal-tered and looked back for assurance that his wife was behind him, only to see his beloved maiden, Eurydice, swept back into the underworld.

The myth continues to show Orpheus not upon the quest he believed he was undertaking, but upon a heroic quest in line with goddess ideology, presided over by the maidens of the myth, so far presented as Eurydice and Persephone. The myth confirms that Orpheus went upon a heroic quest within the underworld, often the final stage of the hero's journey before the hero attains apotheosis, because of the death of the maiden Eury-dice. Because of the intervention of another maiden, the divine maiden Persephone, Orpheus was portrayed as learning to accept both the fac-tuality of death, when he was forced to leave behind Eurydice, but also the promise of everlasting life that is assured in nature, as he ascended out of the underworld in symbolic resurrection. This lesson of rebirth is quite befitting Persephone as she was mythically shown to reside in the underworld during fall and winter, in symbolic death, but to symbolically resurrect each spring. Orpheus's spiritual transformation is portrayed in the myth when he played his lyre for the animals and plants of the for-est after the moment of his symbolic resurrection. The myth shows that the music Orpheus played, that was based on his experience in the under-world, was quite evolved from the music he played before his experience in Hades, as his new music initiated all of the elements of nature to respond to him, moving close to him and listening intently to his song. To fur-ther illustrate Orpheus's embrace of Persephone's message of everlasting life in nature, the myth continues to show Orpheus's death at the hands of the maiden followers of the god Dionysus—the maenads. The maenads were shown to be so enthralled by Orpheus's music that they entered into a frenzy and killed Orpheus by tearing his body to pieces and spreading the pieces of his corpse across the land. This type of mutilation of mythic males in connection to mythic fertility goddesses is common in global mythology, such as is portrayed in the Egyptian myth of Isis and Osiris and the Canaanite myth of Baal and Anat, both of which portray the gods Osiris and Baal experiencing a similar fate to that of Orpheus in order to symbolically show the necessity of death to renew the earth. To solidify that Orpheus obtained the apotheosis of the goddess as a result of his heroic quest, that was guided by myriad maidens, the myth shows that his decapitated head continued to play his enlightened music, similar to how the gods Osiris and Baal were resurrected by the fertility goddesses Isis and Anat after their deaths and mutilations in their respective myths. The fact that a part of Orpheus, his music, remained unchanged even after his death shows that Orpheus finally learned the goddess-oriented lesson of accepting the cycles of nature that demand death, but also promise everlasting renewal.

Additionally, the Greek myth of "Jason and the Golden Fleece," which, in oral form, may have originated as early as the thirteenth-century BCE, shows the maiden Medea as directly teaching the heroic Jason about the necessity of embracing death as part of nature's cycles. In this myth, Jason partook on a typical male heroic quest to secure his right to rule. He ventured, with his male crew, the Argonauts, to Colchis to obtain the Golden Fleece. Once he arrived in Colchis, he was helped by Medea, the princess maiden who was identified as a priestess of Hecate, the goddess of magic who was associated with to the underworld. Besides her connection to Hecate, Medea was shown to directly hold tenets in line with goddess worship, or to even be a goddess remnant herself, as she possessed mystical skills that every step of the way aided Jason in his heroic quest. To obtain the Golden Fleece, Jason had to first plow a field using fire-breathing bulls, and then bury dragon teeth in the soil as if planting them like seeds. The dragon teeth would then cause dead warriors to emerge from the soil, like botanical agents, showing Jason a glimpse of the fertility goddess's message of death and rebirth. Jason would then have to defeat these resurrected warriors in order to make his way to the Golden Fleece, which was protected by a quintessential symbol of the goddess—a giant serpent. Because the maiden Medea mystically helped Jason, he easily and quickly accomplished these elements of his seemingly impossible quest. The agricultural imagery of Jason's quest tasks, of which Medea knew the secrets, further suggests that Medea serves as a remnant of a Neolithic fertility goddess meant to teach Jason that the cycles of life for humans follow the same pattern of death and renewal as found in the harvest.

Medea is explicitly portrayed as connected to Neolithic concepts of divinity when she demonstrates skills that only goddesses possess. Before Jason attempted his impossible tasks, he was killed by Medea, cut up into pieces, and thrown into her cauldron. He then was resurrected by Medea; "the stranger's body now became restored and renewed as it cooked in boiling broth. And so the maiden now lifted him from the broth and laid him, once again upon Mother Gaea [or Gaia] ... and so Jason awoke from his death-like sleep" ("Jason" 191). Nauwald points out that the cauldron of rebirth in the hands of a fertility goddess is an old tenet of many mythological traditions around the world, such as the Celtic Ceridwen's cauldron of rebirth discussed in Chapter 2 of this book (Nauwald 144). Therefore, the ability on the part of Medea to both kill and resurrect Jason assuredly identifies her as at least a remnant of a Neolithic fertility goddess who may have been revised over the centuries when the myth moved from its many oral renditions to written form. Lusnhnig concurs, stating that Medea's "origins are divine" (Lusnhnig viiii). Thus, Jason certainly was presented with the heroic opportunity to learn about death and renewal through the guidance of the goddess-like Medea, but the tale presents Jason as struggling to learn the spiritual lessons of the goddess, as he was shown later in the myth to reject Medea, and thus reject goddess ideology.

The myth continues to show that Medea went with Jason back to Greece. On the way, Medea and Jason were married within a cave, according to the old customs of goddess worship, as caves were once believed to be the womb of the Greek Earth Mother Gaia. In time, Medea birthed two sons with Jason. However, after many years passed, Jason grew tired of Medea, so he declared that their marriage was false because it was done according to the old religious ways and not the new patriarchal standards of marriage within Greece. Jason then told Medea that he intended to marry the princess of Corinth, Creusa/Glauce, and thus become king of Corinth after the current king, Creon, died. Medea, as a fertility goddess representative, reacted by denying kingship to Jason in a reversal of the Neolithic Sacred Marriage act of mythology, that again showcased a fertility goddess approving of the kingship of a worthy male through union with him. Medea, instead of serving as a figure of fertility and fecundity in accepting the worth of the next king, reacted as a wronged fertility goddess often behaved in mythology, such as when the Mesopotamian Gilgamesh shunned the goddess Ishtar who, in retaliation, ravaged his kingdom of Uruk. In order to force Jason to face the necessity of death within goddess-ideology, as Orpheus had to face, Medea killed Jason's fiancé Creusa/Glace, her father King Creon, as well as the two sons she had with him. Though Medea proved that she possessed the ability to bring back people from death, she did not do so with her own two sons. Instead, Medea left Jason forever, as she climbed aboard two flying dragons, signaling again her divine status, and went on to marry Aegeus, the king of Athens, assuring his legacy through the birth of sons.

When Medea left Jason, he was portrayed as a failed hero, who did not learn the lessons of death and renewal from his goddess representative Medea. However, the ending of Jason's mythic narrative suggests that Medea's instruction of Jason was not over when she left him. The end of Jason's heroic quest shows him dying when the mast of his former ship, the Argo, fell on him and killed him. This ending suggests that Jason may have indeed finally learned that his initial heroic quest, that displayed only might and bravado, as well as his longing for power and wealth as king, again typical tenets of patriarchal male heroic quests, did not teach him about heroism according to the standards of goddess ideology. Presenting Jason as coming back to the site of his initial heroic quest and dying by the mast of his ship, which was built from a sacred oak tree taken from the shrine of the goddess Gaia or Rhea, both Greek Earth Mothers, at Dodona, could show him as finally sacrificing himself, as Orpheus did, in acknowledgment of the power of the goddess he failed to embrace earlier within his quest.

Similar to the myth of Jason and Medea, is a folktale entitled "The Prince and the Three Fates" (Phelps, *Tatterhood*, 17), which comes from the Sudanese region of the Nile River and was adapted from an older Egyptian tale. In this folktale, a prince was born, and when peris, supernatural spirits, visited his mother and father, they revealed that their son was fated to die by either "a dog, a serpent, or a crocodile" (Phelps, *Tatterhood*, 17). Devastated, the king and queen tried to keep their son hidden away from life, sequestering him within royal grounds, but when the prince reached maturity, he dismissed his parents' fear as ridiculous, as he felt young and strong, so he decided to finally leave his royal compound. Because the prince was portrayed as believing himself immune to mortality, as many strong, brave, and adventurous male heroes believe at the start of their heroic journeys, the tale immediately provides him with a teacher in the form of a beautiful maiden to marry. The tale shows that one night a serpent entered the couple's bedchamber and threatened to bite the prince while he slept, but the maiden, showing skills similar to the Egyptian goddesses Isis and Wadjet/Wadjit and the Sudanese goddess Abuk, who were all connected to fertility and serpents, killed the serpent with ease, awakened the slumbering prince, and presented him with the evidence of his first brush with death.

Next, the folktale shows the prince out hunting one day when he encountered a crocodile that told him that it would not eat him if he could dig a pit in sand, fill it with water, and then make sure the pit remained full of water. The prince went back home and fiercely tried to think of any means to escape his death. When the prince told the maiden what the crocodile said to him, she was depicted, as many maidens are in quests of male heroes, as possessing mystical knowledge connected to the natural world that allowed her to come up with a plan that she said would save her husband, but in reality, forced him to face his own death for a second time. The maiden declared that she knew of a magic plant that would keep water in a pit for a year, so she ventured into the vast desert on a long quest, easily overcoming trying obstacles, until she finally found the magical plant. The maiden's ability to accomplish components similar to a typical male heroic quest with apparent ease also presents her as a goddess remnant. When the maiden finally made it back to her husband, the prince, who after waiting for such a long time while thinking of his impending doom, quickly and nervously filled the pit he had dug with water and watched as his wife threw in the magic plant. To the prince's great relief, the water stayed within the pit and did not drain out, so the crocodile told the prince that it would not eat him. However, the crocodile also told the prince, "'You cannot escape from me…. I am your fate, and wherever you go, you will always find me before you'" (Phelps 20). The crocodile's utterance here is important, as it solidifies the fact that the maiden is not helping the prince evade death, as the crocodile reminds the prince that his death is assured, as it is for all living beings, but instead the maiden is actually helping the prince face his eventual demise. The tale shows the prince as being forced, in small steps, to face the concept of his own mortality—first when he faced the evidence of the deadly serpent in his bed, and then when he was forced to wait with the crocodile for his wife to return from her, seemingly intentionally long, quest to find the magic plant. Finally, to force the burgeoning hero to fully face his mortality, so that he can overcome the required underworld stage of his heroic quest, the folktale presents him with his longest brush with death.

When the prince wrongly thanked the maiden for saving him from facing death, death immediately came for him a third time, as if initiated by his maiden wife to make sure that he faced the reality of mortality. A duck flew up from the marsh near them, which caused a dog to run past him, making the prince stumble backwards into the Nile River, where he immediately became entangled in the deep mud and reeds. Now fully immersed in the experience of death, the prince thrashed about in the water, trying to use all of his strength to find a way to live. However, once he realized that there was nothing he could do to escape, he accepted his death. After enduring a moment of fully facing the fact of his own mortality, the maiden, again with the ease of a goddess, grabbed a hold of her husband and pulled him to shore, so that he could become an apotheotic king, who did not foolishly believe himself immune to death, but knew fully the value of a fleeting life, as well as the value of his goddess-like wife and her ideology.

Likewise, in a Scottish folktale entitled "The Sea-Maiden" (Caldecott 207–15), a fisherman and his sons were also educated by a sea-maiden, and other mystical women, about life and death. In this folktale, the fisherman encountered a sea-maiden one day as he was trying, unsuccessfully, to fish. The sea-maiden told the fisherman that if he would give his first-born son to her, then she would fill his net with fish. He declared that he had no son, and his wife was past childbearing years; all he had, he told the sea-maiden, was his wife, his mare, and his dog. Hearing this, the sea-maiden told the fisherman to take grain she presented to him home, give the grain to his wife, mare, and dog, and his wife would bear him three sons, his mare three foals, and his dog three puppies. The sea-maiden also instructed the fisherman to plant the remaining grain, which would cause three trees to grow. The sea-maiden told the man that the trees would serve as a sign to him if his sons' lives were ever threatened. In exchange for the magical grain, the fisherman agreed to the sea-maiden's request of giving her his first-born son in three years. The fact that a mystical woman, the sea-maiden, lives in the sea and can provide grain that will allow humans, animals, and plants to reproduce, certainly depicts the sea-maiden as a remnant of a Celtic fertility goddess. The fisherman in the tale went home and was indeed delighted to see that everything happened as the sea-maiden foretold. However, after three years passed, the fisherman was unable to give his son to the sea-maiden. He journeyed to her but did not bring his son; instead, he lied, stating that he forgot what he was supposed to bring. The sea-maiden immediately saw through his lie and told him that he could wait four more years, as it might be easier after this time to part with his son. After four years, the man again feigned to forget his son, and the sea-maiden again granted the man seven more years, of which he thought he might die in that time, thus escaping his return to the sea-maiden.

However, the man did live seven more years, and when his oldest son learned of his father's bargain, he chose to also evade the mystical sea-maiden and flee to a faraway land. The young man made his way to a new kingdom where a female sea-creature with three heads was threatening the community. The fact that the male protagonist is visited by another female creature who resides in the sea suggests that this second sea-creature is aligned to the first sea-maiden. The young man, showing only might, again a heroic trait of many male heroic quests that are not guided by goddess representatives, easily chopped off all three heads of the sea-creature, and thus was able to marry the princess of the kingdom. However, proving the tale to be about a quest for the male hero, and his father, to learn about how to become a hero in alignment with goddess ideology, thus learning about life, death and rebirth, the male protagonist was forced to again contend with the sea-creature when she returned with three new heads, solidifying her alignment with the sea-maiden who also was an expert of renewal and regeneration. When the sea-creature returned, she abducted the wife of the male protagonist. To retrieve his wife and further his heroic quest, the young man had to go to the sea-creature's island, find a "white-footed hind" that produced a crow from its mouth, convince the crow to reveal a trout within its mouth, and then convince the trout to reveal an egg within its mouth, so that the man could find the "soul of the monster" (Caldecott 210). This plot structure, that is similar to the Scottish folktale of the trapped maiden discussed earlier in this chapter, reveals the necessity of the food-chain, and thus the cycle of life, death, and rebirth within nature, in a style that is found in many Celtic myths of fertility goddesses. Thus, again, the sea-creature, just like the sea-maiden, is shown to teach the male protagonist about the goddess-oriented lesson of natural cyclicity. When the burgeoning hero found the egg, the female sea-creature rose out of the water and begged for her life. The man demanded his wife back in exchange for the sea-creature's life, but when his wife was returned to him, he smashed the egg and killed the sea-creature, thus deceiving two mystical female creatures within his lifetime, and proving that he, like his father, had not yet learned the lessons about life and death that the goddess representatives of the tale were trying to teach him.

After this escapade, the royal couple, again to continue the education of the male protagonist, and the father, came to an old woman's house in the woods. The princess, showing her to possibly be aligned with the mystical females of the tale, warned her husband to respect the old woman, but her husband ignored her, went right into the old woman's house, and ended up getting hit on the head by the old woman and dying, thus forcing him to experience death. When this happened, the old fisherman from his home saw that one of the trees planted by the grain given to him by the sea-maiden had withered and died, so the old father knew that his eldest son was dead.

The fisherman's second son went to avenge his brother, and eventually came to the old woman's home, where he received the same fate as his older brother, causing the second tree to wither and die, proving him to have also failed the same heroic tests of his father and older brother. The third and youngest son also sought revenge for his brothers, so he too eventually came to the home of the old woman. Once there, she tried to trick the brother inside, so she could also hit him upon the head and kill him, but the third son was more cautious than his older brothers, so he told the old woman to walk in front of him, which allowed him to draw his sword and cut off her head. However, as this was only an act of strength and bravado, typical of patriarchal male heroic quests, as soon as he did this, the old woman simply picked up her head and put it back on her shoulders, undeniably connecting her to portrayals of mythic fertility goddesses, as well as to the sea-maiden and sea-creature of this tale as her mystical abilities of death and regeneration aligned directly with theirs. The resurrected old woman and the young man then went on to wrestle with one another for a time, symbolic of the youngest son wrestling with his belief systems, until the young man finally realized what his father and brothers did not— he understood that the only way to survive was for him to acknowledge the power of this goddess representative, and thus embrace the ideology she embodied. So, in an act of acceptance of goddess ideology, the youngest son wrenched away the tool of the goddess, her club that she used to kill her advisories, and hit her upon the head with it, thus killing her, but also showing that the youngest son had accepted the fact that he would one day meet a similar fate. To solidify the fact that the youngest son of this folktale had attained the goddess-oriented apotheosis that his father and two older brothers could not, he performed the quintessential act of many fertility goddesses within global mythology—he found the corpses of his brothers, and when he touched them with the goddess representative's club, that signaled his embrace of goddess ideology, they immediately resurrected. The trees that had withered at their father's home also resurrected before the father's disbelieving eyes.

This tale presents the initial sea-maiden as taking on the form of three mystical women to teach multiple male characters about heroism in line with goddess ideology. The triad presentation the sea-maiden uses aligns directly with Celtic representations of fertility goddesses, such as the Morrígan, who was a triple goddess associated with death and fertility. In addition, as discussed in Chapter 2, the fact that the sea-maiden appears first as a maiden and finally as a crone is also significant, as many Celtic goddesses interchangeably appeared as young or old women in order to convey mythic messages about the natural cycles of life. Thus, the sea-maiden in all of her forms, served to teach the male characters of this folktale what she attempted to teach the father at the start of the tale with her abundant examples of birth and fertility. The father proved that he did not understand the sea-maiden's lesson that all elements of fertility and renewal must also incorporate death. Therefore, though he was bestowed with the prosperity of the goddess in having the fertility of his wife, mare, and dog restored, he could not accept the loss, perhaps death, of his son as the cost of such prosperity. The sea-maiden thus appeared in two more forms, that of a sea-creature and murderous crone who both resurrected after being decapitated, to teach the old father and his sons that death is not final in nature; it only serves as the means to initiate prosperity, renewal, and rebirth. However, the father and the two oldest sons were portrayed as still not learning the lesson the sea-maiden strove to teach them, so she forced the two sons, and through them their father, to experience death as part of their heroic journeys. The youngest son, as stated, finally proved that he understood the lesson the goddess representatives of the tale were trying to teach when he was able to perform the act of resurrecting his two brothers, just as his female teachers had taught him. The tale ends with the assurance that, like the youngest son, the two older sons, by experiencing death and resurrection firsthand, as well as their father, by seeing his sons, and their symbolic trees, die and be reborn, ultimately learned the lesson that the initial sea-maiden tried to teach them—that in nature, death is necessary, but from death, ceaseless life is assured. Therefore, all four men of the folktale finally became apotheotic heroes in accordance to goddess ideology.

Otherworldly Women

The presentation of the otherworld is a common element found in myths, folktales, and fairy tales around the globe. The otherworld is often portrayed as a place of vibrant abundance, as unlimited food, drink, women, sex, love, fulfillment, etc., often abound in the otherworld. When male protagonists discover the otherworld, they are often led there by mystical women, or they encounter mystical women once within the otherworld. The otherworld, and the otherworldly women who reside there, often teach male protagonists lessons that are similar to those taught by maidens who resemble traditional fertility goddesses, such as when to embrace times of abundance and fertility, and when to let go and accept age and death, thus reaching heroic apotheosis.

Celtic mythology presents myriad examples of the otherworld. The Celtic myth of the "Voyage of Bran" portrays the male hero Bran as being invited to the otherworld, identified in the myth as the Isle of Women, by an otherworldly woman who resided there. Once at the Isle of Women, Bran, along with his crew of men he commissioned to join him, found that it was filled with natural splendor and unlimited resources. Also, fitting the title of this particular otherworld, the Isle of Women, all the men found that they were each sexually paired with a beautiful maiden, which immediately signals elements associated with the worship of fertility goddesses. However, like many myths, folktales, and fairy tales of maidens who appear as representations of traditional fertility goddesses, the women of this otherworld were also harbingers of death. After a year had passed, the myth shows that one of Bran's men wished to return to Ireland.

The crew agreed to take him to see his home once more, but they were warned by the otherworldly women not to step on Irish soil, or they would die. Once in Ireland, the man who wanted to return home did not heed the warning of the otherworldly women and stepped onto Irish soil, whereupon he immediately turned to ash. At this, Bran called out to the people on shore that he had returned from his long voyage, but no one knew who he or his men were, as hundreds of years had passed in the human realm. The men then realized that the otherworld, with all of its vast resources, was also a place of death, as they were now dead to their former lives. However, the myth continues to present the men returning to the otherworld to live on, portraying the otherworldly women as also agents of renewal. Thus, the women of the otherworld, similar to many fertility goddesses, were shown to transform the males of this myth into heroes when they learned the necessity of embracing both life and death.

Arthurian tales also portray many examples of otherworldly women and their impact on male heroes. Again, because many Arthurian tales were inspired by Celtic mythology, the otherworldly women in Arthurian legends were often directly conceived of as divine women. For example, an Arthurian tale in the Welsh *Mabinogion*, entitled "The Lady of the Fountain," portrays the male hero Owain as spiritually growing because of his experience with an otherworldly woman. Owain, as one of Arthur's Knights of the Round Table, desired a quest, so he sought out a sacred fountain. Sacred wells or water sources, as discussed in Chapter 1, were often connected to earth goddesses in Celtic religious belief. To find the fountain in this tale, Owain journeyed through dense wilderness, until he finally found the fountain, but he saw that it was protected by a mighty knight. Owain also found that an enormous storm picked up while he was in the vicinity of the fountain. Owain proceeded to battle both the knight and the natural elements and came out of the ordeal successful, as he killed the knight and survived the storm. The death of the knight immediately thrust Owain into the otherworld.

Once immersed in the otherworld, Owain found a castle inhabited by the Lady of the Fountain, who was now a widow, as she was married to the knight Owain killed. The otherworld in this tale, like the Isle of Women, was again full of abundant resources. While immersed in this otherworldly environment, Owain lost all desire for his previous life, and soon married the Lady of the Fountain, becoming the new defender of the sacred fountain. The fact the Owain forfeited his old life and identity to unite with the Lady of the Fountain signals that he was being educated by the wisdom of this otherworldly woman, who is explicitly portrayed in the tale as a representation of a Celtic fertility goddess.

Owain, in his new life, guarded the fountain for years, until Arthur one day came searching for him. At first, Owain did not recognize Arthur, which indicates his growth beyond the character he was at the start of his quest. Finally, Owain's memory returned to him, and recognizing Arthur, Owain agreed to leave with him and return to Camelot. However, once in Camelot, Owain immediately realized that he no longer fit in amongst his old life. So, Owain left Camelot once more and sought refuge, not with the Lady of the Fountain, but in nature. Living in the wilderness, Owain became a wild man; "he wandered about ... until all his clothes disintegrated and his body all but gave out and long hair grew all over him; and he would keep company with wild animals and feed with them until they were used to him" (*Mabinogion* 131). Because Owain proved himself capable of fully merging with the natural environment, he was finally rewarded at the myth's conclusion by being reunited with the Lady of the Fountain and staying with her in the otherworld forevermore.

Upon his quest, that was guided by the Lady of the Fountain, Owain learned that death was necessary for the cycles of life to continue. This lesson of mortality was embraced by Owain when he tried to return to his old life in Camelot, but instead realized that his former identity had died away. Owain's final experience in nature also forced him to see the cycles of nature firsthand, and it was this that made him fully ready to embrace his new selfhood as symbolic male consort to the everlasting goddess representative—the Lady of the Fountain. He learned that just as he killed the former guardian of the fountain, thus replacing him as the husband of the Lady of the Fountain, he too would one day be replaced by a new male consort. Thus, the Lady of the Fountain, like the Celtic goddesses, such as Brigid, who presided over sacred wells, accepted the sacrifice of Owain's former selfhood and renewed him as an enlightened hero.

A folktale from China (Young 112–3) also shows two young boys transformed when they encountered otherworldly women within the otherworld. The boys were shown in this folktale to be walking in the wilderness when they discovered a cave. Deciding to enter the cave, the boys immediately saw that they had transgressed into the otherworld. When the boys looked around, they saw otherworldly women playing chess. At first, the otherworldly women did not pay any attention to the boys, so the two youths simply sat down and watched the game for hours. They saw that as the otherworldly women played chess, a rabbit jumped up and down next to the women. When the mystical rabbit rose, "flowers bloom[ed], and when it descend[ed], they fade[d]" (Young 112). As apparent in the previous folktale, the connection of the otherworldly women and nature, portrayed in this tale by the rabbit which is an animal often associated with Chinese goddesses such as Chang'e, as well as the mystical budding and wilting of the flowers which shows the boys the cycles of growth and dormancy in nature, presents the women as representations of traditional Chinese fertility goddesses.

The folktale shows that eventually the otherworldly women finally stopped their game of chess and looked directly at the boys. The women told the boys that they might as well stay with them in the otherworld, since if they tried to return home, no one would ever be able to recognize them, as time within the otherworld was slower than in the human realm, just like it was portrayed in the Celtic myth of Bran. The boys, however, did not choose to stay in the otherworld, as like Bran's obstinate man who did not heed the otherworldly women's warning, the boys left the otherworld and tried to return home. However, when the boys returned home, they found that "seven generations have passed" (Young 113). The boys tried in vain to find the cave that granted them access to the otherworld, but they found that because they did not listen to the advice of the otherworldly women, the entrance to the otherworld had closed to them forever.

The otherworldly women of this tale, who resemble the divine women found in myriad Chinese myths who live in otherworldly realms, strive to teach the boys about death, as they experience a symbolic death during their time in the otherworld. The reference to the boys journeying into a cave to enter the otherworld signals traditional earth goddess ideology that identifies caves as entrances to the underworld, or the womb of the earth, that both harbors the dead and initiates the process of rebirth. Thus, the boys entering into this otherworld, surrounded only by women, are presented as symbolically dying in the folktale. However, the tale also references birthing images, as the boys, though dead to their old lives, have been, because of the guidance of the otherworldly women, birthed into their new lives in a new world where they, as reborn heroes, can impart wisdom about their former lives, and their experiences in the otherworld, to the generations to come.

The Japanese folktale "Urashima the Fisherman" displays another example of a male character transforming into a hero because of his experience with an otherworldly woman. This tale presents a fisherman, named Urashima, out alone on a fishing trip that produced no fish. After three days and nights upon the sea, Urashima still had not caught any fish, but he was surprised to see that he caught a sea turtle. Soon, the turtle miraculously transformed into a beautiful woman. The otherworldly woman told Urashima that she was an immortal who lived in the Dragon Palace beneath the waves, an explicit identification of the woman as a goddess. She told Urashima that she would be willing to take him to her otherworldly palace if he wished. Urashima readily agreed, showing him to be a male protagonist who was willing to learn from his female guide. Urashima found that the Dragon Palace met the requirements of the otherworld, as it was full of natural beauty and unlimited resources. Like Owain, Urashima married the otherworldly woman, and spent three blissful years with her, signaling a transformation on his part. However, for reasons he could not fully comprehend, Urashima began to grow homesick. He asked his otherworldly wife if he might go home to see his aging parents once more. His wife agreed, but before he left, she gave him a magic box that would bring him back to her if he held it against his chest, but she warned him not to open the box. Thus, Urashima made the voyage back to his homeland, but when he stepped on shore, he was distraught to see that his village had greatly changed; in fact, he hardly recognized it. Where his small village once was, he now saw many villages, and he did not recognize anyone around him, though he once knew everyone in his village. Urashima soon learned from the villagers about a legend of a man with his name who disappeared three hundred years ago. Forlorn, Urashima remembered the box his otherworldly wife had given him, but instead of only holding the box close to his chest, he opened it. When Urashima opened the otherworldly box, he found that the years took their toll upon him, as his body aged on the spot, until he became nothing but dust and floated away.

The physical death of Urashima, when he opened the box, revealed his final spiritual transformation, as he, like the Greek Orpheus, showed that he finally understood fully the necessity of the cycles of life. Urashima did not become immortal in the tale, like his otherworldly wife, because he was mortal, and as such, he had to replenish the cycles of nature. However, this folktale suggests that Urashima's spiritually enlightened message, taught to him by his otherworldly wife, would live on for the people who learned about his tale.

As this chapter discussed, maidens and otherworldly women within myths, folktales, and fairy tales often serve as guides to male protagonists. Young, beautiful, often royal, mystical women repeatedly entice male characters to complete heroic quests. When one closely examines these folktales and fairy tales that hold maidens and otherworldly women, one can see that the women of the tales are not merely meant to represent prizes of beauty and fertility for male characters; instead, they often are presented as the superior educators to male pupils, teaching male characters that heroism comes from learning to embrace lessons associated with traditional goddess worship. Likewise, many male quest myths, folktales, and fairy tales also portray female characters in monstrous, seemingly wicked, or ghostly forms, and at first glance, these tales seem to portray women in a negative light, but again when examined more closely, one can see that these monstrous females also serve to educate male heroes about lessons related to the goddess worship of bygone days.

4

Monstrous and
Ghost Women

Just as many folktales and fairy tales around the world preserved once divine women in their representations of earth mothers, animal brides, wise old women, and irresistible maidens, so too did many folktales and fairy tales preserve goddess ideology within their portrayals of monstrous and ghostly women. In fact, similar to many folktale and fairy tale old shamanic women, maidens, and otherworldly women, monstrous or ghostly women often impart messages associated with the goddess-oriented lesson of death and rebirth.

There are many cultures that worshipped goddesses associated with death and the underworld, such as the Norse goddess Hel and the Japanese goddess Izanami, who were both described as showing the reality of death on their bodies through decay. The Akkadian underworld goddess Ereshkigal was shown mythically to teach her sister, the goddess Ishtar, the reality of death when she stripped her of all royal attire, gave her every illness known to humankind, and then hung her lifeless body from a meat hook. The Indian goddess of death, Kali, wears "severed arms as a girdle, freshly cut heads as a necklace, children's corpses as earrings, and serpents as bracelets. She has long, sharp fangs, is often depicted as having claw like hands with long nails, and is often said to have blood smeared on her lips" (Kinsley 116). Similarly, the Aztec goddess of the dead and the underworld, Mictēcacihuātl, possessed a "lower face [that] was made only of bone ... [and] jaws [that] were wide open waiting for victims" (Larrington 371).

In addition, many other mythic females were also associated with death, such as the Norse Valkyries, who took fallen warriors to Valhalla and served as "intermediaries between humans and gods, guides for the dead, and the means to rebirth" (Young 53). The Greek Fates and Norse Norns designed the lives mortals would live and thus knew when they would die. In addition, the Greek Furies were chthonic figures who relentlessly pursued wrongdoers who committed blood crimes. The Hindu and

Buddhist apsarās were portrayed as highly erotic beings who promised new life through their voluptuousness, but were ultimately "connected to death" (Young 118). Likewise, fairies in many cultures were also often connected with death, such as the fairy in "Sleeping Beauty of the Wood" who induced the princess to enter a death-like sleep, or the otherworldly fairy women of Celtic and Asian tales who took men to the otherworld, indicating their death.

Many mythic goddesses were connected with death because they represented the natural aspects of the life cycle, as the "other side of the Goddess who gives life is the Goddess who takes it away, the Mother of Death" (Johnson 79). Therefore, mythic goddess of death and the underworld were often conceived of as goddesses who also enabled rebirth. However, due to invasion, conflict, trade, colonialism, diffusion, etc., many cultures around the world began to overly associate women with death and destruction within their mythological tales in an effort to demote the position of powerful goddesses who commanded over the life cycle of all living beings. For example, the arrival of the Indo-Europeans into the Middle East, Mediterranean, Europe, India, etc., transformed and often decimated the cultures that worshipped indigenous goddesses as centrally important. The Indo-Europeans were said to come from the steppes north of the Caspian and Black Seas "as Hittites in Anatolia and Syria; Mitanni and Kassites in Mesopotamia: Achaeans and then Dorians in Greece; and Aryans in the Indus Valley ... [and] wherever they penetrated, they established themselves as the ruling caste" (Baring & Cashford 156). The influx of Indo-European beliefs occurred in different regions at different times and happened over centuries. Quite often, the traditional beliefs of many Neolithic goddess-worshipping populations were modified to varying degrees because of the introduction of Indo-European values that revered superior male deities, male leadership, and warfare. For example, within many cultures introduced to Indo-European concepts, once superior goddesses were often either replaced by or married off to male gods in order to lessen their authority, such as mythically occurred when the Greek Hera married Zeus and the Norse Frigg married Odin. Likewise, many myths from the regions affected by Indo-European belief systems began to mythically show once powerful goddesses in new monstrous forms in an attempt to demonize these goddesses and their associations. Many of these myths that presented monstrous females strove to display only one aspect of the traditional goddesses they represented—that of death, fully ignoring the goddesses' associations with rebirth and renewal. Decisive measures went on for millennia in the regions influenced by Indo-European ideology to systematically transform the existing spiritual beliefs of the people, such as destroying images of goddesses and places of their worship, as well as modifying the myths that portrayed the lessons of these goddesses as significant. Therefore, over time, many people replaced their traditional belief systems surrounding goddess worship with religious beliefs centered upon superior gods. The portrayal of gods as supremely powerful, instead of goddesses, paved the way for the adoption of the monotheistic religions of Judaism, Christianity, and Islam, which initiated out of regions influenced by Indo-European and Semitic concepts.

Other regions of the world followed similar patterns when it came to lessening the reverence of once powerful goddesses. For instance, in China, and other Asian countries affected by Chinese culture, such as Korea and Japan, the adoption of Confucianism, and later Buddhism, greatly demoted the role of goddesses throughout these regions. Similarly, in places where indigenous cultures were dominated by conquest and colonialism, such as Africa, Australia, and the Americas, beliefs in once powerful goddesses were also often eradicated with the enforced adoption of monotheistic faiths. For example, in Australia and the Americas, many once formidable earth goddesses were replaced by Christian concepts of a monotheistic God, as efforts of colonizers labeled indigenous beliefs regarding goddesses as pagan and therefore evil.

The result, thus, in many regions around the globe was that once powerful and sacred goddesses, and the mythic females who were associated with them, became reassigned as negative, even evil, as they began to be portrayed in myths, as well as within folktales and fairy tales, as monstrous, conniving, untrustworthy, and as harbingers of death and destruction.

Monstrous Females

Female monsters are rampant in myths, folktales, and fairy tales from around the world, and in many instances, the presentation of the monstrous female is intentionally done to portray goddesses, or the women associated with goddess ideology, as sinister.

Greek culture certainly experienced a marked change from Neolithic Minoan religion to religious concepts in line with Indo-European ideology. The Indo-European Mycenaeans brought a reverence for warfare and male gods, and this in time, along with the influx of other Indo-European groups within Greece, influenced the degradation of traditional Minoan goddesses. After centuries, the god Zeus eventually became the head of the Olympian pantheon along with other male gods, such as Hades and Poseidon, and once supremely powerful goddesses, such as Aphrodite and Hera, became stereotypical representations of acceptable females under a newly created patriarchy. Other mythic females, who traditionally carried more divine significance, became portrayed in monstrous forms in a societal, political, and religious effort to demote their power. The Greek monsters Scylla and Charybdis are prime examples of this.

Scylla in her mythological background was said to once be a divine water nymph who was turned into a monster with the upper body of a beautiful woman and a lower body composed of six ferocious dogs that would consume anyone who came too close, such as Odysseus's men in Homer's *Odyssey*. Similarly, another monstrous female, Charybdis, was portrayed in the *Odyssey* as residing opposite of Scylla in the sea as a monstrous whirlpool, so that when ships needed to pass, they would have no choice but to face one of these fearsome females. Charybdis was mythically said to once be the beautiful daughter of the Earth Mother Gaia, but she offended Zeus, so he threw a thunderbolt at her, which thus transformed her into a "disembodied mouth" that destroyed whole ships (Rose 77). The presentation of once divine women being transformed by leading male members of the Olympian pantheon is a common theme in Classical and Hellenistic Greek mythology. Zeus, or other Greek gods or male heroes, often punished older representations of goddesses and mythic women in Greek mythology. In addition, goddesses, such as Athena or Hera, who often served as patriarchal representations, also often punished former goddesses within Greek mythology, such as is seen in the myths where Hera, as the jealous wife of the unfaithful Zeus, punished the once divine Leto, Io, Europa, Semele, etc., for being essentially raped by Zeus. All too often, the punishments these traditional goddess figures received were for them to be transformed into hideous monsters in mythic tales so that audiences would, in time, disassociate the goddesses' former sacrality with new associations of disdain. One mythic example is articulated in a myth that shows Hera, again because of her jealousy at Zeus's infidelity, as punishing Lamia, a former Libyan goddess, by transforming her into a monster who stole and ate children.

Greek harpies and sirens were also monstrous women of mythology who once held roles of more religious significance. Rose states that "harpies were originally wind spirits personifying the storm winds, hurricanes, and whirlwinds and [were] later transformed to the role of vengeful, hideous, monstrous fiends" (Rose 168). In their monstrous role, harpies took on the form of a bird, "with the heads and torso of an ugly woman … having arms with talons for fingers"; they were also said to be "foul-smelling … contaminat[ing] whatever they touched" (Rose 168). They also killed newborn babies and stole people's souls (Young 48). Likewise, the sirens of Greek mythology were said to be malicious female creatures who possessed part human and part animal features, usually that of a fish or again a bird. The monstrous sirens lured men to their deaths by singing enticing songs that men were unable to resist. However, again there appears to be traditional elements in line with goddess worship connected to the sirens of Greek mythology, as they were often depicted as knowing "the past and the future" (Young 48). The sirens were also said to be able to "accompany the dead to the underworld. From very early times, they were seen as protectors of the dead and singers of funeral dirges and were carved on the tops of tombs" (Young 48). This early depiction of the sirens portrays them as connected with traditional Greek goddesses who served as chthonic figures, such as the goddess Hecate or the Furies. Thus, as with both the harpy and the siren, the transformation from divine figure into monstrous creature clearly shows the cultural attempt to degrade once more powerful divine figures to meet transformed, patriarchal belief systems.

Many folktales and fairy tales around the world adopted the same trend found in many ancient mythologies that marked once sacred women as monstrous.

For example, monstrous females abound in Russian and Slavic folktales and fairy tales, such as the poludnitsa, who was represented as being as tall as "a stalk of corn"; and when she walked the cornfield in the relentless summer heat, anyone who met her became instantaneously insane (Phillips & Kerrigan 74). As discussed in Chapter 1, Russia has an extensive history of goddess worship, as well as a history of denigrating once powerful goddesses. Phillips and Kerrigan explain that the "belief of a mother goddess ... as the generator and nourisher of the Earth and its people ... has been central to Slavic spiritual beliefs for millennia" (Phillips & Kerrigan 56). However, when Indo-European Slavic concepts merged with existing cultures in Russia, divine pantheons became ruled by male gods, such as Perun, the thunder god, and Veles, who ruled the underworld. Thus, the position of powerful female deities became lessened. This demotion of goddesses further occurred during the ninth to twelfth centuries CE with the adoption of Christianity by many Slavic people. Therefore, many female divinities became, over these centuries, the mere figures of folklore and fairy tales in an attempt to propel patriarchal social and religious messages.

The rusalki portray a good example of once divine figures who became presented as possessing monstrous qualities as patriarchal concepts gained dominance in Russia. The rusalki are believed to be remnants of pagan earth goddesses within Russia. In this form, they were believed to initiate the coming of summer, as they were mythically said to leave their watery abodes every year in summer in order "to dance together in woods and fields ... [to] celebrate the triumph of summer over the deadly cold of winter" (Phillips & Kerrigan 67). In fact, the festival of Rusal'naya was once a beloved celebration to honor the rusalki, where villagers would dance, and village maidens would bring flowers to the rivers to pay the rusalki homage (Phillips & Kerrigan 67). However, in time, the rusalki became known in the monstrous folkloric form of spirits of drowned women, who in their sadness and rage, lured men to their deaths. Phillips and Kerrigan state that to see a rusalka "was to ache with desire. Her victims, however, never did simply see her. They felt in the summons of her sad, yearning eyes an overpowering longing.... Even the wariest traveler, caught up alone by a discreet riverbank or lakeside, might find himself plunging heedlessly, even joyfully, to his doom.... For the embrace of the *rusalka* meant inevitable death" (Phillips & Kerrigan 66). These types of cautionary tales, that were aimed at men for being enticed by supernatural women, again portrays a social effort to mark women who were connected to former goddesses as evil, thus warning men not to trust such women or their ideology.

Many folktales around the world also portray female characters who take on the form of a succubus who seduce men toward their demise, much like the Russian rusalki. A succubus is said to be a demonic seductress who appears to men who are asleep in order to have sex with them. A folktale from New Mexico shows a husband finding out that his wife was a succubus when he saw her eating human flesh at a cemetery (Leavy 161). Moroccan folklore tells of Aicha Kandisha, sometimes Aicha Qandicha, who is a succubus who appears with the upper body of a beautiful woman and the legs of a goat. She seduces men and possesses their souls or kills them at will. A Scottish folktale likewise shows a blacksmith being "victimized by a female demon ... who 'put a magic bridle' on him and ... [rode] *him* to the wild moors" (Leavy 161). The brother of the blacksmith, who was a hunter, hunted down the succubus, found her in the form of a horse, and had his brother fit her for horseshoes. When the woman transformed back to her human form, she still had horseshoes nailed to her hands, so it was confirmed to the community that she was demonic, and the townspeople condemned her to death.

Another monstrous female in Japanese folklore is known as Yuki-onna, the Snow Maiden. Yuki-onna lives within the wilderness in the winter and is said to be so irresistibly beautiful that when any man encounters her, he is so drawn by her beauty, that he does not realize that he is in the clutches of hypothermia (Allan, Kerrigan, & Phillips 115). One such tale of Yuki-onna (Allan, Kerrigan, & Phillips 115) tells of her coming to a pair of men who found themselves in the mountains during a blizzard. The men found an abandoned shack and tried to escape the ferocity of the storm for the night; they attempted to fall asleep, but one of the young men saw that in the night a woman appeared beside the bed of his travel companion. The man watched as the woman bent down low to the other man and appeared to breathe out slowly on his face. Struck by fear, the young man could do nothing to save his friend. The monstrous woman then made her way to him. She also bent down close to his face and whispered that she would let him live if he never spoke of this to anyone. The man nodded his agreement, and the woman, who was Yuki-onna, disappeared. The young man left the shack as soon as the storm abated and went back to his village, never telling anyone about what happened to him. Years later, though, he fell in love and married a beautiful, young woman, named "Yuki, a common enough name, even though it means 'snow'" (Allan, Kerrigan, & Phillips 115). The man always felt that his wife looked familiar to him, though he could not understand why, until one night he saw his wife's face in the moonlight. The man instantly understood that his young wife looked identical to Yuki-onna, who had visited him years earlier. He told his wife then about that night with Yuki-onna, and immediately his wife reared up before him in her true form, as Yuki-onna, and told him that as he had broken his promise to her, she should kill him, but because they had children together, she would instead leave him forever, which she did, and was never to be seen by him again.

Dakinis of Tibet likewise often appear to men first as beautiful maidens, but in time they reveal their true identity, showing them as "dressed … in mail made from human bones, or as hideous toothless hags" (Kerrigan, Bishop, & Chambers 39). Some dakinis in Tibetan folklore appear with five heads and swim in blood; some ride on birds, "while eating human entrails," and others possess "many hands, which they use to carry corpses, animals, and their own decapitated heads" (Kerrigan, Bishop, & Chambers 39). Certainly, such tales of seductive women who appear irresistibly appealing to men, but in time reveal their "true" nature, which is identified as evil or sinister, carry a message to audiences that they should not revere traditional goddesses who may appear sacred, but are instead, when examined under revised patriarchal standards, suspect or even dangerous.

Folktales of were-animals, like the werewolf, have also preserved themes of mythic goddesses, such as the ability in many cultures for goddesses to shapeshift from human to animal form at will, as is seen with the Norse Freyja's ability to take on falcon form or the Chinese Queen Mother of the West's ability to become part tiger. However, unlike tales of animal brides who are often portrayed as sacred, as discussed in Chapter 1 of this book, folktales and fairy tales that present monstrous female were-animals most often display them as sinister. For instance, one German folktale (Leavy 169) shows a man encountering a werewolf in the woods. When the werewolf attacked, the man managed to survive by cutting off one of its paws, forcing the werewolf to flee. However, the man was shocked to find that the disembodied paw transformed into the hand of a woman. And, when the man looked closer, he saw that the ring on the finger belonged to his wife. He went home at once and saw his wife hiding her hand beneath her apron. When he forced her to show him her hand, he found only a bloody stump. He then had her burned alive as a witch (Leavy 169). Folktales and fairy tales of weretigers, werepanthers, and wereleopards also abound around the world, and often these tales show females transforming into these animalistic forms to wreak havoc upon mostly male victims, thus revealing the tales' intent of proving that women who hold mystical abilities are evil.

Mermaids, merrows (Ireland), selkies (Scotland), havfrue and nixies (Scandinavia), bonito maidens (Solomon Islands), ningyo (Japan), etc., who have the upper body of a woman and the lower body of a fish, also appear in many folktales and fairy tales from around the world (Rose 244). Mermaids and their variants are often portrayed as beautiful, but malevolent creatures, who can spell "misfortune and disaster" to mostly male sailors (Rose 244). For instance, nixies appear in the folklore of Scandinavia as malevolent beings. The nixie is often identified as a "malicious, predatory being that uses … [her] beautiful image to entice mortals to their doom in the waters" (Rose 268). Sometimes nixies appear in elevated monstrous terms, "wizened with green skin, teeth, and hair" (Rose 268). Sometimes mermaids and their variants can appear as benevolent though, such as the Scandinavian havfrue, who can provide humans with the "knowledge of herbal cures for fatal sickness, other rich gifts, and warnings of storms" (Rose 244). Like the wereanimals of global folklore, the portrayal of mermaids and their variants as half human, half fish creatures, who live within the sea and often hold mystical abilities, certainly connects them to traditional mythic goddesses. Baring and Cashford support this, stating that mermaids and their variants are often believed to be remnants of fish goddesses found in many ancient civilizations, such as in Yugoslavia and Egypt (Baring & Cashford 63).

A folktale entitled "The Seven Mermaids" (Sax 246–7) from the Frisian Islands presents mermaids who appear as malevolent. The tale shows a sailor, who before setting sail, "raised his hand and solemnly pledged his loyalty to the sea. If the waters would be gentle to him, sparing his ship and his cargo, he would remain faithful to the sea until death" (Sax 246). It just so happened that seven mermaids heard his vow and decided to help him, if he indeed remained faithful to them. The sailor found that he enjoyed much success upon his voyage and accumulated much wealth in trade. One day, he saw a beautiful maiden living on an isolated island; he fell immediately in love with her, and the woman agreed to marry him.

However, on "the night of his marriage, as the sailor rested in the arms of his beloved bride, the seven mermaids rose by the bank of the sea and sang an unearthly melody. An enormous wave leaped over the dike" and destroyed the couple's home, and more waves came and carried the man away in the sea (Sax 246). The seven mermaids grabbed the man and carried him to their home beneath the waves, since he had vowed his fidelity to them.

Folktales in medieval Europe often depicted the mermaid as "the agent of the devil and a symbol of deceit" (Rose 336). In fact, mermaids were "often depicted on church furniture holding a fish, which symbolized the entrapment of the soul of the Christian drawn to sin by charms and flattery" as presented to men by women (Rose 336). Similarly, in Europe the image of the Greek siren, another mermaid-like creature, was often used in Christian symbolism to represent vanity, "for her attributes were the comb and mirror of vanity; the fish or eel symbols of the entrapped Christian soul ensnared by luxury and vice" (Rose 336). Additionally, sirens were often portrayed in medieval Christian imagery as having a "liaison with the devil ... her nakedness, taken as a sign of her wanton sexuality" (Rose 336). Portraying mermaid figures that hold attributes of traditional goddesses as monstrous, vain, or evil in medieval European representations certainly shows a direct attempt by Christian institutions to portray traditional concepts of sacred women as negative.

As discussed in Chapter 3, the monstrous figure of the serpent or dragon within mythology, folktales, and fairy tales is also often connected to traditional representations of goddesses in many global regions, such as the Middle East, Mediterranean, India, Asia, Mesoamerica, Australia, etc. Frankel explains that the serpent "reflected the Great Goddess, changing from young to old and then cycling back to young as the world renewed in the spring. It ... shed its skin, like a woman birthing a new organism from itself. Depicted coiled in several successive rings, the serpent mimics cyclical evolution and reincarnation" (Frankel 70). Thus, many cultures displayed traditional goddesses in serpent form, such as the Chinese Nü Wa, Mesopotamia Tiamet, Greek Eurynome, the Egyptian Wadjet/Wadjit, the Australian Rainbow Serpent, etc. Many myths also involved serpents who protected the domains of goddesses, such as the Greek python that guarded Gaia's oracle at Delphi, the serpent Lydon that protected Hera's golden apples in the Garden of the Hesperides, and the serpent guardian of the Golden Fleece of Colchis, discussed in Chapter 3. Most often, these serpent goddesses or their serpent guardians ended up being killed by male gods or heroes within myths meant to elevate patriarchal ideologies. And as was seen with many other tales of monstrous women thus far, as new ideologies swept into existing regions, myths, folktales, and fairy tales began to portray serpents in relation to females as evil, as is portrayed when the biblical Eve was tempted by a serpent to eat fruit from the Tree of Knowledge of Good and Evil.

Dragons are often viewed as an extension of the serpent in myths, folktales, and fairy tales. In China, for example, many myths and folktales present dragons, serpents, or other water creatures as connected to female deities. As was discussed in Chapter 1 with the Chinese tale of the serpent bride of West Lake, the representation of dragons and serpent-like creatures as sacred females is believed to date back to Neolithic and Bronze Age China (Shafer 38). Many female dragons or serpents in Chinese mythology were portrayed as beneficial for their ability to bring rain and aid in the fertility of the environment. Even the creator goddess Nü Wa was sometimes portrayed with the tail of a serpent. However, as China became more patriarchal, largely with the introduction of Confucian values, these mythic dragon/serpent women were transformed in folklore into representations of the "flaunting and arrogance of female power, to the detriment of the established order" (Shafer 28). As discussed in previous chapters of this book, by the end of the Zhou dynasty "the masculinization of upper-class life required by official 'Confucian' policy ... tended to erase surviving female elements, not only in social life and politics but also in the officially supported religion. The subtle devotions owed to the ancient [goddesses] ... came to be regarded as sinister" (Shafer 59). Therefore, once powerful Chinese goddesses became culturally demoted. Shafer states that this demotion of goddesses can be seen in Chinese folklore when traditional goddesses began to be portrayed as "inhuman, weird and scary, scaled or fishlike" (Shafer 90) in an effort to convince audiences that the power of traditional goddesses to shapeshift, showing their command of the natural environment, now made them sinister. In addition, many Chinese folktales displayed young females needing to be sacrificed to a male dragon or serpent, often through ritualistic drowning (Shafer 33). Such tales were a distortion of myths where the dragons or serpent creatures actually represented earth goddesses. Shafer concurs, stating that in China, the male dragons/serpents "were probably a later inversion of power that was held in the hands initially of female divinities.... [Thus,] female water deities became replaced by male water deities who required female sacrifices" (Shafer 34). In showing a helpless maiden being abused by a fearful creature, the tale identifies the former sacred symbol of the goddess as dangerous and evil for harming one of the goddesses' own—the virginal maiden.

In many Chinese folktales, though, female characters are often portrayed as needed to either control dragons and serpents or to harness their power. One Chinese folktale (Shafer 29) displays a dragon ransacking a community during the Zhou dynasty, and only female shamans are the ones who can subdue the dragon (Shafer 29). Another folktale (Shafer 30) from the ninth-century CE shows a widow finding five dragon eggs, whereby she "acquires miraculous powers, along with the title 'Mother of Dragons'" (Shafer 30). Shafer believes that this folktale might be a later rendition of an archetypal tale where the mother "actually laid the dragon eggs herself," but the folktale was tamed down in later generations (Shafer 30). Also, many Chinese folktales show women birthing dragon children after bathing in a river, and their offspring often became "great hero[es]" (Shafer 29). In fact, many ancient Chinese records indicate that kings resulted from female and dragon copulations. One folktale (Shafer 30) from the early days of the Wei dynasty "tells how a remote ancestor of the dynasty, a steppe-roving hunter, meets a mysterious beauty who announces that she has been divinely ordained as his mate. After the happy union, she disappears 'like wind and rain.'" (Shafer 30). The tale shows that the "following year the rain goddess" appeared to the chieftain in her true form as a dragon and presented "him with an infant son, the destined founder of the dynasty's fortunes" (Shafer 30). Another folktale from the later Wei dynasty explains how "a great lady of the palace dreams that she is pursued by the sun. That luminary finds her cowering beneath her bed. It changes into a dragon and coils around her. From this strange mating came T'o-pa K'o," a monarch of the Wei dynasty (Shafer 30–1). This type of explanation about how rulers were the sons of human and dragon encounters was not only common in China, but also appeared as the explanation of the conception of both the Macedonian Alexander the Great and the Roman emperor Augustus, as the mothers of both men were said to have copulated with dragons (Shafer 31). These folktales show that though female sacrality was demoted in China, women were still often portrayed as needed to harness the power of dragons within Chinese folklore. Shafer concurs by stating that even though mythic dragons and serpents began to often be misrepresented in Chinese folklore, they were still "directly connected to early conceptions of female power" (Shafer 37).

In Australia, the Bunyip, a female monster associated with water and fertility, appears much like the dragons of China. An Australian folktale of the Bunyip (Cole 608–10) shows a group of young men gathering bulrushes in pools of water. However, one man stated "'why should we waste our time in doing work that is only fit for women and children? Let them come and get the roots for themselves'" (Cole 608). The men agreed with their companion and decided to do work that they deemed more appropriate for their sex, so they began fishing the deeper sections of the pools. As the men fished, one of them began to scream for help, as he caught something that threatened to pull him into one of the pools; the other men ran to his aid and helped him reel in a "creature that was neither a calf or a seal, but something of both, with a long, broad tail" (Cole 609). Then at once, all the men knew that it was "the cub of the awful Bunyip" (Cole 609)! When the men registered this, they immediately heard a wail from the depths of the pool and were horrified to see the mother of the cub rise from the depths and race toward them, with "rage flashing from her yellow eyes" (Cole 609). The same man who declared that the group should not do the "women's work" of gathering bulrushes insanely yelled at the Bunyip that he was going to keep her baby and let his family feast on it for three days. Then this disrespectful man flung his spear at the Bunyip and ran further inland. The man's companions looked at their friend in dreadful shock because they knew that one must never insult the Bunyip. And indeed, they were right, as the water began to rise before them and started to flood the whole plain. The men ran as fast as they could to higher ground, and in time, they finally made it back to their homes where they threw down the Bunyip's baby. The people of the community looked at the cub in horror, but they were more terrified when they saw that the water had followed the men back and was beginning to flood their homes. The people all began to run and climb trees to escape drowning. The man who insulted the Bunyip and stole her cub also tried climbing a tree, but he felt that something was wrong with him, as his feet had transformed into bird's talons. The man looked at his family and the people of his community for help, but he was horrified to see that every one of them had also begun to metamorphose into black swans, just like him. The tale ends with the Bunyip reclaiming her baby and enjoying the deep recesses of the vast pools of water that were now her new home.

The fact that the Bunyip is portrayed as a female monster who lives within the natural environment and is able to transform both the environment and humans to suit her will portrays her in supernatural terms. In Aboriginal Australian belief, supernatural figures are often considered to be the sacred ancestors of the people, who in the time before human existence, Dreamtime, helped to create the natural environment. After these acts of creation, many ancestors became elements of nature, such as hills, pools of water, rocks, etc. Concepts also exist in some regions of Australia of a central mother ancestress, known in some regions as Milapukala or Kunapipi, who "commanded all manner of animal and plant life to come" (Allan, Fleming, & Kerrigan 35). Therefore, this folktale of the Bunyip may hold connections to these traditional conceptions of female ancestresses who manipulated the natural world at will, as the Bunyip is portrayed as a female monster who can easily influence the natural environment in order to teach the people to have the proper respect for nature.

Male Heroes and Female Monsters

Similar to the guidance of myriad females upon the quests of male heroes, monstrous females often serve to educate male heroes about goddess ideology during their heroic quests within myths, folktales, and fairy tales.

As discussed in Chapter 3 of this book, the male heroic journey often requires heroes to face the fear of their own death; this can be done by journeying to the underworld, or it can be done by facing a terrifying opponent. Oftentimes, this mythic requirement of facing death is portrayed by male heroes encountering females who help them in this psychological stage of their quest, as was discussed in Chapters 2 and 3 of this book when wise old women and maidens guided male heroes through aspects dealing with death and renewal. The representation of a wise old woman or maiden serving as a teacher to a male hero seems most in line with true forms of traditional goddesses, as in Neolithic or other earth-based ideologies, when male heroes encountered a goddess associated with death in mythic narratives, they did so to learn about renewal and rebirth within nature's ceaseless processes. However, many male heroes of mythology, folktales, and fairy tales often face encounters with terrifying, confusing, even evil, female characters, who seem to hinder their heroic quests. Again, as discussed, the presentation of narratives that show female monsters battling male heroes is seemingly a result of the religious revision, that held male divinity as superior to female divinity, experienced by many cultures, such as following Indo-European invasions in many regions or through colonialism that brought Western values to indigenous cultures. Once goddesses became demoted in these cultures, many myths began to showcase males upon their heroic quests encountering monstrous females who only represented death and violence for the sake of destruction and not renewal. For example, following the Neolithic period in such regions as India, Europe, the Middle East, the Mediterranean, etc., the introduction of Indo-European values presented, "a virile male figure whose principal significance … explicitly concerned war" (Cauvin 126) as central to myriad mythological narratives. This Bronze Age male hero possessed a new-found "dominant self-confidence" (Cauvin 125), which began to be showcased in myths as male characters who resisted serving only as a personification of the necessary sacrifice male consorts, like the Mesopotamian Dumuzi, must make to Neolithic goddesses for the continuation of nature's cycles. Instead, many Bronze Age myths focused on the importance of the individual male hero, and the legacy he left behind. Thus, when a mythic male hero killed a monstrous female, who symbolized once formidable goddesses, then audiences of the myth received a justification of why the Neolithic values of goddess worship, that did not recognize the importance of the singular hero, should be replaced with new patriarchal ideologies. For instance, the Mesopotamian god Marduk brutally murdered his own mother Tiamet, who appeared in his myth as a giant serpent, so that he could declare his right to rule a new pantheon and thus be worshipped by the people for generations to come.

The Greek myth of Perseus and Medusa is a prime example of a male hero defeating a fearsome female monster, who is almost certainly a remnant of once powerful female deities in Greece. Mythically, the snake-ridden gorgon Medusa was deemed evil, so King Polydectes demanded that Perseus kill her. The goddess Athena, often presented as the female spokesperson for Zeus, since she was directly birthed by him and not a mother, hated Medusa, so she agreed to help Perseus in his quest. Athena instructed Perseus to obtain the elements needed to kill Medusa, all of which came from male gods, such as the winged sandals of Hermes, the helm of darkness from Hades, and a sword from Zeus. The myth then shows a pompous Perseus going to the lair of Medusa, where she lived with her gorgon sisters. Medusa's lair certainly meets the requirement of the heroic stage of facing death for Perseus, as it evokes symbolism of the underworld, since it is within the earth and also could easily spell his demise if Medusa set her gaze upon him and turned him to stone. However, the myth states that Perseus used all his divine tools to slip into Medusa's lair unseen, find Medusa's reflection in his shield, as she was sleeping, and easily slice off her head. To tidy up the end of this myth of male dominance over a monstrous female, Perseus took Medusa's head and used it to save the princess Andromeda moments before she was sacrificed to a sea monster, as Medusa's decapitated head made the creature turn to stone. Having finished his quest, Perseus received the reward of the maiden Andromeda in marriage.

In consideration of this myth, one must ask what Perseus really learned upon his heroic quest, as true mythic heroes, like the Greek Orpheus, must transform psychologically and/or spiritually at the resolution of their journeys. Perseus, though, succeeded far too easily upon his quest, which mostly allowed him to remain psychologically and spiritually the same as when he began his journey; "Perseus—armed to the teeth with miraculous aids from a plethora of supernatural entities, slaying the monster as she sleeps, and then escaping by donning a cap of invisibility—doesn't seem terribly heroic" (Wilk 90). Thus, this lack of transformation on the part of Perseus signals this myth as being mere propaganda to perpetuate patriarchal social and religious messages meant to portray once powerful Greek goddesses, like the Neolithic Minoan goddesses who often were portrayed with snake imagery, as sinister and thus in need of revision. To support this, Medusa's history in Greek mythology indeed portrays her as more than just a fearsome monster in need of being disposed of by a male hero. In Greek religion, the image of the gorgon was a very old symbol connected to Neolithic goddesses. For example, a temple in Minoan Crete, from the sixth-century BCE, shows two gorgons as representations of earth goddesses. In addition, at Corfu, an artistic representation shows Medusa "as the Great Mother," as she stands amidst various animals in complete control of them (Frothingham 357). However, Lubell explains that by the fifth century BCE, Medusa became identified "as the quintessential icon of *aidomai*, of fear and shame, with only a faint trace of reverence still clinging to her. For Greek women had by this time come to be regarded as inherently flawed beings … inferior to men, and Medusa had come to represent the sum total of male fears about the power and dangers of [the] female" (Lubell 111). Therefore, knowing that Medusa was once represented as divine, Perseus's murder of her does not prove him a hero, but instead reveals a myth used to supersede the power of former goddesses in the eyes of the Greek people. This mythic technique of demoting once powerful goddesses into monstrous females became popular in Classical and Hellenistic Greece, so that almost every Greek myth depicting a male hero showed a female adversary attempting to stand in his way, such as Heracles battling Hera's many attempts to kill him, Odysseus evading Scylla, Charybdis, and the sirens, Jason and the Argonauts fighting the harpies, etc.

Many folktales and fairy tales around the world also portray female characters in ways similar to the myths that display male heroes taking down once powerful representations of goddesses in what appears to be patriarchal propaganda.

For instance, an African folktale from the Yoruba, entitled "The Hunter and his Magic Flute" (Cole 638–42), shows a monstrous woman, called by the apt name the Mother of the Forest, who is killed by the patriarchal male hero Ojo. In order to hunt, Ojo came to a place that was further than he ever traversed and set up camp, but he felt unsettled, as he heard many stories from his people that talked about the dreaded Mother of the Forest. The Mother of the Forest was said to be the "size of ten full-grown men and her body was covered with hungry mouths" (Cole 639). Still, Ojo tried to sleep that night, but he could not dispel the fear that something was watching him, and indeed, later in the night the Mother of the Forest actually appeared before Ojo. Too afraid to run, Ojo could only stare at her in awe, and seeing this, the Mother of the Forest began to speak to Ojo, stating, "'Have no fear, hunter. I know why you have come to my domain and I will not devour you if you do me no harm'" (Cole 639). With this warning, the Mother of the Forest disappeared from Ojo's sight.

Feeling scared, but deciding to trust the Mother of the Forest, Ojo tried to sleep once more. In the morning, seeing no sign of the Mother of the Forest, Ojo went hunting and found that the land was the most productive he had ever hunted, as he brought back plentiful game to his camp. He prepared the game into the night, fell asleep, and went again to hunt in the morning. However, when he returned that afternoon, he saw that the Mother of the Forest had stolen all of the meat he had prepared the day before. Ojo felt that the Mother of the Forest was owed a day's offering, so he simply prepared the game he obtained that day and fell asleep for the night. In the morning, Ojo once again hunted in the bountiful forest; however, again, when he came back to camp, he saw that the Mother of the Forest had once more stolen the meat he had prepared. This same pattern happened for six days. On the seventh day, Ojo grew angry and decided not to hunt, but instead yelled out to the Mother of the Forest: "'Why have you eaten all of my meat, you old hag? Do you steal from every poor hunter who enters your forest'" (Cole 640)? When Ojo uttered these insulting words, the Mother of the Forest crashed into Ojo's camp in fierce anger, and when Ojo saw her, he knew that he better run.

Ojo ran as fast as he could, but the Mother of the Forest easily trailed him. He climbed a tree to try and escape from her, but to his horror, he saw that the Mother of the Forest easily began using her enormous mouths to chew the base of the tree to shreds. Having only seconds left, Ojo took out his magic flute and called for his hunting dogs, that were far from him at home, to come and help him. His dogs, named Cut to Pieces, Swallow Up, and Clear the Remains heard his magic flute, and were able to come to Ojo in a flash. Though it was a tremendous fight, the dogs, "living up to their … names," tore through the flesh of the Mother of the Forest and consumed every bit of her (Cole 641). Relieved at having survived an encounter with the Mother of the Forest, Ojo climbed down from the tree and found that he was then greeted by a beautiful maiden, who stated that she was released when the Mother of the Forest was killed, as the monstrous woman had kept her trapped by a spell. The maiden asked Ojo if she might become his wife, and seeing her great beauty, Ojo readily agreed. However, after a few nights, Ojo's wife began to transform into a hideous monster with many ferocious mouths, as she was the sister of the Mother of the Forest. But, again Cut to Pieces, Swallow Up, and Clear the Remains sensed that something was wrong, and finding the monster in their master's home, they too tore the sister of the Mother of the Forest to shreds.

Because this folktale portrays the Mother of the Forest in only a monstrous form, though her title and supernatural powers to control nature portray her as a traditional earth goddess, it shows a demotion of goddess reverence among the Yoruba. The arrival of Christianity and colonialism in West Africa greatly affected the worship of goddesses and the social positioning of women in the region. European colonizers often annihilated many of West Africa's "customs, morals, and religious institutions," including those of the Yoruba (Ogunleye 214). Many Yoruba goddesses were thus deemed to be false, pagan figures that were oftentimes identified as evil by colonizers. In addition, since many African myths and folktales were only written down after contact with Western colonizers, many aspects of these tales portray the legacy of colonization upon traditional goddess worship. As a product of this history, the Mother of the Forest in this folktale is portrayed as a monster who must be dealt with by the patriarchal hero Ojo and his ferocious dogs, but she is also presented with a degree of awe and respect in the folktale as she still maintains clear authority over her wilderness environment, making Ojo's heroism questionable for his massacre of her and her daughter.

Similarly, in a Kashmiri folktale entitled "The Chinese Princess" (Carter 146–7) a monstrous woman is again defeated by a patriarchal male hero. This tale makes it clear that the female character, who can shapeshift at will and thus is instantly portrayed as a goddess remnant, is to be treated with disdain, as the story identifies her as evil. The tale relates a time of flux when an Islamic governor named Ali Mardan Khan ruled Kashmir. The tale begins with Ali Mardan going out into the wilderness by himself to hunt, which is often a requirement for male heroes setting out upon their quests, as was just portrayed in the previous Yoruba folktale. While alone in nature, Ali Mardan found a beautiful woman who was also all alone. Again, this is a common plot devise in folktales and fairy tales to signal that a sacred message will be imparted by the female character to the male character, as was seen in Chapters 1, 2, and 3 of this book when animal brides, old wise women, and maidens often approached male protagonists within remote wilderness environments. Immediately, smitten with the beautiful woman, who stated that she was a Chinese princess who escaped persecution in her country, Ali Mardan vowed to make her his wife. The woman asked Ali Mardan to build them a home upon the banks of the nearby Dal Lake, which he did, and the couple prospered there. However, in time, Ali Mardan mysteriously became ill, and none of the male experts in his region could identify the cause. One day though, a yogi happened upon the house of Ali Mardan and his wife. The yogi identified the cause of Ali Mardan's illness, stating that it came from the bewitchment of his wife. Therefore, the yogi, with the help of his guru, instructed Ali Mardan to spy on his wife at night. When Ali Mardan did this, he found that his wife transformed into the shape of a snake and left their home to enter Dal Lake. Once the Hindu guru confirmed that Ali Mardan's wife was indeed a "Lamia—a snake woman" (Carter 146), he explained the origins of the Lamias to Ali Mardan, stating that after one hundred years if no human saw a particular snake, then it would become "king of the snakes," and after another hundred years of no human contact, the king of the snakes would become a dragon, and after three hundred years of no human contact, the dragon would become a Lamia, a shape-shifter, who most often preferred to take on the form of a woman (Carter 146). The Hindu guru told Ali Mardan that he must murder the Lamia by pushing her into their stove when she was cooking for him, and then set their house on fire, which Ali Mardan did once he returned home. Once Ali Mardan murdered his wife, he found that a pebble appeared out of the pile of ashes that were her body. When Ali Mardan showed the pebble to the guru, he told him to choose between taking the pebble or the ashes. The story ends with Ali Mardan choosing the pebble, which provided him the ability to change all metal into gold, and the guru taking the ashes, but never revealing their power.

This Kashmiri folktale has many elements that suggest a more ancient past intermingled with new belief systems to the region. The tale is culturally diverse, as it portrays the woman as Chinese, the yogi and guru as Hindu, and the governor as Muslim. Cultures within China, the Middle East, and India all maintained the worship of Neolithic goddesses for centuries, and many of these cultures also connected images of the serpent/dragon to representations of these goddesses. In India and Indian Kashmir, naga worship, which connected both gods and goddesses to snake imagery, existed before the Indo-Aryans, a sub-group of the Indo-Europeans, made contact with the indigenous cultures of India and Kashmir. Additionally, in parts of Kashmir, Manasa was worshipped as a tribal goddess of snakes potentially before Indo-Aryan contact. These historical examples of goddess worship in connection to snakes in Kashmir makes the portrayal of the Lamia as a monstrous woman in this folktale intentional. The Lamia in this tale is clearly demonized for her goddess-like attribute of shapeshifting from serpent to dragon to human form over centuries. The destruction of this woman in such violent terms, pushing her into an oven, shows a similar plot structure of many tales that reject traditional representations of goddesses to adopt new patriarchal beliefs. In Kashmir, Indo-Aryans revised indigenous belief systems with Hindu concepts, which in time demoted many goddesses to stereotypical positions. Though goddesses continued to be worshipped within what would become Hindu ideology, the supremely powerful positions of these pre–Indo-Aryan, indigenous goddesses would be greatly lessened under patriarchal standards. For instance, starting about 200 BCE in the Classical period, religious beliefs primarily focused on the superior male gods Brahma, Vishnu, and Shiva as the leaders of the Hindu pantheon, while

Hindu goddesses, such as Saraswati, Lakshmi, and Parvati, were often portrayed as subdued consorts of their male counterparts. In addition, the arrival of the Muslims into India in the seventh century CE, and in Kashmir in the eighth century, also revised existing religious concepts, oftentimes eradicating goddess worship in favor of a monotheistic Allah. These multi-faceted belief systems in Kashmir are represented as merged within the tale, as the Islamic governor, Ali Mardan, is shown to value the advice of the Hindu yogi and guru. However, both cultures make it clear that the power of the mystical female in the tale is abhorrent, and thus she is deemed monstrous. Therefore, the tale makes it clear that the male characters must eradicate this traditional goddess representative. However, the mysterious ending of the tale, where the remains of the snake woman still hold power, suggests a communal maintenance on the part of the people of Kashmir for their once powerful goddesses. This ending suggests that neither Ali Mardan or the Hindu yogi and guru reached true heroism for their defeat of the Lamia, as none of these male characters were shown to psychologically or spiritually transform as a result of their actions; instead, they were only portrayed as stealing the power of a female who was clearly connected to more ancient ideology.

A Japanese folktale (Allan, Kerrigan, & Phillips 83) displays another example of a male patriarchal hero defeating a monstrous female who again seems to have connections with traditional goddess worship. The folktale begins with a male hero named Yorimitsu upon a quest with his trusted male companion Tsuna. As they rode through the forest, the pair saw a skull floating in the air. They followed the skull to an old mansion. Once inside, they were greeted by a monstrous woman who appeared as "a wizened, white-haired crone … [with] eyelids falling back over her head like a hat" and "breasts [that] hung below her knees.… She was 290 years old" (Allan, Kerrigan, & Phillips 83). However, just as Yorimitsu drew his sword, he saw that the monstrous woman disappeared and was replaced by the most beautiful maiden he had ever seen. Yorimitsu could only stare at the beautiful maiden, until he realized that as he stood there, he was being covered with sticky webbing. At this, he pulled out his sword and stabbed the woman, who vanished. Yorimitsu and Tsuna searched the compound until they found that the maiden had metamorphosed again, this time into a giant spider that was quite wounded. The two men then killed the spider by stabbing it to death and found that within its body were "thousands of human victims" (Allan, Kerrigan, & Phillips 83).

Again, the woman in this folktale holds abilities in line with traditional Japanese goddesses, as she can transform from youth to extremely old age and metamorphose from human to animal form, just like the divine Japanese Inari who could transform from fox to human form.

However, instead of revering these qualities in this goddess representative, the folktale makes it clear that its intent is to eliminate such remnants of goddess worship. As discussed, goddesses were readily revered in Japan for centuries, but in the Kamakura and Muromachi periods, Japanese goddesses, and the women who served them, lost religious status (Aoki 64). In addition, the introduction of Buddhism into Japan spread patriarchal concepts in regards to indigenous goddess worship and the spiritual role of women; for example, Buddhism in Japan viewed women as "less than fit vessels for attaining enlightenment" (Yusa 83). Therefore, there was "a long history of discrimination against women in the Japanese Buddhist world" (Aoki 19). The Edo period (1603–1868 CE) in Japan, which heavily embraced Neo-Confucian concepts, also perpetuated the demotion of goddesses and the social positioning of women, as Neo-Confucian values stressed hierarchal social systems that prized patriarchy. The Meiji period (1868–1912), which introduced Western and Christian concepts into Japan, further demoted memories of powerful Japanese goddesses and decimated any remaining high-standing social and religious positions for women. Therefore, folktales, such as this one, that portray a goddess representative as evil and thus deserving of obliteration by male patriarchal heroes, certainly impart a social and political message intent upon identifying traditional goddess representatives as components of a sinister past. Still, the presentation of the two male characters within this tale as heroes for simply killing the female monster is highly unconvincing, as they are in no way shown to transform psychologically or spiritually as a result of their quest and their interaction with the goddess representative.

As outlined in the examples of folktales just discussed, many males are identified as patriarchal heroes just because they killed monstrous women. As discussed, monstrous females within myths, folktales, and fairy tales often initiated the male hero's necessary heroic stage of facing his own mortality. However, in tales meant as patriarchal propaganda to supersede the power of traditional goddesses, such as the ones just presented, many male heroes are shown to face their own mortality too quickly, as they speedily eliminate the monstrous females who threaten them. Thus, these tales show, at the most, only limited growth of the male hero. However, as was shown in many of the tales that showcased male heroes interacting with old wise women and formidable maidens, the mythic, folkloric, and fairy tale heroes who were in line with goddess ideology did not only prove their skills of bravery and might, but instead grew psychologically and/or spiritually as a result of their quests and interactions with goddess figures. Some myths, folktales, and fairy tales of male heroes and monstrous women do move beyond mere propaganda meant to dispel traditional concepts of goddess worship by showing the heroes as profoundly transforming precisely due to their interaction with the monstrous females they encounter. In these cases, facing the monstrous female forces the male hero to accept his own mortality, which allows him to move beyond a fear of death, so that he learns to embrace the wisdom of goddess ideology that promises everlasting life through cyclical existence, and thus gains heroic apotheosis in line with goddess worship.

For example, the Mesopotamian myth the *Epic of Gilgamesh* is a prime example of a hero who reached apotheosis because he was scared to death by a divine female. As discussed in Chapter 2, Gilgamesh was first portrayed in his myth as an unjust king. The goddess Ishtar intervened and presented Gilgamesh with the opportunity to marry her, which would spell death for him, as all of Ishtar's male consorts ended up dead, befitting her role in the Neolithic period. Gilgamesh refused this terrifying request, so Ishtar unleashed the Bull of Heaven to ransack Gilgamesh's kingdom, and then demanded that the gods kill Gilgamesh's best friend Enkidu. Thus, Ishtar seems like a monstrous villain in this myth, yet when examined further, it is clear that it was precisely these actions of Ishtar that propelled Gilgamesh to begin his heroic quest to, as the text states, escape his eventual death, as the death of his best friend so terrified him that he went on a hero's journey to find a means to evade his demise. Gilgamesh's heroic quest ends with him fully facing the terror that Ishtar, seemingly in monstrous terms, presented to him, so that he learned what Ishtar actually represented—not a monster, but an embodiment of the natural necessity of the life cycle. This goddess-oriented wisdom allowed him to finally become a just ruler to his people, signaling his apotheosis.

Similarly, many Greek myths involving the goddess Hera show her as monstrous to the famed hero Heracles. Hera was said to hate Heracles because Zeus had an affair on her with Heracles's mother Alcmene, which produced Heracles. Therefore, Hera connivingly sent serpents into the infant Heracles's crib in order to kill him, but the infant Heracles merely strangled the serpents. Hera again tried many times to torment Heracles throughout his life; the most significant was when she caused Heracles to momentarily become insane, so that he murdered his own wife and children. It is hard to see Hera as anything but monstrous in her interaction with Heracles, yet her interventions initiated Heracles's heroic quest toward apotheosis, as he sought out twelve impossible labors to heal himself from his psychological pain. Each task upon his twelve labors caused Heracles to gain psychological and spiritual wisdom. To continue Heracles's education, Hera again drove Heracles insane later in life, causing him to murder his friend Iphitus. And, again to absolve himself of his pain and guilt, Heracles became a slave to Queen Omphale of Lydia, who made him complete domestic duties assigned to women while wearing women's clothing, which allowed Heracles to further his psychological and spiritual education. Finally, Heracles's death, initiated when he was tricked into wearing a poisoned shirt which caused his skin to burn away, shows him making his own funeral pyre when he realized that he was dying, setting it afire, and smiling at the moment of his death. This final scene for the famed hero Heracles signals his apotheosis, as he, like Gilgamesh, embraced the fact that he, because of the intervention of Hera in his life, must die a mortal death. Thus, Hera is signaled at the death of Heracles, not as monstrous for seemingly destroying his life every chance she got, but instead, as a guide who forced him to face the hardest elements of life. This presentation of Hera, not as monstrous but as the spiritual teacher to Heracles, is shown at the final moment of Heracles's mythic narrative when he, after living a fully human life, ascended to Mount Olympus to live with the gods. Before being granted immortality, Heracles had to first take part in a symbolic birthing act that defined Hera as his true mother, which he did by crawling under the standing legs of Hera, so that she could enable him to be reborn as an immortal. This birthing imagery between Hera and Heracles provides an exquisite example of the apotheosis of a hero being portrayed as the attainment of wisdom from a goddess. This final scene reveals that Heracles, as Hera's namesake, was thus guided by her throughout his entire life so that he could learn that the horror of death, as presented repeatedly by what seemed to be a monstrous Hera, was really his means toward spiritual rebirth.

The Polynesian myth of Maui and Hine-nui-te-Po, the enormous goddess of death, portrays another myth where a monstrous female teaches a heroic male about the natural lesson of life, death, and rebirth, thus imparting goddess-oriented, apotheotic wisdom to the hero. Maui is one of the most revered culture heroes in Polynesia; he "was seen as the defender of the weak and the protector of the underprivileged" (Allan, Fleming, & Phillips 126). In the myth of Maui's death (Allan, Fleming, & Kerrigan 126), he learns the transformational wisdom of the goddess Hine-nui-te-Po. In this myth, Maui is portrayed as full of conceit, as he believed that he could eradicate Hine-nui-te-Po, who seemed to him to be monstrous, as she was the reason death existed on earth. Maui tried to kill Hine-nui-te-Po by journeying throughout the underworld to find her, and then entering into her vagina, so that he could try and crawl all the way through her body to her mouth, thus killing her from the inside. This symbolic reversal of the birthing process, however, was clearly unnatural, just like Maui's attempt to end all death for the inhabitants of earth. Therefore, Maui, as he tried to climb through Hine-nui-te-Po's vagina while she slept, became stuck in the process, causing the onlookers who saw his attempt to start laughing, which awakened the mighty Hine-nui-te-Po. Once awake, this massive goddess of death used the razor-sharp teeth that were a part of her vagina to cut Maui up into pieces, thus killing the famed culture hero.

Hine-nui-te-Po presents a great example of a goddess who appears as monstrous for her connection to death, but the myth itself serves to send the message to audiences about the necessity of nature's laws. It is significant that the male hero Maui does not defeat the goddess who appears monstrous in this myth, but is instead destroyed by her, as it solidifies for audiences the fact that the goddess, as a representation of nature's cycles, holds the superior position. Even though Maui died as a result of his heroic quest, he still was shown to reach apotheosis in line with goddess ideology. As Maui tried to evade death for himself and every living creature on earth in killing the goddess who appeared to him as monstrous, he learned the central message goddesses often teach apotheotic heroes—that death is a natural necessity to initiate rebirth. In addition, the fact that Maui died while in the vagina of the death goddess sends imagery in line with his symbolic resurrection, as the myth suggests that he will also be reborn by means of the goddess's regenerative womb.

Similar to the myths of Gilgamesh, Heracles, and Maui, an Inuit folktale, entitled "Skeleton Woman" (Estés 134), relates a story about how a monstrous woman, though terrifying, ends up helping a male hero reach apotheosis. This folktale relates how a young woman was thrown over a cliff by her father because she broke one of his rules. The fish in the sea consumed her flesh, until she was just a skeleton. One day a fisherman, quite desperate for food, accidently caught Skeleton Woman. When the man realized that he caught a dead woman, he tried to free her from his line, but he was horrified to see that the Skeleton Woman appeared not to be entirely dead, as she held on to his line behind his kayak, until she followed him on shore and chased him over the land. However, when Skeleton Woman realized that she was on land again, she began to gorge on food. When the man saw Skeleton Woman's hunger, he finally was able to calm his fear down enough to see her for what she was, a woman's skeleton in an uncomfortable heap of bones because she was still entangled in his fishing line. So the man forced himself to do the right thing and disentangled Skeleton Woman from his line, one bone at a time, until her skeleton appeared as it should. The man then took Skeleton Woman to his home, wrapped her up in furs, and set her by his fire. The man then huddled down by the fire himself and fell asleep, shedding a single tear for Skeleton Woman. When Skeleton Woman saw the man's tear, she pushed herself up and crawled over to him. Skeleton Woman then drank up the water from the man's tear, and as she tasted the water, she finally felt relieved of the terrible thirst she felt during her years under the sea. Once satiated,

Skeleton Woman then reached inside the chest of the man and pulled out his heart. Skeleton Woman then beat like a drum upon the man's heart and sang "'Flesh, flesh, flesh! Flesh, flesh, flesh!' And the more she sang the more her body filled out with flesh" (Estés 134). In no time, Skeleton Woman's frame was covered fully in flesh once more, and she again had organs within her body, and her hair, skin, and eyes reappeared. Skeleton Woman then sang the clothes off the man, and at last stopped singing and crawled next to him, placing his heart back within his own chest. After this, the woman, physically resurrected, and the man, psychologically and spiritually resurrected, lived out the rest of their lives together.

This folktale shows many features that tie Skeleton Woman to a traditional goddess representative, as she is able to live on after her death within the sea, and she is able to resurrect herself and the male hero. In addition, Skeleton Woman could not be a better representation of the reality of death. Her monstrous form, and the symbolic message of the assurance of death that she sends to the man of the tale, just by the sight of her, truly terrifies him at first. However, the man becomes a true hero when he is able to dispel his fear of Skeleton Woman as monstrous, and instead see her for what she really is—a representation of the cycles of life. The man's taking the monstrous woman into his home, and then crying for her, shows that he accepts the wisdom of the goddess. His subsequent death and resurrection, which initiates the rebirth of Skeleton Woman, shows that the man reached apotheosis and thus became a true hero of the goddess. As seen often in this book, many myths, folktales, and fairy tales signal that a male character has successfully completed a spiritual quest when he is rewarded with the love of a woman, and this is certainly the case in this folktale, as Skeleton Woman transformed from her death-like state to a young, beautiful woman, which is a common skill of goddesses.

Female Spirits

Many folktales and fairy tales contain portrayals of female spirits, who like many monstrous females are often linked to former conceptions of goddesses within their respective cultures. For instance, many Chinese folktales display female spirits who are directly linked to conceptions of divine women. Chinese folklore often mixed "indigenous beliefs about divine women" with tales of "ghosts of immortals who ... might either benefit humans or bring them harm" (Young 112). However, as, "Chinese society became increasingly male-oriented, these female spirits became less benevolent" (Young 112).

In Ireland, Scotland, and England, female ghosts are also often portrayed in folklore, and their presentations additionally hold connections to former conceptions of goddess worship. For example, the banshee in Irish and Scottish folklore appears in female form to signal the approaching death of a loved one within a certain family or clan. The banshee is said to appear as a woman wearing a long white, or sometimes red, dress. She has long, flowing hair and red eyes from weeping for the upcoming death. Some accounts of the banshee depict her by other names, such as the Bean Si or Little-Washer-by-the-Ford, and some show her not as a beautiful, mournful woman, but as a creature with "one nostril, a large protruding front tooth, red webbed feet and long pendulous breasts" (Guiley 30). Some accounts connect the folkloric banshee to the Celtic goddess Clíodhna, who was the goddess of love and beauty, and sometimes referred to as the Queen of the Banshees. Clíodhna mythically was said to possess three birds who ate mystical apples, which gave them the ability to sing songs that healed the ill. The demotion of this goddess to the female spirit of the banshee, who only weeps from sorrow, sends a message about the enforced degradation of this goddess, as the folkloric banshee's incessant sorrow could reflect the people's sorrow for losing their once revered divine woman.

In English folklore, ghosts of women known as White Ladies abound, and often the female spirits in these folktales, like the banshee, portray a remnant of traditional goddess worship. For example, a folktale from England (Phelps, *Tatterhood*, 79–82) presents an old woman who lived by herself at the edge of "a great wild moor" (Phelps, *Tatterhood*, 79). One night the old woman saved a rabbit whose life was endangered within the moor. The old woman was immediately astonished to see that the rabbit metamorphosed into a ghostly lady dressed all in white. The White Lady then presented the old woman with gifts suitable of a goddess—the assurance that her hens will always lay eggs, her cows will always give milk, and she will always yield a bountiful harvest. The gifts bestowed to the old woman by the White Lady for saving an element of nature, as well as the White Lady's ability to metamorphose from animal to human form, makes it clear that she serves as a representation of a goddess, as folkloric White Ladies were believed to be remnants of "early pagan deities who gave fertility to land and livestock" (Phelps, *Tatterhood*, 82).

In addition, like monstrous females, when folktales and fairy tales include female spirits, they are often used as narrative devices meant to teach male characters goddess-oriented lessons about the role of death within the cycles of life.

For example, a Japanese folktale (Allan, Kerrigan, & Phillips 118–9) about a man named Ito who traveled to a strange location filled with ghosts presents classic lessons tied to goddess worship. In this folktale, Ito was met by a servant girl who told him that he must follow her to an "urgent meeting," so he "unquestionably" did so (Allan, Kerrigan, & Phillips 118). Ito saw that they arrived at an abandoned home in the middle of a deep, dark forest. Inside, he saw many guests, all of whom were ghosts. However, instead of being afraid, Ito felt comfort, as the guests treated him with warmth and kindness. In time, Ito met a beautiful maiden, who said that she was the daughter of the "famous Shigehira … a warrior of the Taira clan who had been executed by Yoritomo … six centuries earlier" (Allan, Kerrigan, & Phillips 119). Feeling overcome with love for this maiden, the two were married immediately, and Ito enjoyed a night of unearthly pleasure. However, when morning came, Ito's new bride told him that he would have to wait ten years before he could see her again. Ito simply stated "For another such night, [I] … would wait a lifetime" (Allan, Kerrigan, & Phillips 119). So, Ito went back home and waited ten years for his ghost bride to return to him. In those ten years, the people who loved Ito saw his body grow weak and frail, as he longed for the time to pass. On his deathbed, after almost ten years were up, Ito revealed to his mother what had happened to him, and how happy he was that he would soon be reunited with his bride. His mother "did not know whether to weep or rejoice. Had her son died in a delirious dream, or had he moved on to a life of rapture with his chosen lover" (Allan, Kerrigan, & Phillips 119)? This folktale displays the ghost woman in terms that could be described as divine, as she, and the other ghosts around her, live in a supernatural otherworld. The woman additionally appears as the pinnacle of maidenhood and beauty, but, as a ghost, she is also clearly connected with death. Thus, the ghost woman of this folktale teaches Ito, as many goddess representatives teach male characters, that his death is no death at all, just a transition.

Sometimes the portrayal of female spirits in folktales and fairy tales is meant to reflect the anger women felt at being forced to maintain demoted positions in patriarchal communities. For instance, in Persia female "witch-like spirits who transformed themselves into beautiful maidens … lead men astray" (Allan, Phillips, & Kerrigan 118) in order to kill them. In India, a churel is identified as "the evil ghost of a woman" (Guiley 64), who appears to men as a beautiful woman who wishes to lure men to premature deaths (Guiley 64). Churels are said to be the ghosts of young women who died in childbirth; therefore, in their spirit states, they are said to unleash on men a fate that is closely related to the fate they had, of dying in their prime. Similarly, in a Sinhalese folktale, a female demon named Bodrima was said to be "the ghost of a woman who died in childbirth in great agony" (Leavy 187). Because of her painful death, she holds "vindictive feelings against men, whom she chokes to death whenever the opportunity presents itself" (Leavy 188).

There are also often folktales that portray ghostly women "who react violently against their subordination to male power" by "frequently act[ing] out their fury through infanticide" (Leavy 187). For instance, again in England, Gray Ladies are sometimes said to be the "ghosts of women who reportedly died violently for the sake of love or pined away from loss of love" (Guiley 143). These apparitions appear as women clad in gray and are said to haunt a particular place waiting for a loved one. One such tale shows a woman of a low social position who became pregnant while unmarried. The man, a knight of high social position who got her pregnant, only mocked her when she wanted to get married to him and thus legitimize the baby. Enraged by his treatment of her, when the woman met the man in the streets "she threw their child under his horse's feet, tore the sword from his scabbard, and stabbed him" (Leavy 187). The man died as a result, and the woman was executed. However, the woman in some folkloric accounts even today is said to appear as a Gray Lady who can be seen "at the spot of the double murder ... [where she] attempts to lure young men with her pale beauty. [But,] ... all who speak with her die within the next few days" (Leavy 187).

Also, in Mexican folklore, La Llorona (the Weeping Woman) was a woman who fell in love with a man and had a child, or children in some versions, with him, only to be later shunned by him when he married another woman. In anger and sadness, La Llorona murdered her child/children by drowning them and then also drowned herself. La Llorona is also said even today to haunt bodies of water in despair as she searches for her drowned child/children. Though most folktales about La Llorona present her as only wandering near bodies of water searching for her child/children and not harming anyone, some tales do show her as enticing men to their deaths. Leavy points out that there are certain La Llorona tales where she "attacks men who in one way or another have already denigrated women.... Hence her victim is portrayed as a woman's victimizer, and if the man does not die, he 'suffers extreme fright or becomes insane'" (Leavy 187). Guiley states that "most folklorists believe that the legend derives from Aztec mythology. The goddess Civacoatl ... dressed in white and carried a cradle on her shoulders. She walked among Aztec women and left the cradle, which was discovered to contain an arrowhead in the shape of a sacrificial knife. Civacoatl also walked the cities, screaming and crying, especially disappearing into lakes" (Guiley 190). Another basis for the folktale of La Llorona comes from a historical account from Mexico City in 1550 CE that shows a nobleman, Don Nuno de Montesclaros, agreeing to marry a woman, Doña Luis de Olveros, but then marrying another (Guiley 190). The Doña then murdered her children and was found guilty of sorcery and hung (Leavy 186). Whatever the origins are, the tale makes it clear that the ghostly form of La Llorona is meant to unsettle people, especially men, as she appears in folktales to seek revenge upon the man who wronged her, but also presumably, to serve as a statement to society about the lasting effects of acts against women.

Hans Christian Andersen's "The Little Match Girl" (1845), likewise serves as a fairy tale that uses a ghost-like female figure to make a statement about injustice against women. In this fairy tale, a young girl comes from a poverty-stricken household with an abusive father and a dead mother. In order to survive, she was forced to wander the streets trying to sell worthless matches to upper class men, who all ignored the fact that she was near death. The fairy tale ends with the young girl freezing to death because of her social situation in a patriarchal culture in which no one notices or cares about her. The ending of the fairy tale proves misleading as it portrays the little matchstick girl as finding solace from her hunger and her hypothermia at the moment of her death, when she believes she sees, as she strikes her leftover matches in a futile effort to warm herself, her dead grandmother. At this moment, the tale reflects a triad of female characters through the common plot device, as discussed in Chapter 2 of this book, of a maiden, mother, and crone, but in this fairy tale, all of the females have either already died or will die. Therefore, the death of the grandmother and mother symbolically suggest a dying out of traditional goddess-oriented concepts associated with such fairy tale figures, as grandmothers and mothers in fairy tales often nurture and guide their granddaughters and daughters. This legacy, that should protect the little girl, is gone, and she is left without care at the hands of an abusive father and a society filled with men who do not care about her. Thus, all three dead females in this fairy tale, serve as ghostly figures meant to haunt audiences in their demand for reflection upon the cost of a purely patriarchal society.

Myths, folktales, and fairy tales that portray monstrous or ghostly women do so to remind audiences about the once revered and powerful wisdom of many goddesses. Monstrous women, who are often representations of traditional goddesses, terrify male protagonists in countless myths, folktales, and fairy tales. Some male protagonists do not face the monstrous female but merely eradicate her; these males only serve as societal heroes who promote patriarchy. Other male protagonists become psychological and/or spiritual heroes in line with goddess ideology when they indeed face the monstrous female, who reveals to them the laws of mortality as well as the promise of natural immortality. Ghostly women within folktales and fairy tales also help male characters face the reality of death in similar ways, as their very appearance shows the factuality of death in human form. However, spirit women in folktales and fairy tales often additionally provide voice to the voiceless women within many global societies who were wronged by men and patriarchal structures. Showing an angry female creature or ghost that refuses to be silenced, or even strikes out at men, shows the anger at centuries of injustice done to women in societies that degraded goddesses and subsequently destroyed powerful social roles for women.

However, folktales and fairy tales do not just provide stories of victimized women, just as they do not only portray female characters who serve solely to help the quests of male heroes. Remarkably, despite centuries of degradation to goddesses and the women who revered them, folktales and fairy tales around the world preserved more examples of capable, resourceful, and brave females upon their own heroic quests than are found in global mythology. Therefore, the last half of this book will now turn to the heroines who partook on their own heroic quests.

5

Defiant Women and Women Warriors

Often mythology from around the world shows examples of women who held superior social, political, and religious roles in many communities, such as that of queen, regent, warrior, monster-slayer, savior of the people, etc. However, in many myths, these powerful women are often portrayed as defiant remnants of the last semblances of goddess worship within their respective cultures who fight against in-coming patriarchal restrictions that seek to strip them of their power and autonomy. Many folktales and fairy tales likewise portray stories that display powerful, independent women who defy their societies' patriarchal structures. These folktales and fairy tales, though, often are anomalies, as the cultures that produced and embraced them often dispelled the worship of powerful goddesses centuries earlier, and thus maintained long-held restrictions against the rights of women. Therefore, many folktales and fairy tales that showcase defiant women serve to preserve an ancient ideology based on goddess worship that historically enabled many women within various cultures to hold leading societal, political, and religious roles, while at the same time, sending a clear message to audiences that the women who are restricted within patriarchal cultures are not content holding inferior positions.

Defiant Women

As stated, there are many defiant women portrayed in world mythology. For example, as discussed in Chapter 4, ancient Greece experienced centuries of degradation in regards to the positioning of divine and authoritative women. In Greece's Classical and Hellenistic periods, women held severely inferior positions, as they were viewed as the property of their fathers and husbands and were considered legal minors

(Vivante 241). The famed Greek philosopher Plato referred to women as being connected to "children and servants" (Kidwai 6). Women in Athens were required to live out their lives within the household. Married Greek women were required to be veiled, so as not to be seen by another male. Because Greece once held high social positions for women, when powerful Minoan goddesses were worshipped, but then experienced a decline in this positioning of women when male gods and male heroes began to dominate with the introduction of Mycenaean values, many Greek Classical and Hellenistic myths capture a complex view of women who refused to fall into the patriarchal social restrictions demanded by their culture. As discussed in Chapter 4 of this book, many women within Greek mythology were portrayed as monstrous for maintaining a degree of defiance toward the in-coming patriarchal structures, and thus they were in need, according to the myths, of being punished by a patriarchal male hero. However, some defiant women in Greek mythology were portrayed as prized women for their defiance. Showing a society that values mythic women who defy the rules set forth by their own patriarchal standards is odd, but nevertheless, these myths of defiant women were beloved by the Greeks. Therefore, perhaps the Greek people in cherishing these myths of defiant women were preserving memories of when women indeed once held superior social, political, and religious roles in Greece.

For instance, some Greek myths, such as those portraying Jason or Heracles, display strongholds of societies governed only by women, and the women of these matriarchal societies are portrayed as irresistible to Greek male heroes. When the Argonauts journeyed toward Colchis, they made a stop at the island of Lemnos, which was inhabited, and governed, by only women. Mythically, the people of Lemnos were said to have once offended the goddess Aphrodite, so she cursed the women of the island by making them smell so bad their husbands had affairs with Thracian women. In revolt, the women of Lemnos murdered all their husbands and went on to live peaceably in a self-governed matriarchy. Unable to forget the fiercely independent women of Lemnos, the Argonauts were said to make a return trip to the island after retrieving the Golden Fleece in order for many of the male heroes to marry the enthralling women of Lemnos. Scholars, like Barnes, suggest that historically in Greece there may have been island strongholds governed by women in accordance to older Minoan belief systems, as the many islands of Greece were the last places to adopt Indo-European ideology. Therefore, the mythical Lemnos may represent a historical matrilineal island that might have indeed existed "at the beginning or even before ... [Greece's] Dark Age, perhaps before the Trojan War" (Barnes 118). The Greek hero Heracles likewise visited the Amazon stronghold of Themiscyra to retrieve Queen Hippolyta's belt during his ninth labor, and also found a matriarchal and matrilineal community of defiant women. Like many of the Argonauts, Heracles also found Queen Hippolyta irresistible for her powerful independence, but in a moment of confusion, initiated by Hera, he ended up killing the only partner that might have matched his heroism. Like the island strongholds of matrilineal practices that may have existed throughout Greece, there is also evidence that the famed Amazon women warriors of Greek mythology might also reference historical warrior women who maintained contact with the Greeks; these women will be discussed more extensively later in this chapter.

Another Greek myth involving the maiden Atalanta presents her as a prime example of a woman who was revered in Greek mythology precisely because she was defiant toward her patriarchal culture. As briefly discussed in Chapter 3, the maiden Atalanta was viewed as prized because of a contest that promised her hand in marriage if a worthy male could beat her at a footrace. As discussed in Chapter 3, many myths, folktales, and fairy tales relate stories of young maidens who must be won by worthy males. Many a father within a myth, folktale, or fairy tale advertises that a display of masculinity, defined in the tale most often as bravery, strength, and endurance, that is unmatched by any opponent, is required to win the hand of the prized maiden. And, at first glance, such tales seem to perpetuate a patriarchal society using daughters as the means to secure wealth and reputation for fathers, and though many tales may only be a display of such things, this myth certainly is not, because it is Atalanta herself who stated the conditions of her marriage by orchestrating the competition to win her hand in marriage. Furthermore, it was also Atalanta who declared that all defeated males who failed to win her hand must die. It would seem that such an outlandish contest would identify Atalanta as an evil seductress to any man who should attempt such a contest, as women in Greece, as discussed, were viewed as the property of their male relations and would not be allowed to articulate such demands for their futures, but the opposite is true in this myth, as indeed many men tried, and failed, to meet Atalanta's deadly challenge.

The myth states that Atalanta's father, King Iasos, wanted only sons, so at her birth, she was left alone to die at the top of a mountain in Arcadia. She was found by a she-bear who nursed her and raised her as its own. She, thus, became an extraordinary huntress, quite at home in her wilderness environment. Hunters discovered her one day and gave her the name Atalanta, meaning "equal in weight." Atalanta was "self-reliant, with a 'fiery, masculine gaze'"; she could "wrestle like a bear and could outrun any animal or man" (Mayor 1). Because of her skill, she was permitted to join in on a hunt to kill the Caledonian Boar that ransacked southern Greece. Some of the men refused to hunt with a woman, but a man named Meleager, who was in love with Atalanta, insisted that she accompany them upon the hunt, and soon she proved her worth, as she and Meleager slew the mighty Caledonian boar. Meleager gave the hide and head of the boar to Atalanta because she struck the first blow. Again, the men of the hunting party saw this as a disgrace, and when Meleager fought against his own kinsmen to defend Atalanta's right to the trophy, this set about a series of events that ultimately led to Meleager's death.

After this, Atalanta's father, finally seeing her worth, accepted her back into his kingdom, but he demanded that she marry, so Atalanta created the nearly impossible challenge of having men try to beat her at a footrace. Even at the threat of death to those who lost, many men were enticed by the fortitude of Atalanta, so many men tried to race her, but as a result, many died. Nonetheless, a young man named Hippomenes asked for the help of the goddess Aphrodite to win the race against Atalanta. Aphrodite gave Hippomenes three golden apples to use along the race to entice Atalanta to stop and pick them up, thus slowing her down, so that Hippomenes could win. The divine intervention worked, and Hippomenes won the race, so the two were indeed married. But Mayor states that "theirs was not a typical Greek marriage, however, [as] Atalanta and Hippomenes spent their days as hunting companions and impetuous lovers," who accidently had sex is a sacred place and were thus turned into a pair of lions (Mayor 3).

This myth "expresses the powerful mixed emotions that Atalanta's independence and physical vigor aroused among Greek males. Some men, like [the men of Meleager's hunting party], reacted with anger and violence. But other men, like Meleager and Hippomenes, thought Atalanta deserved to live as she wished" (Mayor 7). This common aspect in Greek mythology of portraying men who were enticed by women who defied the strict patriarchal standards of their own culture may represent the unease felt by some men who lived in a patriarchal culture that held women as inferior, or perhaps these types of myths present a dissatisfaction on the part of men who married women who were raised to believe they were inferior minors. The unease or dissatisfaction at the role of women that seems to have been felt by some Greek people, as the popularity of this myth suggests, may result from the transition in Greek culture from traditional times in Greece when formidable goddesses were worshipped, and women held roles of social importance. For example, Minoan culture shows myriad examples of women who resemble Atalanta; one of the most famous is a fresco from the palace of Knossos in Crete that depicts women leaping over bulls in open competition with men. Furthermore, mythically Atalanta was said to have worshipped Artemis, the goddess of the wilderness and hunt, who had connections to Minoan religion as Potnia Theron, the Mistress of Animals. This worship of Artemis by a woman who hunts like a bear because she was raised by a she-bear, a symbol of Artemis, suggests that Atalanta's independent nature was a result of her worship of a goddess who demanded her own independence, as Artemis was repeatedly portrayed in Greek mythology as fiercely autonomous. Therefore, the lasting embrace of the people for Atalanta suggests at least a remnant of dissatisfaction for their present circumstances in producing women who no longer resembled Greece's traditional goddesses.

Like the myth of Atalanta, many folktales and fairy tales also present tales of defiant women within strict patriarchal cultures. For example, in a Chinese folktale (Don 6–14), a defiant girl named Li Chi is shown to be the only one who can save her community from a fearsome dragon with seven heads. The tale begins with a dragon that threatened the whole community, unless the people, upon decree of the emperor, sacrificed a young girl to it annually. For years, Li Chi watched as her community made impossible decisions as to which young girls would be sent to their deaths. When it was time for her community to choose another girl, Li Chi, still a young girl herself, stepped before her people and declared that she wanted to be sacrificed to the dragon. Li Chi's father swore that he would never permit this to happen, but Li Chi defiantly insisted that despite her father's authority over her under Confucian ordinances, she was going to do as she wished. So, filled with anguish, her father finally relented to his defiant daughter. Before she went to be sacrificed to the dragon though, Li Chi, proving her intellect at having devised a plan, asked that her community grant her three requests: provide her with a sword; give her as many barrels of sticky rice as they could spare; and secure her privacy for her walk up the mountain to the dragon's cave. Li Chi was granted her requests and trekked alone up the desolated mountain to the entrance of the dragon's cave, proving her bravery. Once at the entrance of the cave, she did what no one before her had done; she chose to observe the dragon in its natural habitat in order to learn about its behavior. For days, Li Chi watched what the dragon did each hour of the day, until she was confident that she could successfully utilize the elements she brought with her. Li Chi learned that the dragon was most hungry first thing in the morning, so she put the barrels of rice outside the entrance of its cave and waited for the dragon to gorge on the food. When the dragon did as she anticipated, Li Chi grasped her sword, ran straight at the dragon, and killed it. When the young Li Chi had accomplished the nearly impossible mission of killing the dragon, her people held her up as their savior, and she went on to live in a place of prominence in her community until the end of her days.

It is important to point out that this folktale focuses upon Li Chi's heroism; however, Li Chi does not appear as a heroine upon a journey toward discovering who she is and what she is capable of. Instead, Li Chi is presented as being a fully formed heroine at the start of her journey. The tale shows the community greatly needing her, so, possessing all the skills required to meet her community's need, Li Chi simply steps forth, ready and capable of saving them. This element of presenting a fully formed heroine, who accomplishes a task no one else can achieve, suggests that this is not a tale to teach women the importance of embarking on their own heroic quests in order to elevate themselves psychologically and spiritually, which will be the focus of the last three chapters of this book; instead, this folktale, and others like it that show a fully formed heroine in the role of savior to her people, seems to have a different message meant to remind audiences of older ideologies associated with traditional goddess worship. This is evidenced by the tale's insistence that no male authority within the village, not even the emperor of China who decreed that children must be sacrificed to the dragon in order to appease it, was capable of contending with the dragon. Therefore, this tale, which is said to be over 2000 years old (Don 110), may hold qualities that connect it to a time when superior goddesses were worshipped in China, and Chinese women thus held more prominent social and religious positions. The fact that Li Chi is the only one capable of killing the dragon, especially in such an ancient tale, gives special attention to the power females once were believed to possess in controlling supernatural agents, which as discussed in the first four chapters of this book is often an attribute given to folkloric and fairy tale females who serve as representations of traditional goddesses or the women who served them. Perhaps then the long embrace of this tale by the Chinese people, even though it presents a defiant female who certainly does not meet later patriarchal standards of femininity in China, suggests conflict on the part of the Chinese people to eradicate their traditional forms of goddess worship.

"The Tale of the Oki Islands" (Cole 512–6) is a folktale from Japan that also displays a defiant girl who disobeys the rule of an emperor. This tale begins in the year 1320 CE when Emperor Hojo Takatoki ruled. Emperor Hojo Takatoki was said to be a powerful ruler who was easily displeased, and when the samurai Oribe Shima accidentally made a mistake that the emperor did not approve of, the emperor banished Oribe to the isolated Oki Islands. Oribe was miserable there because he lived in complete isolation and desperately missed his daughter Tokoyo, whom he was forced to leave behind. Tokoyo, however, "was a brave girl and knew no fear," so she decided to make the dangerous journey to the Oki Islands "or die in the attempt" (Cole 513). Again, from the start of the folktale, Tokoyo is presented as a fully formed heroine, even to the point of having her appear unrealistic in her superior skill, fortitude, and bravery. Therefore, this is not a tale of a heroine's journey where Tokoyo will learn important psychological and spiritual lessons; instead, this folktale appears as a reminder to the people of a traditional time when females were revered as spiritual leaders and protectors of their communities, countering the restricted role of women in Japan at the time of the tale's construction.

The folktale continues to show that although no one was permitted, by the decree of the emperor, to visit the people who were banished to the Oki Islands, Tokoyo did not heed this command, showing her to be a fully formed heroine who, unlike her father, does not bow down to patriarchal rule. The tale shows Tokoyo getting a small boat and confidently fighting the waves and wind to make it to the Oki Islands. Once there, Tokoyo asked a man if he knew where her father was, but he only warned her not to ask anyone else about her father's whereabouts, as doing so could risk his life. In the days to come, Tokoyo traveled over the inhospitable island searching for her father. One night, Tokoyo found a shrine where she prayed to the Buddha to help guide her. Tokoyo was immediately astonished to see a young maiden come to the shrine, who was openly distraught. The maiden was accompanied by a priest. Tokoyo peered at them, but soon she grew horrified when she saw the pair walk to the edge of a cliff, where it became evident that the priest was about to push the maiden off the cliff into the churning sea below. Seeing this, Tokoyo dashed up and stopped the priest. The priest looked sadly at Tokoyo and then explained that he was only following a required custom of the people of the Oki Islands that demanded that each year, a maiden had to be sacrificed to the "evil god…. Yofune-Nushi" (Cole 514), or else the god would cause great storms. Hearing the priest's story, Tokoyo did the unthinkable—she declared that she wished to be sacrificed instead of the maiden whom she just met.

Tokoyo removed the ceremonial white robe the maiden was wearing and adorned herself with it instead; then she prayed for the courage and strength to kill the god Yofune-Nushi. It is fitting that Tokoyo, as a fully formed heroine like Li Chi, is the one who must contend with the supernatural agent in the story, as this power in both China and Japan was once believed to be in the hands of female shamankas (China) and miko (Japan). Used to diving for oysters in her youth, which in itself is a dangerous task, Tokoyo rose from prayer and "withdrew from her clothes a beautiful dagger that had belonged to her family, and placing it between her teeth, she dived into the roaring sea and disappeared" (Cole 514). Tokoyo swam fast and expertly to the bottom of the sea, until she came to a cave. She peered inside the cave and saw what appeared to be a man sitting inside. Tokoyo grabbed her dagger and bravely entered the cave, but she saw that what looked like a man was only a wooden statue of the emperor who had banished her father. Taking out her anger at this patriarch, she began thrashing at the statue. However, after a moment, "she changed her mind. 'What good will it do? I'd rather do good than evil,' so Tokoyo decided to rescue the statue instead. Tokoyo undid her sash and tied the statue to herself" (Cole 515) and began swimming out of the cave back to the sea's surface. However, as she left the cave, Tokoyo saw the creature that she sought— Yofune-Nushi, the evil sea god. Yofune-Nushi was a terrifying "snakelike creature covered with horrible scales and waving tiny legs" (Cole 515), but again, because Tokoyo was a fully formed heroine, she did not give way to her fear. Instead, Tokoyo grasped her dagger hard and thrust it into the monster's eye. Yofune-Nushi tried to swim into his cave, but being half blinded, he could not find the entrance, so Tokoyo swam up from behind and was able to stab him again, this time in his heart, killing him. The fact that Tokoyo, a young girl, is capable of killing a divine sea god, again shows her to be a fully formed, even goddess-like, heroine. Thus, freeing the people from the evil sea god, Tokoyo, with the statue of the emperor strapped to her body, dragged the corpse of the sea god up to the surface of the water with her. The priest and the maiden saw her and helped Tokoyo ashore with her spoils. All spoils were taken to the island's lord, who immediately sent word to the emperor. When the emperor learned of Tokoyo's astonishing bravery, he felt overcome with emotion. He had been suffering greatly from a curse placed upon him by an unknown source, "someone who had carved his figure, cursed it, and sunk it in the sea," but when he heard the story of Tokoyo, he felt himself immediately relieved of the curse (Cole 515). Furthermore, when the emperor heard that Tokoyo was the daughter of the samurai he banished, he immediately released Oribe Shima and returned all of his land to him, and Tokoyo was forever embraced by the people of Japan as their savior.

Tokoyo, like Li Chi, is presented as an exceptional fully formed heroine, who is strong, wise, and brave right from the start of the folktale. However, it is Tokoyo's defiance of the patriarchal ordinances against her and her people that forces the community to see her for the heroine she is. This feminine defiance, as with the myth of Atalanta and the folktale of Li Chi, is an odd element for a people to embrace in a time when women were viewed as socially inferior, as Japanese women in the Kamakura and Muramachi periods, the era presented in this folktale, were oppressed by severe social restrictions. Thus, the folktale's popularity suggests a lingering embrace by some Japanese people for their ancient past, such as in Japan's Jomon period, when goddesses held superior roles, and women "enjoyed freedom and high position in their communities," often serving as matriarchs (Aoki 69–70). Therefore, Tokoyo's ability, as a heroine, who is not in need of a heroine's quest to grow psychologically and spiritually, but who is instead fully formed and ready to save her people through her mastery of supernatural agents, even to the point of killing a god, suggests that the defiant Tokoyo may be best understood as a remnant of a goddess herself.

A folktale from India entitled "Princess Sivatra" (Barchers 211–4) also portrays an exceptional example of a defiant heroine. Princess Sivatra is shown in the folktale to leave her castle compound at age eighteen to seek wisdom from life within the secluded forest. Leaving civilization behind is a task most often assigned to male heroes in Indian folktales, as Hindu males were often encouraged to seek spirituality in the seclusion of the forest during Vanaprashta, so Princess Sivatra's willingness to adopt this lifestyle signals her as a fully formed heroine who already possesses spiritual wisdom at the start of her tale. While Princess Sivatra was in the forest meditating, she met the son of an exiled king, who was left poor and blind by enemies of his kingdom. When Sivatra returned home, she told her parents that she wished to marry the exiled prince, Sayavan. But, Princess Sivatra's father refused to allow her to marry Prince Sayavan as he had been socially outcast, and furthermore, Sivatra's father had learned from the kingdom's seer that Sayavan only had one more year to live. However, Sivatra's defiant nature finally convinced her royal father to succumb to her demand, and the two were married.

Princess Sivatra was unafraid of the prophecy against her husband; this lack of fear, that was evident in both Li Chi and Tokoyo, further shows Sivatra to be a fully formed heroine who is not in need of a quest to allow her to grow psychologically and spiritually. The tale continues to show that Sivatra and Sayavan relished in each other's company while they were married. However, when there was only five days until the prophecy said her husband would die, Sivatra, in full command of her spiritual powers, went again to the seclusion of the forest to meditate. For four days and nights, she stood alone, resisting food and rest. Her husband tried to stop her asceticism, begging her to rest, or to at least tell him why she prayed so fervently, but Sivatra remained unmoved. On the appointed day of her husband's death, Sivatra stopped her meditation and went with her husband. Husband and wife spent the whole day together, until Sayavan approached Sivatra, stating, "'My dear, I can hardly see you. My head hurts dreadfully. I must rest'" (Barchers 212). After this utterance, Sayavan fell into a comatose state. Sivatra held her husband's head in her lap, until she saw a man come near him; immediately, Sivatra knew that the man was Yama, the god of the dead, who had come to take her husband (Barchers 212). The tale shows that Sivatra stood in front of the Hindu god of death, and in her defiance, refused to let him take Sayavan. Seeing Princess Sivatra's defiance over even the laws of death, Yama felt admiration for her. Yama stated that he would not give life back to her husband, but he would grant her a wish instead. So, Sivatra wished that her father-in-law, the exiled king, could have his sight returned, and Yama granted this wish. However, Sivatra again disregarded the divine Yama and refused to give up her husband to him. So, Yama granted Sivatra another wish. This pattern goes on in the folktale until Sivatra got her father-in-law his kingdom back, a son for her parents, and a son for herself. Finally, with Sivatra still refusing to let go of her husband in death, Yama became so frustrated with her that he remarked that he would give her anything she desired as a final wish. So, Sivatra promptly responded that she wanted her husband to resurrect, and with that, Yama disappeared, and Sayavan came back to life.

Like Atalanta, Li Chi, and Tokoyo, Princess Sivatra is shown in this folktale to be a defiant, fully formed heroine throughout the work's entirety, as she defiantly insists on her own spiritual and emotional well-being. But, her ultimate act of defiance, to what appears to be an insurmountable obstacle, the male god of death, suggests that Princess Sivatra may be a remnant of traditional goddess worship in India; in fact, Sivatra seems to be connected to the Hindu goddess Parvati. Parvati, the goddess of love, marriage, and fertility, is the consort of the god Shiva, the god of destruction. In order to win Shiva's love, Parvati mythically was said to practice extreme ascetic meditation, until her strong devotion was noticed and valued by Shiva. This explicit connection to Hindu goddesses, like Parvati, in the folkloric character of Sivatra may explain why she is presented at the start of the folktale as possessing all of the wisdom, skill, and bravery she needs to accomplish the task she alone deems worthy, which is essentially to resurrect her dead husband, a task often mastered only by goddesses and their representatives. This presentation of a fully formed heroine seems to again purposefully send a message to audiences about the power of India's goddesses and the once high position Indian women, in pre–Indo-Aryan times, held as representatives of these goddesses.

A classic defiant heroine can also be seen in the Middle Eastern folktale collection of *One Thousand and One Nights*. The narrative begins with two brothers of the Sasanian dynasty, the elder King Shahryār, who ruled over China and India, and the younger King Shahzaman, who ruled Samarkand. Both brothers found that their wives were cheating on them with their servants. Enraged, the brothers put their wives to death and went upon a quest to try and prove if all women were as deceitful and unfaithful as their wives. The brothers quickly ended their quest, which was hardly a quest giving its short duration and lack of psychological or spiritual maturation on the part of the brothers, when they found what they were looking for in the form of a woman who was stolen by a demon and was kept in a chest. The brothers found that this entrapped woman had discovered a way to maintain the only act of rebellion that she could as hostage to a demon, which was to have sex with ninety-eight men without the demon knowing. The captive woman then had sex with the two brothers, so that she could reach her goal of one hundred moments of deceiving her demon captor. After this, the brothers felt justified with their hypothesis that all women were deceitful, so they returned to their kingdoms. Over the next three years, in a perfect example of a heightened patriarchal culture, King Shahryār married, one by one, all the available women in his kingdom, had sex with them on their wedding night, and then had them killed the next morning. Things began to become dire for the community, as after three years, they started running out of available maidens for the king. However, another fully formed heroine, named Scheherazade, stepped into the situation, ready to save her people. Fully aware of the immense risk to herself, Scheherazade volunteered to marry King Shahryār. Scheherazade's father, the king's vizier, whose job it was to put to death the maidens who married King Shahryār, tried forbidding his daughter to marry the king. The vizier even threatened to beat Scheherazade if she disobeyed him, showing again the heightened patriarchal culture in place, but Scheherazade still defiantly insisted on marrying the ruthless king in order to save further women from being killed by him.

The text shows Scheherazade marrying Shahryār, but on their wedding night, she began to unravel an enticing tale to him, since she, as a fully formed heroine already possessed at the start of her tale a full plan to educate the extreme patriarch. When dawn approached, which should have been the time for her death, she abruptly stopped the story before she finished it. Enthralled with the story, Shahryār vowed to wait to execute Scheherazade until she finished her tale. This pattern, thus, continued for one thousand nights, and during that time, she bore the king three sons. At the end of one thousand nights, Scheherazade brought forth her children to the king and stated that she had finally run out of stories. Shahryār then declared that he had long ago fallen in love with her and would cherish her for the rest of his days, and thus would not abuse any more women in his kingdom.

The tales within *One Thousand and One Nights* were compiled over many centuries, and Middle Eastern women lost social status in the timeframe between the earliest to the latest tales within the collection. With the region's embrace of Semitic values and the religions of Zoroastrianism and later Islam, Middle Eastern women in many cases experienced a shift in autonomous power when the worship of goddesses was eventually eradicated with the new faiths. Over centuries, women became more and more socially degraded and devalued, until they were in most cases believed to be entirely inferior to men. However, Scheherazade does not adhere to the societal requirements of her era; therefore, as with other defiant women in folktales, it appears odd that Scheherazade was so embraced by a culture that did not value such women. Thus, the presentation and continued embrace of Scheherazade, as a fully formed heroine, may suggest that she is meant to serve as a potential goddess remnant. As discussed in Chapter 2 of this book, Middle Eastern goddesses, such as Inanna/Ishtar, and the powerful women who served them as priestesses, were often portrayed as granting kingship to eligible males through Sacred Marriage rituals. Like the Sumerian Inanna in her interaction with Dumuzi, Scheherazade, through "the power of ... ritual and renewal" (Tatar 463), done by her manipulation of storytelling, serves to spiritually elevate the man in the highest office of her community, making him a just king of an empire that, because of Scheherazade, can once again regain its fertility and prosperity with the preservation of fertile women. Also, similar to the presentation of Ishtar within the *Epic of Gilgamesh*, Scheherazade is the only one who knows how to handle an unruly king. Therefore, Scheherazade as a fully formed, socially defiant, heroine may indeed preserve remnants of Middle Eastern goddess worship.

The Norwegian folktale, "Tatterhood" (Phelps, *Tatterhood*, 1–6), displays another defiant, fully formed heroine. The tale presents a queen who was unable to have children, and feeling the need to have kids around her, she invited her nieces to stay at her castle for a time. As the queen watched her nieces play one day, she noticed that they were playing with a girl dressed in "tattered clothes" (Phelps, *Tatterhood*, 1), so the queen went up to the girl and told her to leave, as peasants were not welcome on royal grounds. However, the tattered girl told the queen that if she knew the magical powers of her mother in being able to tell women who struggled with infertility how to become pregnant, she would not send her away. Hearing this, the queen immediately ordered the girl to bring her mother to the palace. The girl ran to fetch her mother, who was selling eggs at the market, and brought her before the queen. In time, "the egg woman" (Phelps, *Tatterhood*, 2) told the queen a magic exercise to become pregnant, telling her to get "'two pails of water ... before you go to bed.... In each of them you must wash yourself, and afterward, pour away the water under the bed. When you look under the bed the next morning, two flowers will have sprung up: one fair and one rare. The fair one you must eat, but the rare one you must let stand. Mind you, don't forget that'" (Phelps, *Tatterhood*, 2). The queen did as instructed, but she disobeyed the last part of the charm by eating both the fair and the rare flowers. As shown in numerous folktales and fairy tales thus far, presenting a female character who holds the wisdom to mystically aid in fertility, as the aptly named "egg woman" does in this text, is a common archetype that dates back to ancient mythic narratives of fertility goddesses. In time, the queen found that she was indeed pregnant. She gave birth to two girls, one fair child, and one certainly rare child, as the baby came out of the womb riding a goat and carrying a wooden spoon; she could also immediately speak. The presentation of the rare twin as possessing exceptional abilities at birth is often presented in myths meant to signal divinity. Therefore, like the other fully formed heroines within this chapter, it appears that this female character may also possess qualities that connect her to traditional conceptions of Norse divinity.

Over the years, the twins grew to deeply love each other and were constantly in each other's company, but they were very different from one another. The fair twin remained fair, but the rare twin was nicknamed Tatterhood because she always appeared to be dressed in tatters, since she often took part in escapades that left her dirty and disheveled. One Christmas Eve night, the girls heard a great tumult outside. Their mother then revealed to them that every seven years, the castle was ransacked by trolls, and there was nothing anyone could do to stop them. Hearing this, Tatterhood, undaunted, declared that she would rid the household of the trolls once and for all. Her mother and all the servants of the household tried to stop Tatterhood, as the trolls "were too dangerous," but Tatterhood paid them no heed and went to attack (Phelps, *Tatterhood*, 2). The household could only listen behind closed doors to what sounded like a mighty battle, as Tatterhood killed troll after troll with her wooden spoon. Again, here the tale presents Tatterhood as a fully formed heroine who possesses mystical skills that further connect her to traditional conceptions of Norse divinity, as many Norse myths show divine beings interacting with formidable trolls.

Tatterhood's sister, who is significantly unnamed in the tale, seemingly because her fair nature only identifies her with any other traditional female of her era and culture, could only worriedly peak in at the battle her sister was fighting. However, when she did this, one of the trolls cut off her head and replaced it with the head of a calf. The once fair girl then retreated to her mother, with the head of a calf, on all fours, mooing like a cow. This metamorphosis recalls mythic narratives that show goddesses, who can transform into myriad guises or cause others to metamorphose. In Egyptian mythology, for instance, the mother goddess Isis too had her head cut off by her son Horus, but she, like Tatterhood's sister had done to her, merely replaced it with the head of a cow and carried on, signifying her role as a goddess.

This Norwegian folktale continues to show Tatterhood emerge from her battle with the trolls victorious. However, when Tatterhood saw the state of her sister, she ordered a ship with full provisions to be prepared, so that she could go upon a quest to save her sister. Though the role of women in Norway at this time did not condone such behavior for women, as Norse women lost considerable social status once Christianity was adopted over Norse religious beliefs, Tatterhood's father realized the formidable nature of his daughter and ordered the ship she asked for, but he demanded that Tatterhood take a male captain and crew with her. However, staying true to her defiant nature, Tatterhood refused her father's order, confirming her to be a character who ignores the rules of patriarchy set forth by her father/ king. When the ship and provisions were ready, Tatterhood and her sister sailed to the land of the trolls, where Tatterhood again fought bravely, until she was able to retrieve the head of her sister. Making her way back to the ship, where he fair sister only waited patiently, Tatterhood replaced her sister's head, helping her metamorphose back into a human once more. Tatterhood's ability to aid in her sister's metamorphosis further connects her to traditional Norse goddess worship, as the goddess Freyja was said to be able to transform others into animal shape and could herself metamorphose into falcon form.

Next the tale presents Tatterhood as wanting to "'see something of the world'" instead of go directly back home after her defeat of the trolls, so the sisters set sail for distant lands (Phelps, *Tatterhood*, 4). In time, the sisters came to a kingdom where messengers, seeing that a huge ship was only directed by two young girls, asked that they go up to meet the king of the land and his two sons. The defiant Tatterhood refused, saying, "'No…. Let them come down to the ship if they wish to see us'" (Phelps, *Tatterhood*, 5). The elder prince took up this invitation and went to meet the girls, and when he saw the fair sister, he fell in love with her and asked her to marry him. However, the fair sister said that she would only marry when Tatterhood married. At this, the prince invited the girls to a feast at the castle and begged his younger brother to consider marrying Tatterhood. In preparation for the feast, Tatterhood's sister asked her to change out of her tattered clothes and ride to the feast on a horse instead of her goat. But, Tatterhood, always being herself, refused. When the younger prince saw Tatterhood, he immediately felt disdain for her and refused to speak to her. Tatterhood asked him why he remained silent, but the prince only scoffed at her insistence to ride a goat instead of a fine horse like her beautiful sister rode. At this remark, Tatterhood again showed herself in the folktale to possess qualities more like a Norse goddess than a mortal maiden when she told the prince, "'I can ride on a horse if I choose'" (Phelps, *Tatterhood*, 6), and then proceeded to transform her goat into a fine steed before the eyes of the prince. The prince next asked Tatterhood why she always wore a tattered hood, and Tatterhood instantly transformed her appearance into a mystifyingly beautiful woman. Feeling more and more drawn to her, the prince inquired about her large wooden spoon, so Tatterhood changed it into "a gold-tipped wand of rowan wood" (Phelps, *Tatterhood*, 6). Thus, Tatterhood was finally revealed to be what she truly was all along, a representation of a goddess. Seeing Tatterhood is her full splendor, the young prince immediately fell in love with her. At this, Tatterhood returned back to her ordinary state of tatters, and the prince still loved her wholly and completely, so both sisters thus married their princes.

Tatterhood's mystical abilities in this tale immediately and repeatedly point to her being a fully formed heroine who is meant to remind audiences about the powerful divine females who were once embraced by their communities. For instance, Tatterhood serves as a capable warrior and mystical agent in this tale, similar to the goddess Freyja, who often led the frenzied Wild Hunt; the divine Valkyries, who rode the battlefield to choose the best of the fallen warriors; and the goddess Frigg, who could transform natural elements at will. Thus, when Tatterhood transformed into her seemingly divine form at the end of the tale, holding a piece of rowan wood, which in Norse mythology was the wood in which womankind was first created, she sends a message to audiences that women should no longer hold themselves under patriarchal restrictions that define them in terms of Tatterhood's unnamed sister; instead they should be like Tatterhood, and the goddesses who came before her—defiant, brave, mystically knowledgeable, and demanding.

Charles Perrault's fairy tale "Bluebeard" (1697) also presents a heroine who defies the patriarchy of her community, and thus holds connections to traditional goddesses. The tale of "Bluebeard" shows a heroine marrying a husband who left her in his opulent castle one day early in their marriage with only one rule—not to open a particular door, though he provided her with keys to open all of the castle's rooms. The heroine of the tale, however, did not follow the order given to her by her husband, because the tale presents her as defiant in her quest for knowledge. The heroine thus used the forbidden key to enter the forbidden room, and it was a good thing she did, because she discovered the truth of her new husband—that he had murdered all of his many wives who came before her, hiding their corpses in the forbidden room. The protagonist's curiosity and defiance thus end up being the precise elements that save her from succumbing to a similar fate as Bluebeard's previous wives.

Tatar states that Perrault's "Bluebeard" almost certainly was meant to connect its heroine to "literary, biblical, and mythical figures," such as the Hebrew Eve and Greek Pandora (Tatar 185), who received a bad reputation for their curiosity, but who initiated the necessary elements of existence because of their defiance. For instance, because Eve, who ate the forbidden fruit from the Tree of Knowledge, and Pandora, who opened the forbidden box given to her by Zeus, were curious and also defiant toward the divine patriarchs who demanded they follow their orders, both women were said to be responsible for unleashing the world's ills, including death, to humankind. The patriarchal ideology of each tale shows both Eve and Pandora in a negative light, as weak for succumbing to their curiosity and wicked in their defiance to their patriarchs, so they were punished by a Hebrew Yahweh and a Greek Zeus. Many global mythological narratives in cultures that revered goddesses often attributed goddesses as creating the earth with both positive and seemingly negative elements to balance existence, but presenting Eve and Pandora as only being responsible for creating the seemingly negative aspects of existence, shows that their creation in Hebrew and Greek ideology was intentional to perpetuate patriarchal belief systems that labeled women as sinister in order to elevate the status of male gods and their male representatives. The presentation of the wife of Bluebeard does connect her to such figures as Eve and Pandora for her curiosity and defiance to patriarchy, but the result of her defiant action appears as the opposite of the destruction unleashed by Eve and Pandora. Instead, the curiosity and defiance of Bluebeard's wife are shown in the tale to be the precise elements that allowed her to save herself and myriad future victims from the extreme patriarch of Bluebeard. Therefore, this fairy tale of "Bluebeard" may help reassign the curiosity and defiance of Eve and Pandora as positive traits that gave the women, and thus humankind, knowledge about the reality of existence. To support an analysis that Bluebeard's wife may serve to define the curiosity and defiance of women within patriarchal cultures as positive traits, there are numerous other folktales similar to "Bluebeard" that portray exceedingly curious and defiant heroines as remarkably similar to traditional goddesses, suggesting that the curious and defiant heroine may preserve elements of traditional goddess ideology in patriarchal societies.

For instance, the Grimm brothers' "Fitcher's Bird" (J. Grimm & W. Grimm 146–8) is remarkably similar to "Bluebeard," and it presents a prime example of a heroine whose curiosity and defiance toward a murderous man explicitly connects her to traditional goddess ideology. The heroine is described as the youngest daughter of three daughters in her family. Her oldest sister married a mysterious man, but soon after the marriage she disappeared. The heroine's second sister married the same man and also disappeared. So, the youngest sister, as a fully formed heroine, agreed to go the man who married her two sisters and discover what he had done to them. The man turned out to be a powerful sorcerer, solidifying his role in the tale as a patriarch who held authority over his wives in marriage, but also held mystical abilities that allowed him to further control his wives. When the heroine found herself in the sorcerer's compound, he warned her not to look in a secret room, again after he gave her the key to do just that. The heroine's first two sisters evidently were not defiant and did just as they were told by their patriarchal husband, becoming his prey. However, the youngest sister did defy the male sorcerer and went into his secret room, where she found her sisters' remains. Instead of just showing the heroine flee the murderer's compound, as Bluebeard's wife did, the heroine of this fairy tale acted as a fully formed heroine, even a goddess, when she proceeded to resurrect her dead sisters; "When she found her sisters in the bloody basin, she looked all over the place for their missing parts and put them all together—head, body, arms, and legs. So the two sisters came back to life" (J. Grimm & W. Grimm 146). Furthermore, the heroine of "Fitcher's Bird" goes on to save herself and her sisters by metamorphosing into a bird and tricking the sorcerer outside of his compound, which allowed them all to return home safely. Thus, the heroine of this tale is explicitly presented as a fully formed heroine who undeniably possesses skills that are in line with traditional goddesses, such as resurrection and metamorphosis, proving her to be an advocate for goddess ideology. The fact that this goddess-like heroine defiantly trusted her own curiosity, and then proceeded to confidently use an array of mystical skills to supersede the power of the murderous male sorcerer within the tale, portrays her as a superheroine who sweeps in to shed light on the dark, but potentially hidden, like Bluebeard's and the sorcerer's hidden rooms, side of patriarchy that imprisons, oppresses, and even murders women. The fully formed, goddess-like, superheroine of "Fitcher's Bird" therefore serves as an inspiration to women to be like Bluebeard's wife, Eve, and Pandora—consistently curious and defiant until the truth of patriarchy is revealed to all.

Warrior Women

Aside from being merely defiant in the face of patriarchal structures, many women in mythology, folktales, and fairy tales disregard definitions placed by patriarchal structures all together; these women are portrayed as warriors.

Many goddesses in world mythology are portrayed as warriors. For instance, the Indian goddess Durga is a warrior goddess who projects strength and power to her subjects. Durga is often depicted as riding atop of a lion while she holds multiple weapons. It is her job to battle demons who threaten the gods of the Hindu pantheon, such as when she defeated the buffalo demon Mahisasura, when Brahma, Vishnu, and Shiva were unable to do so. The Greek goddess Athena and Roman Minerva also were envisioned as wearing full battle attire, as the goddesses of strategic warfare. The Celtic the Morrígan, Egyptian Sekhmet, and the Norse Freyja were also identified as goddesses of warfare. Likewise, many myths from around the world displayed powerful human women in the role of warrior, and often these women were portrayed as exceptionally formidable in battle because of their tie to warrior goddesses within their respective cultures. For example, the Scottish Scáthach in the Celtic *Tain* taught the protagonist Cúchulainn the proper battle techniques to be a mighty warrior, though she herself was portrayed as an old woman; therefore, Scáthach was probably at one time worshipped as a Celtic goddess who underwent some demotion in myth to be presented as a mortal woman. Matthews concurs, stating that Scáthach was probably once "the eponymous goddess of the Isle of Skye" in Scotland, since she possessed seemingly divine wisdom about the art of warfare (Matthews 75).

Perhaps the most famous women warriors in mythology are the Amazons of Greek mythology. In almost every myth portraying an Amazon, the woman warrior is presented as a fully formed heroine, as she almost always exudes defiance and emanates masterful skill and bravery above most men. One of the most famous myths displaying the Amazons appears in one of Heracles's twelve labors, as discussed briefly in this chapter. The myth shows Heracles going to Themiscyra on the southern shore of the Black Sea and meeting Hippolyta, the queen of the Amazons. Heracles explained to Hippolyta his need for her mystical golden girdle, stating that retrieving it was one of the labors assigned to him by King Eurystheus. Hearing this, Hippolyta graciously agreed to give it to him, because it was clear that he had come in peace and viewed Hippolyta as his equal, as each of them were "aware of each other's athletic physique, military bearing, and confidence," and each assessed "the other's weapons, splendid armor, and impressive contingent of bodyguards" (Mayor 250). The myth also shows that Heracles and Hippolyta became attracted to each other, but before they could have further contact, Hera was said to intervene by disguising herself as an Amazon warrior who alerted the other Amazons that Heracles was trying to abduct Hippolyta, which caused a battle to ensue. Heracles at once assumed that Hippolyta was trying to trick him, so he killed her and stole her girdle.

Perhaps, the injustice portrayed in this myth speaks toward the injustice women must have felt at the shifting tides of patriarchal rule in Greece, as discussed in the previous chapters of this book. In this myth, the Amazons were mythically portrayed as living peacefully until Heracles arrived. Though Heracles initially did not mean to harm Hippolyta, he certainly did not pause to think through what was happening when the battle alarm rang. He acted only with extreme violence, immediately killing off any potential he could have had to merge with an equal partner such as Hippolyta. This brutal killing of Hippolyta could be another example of a male hero killing a powerful mythic female to project the superiority of patriarchal ideology, yet the myth itself makes it clear that this is not its intent, as it shows the death of Hippolyta as a misunderstanding, which suggests commiseration on the part of the Greek people for the Amazons.

Another Greek myth of the Amazons shows them on a war campaign across the Aegean, until they finally invaded the Acropolis in Athens. Plutarch wrote about the battle in Athens as "'anything but a trivial or womanish affair'" (qtd. in Mayor 271). The battle was said to begin because Theseus kidnapped an Amazon woman named Antiope. When the Amazon Queen Orithyia heard about this, she remembered the death of Hippolyta by Heracles, so she sought revenge. In Athens, the Amazons secured high ground, making it impossible for the Athenians to leave the city or gain supplies. The intense battle ensued for four months, with many casualties on both sides. Finally, the battle ended with the Athenians as victorious. Though the Amazons were the defeated enemies of the Greeks, their portrayal in this Greek myth was one of extreme respect for these formidable women warriors who were almost able to take over the most powerful city-state at the time in ancient Greece.

One of the most famous depictions of the Amazons appears when the Greek hero Achilles encountered Queen Penthesilea in the Trojan War. Homer's *Iliad* recounts how after the Trojan prince Hector was killed by Achilles, Troy's last hope fell upon the aid of the allies to Troy—the Amazons. The *Iliad* closes with the anticipation of the arrival of the Amazons. In the *Aethiopis* by Proclus, and later in *The Fall of Troy* by Quintus, the remainder of the story is told, showing Penthesilea as the sister of Antiope and Hippolyta, who ruled after Queen Orithyia (Mayor 289). Quintus relates that "Amazons from Pontus accompanied Penthesilea to Troy," with an entourage that resembled "a resplendent goddess surrounded by her noble escort…. [Thus,] the spectacle of the proud Amazons with their bows and spears astride horses glittering with finery lifted the Trojans' spirits" (Mayor 292). Penthesilea, as a fully formed heroine, approached the Trojan King Priam with confidence and assured her success. She entered battle with "her half-moon shield and two spears," a battle-axe that she designed herself, and her bow and arrows on her horse. Battle ensued between the Amazons and Trojans against the Achaeans. Penthesilea quickly and easily killed eight Achaean men, and her Amazon companions also wreaked havoc upon the Achaeans. Penthesilea called out in her battle rage to Achilles to face her. Quintus's text states that the Trojan women watching this event were inspired to join the battle themselves; "One young woman, Hippodamia ('Horse Tamer,' an Amazonian name), was seized with an impulse to join the Amazons. She jumped up and urged the other young women to take up arms: 'Let us fill our hearts with courage and take an equal share of the fighting. Our bodies are as vigorous as men's; we have the same light in our eyes and we breathe the same air! ... Far better to die fighting than to be enslaved'" (Mayor 294)! At these words, the Trojan women were ready to enter battle, but they were stopped by an old woman who told them that they were equal to men, but that because they lacked training, they would be unable to defeat the men in this battle. Penthesilea and the remaining Amazon women were depicted as fighting on, until they began to drive the Achaeans back to their ships. Ajax and Achilles saw this and joined in the fight. It was then that Achilles killed the Amazon warriors fighting alongside Penthesilea. Penthesilea saw this and threw her spear at Achilles, but it could not penetrate his shield. She then charged both Ajax and Achilles upon her horse, and again threw a spear, this time at Ajax, but again it could not pierce his armor. Achilles chose to then mock Penthesilea "for presuming that a mere woman could take on the 'two greatest warriors in the world,'" whereupon he threw his spear at Penthesilea, which successfully struck her chest (Mayor 294). Achilles then threw another spear at Penthesilea, which impaled her and her horse. She and her horse fell to the ground, and the Trojans fled in terror.

Achilles approached Penthesilea, full of pride, stating, "'Poor woman.... What lured you to abandon women's work to face me, the best of the Greeks'" (qtd in Mayor 296)? Achilles then bent down to her and removed her helmet, suddenly realizing his remorse at his harsh actions when he saw the beauty of Penthesilea. At the sight of Penthesilea's face, Achilles immediately suffered "'bitter grief as profound as he had felt at the death of his best friend Patroclus'" (qtd in Mayor 297), presumably because he, like Heracles, lost his chance to gain a partner who was his equal. As Penthesilea died, the myth compares her to "'the immortal goddess Artemis asleep after a day of hunting lions in the mountains'" (qtd in Mayor 297). Therefore, this portrayal again shows both commiseration for Penthesilea as well as contention over the fact that Greek civilization eradicated the possibility for women who resembled their goddesses of old to thrive within their revised patriarchal culture.

For centuries, Greek mythology that displayed Amazons as "fiercely independent women warriors, was considered the stuff of legends, not history" (Davis-Kimball 54). However, Davis-Kimball states that kurgans from the sixth-century BCE were discovered that contained the remains of what appears to be women warriors who were buried with "weaponry, armor, and riding gear" (Davis-Kimball 54), suggesting they may be historic examples of women similar to the Amazons of Greek mythology. The Amazons discussed in various Greek myths were often identified as coming from the Caucasus region of the northern Black Sea, which is now southern Russia, so they could feasibly have been the descendants of the steppe nomads of Scythia (Mayor 17). Even Plutarch stated that the Amazons "'were of Scythian origin,' and that long ago, 'after their husbands had been massacred, the women had taken up arms and proved by their valor that Scythian women were as spirited as men'" (qtd. in Mayor 272). The Scythians, being an oral culture, left behind no written record, so it is difficult to gain an accurate portrayal of their warrior women, since most of what has survived comes from Greek sources. Because of this, there are many inaccuracies that have been captured throughout history, such as the Greeks' claim that Amazon women cut off their right breast so that they may better control their bows. The Greeks encountered the Scythians in the seventh century BCE (Mayor 18). After encountering the Scythians, "Rumors of warlike nomad societies—where a *woman* might win fame and glory through 'manly' prowess with weapons—fascinated the Greeks. The idea of bold, resourceful women warriors, the equals of men, dwelling at the edges of the known world, inspired an outpouring of mythic stories, pitting the greatest Greek heroes against Amazon heroines from the East" (Mayor 19). Again, it is telling that a culture would want to display women in their mythology as powerful when they were currently squelching the rights of women within their own culture. Perhaps, therefore, the mythic embrace of the Amazons signaled a nostalgic longing for an earlier way of life in Greece when powerful goddesses were revered, and strong women were allowed to play an equal part in society.

Like the Scythians, many cultures included women who served in the role of warrior. Scythian women warriors came from a long line of ancient steppe tribes, including the Saka and Sauro-Sarmatians who openly "embraced women of power" (Davis-Kimball 44). It is well documented that Scythian, Saka, and Sauro-Sarmatian women were entrusted with protecting their herds and pasturelands from predators and invaders, and they often took part in battle (Davis-Kimball 65). In addition, many Mongol women, in history, myth, and folklore were also identified as warriors. Many of them, such as the renowned Khutulun, were said to better any man at skills in warfare, such as wrestling. Folktales of Khutulun, like many myths of the Amazons, portray her as a fully formed heroine, as she towers above all others around her in her skill, bravery, and wit. Folktales often present Khutulun only agreeing to marry a man who could beat her at wrestling, and if they lost, they had to provide Khutulun the payment of one of their prized horses. Most men failed the challenge, which enabled Khutlun to tremendously increase her wealth, as she was said in folktales to have amassed a herd of ten thousand horses. Semi-historical folktales such as those of Khutlun were made possible by the fact that real Mongol women were permitted to hold high social positions. For example, Mongol women shared "openly in governing" and were often "awarded appendages ... [or] properties" (Jackson 8). Also, Mongol princesses "ruled and taxed their own fiefs separately from the state domain. Completely independent of the *khan*, they signed decrees and made major administrative decisions" (Jackson 8). After the death of Genghis Khan in 1227 CE, Mongol warrior queens, such as Sorqaghtani Beki, Törogene, and Oghul Qaimish, proved to be the "stabilizing force, holding the nation together during the political turmoil that preceded the election of each subsequent khan" (Davis-Kimball 223). Davis-Kimball states that "these queens were warrior women, brilliant politicians, astute businesswomen, holders of immense properties, who had become steeped in wisdom, and upon the death of a khan were powerful agents in choosing the next one" (Davis-Kimball 223).

In Kazakhstan, Kyrgyzstan, Uzbekistan, and Afghanistan, the Kyrgyz, who descended from the Saka-Scythian-Siberian groups from the Altai region, also revered women warriors, evidenced by their production of "opulent graves of women warriors dressed in gold and buried with their weapons" (Mayor 399). The Kyrgyz created the *Manas* epic cycle, which recounts women who were "'as heroic and militant as men'" (Mayor 399). The central heroine of the *Manas* tales is Saikal. Saikal "becomes the leader of her tribe because her husband, the chieftain, is a drunkard" (Mayor 401). Therefore, Saikal is presented as a fully formed heroine who is shown as fighting skillfully in numerous battles and "horse-wrestling with the best male champions" (Mayor 401). In addition, the *Manas* shows another formidable female in Mana's wife, who avenges her husband's death by "killing his murderers and drinking their blood" (Mayor 399).

The Central and Inner Asian tribes of the Saka-Scythian-Sarmatian, Mongol, Turkic, Altaian, Tocharian, Uralic, and Iranian people also had a long tradition of women warriors (Mayor 422). These cultures often battled against the Chinese, resulting in the Chinese becoming influenced by the customs of these people (Mayor 422). For example, Mayor states that many Chinese folktales began to portray female characters who were similar to the real women from these tribes, who were "expert riders and archers just like the men, and ... taught the boys and girls how to ride and handle bows and arrows. The women also rode beside their men into battle and valiantly defended against attacks" (Mayor 422). Because of this, "Historical and legendary women warriors became favorite characters in [Chinese] folktales, and the popularity of such tales "was due in part to the subversive themes of outsider women opposing Chinese male rulers and challenging expected gender roles" (Mayor 422). For example, one famous folktale of a Chinese warrior woman is the legend of Hua Mulan. Mayor states that Mulan, which means Deer or Elk, is a non–Chinese name that "reveals that the warrior woman glorified in … folktales, poems, and lore as China's ideal brave female fighter has roots in the peoples of the north-western regions of Inner Asia" (Mayor 429). Mulan is therefore likely to be a "warrior woman of nomadic origins" (Mayor 429).

Chinese folktales of Mulan certainly portray her as a fully formed heroine. Mulan is presented as a young maiden who was uninterested in traditional female duties, such as weaving and marriage. Instead, when each household was called to provide one warrior to fight against the nomads outside the Great Wall, she snuck away from her household, dressed as a male soldier, and joined the military. Tales of Mulan state that "for ten or twelve years Mulan … [rode] her 'flying' horse over ten thousand miles, enduring hardships, fighting the steppe nomads with great valor, winning victories for the emperor," and during this time, no one was able to identify Mulan as a woman (Mayor 427). It is again significant that at the time the folktales of Mulan were embraced, there were heavy restrictions in China regarding the role of women. As discussed, with the introduction of Confucian values and other patriarchal elements, Chinese women suffered from strict regulations that placed them beneath the over-sight of the male relatives of their families. However, because many Chinese people adopted and embraced folktales that portrayed strong women who defied Chinese restrictions, like Mulan, perhaps a longing to return to a traditional way of life, when Chinese goddesses and powerful women were once revered, was preserved.

In addition to Mulan, Chinese historical records and folktales tell of more renowned women warriors within China. One such example is Xun Guan, identified in the *Historical Records of the Jin Dynasty* in 265–316 CE, who led warriors through enemy lines in order to save her city (Mayor 420). Also, during the Jin dynasty in 317–420 CE, a legend recounts a woman named Mao who was a "horsewoman archer who killed seven hundred foes with her bow before she was captured and killed for refus-ing to marry the enemy commander" (Mayor 420). In addition, legends of Lady Mongchi state that she "commanded her husband's fortress in 503 [CE] and routed the imperial army at Changyang" (Mayor 420), while in 515 CE, "another female general, Lieouchi, defended Tsetong from imperial armies" (Mayor 420). Woman warrior Mu Guiying, who fought during the Song dynasty (960–1279 CE), was said within her folktales to have become a trained warrior since she was a child. Folktales state that a renowned male warrior named Yang Zongbao tried to overrun her community, but Mu Guiying battled him in a duel. Losing to Mu Guiying, Yang Zongbao pleaded for her to kill him for his dishonor, but Mu Guiying was said to instead fall in love with Yang Zongbao because he was the only man she knew who nearly matched her own warrior abilities. Mu Guiying proposed marriage to Yang Zongbao, and though he agreed, his father Yang Yanzhao refused the disgraceful marriage, so Mu Guiying engaged in battle with Yang Yanzhao, also defeating him. After Mu Guiying proved her superior warrior prowess, folktales state that Yang Yanzhao accepted the marriage and commissioned Mu Guiying to become one of his most trusted warriors.

Similarly, in Vietnam, the historical Tru'ung sisters (12–42 CE), Tru'ung Trac and Tru'ung Nhi, led a rebellion against the Chinese during the Han dynasty (Cross & Miles 40) and became folkloric heroes because of their efforts. Tru'ung Trac and Tru'ung Nhi were said to be instrumental in capturing over sixty-five cities (Cross & Miles 40). The sisters had many women followers who joined them in battle, such as Phu'ing Thi Chinh, who legend says joined the battle heavily pregnant, gave birth while fighting, and then tied the baby to her back, so she could continue the fight (Cross and Miles 40). The Tru'ung sisters, and Phu-ing Thi Chinh, were ultimately defeated by the Chinese and committed suicide rather than be taken captive. Because of their "formidable fighting spirit and aptitude," the Tru'ung sisters, as fully formed heroines, "earned their place in Vietnamese history as the leaders of the first resistance movement after nearly 250 years of [Chinese] subjugation" (Cross & Miles 42). In addition, the goddess-like Vietnamese figure of Trieu Au, who was claimed to stand over nine feet tall, had breasts that hung down a yard, and could walk over 1,500 miles a day, was said to have led another revolt against the Chinese in 248 CE. In her folktales, her brother tried to stop her from acting in what he deemed an inappropriate fashion for a woman, but she retorted "'I only want to ride the wind and walk the waves, slay the big whales of the Eastern sea, clean up frontiers, and save the people from drowning. Why should I imitate others, bow my head, stoop over and be a slave? Why resign myself to menial housework'" (qtd in Cross & Miles 42)? Therefore, as a fully formed heroine, Trieu Au and her followers were able to defeat the Chinese in many battles, but again, she too was finally defeated and subsequently committed suicide.

In Japanese folktales, many heroines also appear as warriors who were likely inspired by goddesses who were depicted mythically as women warriors, such as the goddess Amaterasu, who donned full battle attire to fight against her divine brother Susanoo (Allan, Kerrigan, & Phillips 39). For example, Japanese folktales of Tomoe Gozen (ca. 1161–1184 CE) present her as "a consummate woman warrior ... versatile with many different weapons" (Cross & Miles 43). Tales surrounding her life state that at the time of the rise of the samurai, Tomoe Gozen was the wife or concubine of Minamoto no Yoshinaka, and she rose by skill to be a senior officer in the struggles against the Taira and Minamoto clans (Cross & Miles 43). She was described in the *Heike Monogatori* as "'a remarkably strong archer, and as a swordswoman she was a warrior worth a thousand, ready to confront a demon or a god, mounted or on foot…. Whenever a battle was imminent, Yoshinaka sent her out as his first captain, equipped with strong armor, an oversized sword, and a mighty bow; and she performed many more deeds of valor than any of his other warriors'" (qtd in Cross & Miles 43). Some folktales state that when Yoshinaka was finally defeated and killed in battle, Tomoe Gozen refused to flee and died fighting next to her husband; other tales state that she flung herself into the sea holding the decapitated head of her husband, and still others say that she survived to join a religious order (Cross & Miles 43). Likewise, legendary Japanese woman warrior Jingū was said to be a warrior queen (Allan, Kerrigan, & Phillips 87). When her husband, Emperor Chuai died before invading Korea, Jingū was said to have finished her husband's military campaign herself. In fact, some folktales of Jingū portray her in a goddess-like state by claiming that her baby stayed in her womb for three years, so that she could continue to fight. Also, folktales of Jingū state that she was successful in her battles because she, again similar to the portrayal of a mythic goddess, utilized magical elements that could sway nature to serve her endeavors; for instance, she was said to possess "'Jewels of the Sea' that allowed her to cause the tide to ebb, leading to a Korean fleet of ships [becoming] stranded, and then she caused the tide to resume, which in turn drowned her enemies" (Allan, Kerrigan, & Phillips 87).

Also, in India, warrior goddesses, such as Durga and Kali, likely inspired myriad tales of formidable women warriors. For example, "ancient legends about warrior women were recorded in Sanskrit epics as early as 850 BC[E]" (Mayor 406). For example, the *Rig Veda* included women warriors, such as Mudgalani who "drove her husband's chariot to victory on the battlefield," and Vishpala, meaning "'Strong Defender of the Village' [who] lost her leg fighting the enemy" (Mayor 408). Megasthenes's *Indica* (ca. 300 BCE) also portrays a "company of trained female bodyguards who surrounded Chandragupta at all times" (Mayor 407). In addition, India's epic *Ramayana* presents Queen Kaikeyi who "served as a charioteer for her husband, King Dasaratha, in a battle and saved his life" (Mayor 408). A civilization of warrior women also appears in the *Mahabharata* (Mayor 409). In addition, many ancient artistic depictions in India display females as bow hunters and mounted soldiers (Mayor 408). The ninth century CE text, the *Agni Purana*, which is based off of tales from India's oral tradition, declares that "both men and women in India practiced fencing and archery" (Mayor 408). Also, historically Indian queens were credited for their strength in warfare, such as Queen Abbakka Chowta (1525–1570s CE), Queen Durgavati (1524–1564), Queen Keladi Chennamma (died in 1696), and Queen Tarabai Mohite (1675–1761), who all were revered for fighting against the Mughal Empire (Datta). A folktale from India (Ragan 167–9) shows a woman warrior, named Shuka Dei, who was said to be an equal warrior to her renowned warrior husband Dhanurjaya, the Raja of Banki. When Dhanurjaya fell in battle against Khurda, Shuka Dei rose such fervor in her community that they fought against the state of Khurda even though their state of Banki was much smaller. Shuka Dei's bravery encouraged her Banki warriors to fight harder than they ever had before. In time, the Banki army caught the Raja of Khurda, who felt great shame at being captured by an army led by a woman. The Raja of Khurda thought that he surely would be killed by his captors, but when he was brought before Shuka Dei, to his surprise, she ordered him to be set free, stating, "'Sir, you are my prisoner and if I like I can have your head cut off. But what good would such an act produce? I am a widow. I have a woman's heart. My husband is dead and my grief is too heavy to bear. How can I inflict such a suffering on another woman? No, no, I cannot do this to the Rani of Khurda! I fought with you only to bring back the lost prestige of Banki and not for revenge'" (Ragan 169). This contrary act in wartime, of peace and compassion instead of violence, that was led by a woman, transformed the Raja of Khurda, so that he forever promised that Khurda and Banki would remain united.

Europe also has a history of portraying warrior women in mythology and folklore. For instance, the Celts revered warrior women who were similar to the formidable goddesses of their culture, such as the Morrígan and Cathubodua. Celtic women were permitted to train at "war colleges" (Cross & Miles 35), and they were often feared as formidable warriors. In fact, the Roman historian Ammianus Marcelinus commented that a warrior "'would not be able to withstand one Celt in battle if he calls his wife to his aid. [She is] stronger than he by far ... especially when she swells her neck and gnashes her teeth and swinging her huge white arms, begins to rain down blows mixed with kicks, like the shot from a catapult'" (qtd. in Cross & Miles 35). Celtic mythology portrays Queen Medb in the *Tain* as leading her own army, Scáthach of Scotland training Cúchulainn in the art of warfare, and Cúchulainn himself having to battle the mighty warrior woman Queen Aífe. Queen Boudica of the Iceni became the stuff of legend because of her warrior prowess and connection to the Iceni warrior goddess Andraste. Boudica summoned an army of thousands to drive the Romans out of Celtic regions. Boudica's armies successfully captured the cities of Camulodunum (modern Colchester), Londinium (London), and Verulanium (St Albans), but they were finally defeated by the Romans at the Battle of Watling Street, and Boudica, rather than be caught by the Romans, opted to commit suicide. Some Anglo-Saxon women also were initially revered as warriors largely due to the fact that their Germanic ancestors worshipped powerful goddesses of war, such as Baduhenna and Sandraudiga.

Also, some Slavic communities, such as the Czech Republic, were believed to embrace warrior women. A Czech folktale, that may in part be based on history from as early as the sixth century CE (Hodges 57–9) presents a formidable woman warrior named Divoká Šárka. The tale states that when Slavic tribes first entered Bohemia, the land was ruled by Queen Libuse under a matriarchal system. The folktale shows men trying to secure Bohemia's power after the death of Queen Libuse, but legendary warrior woman Divoká Šárka, along with the other female warriors of Bohemia, fought and succeeded for years to preserve their way of life, though in the end the men won the war and patriarchy dominated Bohemia (Hodges 58). Divoká Šárka, like so many folkloric and semi-historical women warriors like her, refused to be dominated by her male attackers, so she also committed suicide. Though this folktale is largely considered fictional, some scholars, such as Hodges, believe that it may have origins in the "folk memory of the pagan [goddess-oriented] matriarchal society that was around thousands of years before Christianity" in the region of the Czech Republic (Hodges 58).

Scandinavia also embraced powerful divine warrior women, such as Freyja and the Valkyries; therefore, Scandinavian women, identified as shield maidens, were permitted to serve in the role of warrior. A Norse folktale entitled "Hervor and the Cursed Sword" (Don 61–7) presents a female warrior who undoubtedly was inspired by a cultural memory of its traditional warrior goddesses and women. In the folktale, a sword called Tyrfing was made for a man named Sigrlami who forced two dwarves to use their metallurgy skills to forge it for him. The dwarves did as directed, but they put a curse upon the sword, stating that it could not be sheathed again until it had spilled blood (Don 62). Sigrlami, as a mighty warrior, scoffed at this apparent curse, as he thought it would be no problem to consistently drench his sword with blood in the many battles he would fight, and indeed he was right, as Sigrlami lived out his life in violence, and in death passed on his sword Tyrfing to his first-born son, who lived the same way as his father and in death passed Tyrfing on to his first-born son. This pattern continued for many more generations, until Tyrfing finally made its way to the last of the line of first-born sons, Angantyr. The Viking men who were given Tyrfing throughout the generations thought the curse placed upon their sword by the dwarves so long ago must have really been a blessing, as the sword enabled many men to secure myriad victories over their enemies, but it came to pass that this family, who had embraced so much violence, had finally caused all of their male heirs, including Angantyr and his brothers to ultimately die in battle. Therefore, the people of the community came to understand that Tyrfing really was a cursed sword, so they had it buried with Angantyr on a small island to try and end the curse. However, Angantyr, though he had no sons, did have a daughter named Hervor. Hervor did not choose to do the traditional activities her community designated for most women; instead, she felt the insatiable urge to become a warrior like her father, grandfather, and great-grandfather. She spent year after year training for battle, and when she came of age, she announced to her village that she would lead a raiding expedition. But, having no proof of her warrior prowess, no one wanted to go with Hervor upon her raid, so she, showing herself as a fully formed heroine, set off alone to the island where her ancestral sword was buried. The people tried to warn her against retrieving Tyrfing, stating that the island that housed it was haunted, and the sword was cursed, but Hervor felt that it was her ancestral duty to possess her father's sword. As Hervor stepped onto the lonely island, she felt the presence of her father and uncles, and seeing the mound in which they were interred, she stared in respectful silence. However, Hervor was stunned to see that the mound suddenly burst into flames before her eyes, creating a deep pit. Feeling that it was a signal from her ancestors, Hervor bravely leapt into the pit. When she stood up, she was surrounded by twelve men. Though she never met her father, she knew that he stood before her when she saw his sword glowing within his bloody hand; she called to him "'Angantyr. Father. I am your daughter Hervor and I have come to claim my sword'" (Don 65). At this, Hervor stepped before her father and took the sword, claiming the "responsibility of the blood curse" (Don 66). After this, Hervor was transformed into a great warrior. Hervor then went back to her people, and when they saw her with her father's sword, they followed her upon her raiding expedition, knowing that the curse was fated to continue. However, in the female Hervor's hands, the cursed sword became an element that protected them, and Hervor was forever remembered as a respected and proven warrior woman among her community.

Defiant and warrior women within myths, folktales, and fairy tales, who often appear as fully formed heroines for their elevated abilities to save and protect their communities, are connected to portrayals of powerful goddesses who were once worshipped in many communities. Additionally, a culture's embrace of tales about defiant and warrior women, especially when the culture restricted the role of women, might reveal a preservation of a historical memory when women once held more prestigious roles than what they were permitted at the time of a tale's written narration. These tales of powerful women reminded audiences that women were capable of so much more than what their patriarchal communities defined as appropriate avenues for women; they also showed that patriarchal concepts were not always embraced by all members of a community. These fully formed heroines thus paved the way for female characters in folktales and fairy tales to partake on legendary quests that mimicked, and arguably surpassed, the quests of male heroes within myths, folktales, and fairy tales; therefore, the remaining chapters of this book will showcase the quests of these formidable heroines.

6

Heroines on Their Own Quests

Many scholars have discussed the idea that the journey of the heroine looks somewhat different than that of the male hero's journey. Maureen Murdock in her *The Heroine's Journey* (1990) identifies that the journey of the heroine involves such crucial stages as: "The Road of Trials," a stage that forces the heroine upon a quest; "The Initiation and Descent of the Goddess," where the heroine must undergo an experience with mortality; the "Urgent Yearning to Reconnect with the Feminine," where the heroine learns who she really is; and finally the stage of "Finding the Inner Man with Heart" that allows the heroine to move beyond a dualistic representation of male/female within herself, thus achieving self-actualization. Valerie Estelle Frankel in *From Girl to Goddess: The Heroine's Journey through Myth and Legend* (2010) also discusses the heroine's journey as being distinct from the male heroic quest. In this text, Frankel articulates the journey of the heroine often following these stages: "Growing Up: the Ordinary World," where the heroine learns to define selfhood under societal pretexts and is also called to her quest; "Journey through the Unconscious," where the heroine partakes on a physical or symbolic quest toward selfhood; "Meeting the Other," where the heroine encounters alternatives to former definitions of selfhood; "Facing the Self," where the heroine leans how to define her own identity; and "Goddesshood and Wholeness," where the heroine achieves self-actualization. Both of these definitions of a revised quest solely based on the heroine's experience is important, as a heroine's quest undoubtedly appears somewhat different than one experienced by a male hero. This is due to many factors—most predominant is the way that male/female roles have been defined within cultural contexts. For example, women at the start of their quests often have different views of selfhood than male heroes. Women also often have different relationships with mothers, fathers, grandparents, siblings, children, friends, etc., than male characters commonly have. Societal expectations may even proclaim that traditional quests are not fitting, safe, or available for female characters, and these expectations may thwart women from partaking on quests. Women also may have different restrictions placed upon them that make them believe that they cannot or should not embark on heroic journeys, such as the expectation to forfeit selfhood for one's children. If women do partake on a heroic quest, they often have different ways in which they interact with those they meet upon their journeys, such as especially fearing or mistrusting male characters in ways that are different from a male hero's encounter with female characters. Finally, the culmination of the heroine's quest may also appear somewhat different for women as opposed to male heroes. However, this text argues that despite their differences, the journey of the male hero and the female heroine are more similar than they are different, until the final stages of the heroic quest.

As was discussed in the male heroic quests of the first chapters of this book, the heroic quest is ultimately about attaining self-actualization. Though the variables change in every myth, folktale, and fairy tale, both heroes and heroines must leave behind their known communities, even if only psychologically, so that they may forfeit their preconceived notions of selfhood as defined by societal expectations. As stated, female characters often have a longer journey ahead of them to dispel notions of what society expects of women, as many female characters must first strip away beliefs taught to them by patriarchal communities about their own inferiorities in order to realize that they possess the bravery, strength, and determination to complete a heroic quest. Once the hero and heroine ventures upon his or her quest, the format of the quest remains quite similar, showing that the psychological and spiritual quest, which is the goal of the heroic journey, is indiscriminate of sex. Upon the heroic quest, both the hero and heroine must interact with those who serve as helpers and those who serve, or seem to serve, as hindrances. Both hero and heroine must also often encounter unfamiliar landscapes, people, creatures, etc., in order to contend with the reality of the "other," as identified as the otherworld stage of the heroic journey by mythologist Campbell. This otherworld stage prepares the hero and heroine to redefine notions of selfhood. The heroic quest then reaches its climax in the underworld stage of the quest, where the hero and heroine must contend with the factuality of mortality; Murdock's "Initiation and Descent of the Goddess" and Frankel's "Facing the Self" both discuss this stage for the heroine in similar terms. This facing of death finally allows the hero and heroine to embrace a more realistic and appreciative view of life, causing them to fully dispel their old definitions of selfhood and emerge psychologically, and sometimes spiritually, reborn. After this psychological and often spiritual resurrection, both the hero and heroine are identified as achieving, in Campbell's terms, the stage of apotheosis or

"Meeting with the Goddess," and by Murdock's terms, "Finding the Inner Man with Heart," and in Frankel's terms, "Goddesshood and Wholeness."

The striking difference between the hero's and the heroine's quest arguably comes in the final stage of apotheosis. As shown in the first chapters of this book, and as supported by Campbell, the male hero often achieves apotheosis when he learns to embrace goddess ideology that is taught to him by a goddess or goddess representative. Therefore, goddesses in myths, or their animal bride, wise old woman, maiden, or monster representatives in folktales and fairy tales, often teach male heroes, as was repeatedly discussed in the first chapters of this book, that their youthful strength and vigor, their perceived self-importance, their longing for power, and their egotistical desire to leave behind a lasting legacy all have to be forfeited in their acceptance of what the mythic goddess represents— the demands of nature's cycles. As shown thus far in this book, many male heroes rejected the concept of the goddess and either failed their goddess-oriented quests or become identified as patriarchal heroes who did not transform psychologically or spiritually but only served to elevate male-oriented political and religious agendas. However, as also shown in this book, many male heroes did attain the apotheosis of the goddess by being taught by goddesses or goddess representatives how to merge their life with nature's ceaseless patterns of life, death, and rebirth, allowing them to find a psychologically renewed, and often spiritually renewed, life for themselves.

The apotheotic heroine also learns the same message as the hero does about the factuality of death and renewal from the goddess or goddess representative in her myths, folktales, and fairy tales, but there is an added element to the apotheosis of heroines. The heroine often receives the additional confirmation that she herself is a part of the goddess or goddess representative of the tale. The apotheotic male hero learns that he is a part of a greater system of nature; thus, he will one day lose selfhood but will be continually renewed following nature's cycles, just like the mythic male consorts discussed in Chapter 3 of this book. Conversely, the apotheotic heroine learns that she *is herself* nature—and is thus a goddess, or more aptly is a representative of the goddess, just as her mother and grandmother was, and just as her daughter and granddaughter will be.

Because the apotheotic heroine along her journey learns that she is a goddess representative herself, her tales additionally often show her as now being responsible to become an educator to others about the wisdom of traditional goddesses, as myriad female characters did when educating male heroes in the first chapters of this book. Thus, the heroines of folktales and fairy tales often hold the sacred duty of bringing back the traditional goddess wisdom she gained upon her quest to the members of her family and community; this is why folktales and fairy tales often end with women returning to their families and their communities after their quests. Conversely, myths, folktales, and fairy tales of male heroes often end with them attaining the lesson of their quest, and then simply holding the wisdom within them. Therefore, the apotheotic heroine, often unlike the male hero, serves to challenge others to embark on their own heroic quests.

The apotheotic heroine's duty to educate others explains why so many heroines' quests, especially within folktales and fairy tales, involve female characters who openly serve as guides to initiatory heroines upon their new journeys. These female characters, who come in a variety of forms: grandmothers, mothers, stepmothers, witches, etc., have seemingly completed their own heroic quests and now serve to teach upcoming heroines the wisdom they must obtain upon their journeys. Whether female guides are portrayed in a positive light, like nurturing mothers and grandmothers, or as seemingly negative, like combative stepmothers or terrifying witches, they all serve to instruct female heroines upon their quests. This education from woman to woman, which often appears to be transferred to young girls or maidens from older women, secures the preservation of a long line of feminine power that is connected to traditional representations of goddesses around the world. In this way, the fictional female guides within myths, folktales, and fairy tales serve as educators to the real female audience members who listen closely to the messages the goddess representatives impart.

Interestingly, there are far more active heroines in folktales and fairy tales from around the world than there are in global mythology. As discussed, in the centuries following the degradation of myriad goddesses in many global cultures that adopted patriarchal ideologies, goddesses were either eliminated or so demoted and revised that they were hardly recognizable from versions of their former selves. Subsequently, women for hundreds of years lost powerful social, political, and religious roles and entered lives of inferiority and injustice, as has been discussed in the first five chapters of this book. However, as stated in the introduction of this book, folktales and fairy tales were often created, recited, and preserved by women within a community who often portrayed female characters who defied patriarchal restrictions and thus taught audiences about the messages of lost goddesses. For example, it was the intent of the Grimm brothers to collect Germany's old folktales in their pure form to see within them the preservation of "pagan beliefs" maintained through the oral tradition (Zipes, "Introduction," xxv). To gather these tales, the Grimm brothers depended upon mostly female storytellers whose collection of tales included many diverse and powerful female characters who carried with them ancient goddess-oriented concepts. This pattern of female storytellers preserving tales of powerful women that the Grimm brothers encountered when recording their tales was common in the recording of many folktales and fairy tales around the world (Warner 407); therefore, the legacy of these female storytellers is much like the legacy of the female characters within their respective folktales and fairy tales—teaching others transformational wisdom preserved for generations about the lessons of lost goddesses.

Heroines and Nature

Mythology does present some examples of the heroine's quest, though again there are fewer mythological quests than folktale and fairy tale quests involving heroines. In world mythology, when emerging heroines strive to realize their own connection to goddesses, they often must first learn to embrace the sacrality of nature.

For example, the American Indian Tlingit and Haida myth of Rhipsunt, Bear Mother ("Haida"), presents an example of a heroine learning the importance of the environment upon her heroic quest. In this myth, a maiden was picking berries with her friends when she disrespected the bears by cursing them out loud. This scene immediately signals that the maiden will have to learn to respect nature before she can heroically evolve. After her disrespectful utterance, the maiden found that she became separated from her friends and ended up spending the night alone in the wilderness. Again, this tenet of showing a character alone in the wilderness at the start of a quest is common, as was often seen in the male heroic quests discussed in the first chapters of this book. When males begin quests alone in the wilderness, it often signals that they will soon interact with a female goddess or goddess representative; however, for quests involving heroines, their immersion into wilderness environments at the start of their quests prepares them to understand their own goddess-like connections to the sacrality of nature.

While alone, entering into a state of panicked fear, another requirement of the heroic quest, which states that the hero or heroine must be placed in an atmosphere wholly different than that which they are used to so that they may grow past old identifications of selfhood, the maiden met a quest helper in the form of a handsome man. The man instantly reassured the maiden by telling her a lie that her parents sent him to retrieve her and take her to his village as his bride. The maiden was quite happy with this turn of events, so she followed the stranger to his village, which served as the otherworld stage of her quest, because she began to notice that the people of her new husband's village acted a lot like bears. For example, the people of the village would only wear bearskin robes, and they would spend day after day only fishing together. Three years passed with the maiden living with her husband's people, but one day she finally discovered, by defiantly breaking her husband's orders and spying on the private affairs of his family, that indeed the people she lived with, including her husband, were all bears. When the maiden discovered this, her husband reared up at her in full grizzly bear form, but the maiden showed him that she did not fear him but instead loved him despite his animalistic form. This moment marks an important psychological transformation on the part of the heroine, as it shows that she is growing beyond the young maiden who insulted bears, in her disrespect of nature, into a heroine who could fully love and merge with a bear. The myth continues to show the heroine's psychological evolution by portraying her as renouncing her old identity and choosing to live her remaining days with the bears. In time, she gave birth to two bear sons. The heroine's family, though, never stopped searching for her since the day she went missing, and one day they finally found her. Before they arrived, the myth states that the woman's bear husband knew that her people would soon find them and would soon kill him. The woman tried to keep this from happening, begging her husband to run away. However, the bear husband told his wife that he must allow the natural course of events to take place, as death in nature is required to ensure the survival of other beings. Therefore, the woman's people did come, and they did kill the heroine's bear husband before her eyes, thrusting her into the underworld stage of her heroic quest. However, before the heroine's bear husband died, he reminded his wife that death within nature's cycles is only temporary, and that he would assuredly be reborn one day as another natural element. The myth thus ends with the woman's apotheosis, which was signaled when she transformed from the nameless female protagonist into the sacred Rhipsunt, Bear Mother. Staying true to the heroine's quest, Rhipsunt and her bear sons then returned to her people, so that she could impart the wisdom of nature to them.

Apuleius's "Cupid and Psyche" within *The Golden Ass* (second century CE) portrays the mythic maiden Psyche as gaining immortality because of her realization that the wisdom of nature connects her to the wisdom of goddesses. In this myth, Psyche was to be sacrificed to a monster; however, when she met the monster, he was invisible and treated her kindly. Psyche was taken to the "monster's" opulent palace and quickly fell in love with him, seemingly because she suddenly obtained a life of extravagant materialism, signaling her disassociation with the natural environment. The myth continues to show Psyche as needing to evolve, so it presents to her a challenge that stated that she could continue with her life as it was if she never saw her husband. However, Psyche, like her many heroine counterparts, defiantly decided one night that she must break the restriction set upon her, which kept her from truly knowing her husband, so she lit a candle and stole a glimpse of his true form. Psyche found that her husband was not a monster, but was in fact the beautiful god of love Cupid. When Cupid saw that Psyche had broken her promise, he fled, so Psyche felt that she had no choice but to try and find him.

Psyche started her true heroine's quest when she left her opulent, yet psychologically and spiritually blind, life in Cupid's castle. Upon her journey, she found that she had to contend with an angry goddess, Venus, who was Cupid's mother, before she could earn her husband back. Venus invented tasks that were almost impossible for Psyche to overcome. This process of initiation by a female guide, who is often a goddess or goddess representative is common in quest stories, as was seen in myriad tales that featured male heroes; it shows that heroic quests are often created by female guides to help heroes and heroines grow. Most of the tasks that Venus invented for Psyche were heavily tied to elements involving nature. For instance, first Psyche had to separate a massive pile of seeds before morning. Initially, Psyche found this task impossible, and began to fear that there would be no way she could accomplish it by morning. However, Psyche found that she was helped by natural agents in the form of ants that came and separated the seeds for her in plenty of time. Again, as was shown in myriad quests of male heroes, showing animals as helping heroines upon their quests signifies that the heroine is open to receiving wisdom from the natural world, which is especially important for the spiritual evolution of a heroine. For her next challenge, Psyche had to get a piece of wool from golden sheep who threatened death with their bite, but again the natural agent of a reed spoke to Psyche and taught her how to overcome the task safely. Psyche's third trial involved retrieving black water from the River Styx and River Cocytus, both of which were connected to the underworld, but again a natural agent, an eagle, came and helped her. It is significant that the goddess Venus, a fertility goddess, invented tasks that forced Psyche to see that she was capable of uniting with the elements of the environment in order to succeed at what she believed was impossible. This lesson presents the divine Venus as teaching a mortal maiden about how to live as a goddess might live within a mythic narrative. Venus shows that no task is impossible for a goddess who values the power of nature, thus teaching Psyche that if she unites with the natural world, she too can become symbolically divine.

Finally, in order for Psyche to fully learn to become goddess-like, she still had to face the underworld stage of her quest. Therefore, Venus-made Psyche venture into the underworld in order to obtain part of the beauty of the goddess Proserpine. Psyche was helped on this challenge by a speaking tower that told her precisely how to achieve her task. Once having obtained part of Proserpine's beauty in a box, Psyche, like Pandora, could not resist opening it, which immediately sent her into a comatose sleep. The fact that Psyche at this point in her quest valued beauty, an element that fades with age, after her underworld experience suggests that she did not learn the true significance of what the underworld is meant to teach heroines, so she mythically had to be forced to experience a symbolic death through her comatose sleep in order to fully face the fact of her own mortality. Cupid eventually found Psyche in her comatose state and revived her, symbolically signaling that Psyche had finally become spiritually reborn after successfully completing her heroic quest. Further signaling this, the tale ends with Psyche obtaining immortality, indicating her apotheosis, which enabled her to be forever married to Cupid as his divine equal. Therefore, this mythic tale presents Psyche as gaining apotheosis after being systematically taught by Venus, who was traditionally revered as a goddess of nature and fertility as the Greek Aphrodite, how to connect with, and thus utilize, the resources of nature in order to realize her own connection to divinity, so that she finally could see herself as the equal match to the goddess's divine son.

Though myths exist that feature the heroine's quest, like that of Rhipsunt and Psyche, far more folktales and fairy tales involve stories of heroines who go on quests in order to realize the elements of the goddess, such as their deep connection with the natural environment, within themselves. For instance, the classic fairy tale "Little Red Riding Hood" presents a quintessential heroine's quest that teaches Little Red Riding Hood about her goddess-like authority within nature. Many versions of "Little Red Riding Hood" exist around the world, and Tatar believes that these tales might merely be cautionary stories meant to prepare young girls for the predatory aspects of both animals and men alike. However, there are arguably aspects in some of the versions of this tale that prove them to be less about caution as to what girls should avoid and more about what heroines should seek as they move away from childhood into adulthood.

In Perrault's version of "Little Red Riding Hood" (1697), Little Red was portrayed as naïve for trusting the wolf, and for this, explained by Perrault, she was punished, as the explicit moral states: "From this story one learns that children,/ Especially young girls,/ Pretty, well-bred, and genteel,/ Are wrong to listen to just anyone,/ And it's not at all strange,/ If a wolf ends up eating them…. Watch out if you haven't learned that the tame wolves/ Are the most dangerous of all" (qtd. in Tatar 17–8). However, the Grimms' version of "Little Red Cap" (1857) portrays Little Red as a heroine with more depth. Little Red initially trusted the wolf who approached her in the solitary wilderness and talked to it, though her mother instructed her to maintain her course and not stray. Therefore, Little Red upon reaching her grandmother's cottage, after the wolf arrived there and ate her grandmother, was also eaten. However, the Grimms allow Little Red to be saved by a huntsman who saw the evidence of what the wolf had done and cut open the wolf's stomach, freeing Little Red and her grandmother. Once freed, the tale does not end, as Little Red is shown to come up with an idea to fill the wolf's stomach with stones, which she proceeded to do, and ultimately killed the wolf herself. The fact that both Little Red and her grandmother symbolically die and are resurrected in this version of the tale, as well as the fact that Little Red, having been resurrected, goes on to possess the power herself to kill the wolf, suggests that there might be more to this tale than just one of caution against predators.

The Grimm brothers also provided an alternative version to this fairy tale, which showed Little Red as fully knowing the intentions of the wolf she encountered on the path, so in this version, she ignored the wolf and kept walking. In this version, Little Red arrived at her grandmother's cottage and told her about the wolf, and the grandmother, possessing the right wisdom to keep out a wolf, told Little Red to lock the door, so the wolf could not enter. Seeing that it could not enter the cottage, the wolf jumped on their roof to wait until Little Red emerged; however, the grandmother, instead of only being a silent character who simply gets eaten, again had the wisdom to come up with a plan to deal with the wolf. This time, the grandmother instructed Little Red to fill a bucket with the water in which sausages were boiled and then pour it into their trough. Little Red did as instructed by her grandmother, and the wolf indeed could not resist the enticing smell of sausages, so it fell into the trough from the roof and drowned.

This alternative version of the tale shows Little Red as being a brave and smart child as she partakes upon her heroic quest alone into the wilderness, again a quintessential aspect of the heroine's journey, as she knows not to trust the wolf. The fact that the wolf is an animal in the tale, a being from nature, who tests Little Red instead of just immediately eating her when they cross paths, suggests that the wolf serves to teach Little Red wisdom about her own capacities of judgement in connection to the environment, showing her to receive a similar education as that of Psyche by Venus. In addition, in both Grimm versions of the tale, Little Red furthers her quest when she confronts the underworld stage of her journey by coming face to face with death, presented through a wolf who wishes to come up with any means to kill both herself and her grandmother. Little Red especially faces the concept of her own mortality in the version where she experiences both death and resurrection. Little Red is also signaled in both Grimm versions of the tale as being guided upon her quest by the wise old woman archetype that often serves in the role of a goddess representative—her grandmother, in order to come out of her quest transformed. The tale, then, can be best understood as a coming-of-age heroic quest instead of just a cautionary tale to elicit fear of nature and of men within young girls. The fact that Little Red grows wiser because of her solitary expedition into the wilderness, her interaction with the predatory wolf, and the guidance of her grandmother to survive the elements in nature, suggests that young girls, like Little Red, must remember that, like traditional goddesses, they hold powerful and transformative abilities to connect with nature. Thus, the Grimm versions of this fairy tale end with the assurance that Little Red will grow into an apotheotic woman like that of her grandmother, who thrives alone in the wilderness.

A folktale from Korea entitled "The Tiger's Whisker" (Cole 558–60) also shows a woman becoming a heroine upon a quest that, with nature's help, enables her to realize her own goddess-like attributes. In this tale, a young wife named Yun Ok had a husband who came home from war struggling to reenter civilian life. Yun Ok knew that her husband was in need of healing, so she turned to a hermit who resided deep within the forest for help. However, the hermit did not offer to cure Yun Ok's husband; instead, he sent Yun Ok on a quest to get a whisker from a living tiger, as the hermit stated this would cure her husband.

Believing that the whisker of a tiger held magical properties, Yun Ok went into the isolated wilderness and began searching for the dwelling place of a tiger, thus initiating her heroine's quest within the quintessential element of the wilderness. In time, Yun Ok found a cave where a tiger lived, clearly a symbolic underworld, as a cave is a physical entrance to the interior of the earth, and a tiger could easily cause one's demise. Yun Ok worked to control her fear and placed food outside of the tiger's cave, calling to it to come and eat, while she scrambled to hide at a good distance away. The tiger, though, did not trust Yun Ok and did not eat the food she brought, signaling that Yun Ok had more to learn upon her quest. So, the next day Yun Ok brought different food for the tiger, but again the tiger did not trust her and never emerged. Days passed with Yun Ok trying to entice the tiger out of its cave, but it never emerged. Finally, Yun Ok decided to stop hiding and merely waited next to the food she offered. And sure enough, the tiger peeked out from the back of its cave at her. Fear instantly seized her, and she wanted to run, but she forced herself to remain where she was and stared directly at the tiger. Showing the heroic evolution of Yun Ok, as she finally was connecting with her environment, the next day, the tiger got up when Yun Ok arrived and walked toward her. Yun Ok again forced herself to hold her ground and began to speak softly and encouragingly to the tiger, holding out food for it. In response, the tiger walked right up to Yun Ok, and "after looking carefully into Yun Ok's eyes, the tiger ate the food" (Cole 559). Having united with the tiger after months of effort, Yun Ok proved that she had realized her own goddess-like abilities to respect and thus tap into the resources of nature, so she was able to come each day to visit the tiger, who waited for her outside of its cave, and feed it from her own hand. Finally, instead of stealing the tiger's whisker, as many male hero's might have done to achieve their heroic quests, Yun Ok instead asked the tiger for one of its whiskers by telling it about her husband's need. The fact that Yun Ok is portrayed as being able to converse with an animal further shows her realization of her own goddess-like abilities as a result of her heroic quest. The tiger consented and allowed Yun Ok to cut one of its whiskers off. Feeling as if she had successfully completed her quest, she ran at once to the hermit's abode with the tiger's whisker. However, the hermit only smiled at Yun Ok, and then took the tiger's whisker and threw it into the fire. Shocked and infuriated, Yun Ok asked why he did such a thing. The hermit then revealed the true intent of sending Yun Ok on her quest by stating that her time in nature allowed her to win the "confidence and love" of the tiger, just as she must realize that she possessed the ability to patiently gain the confidence of her husband back through her "kindness and understanding"; "'If you can win the love and confidence of a wild and bloodthirsty animal by gentleness and patience, surely you can do the same with your husband'" (Cole 560). Therefore, Yun Ok, because of her heroine's quest, was able to discard the belief that she had to turn to the male authority of the hermit instead of relying on her own devices to help her husband heal. Furthermore, because of her time immersed in nature, she attained apotheosis interacting with the tiger in a way that resembles mythic goddesses who can command wild beasts with ease. Tigers have long been regarded as sacred in Korea, even being connected to Korean deities, so the heroine's connection with the tiger of this tale solidifies her as attaining the heightened spirituality of a goddess.

A fairy tale from Norway entitled "East of the Sun and West of the Moon" (1914), recorded by Peter Christen Asbjørnsen and Jørgen Moe, also shows a heroine upon a quest to realize her own connection to nature. In this tale, a poor couple was visited by a white bear who asked to marry their daughter in exchange for considerable wealth. The tale's presentation of an animalistic husband signals that the heroine will enter upon a quest that will teach her about the wisdom of the natural environment. When the maiden married the white bear and moved into his home, she discovered that he transformed into a man at night; however, the maiden, like Psyche, was forbidden to ever see his human appearance; she could only feel it. The couple lived together happily for some time, until the woman became homesick. Before leaving to visit her home, the bear husband told his wife that she must never disclose the details of their relationship to anyone. However, once home, the woman broke her oath to her husband and told her mother about her husband's ability to metamorphose. The mother convinced her daughter that her happiness was flawed, stating that her husband's human form might actually be the form of a troll. Hearing this, the daughter mistrusted her own happiness with her husband. Like Psyche, when the woman returned home, she took a candle and looked at her husband while he slept and found that her husband was the most beautiful man she had ever gazed upon. However, when the woman broke her oath to her animalistic husband, he left her, stating that he was placed under a witch's spell that made him appear as a bear by day, and because she had broken her promise to him, he would have to go to the witch and marry her daughter, who lived east of the sun and west of the moon.

At this point in the fairy tale, the woman is shown not to be ready to stand as a goddess representative because she was portrayed as falling victim to the perceptions of society, presented through the role of her mother, instead of trusting her own happiness. However, in venturing to find her husband, the woman began her quest to become an actualized heroine. Her quest began again in a remote forest, which signals that she, like many heroines discussed in this chapter, will learn about her own connection to the environment in order to attain apotheosis, which was already suggested in the tale when she agreed to marry her animalistic husband. Along her journey, the woman gained help from an old woman who lived "in the midst of a thick, dark forest" (Asbjørnsen & Moe); this tenet of showing a younger heroine gaining help from an older woman, as discussed in the Little Red tales, is a quintessential component of many folktales and fairy tales involving heroines. The old woman of this tale knew, before the young woman spoke, the reason for her quest, signaling that the old woman held mystical abilities that connected her to remnants of goddess worship, like many other old wise women in folktales and fairy tales. The old woman instructed the young woman to continue her quest through the forest until she arrived at the old woman's neighbor, who was another old woman, in order to gain more help upon her quest. Before, the young woman left, though, the old woman gave her a gift of a golden apple to help her upon her journey. The same pattern continues in the tale two more times, with the second old woman giving the heroine a golden comb, and a third old woman giving her a golden spinning wheel. The gifts, which will prove supernaturally helpful to the heroine upon her quest, as well as the triad presentation of the old women of the forest assuredly connect the old women to representations of divinity.

The heroine continued her journey, until she came to the homes of the east wind, the west wind, the south wind, and finally the north wind, which blew her to the end of the world. The imagery of the heroine needing to journey to the literal four corners of the world in order to fully unite with her animalistic husband shows her as gaining intimate knowledge of the natural world upon her quest. Also, the fact that the heroine allows the north wind to thrust her up into the sky to send her to the edge of the known world signals that she has finally learned to fully trust the natural environment; something she was shown as unable to do at the start of her tale when she distrusted the form of her animalistic husband. The heroine thus made it to the destination she sought—east of the sun and west of the moon. Once there, the heroine perfectly used the magical gifts given to her by the old women of the forest in order to trick the witch's daughter, who was to marry her husband, into allowing her to be reunited with him. The fact that the heroine knew precisely how to use the magical gifts of the three old women shows that she has gained a mastery over the mystical wisdom they possess, presenting her own spiritual growth. When the heroine's husband returned to her, the tale makes it clear that their union was now secured because the heroine, by completing her quest to learn the ways of nature, had proven herself willing to fully unite with her animalistic husband. Thus, having literally journeyed to the heavens and back, symbolic of her psychological and spiritual death and resurrection, the tale ends showing the apotheotic heroine as becoming a goddess representative.

In a folktale from Spain entitled "The Water of Life" (Barchers 69–72), another young maiden proves herself a heroine because she learns to align herself with nature. This folktale begins with three brothers and their younger sister amassing a fortune for themselves and subsequently building a marvelous castle for them all to live in. However, one day an old man came to the castle, looked over its abundant wealth, and stated that though the castle was splendid, it still needed: "'a pitcher of the water of life, a branch of the tree … [with] flowers [that] give eternal beauty, and a talking bird'" (Barchers 69). The old man told the brothers where they would have to go to get the items, but before the old man departed, he left the young sister with a knife, telling her that as long as the blade remained clear, her brothers were fine, but if the blade turned the color of blood, it meant that evil had befallen them. Hearing this, the oldest brother left on his own heroic journey to find the nebulous items. After many days of searching the countryside alone, the oldest brother came to a giant and inquired if he knew where he could find the coveted items. The giant told the brother to walk up the mountain that was before him, while ignoring the cries of the rocks all around him. The brother did as he was told but found it impossible to ignore the cries of the rocks, so he paused to look at the phenomenon, causing him to be transformed into a rock himself. When the sister, back home, saw her knife turn the color of blood, she cried out that something was amiss, and the second brother declared that he would leave at once to save their brother and obtain the mysterious items. But again, the second brother, and then the third, met the same fate of metamorphosing into rocks.

Finally, left only to herself, the youngest sister partook on the very same quest her three brothers failed. The youngest sister left the safety of her known home, that contained her identity as meek and under the protection of her three older brothers, and ventured out into the unknown, where she too, like her brothers, encountered the same giant. However, the sister proved the only one who could heed his warning of not looking back at the rocks, even though she noticed that the voices of her brothers were among the cry of the rocks. This element within the tale is significant as it appears similar to many myths that recall a male hero attempting to retrieve a loved one from death, such as the Greek myth of Orpheus and Eurydice or many similar American Indian myths where males attempt to retrieve dead loved ones. In each of these myths, the male fails the quest by turning back to try and embrace the loved one, even though they are told that they can get the loved one back if they just obey the rule of resisting the proof of sight or touch. Therefore, this scene becomes the underworld stage of the heroine's quest within this folktale, as she hears her brothers crying as stones, symbolic of their death, but she is able to resist the temptation to look back at them, symbolically showing that she has accepted their deaths. By doing this, the maiden connects herself to many mythic goddesses who know well the requirement of death as part of nature's cycles.

The heroine was shown to continue her quest when she successfully scaled the mountain and made it to the pool of water that held the water of life. There, the heroine was able to contain some of the sacred water into a pitcher. She was also able to catch the talking bird, just as she was able to obtain a branch with flowers of everlasting beauty from the tree that grew by the pool of water. The heroine's ability to retrieve these items, which appear often in Iberian/Celtic mythology as sacred, shows her as possessing the ability to harness sacred elements within the environment, which again signals her as learning the ways of the goddess upon her quest. Additionally, when the heroine secured the water of life, she obtained the ability to resurrect not only her brothers, but all the people who were trapped as crying rocks. This ability to resurrect life from death shows that the heroine reached apotheosis and became a goddess representative herself. The folktale ends with the heroine taking the natural elements back to her family castle, where she planted the tree branch and watered it with the water of life, so that it grew another sacred tree to house the bird that she freed in its branches. These natural images of fertility and renewal clearly align the heroine with representations of traditional Iberian/Celtic goddesses and assure that she will now reign in her own castle, not as the dependent of her brothers, but as her own sovereign.

Heroines and Supernatural Wisdom

As discussed with the wise old shamanic and oracle women of Chapter 2, many cultures around the world believed that especially women, as directly aligned to powerful goddesses, were connected to the supernatural and mystical components of life. The ability of women to harness supernatural abilities similar to those performed by goddesses is an element discussed in many mythic narratives; therefore, it makes sense that myriad folktales and fairy tales also showcase women as possessing supernatural abilities. Thus, as was seen with the heroines who realized their connection to goddesses by understanding that power and wisdom comes in connecting with nature, many heroines of folktales and fairy tales also realize their connection to goddesses by learning to master supernatural abilities upon their heroic quests.

Perhaps one of the most well-known tales displaying a female heroine as partaking on a quest to obtain mystical knowledge comes in the Grimm brothers' fairy tale of "Rumpelstiltskin" (J. Grimm & W. Grimm 181–2). This tale has many variants, from "Tom Tit Tot" in England to "Whuppity Stoorie" in Scotland, and scholars believe that it, like many folktales, has ancient roots, as the tale's general format is believed to be over 4,000 years old (Anderson 144). The tale of "Rumpelstiltskin" shows the quintessential tenet of the spinner within folktales and fairy tales. Many tales include spinner characters, who are almost always women, as this was a domestic chore of many women, whose spinning abilities connect them to the fate of the characters within the tale. This connection of spinning and fate comes from depictions of mythic goddesses who are portrayed with these same attributes, such as the Greek Fates and the Norse Norns. Likewise, Davis-Kimball notes that the Sauro-Sarmatians also connected leading spiritual women with the act of spinning, as their grave goods often included "pseudo-spindle whorls, a puzzling item indeed as they were carved from chalk and therefore were too fragile to have functioned as an actual tool ... [; therefore, they] might have possessed a magical significance, perhaps along the line of the old fairy tale about spinning straw into gold" (Davis-Kimball 47). Thus, the tale of "Rumpelstiltskin" carries with it similar tenets that connect spinning with the attainment of mystical wisdom.

In "Rumpelstiltskin," a poor miller lied and told the king that his daughter was capable of spinning straw into gold. In addition to the theme of spinning in tales, the theme of gold objects or treasured items often carries symbolic meaning within many folktales and fairy tales, as often gold or treasure is possessed by guardians who hold important, often mystical, wisdom for the heroes and heroines they encounter. The king in this tale, like many folktales and fairy tales, represents a patriarchal governmental structure. The king immediately is portrayed as abusing his power by demanding that the miller's daughter be brought to him in order to exploit her mystical ability, which thrusts the maiden into her heroic quest. In fact, the patriarchal sentiment is so strong in this tale that the king threatened to kill the maiden if she was unable to spin a room full of straw into gold in a single night. The maiden was forlorn and fearful, as she was forced immediately to face her own mortality in the symbolic underworld stage of her heroine's quest. However, a mystical helper appeared to her in the form of a small man who said that he would spin the straw into gold for her, if she gave him her necklace. Trusting this mystical experience, the maiden at once gave the small man her necklace and found that he kept his promise by spinning all of the straw into gold. It is significant that the tale initially places the knowledge of spinning in the hands of a male; this suggests that the tale will right this wrong by educating the maiden of her own goddess-like power.

The next morning, the king, astonished at the growth of his wealth, became even more greedy and again stated that the maiden must spin all the straw in a larger room the next night into gold. Again, the little man came, and in return for the maiden's rings, he accomplished the mystical task for the maiden, so she would not fall victim to the king. The same event happened on a third night, only the room was larger, and this time, having no jewelry left to relinquish, the mystical little man asked the maiden to promise her firstborn child to him. Feeling that she had no other option, the maiden agreed, and the mystical man spun all the straw in the enormous room into gold. This time, when the king saw the enormity of his wealth, he married the maiden. At this point in the story, it is clear that the maiden is locked within what appears to be unavoidable patriarchy, where she is traded by her father, used by the king, and ill-treated by the mystical little man. Yet, the maiden, who is indeed on a heroic quest, does not remain trapped in this state.

When the maiden, now queen, had her first-born son, the little man indeed came to claim him. The queen begged the little man not to make her keep her dark promise, but he said that she must forfeit her son to him in three days, unless she could figure out his true name. The queen, instead of being a character who only represents passivity, as she was portrayed at the start of the tale when she merely waited for the king to kill her or the mystical man to save her, now becomes presented in the tale as a fully active and capable character. Instead of forfeiting her child to the mystical man, the queen immediately took it upon herself to learn the mystical man's name at all costs. Using the resources available to her as queen, she indeed learned the name of the mystical man—Rumpelstiltskin. Then, upon possessing this secret name, the queen proudly proclaimed it aloud to the mystical man, which immediately dispelled all of his power over her, forcing him to leave her and her son forever. In a similar myth from Egypt, the goddess Isis obtained the mystical wisdom of the god Ra, the head of the pantheon, when she tricked him into divulging his true name to her. This tenet of a true name holding mystical significance is a common element of many myths, folktales, and fairy tales. Lerner explains that in Mesopotamia "Naming had profound influence [as] naming revealed the essence of the bearer; it also carried magic power. The concept lives on throughout the millennia in myth and fairy tale. The person who can guess the name of another acquires power over him" (Lerner 151). Thus, when the queen in "Rumpelstiltskin" proclaimed out loud the mystical man's name, it showed that she had obtained his mystical wisdom, which in turn revealed that she had become more powerful than him, and in so doing, she had become a goddess representative who, in the powerful position of queen, now held the ability to control the supernatural.

The similar Scottish tale of "Whuppity Stoorie" (Ragan 29–31) includes more emphasis upon themes that connect the female protagonist of the tale with tenets of mythic goddesses. For instance, this tale shows the Goodwife of Kittlerumpit as being left by her husband and forced to raise her son with few resources. Her community was shown as refusing to help her, though they clearly saw how destitute she was. The Goodwife, though, remained positive, as she had a sow that could help her. The resourcefulness of the Goodwife helped her and her son survive, yet one day the sow they depended upon fell ill, and the Goodwife began to fear for their future. The Goodwife, in having to raise her son independently while facing starvation, had already begun a heroic quest, but when an old woman appeared to the Goodwife, "dressed in green ... [with] a black velvet hood, and a steeple-crowned hat," carrying "a walking-stick as long as herself in her hand" (Ragan 29), and identifying herself as a "Green Lady" (Ragan 29), the Goodwife began the stage of her quest that would allow her to learn of her own connection to supernatural wisdom. The portrayal of the old woman immediately identifies her as a remnant of a Celtic goddess, as often in Celtic mythology the divine Tuatha de Danann, or Fae, were identified as Green Ladies clad in grand garments that identified them as distinct from regular mortals. Further suggesting the old woman's divinity, she showed in the tale that she possessed magical foresight by stating that the Goodwife's sow was ill and would soon die. So, when the Green Lady presented the Goodwife with a proposition to save the sow if the Goodwife gave her anything she wanted, the Goodwife felt that she had to agree.

The Green Lady chanted a magic spell, which immediately healed the sow, explicitly showing her to be a goddess representative, but the old woman demanded that the Goodwife give her young son to her in return. The Green Lady gave the Goodwife three days to fulfill her part of the bargain, unless the Goodwife could figure out the old woman's true name. Again, learning the true name of a divine being mythically gives the power of the being to the one who discovers it; thus, when the Goodwife spied on the mystical woman, while she was in the act of spinning, which again portrays the Green Lady as a divine figure, she heard her sing out her true name. The Goodwife proudly articulated the name—Whuppity Stoorie—to the mystical woman, and thus showed that she had fulfilled her heroic quest by obtaining the goddess representative's mystical knowledge. The representation of the divine Whuppity Stoorie in this tale, more than "Rumpelstiltskin," makes it decisively clear that in learning the goddess's name, and thus achieving her mystical abilities, the Goodwife become connected to the goddess herself. Instead of just being identified as Goodwife, which connected her to the husband who left her, the tale ends with the assurance that the heroine, because of her possession of mystical knowledge, will now design her own prosperous fate.

In another Scottish folktale, entitled "Janet and Tam Lin" (Barchers 165–6), a girl named Janet also becomes a heroine when she learns to harness supernatural abilities. Janet is presented as being told by her parents never to venture into the forest alone, but as the forest so often is the precise place where females learn who they really are in connection to mythic goddesses, Janet disobeyed her parents and ventured alone into the wilderness. One day within the forest, she met a young man named Tam Lin, and the two became close friends. In time, Tam Lin revealed to Janet that he was under a spell by the fairy folk, as he was a mortal during the day, but at night he was forced into the domain of the fairies where he shapeshifted into a ferocious wolf. Tam Lin then told Janet that every seven years humans who were spellbound by fairies were sacrificed on Samhain Eve, which he told Janet was almost here. Resolved to break the fairy spell, and thus begin her heroic quest, Janet asked Tam Lin for any known advice on how to save him. He told her that there was only one way to save his life, but it would greatly test Janet, as the task was extremely dangerous. Tam Lin stated that Janet would have to wait for the fairy procession to pass on its way to the standing stones where the sacrifice was to take place;

she would then have to grab hold of Tam Lin, in his wolf form, which was not an easy task, and hold him tight for twenty-one heartbeats. If her love for him was true, he would be released from his spell and not be sacrificed. Hearing what needed to be done, Janet resolved to fulfill the task that would constitute her heroic quest.

On Samhain Eve, Janet waited alone in the wilderness near the standing stones, which was something no one in her community ever dared, as the people knew to close their homes up tight on Samhain Eve, the night that the fairies and spirits roamed among the living. Yet, Janet, in being willing to experience what no mortal dared, proved that she was worthy of obtaining the mystical knowledge of the divine fairies, as she saw the fairy procession arrive and saw Tam Lin dressed in a white robe between two druids dressed in black. This scene propels Janet into the underworld stage of her heroic quest, as she witnessed Tam Lin transform into a huge, ferocious wolf in front of her eyes. Though the sight was far worse than she ever imagined, Janet still ran up to the fairy procession and caught hold of Tam Lim. He bit and scratched her, but Janet held fast. The fairies then turned Tam Lin into a massive, slimy "wormlike creature" (Barchers 166), but still she held firm. Then Tam Lin metamorphosed into molten metal that burned her skin, and then the coldest metal she had ever held, but she refused to let go. Finally, twenty-one heartbeats passed, and Janet's love had proved true, as she heard the "fairies weeping and screeching," and then saw them disappear forever (Barchers 166).

Because Janet in this folktale proved herself capable of accomplishing the fairies' test, she gained their mystical wisdom, becoming like them as divine representations. The folktale presents the fairies as clearly demoted figures, who mostly create mischief and sinister acts, instead of as the once divine figures they were imagined as being in Celtic times. However, the explicit inclusion of such Celtic elements in connection to a female heroine suggests that they appear in this tale as reminiscent of a time when goddesses were worshipped, and women were believed to hold abilities especially in tune with the magic of goddesses. So, when Janet achieves abilities that supersede those of the fairies, the tale does not impart a message about how pagan elements are evil; instead, it sends a message that pagan elements must be dealt with only by formidable females who are capable of harnessing the divine magic of the fairies.

Heroines and the Underworld

Like the folktales and fairy tales discussed in this chapter that portray female protagonists as becoming heroines because they learn about the sacrality of nature or learn to perform mystical tasks, both of which connect them to the goddesses of mythic narratives, so too do many mythic, folkloric, and fairy tale heroines reach goddess-like apotheosis because of their heightened experience within underworlds that teach them to embrace the primary lesson of many goddesses from around the world—that of life, death, and rebirth.

For example, many myths involving goddesses focus especially on their journey to learn about the significance of the underworld. One prime example can be found in the Greek myth, discussed in Chapter 3 of this book, that portrays the goddess Persephone going upon a heroic quest to learn about life, death, and rebirth when she was abducted by Hades and forced to become the goddess of the underworld through marriage to him. After facing death, an element not faced by many divine, immortal beings, Persephone was able to learn about resurrection when her mother, the goddess Demeter, demanded Persephone's annual rebirth, which enabled Persephone to become an actualized heroine as the goddess of spring and renewal. Also, the Akkadian myth of "Ishtar's Descent to the Underworld" shows Ishtar going on a similar quest as Persephone's to learn about the reality of death and rebirth by her sister Ereshkigal. Likewise, the Chinese myth of the goddess Guan Yin, also discussed briefly in Chapter 3 of this book, presents her as a maiden whose divinity is revealed by her education of the natural processes of life, death, and rebirth. As discussed, Guan Yin is mythically portrayed as a maiden who was desired by all the men of her village, but Guan Yin refused to marry anyone and instead became a Buddhist nun. Because of her defiance, Guan Yin's father killed Guan Yin for her resistance to his wishes. It is the portrayal of Guan Yin's experience in death that shows why Guan Yin moves in the myth from a representation of a maiden to that of a goddess, or as she is sometimes portrayed a bodhisattva. The myth shows that when Guan Yin descended into the underworld, the opposite of what was expected happened—Guan Yin's presence caused the elements of the underworld, which are most often associated with death, to transform into elements of life. Allan & Phillips state that Guan Yin thus performed the impossible by transforming the world of the dead into "a veritable Paradise" (Allan & Phillips 125). Guan Yin's ability to transform the underworld into a place of vibrant life instead of death shows that she reached a heightened spiritual state that allowed her to see the underworld for what it truly was—a place that harbored the dead to initiate rebirth. Guan Yin's apotheosis, and subsequent portrayal in her myth as a goddess, or enlightened bodhisattva, is further articulated when she left the underworld and resurrected herself, reclaiming her body. After Guan Yin's experience with the lessons of life, death, and rebirth, she became known and revered as the Merciful Mother in China, a divinity/

bodhisattva who, even to this day, the people turn to when they are in need of compassion and strength.

Folktales and fairy tales likewise show female protagonists who go on heroic quests and become heroines when they endure a heightened underworld experience that teaches them about the necessity of nature's cycles of life, death, and rebirth.

For instance, in a folktale from Cameroon entitled "Mbango and the Whirlpool" (Don 52–60) a girl name Mbango went on a journey to the underworld and became a goddess-like heroine because of the knowledge she learned there. Mbango's mother died when she was young, so she was raised by her aunt, whom she feared. Mbango's aunt had a daughter she prized, but she treated Mbango unfairly. One day while Mbango was getting water at the river, she accidently dropped her calabash in the water, and it quickly floated away. Mbango chased it downriver but was horrified to see that the calabash was swept into a whirlpool and disappeared. Fearing the wrath of her aunt, Mbango dove into the whirlpool to try and get her calabash back, but instead of being immersed in water, Mbango found that she had entered a village. Once in this underworld, Mbango found an old woman holding her calabash. The presentation of an old woman within the underworld immediately signals her as a goddess remnant, as powerful goddesses were envisioned as being in connection to the underworld throughout Cameroon and West Africa. The old woman set forth many tasks for Mbango to accomplish before she could fulfill her quest within the underworld. She requested that Mbango fix her roof, patch her walls, clean her pig pens and hut for her, and Mbango gladly did all of these tasks for the old woman (Don 56). At the end of the day, the old woman further tested Mbango by putting a plate of pig dung in front of her to see if she would gratefully accept and eat it. Mbango initially was filled with disgust and almost turned it down, but as she looked into the eyes of the old woman, she remembered the horrible things she forced herself to do for her aunt, whom she hated, so out of respect for the old woman, she resolved to eat the dung. But when Mbango brought the feces to her mouth, she miraculously found that the dung transformed into sumptuous food. Mbango then gratefully ate everything on her plate to the delight of the old woman. This scene is similar to the Japanese myth of Tsukuyomi, the moon god, and Ukemochi, the food goddess. In the Japanese myth, Tsukuyomi did not understand nature's requirements to provide food for the people, so when he saw that the goddess Ukemochi produced food from her own body, he found it disgusting and killed the goddess. In this similar folkloric scene, the old woman taught Mbango, while pointedly within the underworld, the process required for the procurement of food, as feces provides the needed fertilizer to produce the food living beings depend upon. So, when Mbango ate the food of the underworld goddess representative, she became a heroine who learned, in her time in the underworld, about the goddess's lessons of cyclical life, thus enabling her to emerge, resurrected, from the underworld as a goddess representative herself. Mbango's goddess-like apotheosis is further made clear in the tale when she returned to her village and opened three eggs the old woman gave her within the underworld; the eggs, again a symbol of rebirth, provided Mbango with considerable wealth to live out the remainder of her life, free from the confinement of her stepmother or anyone.

A folktale from Kenya (Ragan 203–4) additionally shows a girl named Marwe who reached apotheosis through her experience in the underworld. In this tale, Marwe feared that she let down her family, so she drowned herself. However, when Marwe descended into the underworld, that was portrayed at the bottom of the lake she drowned herself in, she found that she was, like the previous tale of Mbango, greeted by a kind old woman. Marwe found that the underworld was not at all how she expected it to be, as it was not a fearful place full of the dead but was instead filled with young children who were cared for by the old woman in an atmosphere of love. Again, this tale signals the wise old woman character as a goddess representation, as this woman within the underworld is clearly portrayed in terms that show her as caring for the dead until they are ready to be reborn, making the underworld of this tale convey womb-like imagery. As Marwe spent time in the underworld, she too felt loved by the old woman. But, in time, Marwe wished to leave the underworld to resume living life upon earth. Thus, the old woman encouraged Marwe to continue upon her quest, back to life.

To be reborn, Marwe dipped herself into cold water, as instructed by the old woman, and found that she had reentered her life on earth. The simplicity of Marwe just reentering life when she and the old woman felt she was ready further conveys the tale's message of the cyclical nature of life. When Marwe was reborn, she saw that her body was covered in jewels, as a gift from the old woman of the underworld. The jewels that adorned Marwe signaled her apotheosis, as the tale presents her as being reborn into her former identity, just now covered in jewels to symbolize her as spiritually transformed because of the wisdom she learned about life, death, and rebirth while in the underworld. When the men of her village saw Marwe this way, they all wanted to marry her, as she appeared divine to them, but Marwe chose to marry a man named Sawoye who suffered from a severe skin disease. Marwe was able to heal Sawoye, which again signals her goddess-like transformation after her time in the underworld. Marwe and Sawoye lived happily for many years, but the men of Marwe's community killed Sawoye because of their jealousy. So, Marwe performed the supernatural task that is repeatedly shown in many myths to be the greatest ability goddesses possess—resurrection. Just as the Egyptian goddess Isis mythically resurrected her dead husband Osiris, Marwe too, as a folkloric figure, resurrected Sawoye. Thus, in performing this monumental act of resurrection, and proving her full understanding of the laws of life, death, and rebirth, Marwe is presented as having become fully goddess-like because of her quest to the underworld.

In a folktale from the Kewa people of New Guinea (Ragan 296–8), a young girl also becomes a goddess-like heroine because of her experience in the underworld. The tale opens with a young brother and sister living alone together in poverty, with a pig as their only worthwhile possession. One day, an old man came to their home and demanded to marry the sister, and though the brother tried to delay such an unfavorable union, the two siblings knew that they were in no position to resist. The brother suggested to the sister that before the old man came back to claim her, they should kill their pig and cook it, so that the sister could take the meat with her, should she need it. The brother and sister also put a bush knife, an axe, and a bundle of glowing embers in a bag for her to take with her. And indeed, the items she packed helped the sister survive, as when the old man came for her, he led her down a path and demanded that she wait for him while he went back to her home. When the sister saw the old man return for her, she knew that he had killed her brother, so she realized that she was in great danger. In a short while, the old man pushed the sister into a well and left her to either wait for him to return or die. However, the girl, who at the start of the tale was portrayed at the mercy of patriarchal control, saw something in the well that transformed her upon this quest she had forcibly undertaken.

The girl saw that the well was filled with other girls like herself. She found, though, that the girls, who were also thrown in by the old man, were in different states of distress, as some of them were injured; most were starving, and some were dead. The sister remained calm however in this symbolic underworld and moved to create order by opening her bag and cutting wood to start a fire with the embers she brought. She ordered the able-bodied girls to help the injured girls to get close to the fire, so they could warm themselves. The sister also began feeding the starving girls with the pig meat she brought, and soon the sister was surrounded by many healthy girls. The sister discussed the girls' options with them, and they all came up with a plan to seek revenge upon the old man, and thus obtain their freedom. The symbolism of this underworld scene shows the role that female characters in folktales and fairy tales often play in connection to the underworld. Male heroes are often taught in the underworld stage of their quests that they must shed their preconceived notions of power and superiority and accept their own mortality. However, female characters in folktales and fairy tales often intuitively know about the underworld; they often skip the male heroic lesson about accepting the fact of their impending mortality, and instead convey a message about the rebirth that comes from death. This is certainly true in this folktale, as it shows the sister quite at home in this symbolic underworld, as she simply accepted, without fear, the dead girls who did not survive and cared for the girls who were still alive within the well. The capable ministrations of the sister within this underworld stage of her quest shows that she is discovering her own autonomy, as at the start of the tale she succumbed to an unacceptable life just because society deemed it appropriate for her to marry a strange, old man because she was poor and alone, just as it demanded of the other girls within the well.

The underworld girls within the well are shown to unite in order to take their own fate in their hands, thus revealing not only the initial protagonist of the tale as a heroine, but all of the girls who experienced the underworld as heroines. To leave the underworld, the heroines built a ladder; the fact that the girls just had to realize that they possessed within themselves the ability to free themselves by simply building a ladder shows that they have matured into women. This idea is elaborated when the tale next shows the now mature women leaving the underworld, entering a nearby community, and gaining the attention of the local young men who were shocked to see so many young women fill their community. Like many folktales and fairy tales, this tale shows that the heroines will continue the cycles of life by a promise of fertility, as many folktale and fairy tale heroines end their stories with promises of marriage that will presumably initiate the process of birth. This often has been interpreted as the only purpose for the life of domesticated women within folktales and fairy tales, but when viewed in terms of goddess worship, this stage of the maiden becoming a mother can be seen as a realization of the power of an autonomous woman's place within the cycles of nature. Therefore, when the heroines in this tale decide to marry, thus symbolizing reproduction, they become apotheotic, goddess-like symbols of the cycles of life, as they have proven their understanding of the importance of life, death, and rebirth within goddess ideologies. Before the women in this tale married though, they again showed themselves as representations of goddesses when they unleashed death to the old man who entrapped them. The collective group of women found, captured, and killed the old man; they then cut up his body in front of the community. This act of unleashing death and cutting up the corpse is an old theme in many mythic narratives involving goddesses to display an explicit example of the necessity of death to initiate nature's cycle of rebirth, as discussed in Chapter 3 of this book. Thus, the fact that the spiritually reborn heroines commit this act in front of their new community reveals the goddess-like power they will command as wives, mothers, and as members of their community. To solidify the community's acknowledgment of this, the tale ends with them honoring the goddess-like women with a great feast.

A Slavic folktale (Phillips & Kerrigan 97–9) also displays a female heroine who undergoes a heroic journey into a symbolic underworld to discover the lessons of goddess ideology. The tale shows a young maiden named Maruisa who was desired by all the eligible men in her village, but she did not return their feelings. However, one day, a stranger entered her village, and Maruisa immediately fell in love with him, so she promised to wed the stranger. When Maruisa told her mother about her intentions, her mother, proving to be a wise counselor, as mothers often are in folktales that present heroines upon quests, told Maruisa to tie a ball of thread to the stranger and follow it to see where he went at night. Maruisa did so and found that her betrothed went to the local church at night, but when she looked in the church window, she saw, to her horror, that he fed off the dead body of a recently deceased parishioner. Maruisa immediately turned to run, but the stranger saw her flee. When Maruisa came home, she remained hidden for some time, but finally feeling it to be safe, she went to meet her friends; however, Maruisa was again horrified to see that the strange man was there. He approached Maruisa and asked her if she saw him the night before, but she denied it, so he told her that her father would have to die the next day because she lied to him. And, indeed her father did die the next day. The same event unfolded days later when Maruisa saw the stranger once more, and again when he asked her to tell him the truth, she denied it, so he told her that her mother would die the next day, which also happened. Days later, while mourning both of her parents, Maruisa was horrified to see the man she once loved again, and this time he asked her his same question, and again Maruisa lied to him, causing him to say that it would now be her turn to die the next day. Certainly, the tale thus far shows Maruisa as being forced, repeatedly, to face the necessary element of death that is a part of the underworld stage of the heroine's journey, as the mysterious man, who fed off of the dead, caused the death of her parents, and threatened Maruisa's own life, undoubtedly is shown to be a supernatural agent of death.

Distraught, Maruisa sought advice from her grandmother. This scene is important, as it portrays the grandmother in the folkloric wise old woman role shown in Chapter 2 of this book, as she knew exactly what to do to guide her young granddaughter on what begins to appear in the tale to be Maruisa's rite of passage from childhood into womanhood, as many quests of folklore and fairy tale heroines are. The grandmother instructed

Maruisa to face her death, but to also tell the village priest to dig a hole under Maruisa's doorway, so that Maruisa's coffin, along with those of her two parents, could be slid through the hole, and thus not cross the household's threshold. The grandmother then told Maruisa to demand that the priest bury her and her parents at a crossroads. Following this advice, Maruisa indeed went home alone and prepared herself for death; "She had a third coffin brought to the house and laid down in it voluntarily. That evening she passed away" (Phillips and Kerrigan 98). In physically dying, Maruisa is thrust deeper into the underworld stage of her heroic quest. The priest handled Maruisa's corpse according to the grandmother's instructions, which is telling, since the grandmother is portrayed as possessing pagan wisdom that supersedes the wisdom of the priest who is supposed to be the spiritual center of the community.

A flower grew where the corpse of Maruisa was buried, and following another folkloric trope discussed with tales of maidens and young men in Chapter 3 of this book, a handsome nobleman saw the flower and immediately desired it, so he plucked it and took it home with him, replanting it in a pot at his compound. However, this flower was no ordinary flower, as each night it transformed into Maruisa. The fact that Maruisa died and reincarnated as a flower, which could shapeshift back into her human form, shows her as evolving upon her heroic quest, as she is portrayed as connected to representations of Slavic goddesses who could also metamorphose. Eventually, the nobleman saw the flower transform into Maruisa, and immediately he asked her to marry him, and Maruisa at once agreed, which is the second time in the tale she rashly made this decision. However, presenting Maruisa as getting wiser upon her quest, after her symbolic death and reincarnation, she told the nobleman that she would marry him only if he promised to not make her attend church. This scene suggests a shift in belief systems, as the wisdom that Maruisa obtained upon her quest—wisdom that came to her from her grandmother, as again it was her grandmother and not the priest who possessed the knowledge to save her life, as well as the wisdom from her own experience with death and reincarnation/resurrection—is decidedly pagan and therefore likely not tolerated by the Christian church. Thus, Maruisa's declaration that she did not want to go to church perhaps suggests that her wisdom comes from Slavic beliefs that predate Christianity. The nobleman agreed to Maruisa's demand, so they were married. Once married, Maruisa forever shed her flower form and maintained her human form, signaling her as gaining mastery over the skills associated with Slavic goddesses. The marriage seemed happy, and in time Maruisa had a son; however, giving in to the pressure of the community, Maruisa's husband one day demanded that Maruisa accompany him to church. Feeling that she must obey him,

Maruisa reluctantly went to the Christian church, which shows that she, though having intimately learned about the underworld upon her quest, as well as Slavic concepts of rebirth, still had not achieved full goddess-like apotheosis.

When Maruisa went to church, she again saw her former betrothed there, waiting for her, showing that he served as an agent meant to compel her to finally reach apotheosis. The mystical man, who symbolizes death, again asked Maruisa his same question, and she again lied to him, so he told her that the next day her husband and son would die. Because Maruisa continually lied to the embodiment of death in the tale, shows that, even having experienced death and resurrection herself, she still did not learn the goddess-oriented lesson that reveals death in nature to only be a temporary state needed to initiate rebirth. To seek a means to escape the worst experience she could imagine, Maruisa once more went to her grandmother for advice, which again signals that she has not yet fully learned the goddess-oriented wisdom her grandmother possesses. The grandmother told Maruisa that she would have to face her worst fear, as there was no way to evade the deaths of her husband and son. However, the grandmother also told her granddaughter how to bring both her husband and son back to life. The grandmother gave Maruisa two vials of water, "one containing Holy Water and the other the Water of Life" (Phillips & Kerrigan 99). This scene shows again pagan belief systems alongside Christian beliefs, as it connects the Christian idea of Holy Water to the pagan Slavic belief in the Water of Life.

To ultimately teach Maruisa the pagan lesson that death is only a temporary state to initiate rebirth within nature, she was thrust into the full force of the underworld when she had to face the death of those she held most dear. After the deaths of her husband and son, the mystical stranger again approached Maruisa and asked her if she saw him in the church that fateful night. This time, the tale shows Maruisa as finally facing her fear and misunderstanding of death when she at last told the truth to the mystical man and acknowledged that she indeed saw him in the church mystically eating the dead. The fact that Maruisa finally admitted that she saw the mystical man, which the tale suggests is a vampire, in a church, where a vampire should not be able to go, is telling. Vampires have been a part of Slavic belief systems since pagan times, and because the vampire man within this tale is presented as being able to enter and remain for years within a Christian church suggests a view by the people who created this folktale that the church is often incapable of handling mystical components that predate its existence. Many Slavic folk beliefs and customs, for instance, survived after the coming of Christianity, even though they were outwardly condemned by the church. Once Maruisa finally accepted the role of death within nature's cycles, and was additionally able to acknowledge that pagan wisdom may supersede aspects of Christian ideology, as she was portrayed as not fully committing to when she allowed her husband to make her go to church against her will, the tale finally shows her as securing a more traditional knowledge that is connected to the wisdom her grandmother possesses—the wisdom of the old Slavic goddesses, signaling her apotheosis.

It is at this moment of Maruisa's apotheosis that she is portrayed as now being fully in command of the supernatural items her grandmother gave her, as the tale shows her as first sprinkling the Holy Water on the vampire, performing a task usually bestowed to a priest. The Holy Water causes the vampire to turn to dust. The fact that Maruisa, a female maiden who under Christian doctrine would not be viewed as a spiritual authority, could successfully harness the power attributed to male leaders of Christianity shows that she finally fully became an agent of goddess ideology. To reiterate this point, the tale next shows a fully apotheotic Maruisa becoming a representation of a Slavic goddess when she takes the pagan Water of Life and uses her newfound supernatural abilities to sprinkle this water on her husband and son, successfully resurrecting them. This extraordinary mystical act, that was performed by Marwe and the maiden in the folktale from Spain, as well as by myriad mythic goddesses, solidifies that Maruisa, because of her long underworld experience with an agent of death, ultimately stepped into the ancient role of the goddess, just like her grandmother.

In showcasing heroines as becoming like the goddesses of mythic narratives because they took part in quests that taught them about the sacrality of nature, gave them supernatural abilities, and educated them on the lessons of life, death, and rebirth as found in the underworld, audiences are educated about bygone religious components that can encourage all women to become more like the goddesses of old. In folktales and fairy tales that feature mothers and stepmothers, quests involving predominantly female heroines continue, but these additional tales focus on the decisive network of women within the lives of young heroines who hold a responsibility to shape them upon their quests into goddess representatives like themselves.

7

Mothers and Stepmothers

Mothers

Many divine mothers in mythology appear similar to real mothers, acting as protectors, educators, promoters, caregivers, etc. For instance, the Greek goddess Rhea protected her son Zeus from his father Cronus; the Indian Parvati threatened all existence until her son Ganesh was healed; the Celtic Rhiannon humiliated herself when she believed she harmed her infant son; and the Egyptian Isis admonished her son Horus and then took on the full force of his anger. Mythic divine mothers are also often portrayed as guiding their sons upon their heroic quests. For example, the divine Thetis consistently guided her son Achilles throughout his heroic quest, as she attempted to convince him to relinquish battle and instead live a simple life. Likewise, the Roman hero Aeneas was also helped by his mother, the goddess Aphrodite/Venus, on every step of his heroic quest to found Rome.

Similarly, many folktales and fairy tales continue the theme of showing mothers aiding sons upon heroic quests. For instance, one folktale from China, "The Magic Brocade" (Cole 539–44), shows a mother, whose mystical ability to weave brocades of natural elements that looked as if they were real, set in motion heroic quests that were meant to test her three sons. The woman in the folktale was a widow, who lived with her sons in a small community that struggled to survive, as the environment was consistently in a state of barrenness. The mother's skill at weaving, though, provided enough income for her to care for her three sons, as she was quite renowned for her abilities. One day, the mother and her sons were selling her brocades in town, when she noticed another vendor selling a painting of an idyllic house surrounded by abundant nature. The widow could only stare at the painting that actualized her innermost dream, but her two elder sons only laughed at their mother's dream. The mother's youngest son, however, told her to weave the picture into a brocade, and for unknown reasons, this suggestion felt exactly right to the mother. The mother went home and began her creation at once, but she soon became entirely consumed with the act. The mother would weave late into the night, even after her body ached with the endeavor. In fact, she did little else for months, so that in time, the family had no brocades to sell. The elder sons complained to their mother to stop her obsessive weaving of a single brocade, but her youngest son again supported her by simply walking into the mountains each day to cut enough wood to sell to keep the family fed.

A year passed this way, and still the mother wove her brocade that seemed to bring her dream to life. She worked so many hours, sometimes in so much pain that tears fell from her eyes, but she only wove the tears into the brocade, turning them into a river within the pattern. In time, the mother worked so hard that her tears turned to blood, and still she wove the blood into the pattern, allowing the blood to become a "flaming sun and brilliant red flowers" (Cole 540). Finally, after three years, the mother was done with her brocade, and as she gazed at it with its portrayal of the splendid small home that was surrounded by vast and fertile nature, she felt at peace. However, a great wind blew in and stole the brocade, taking it far out of her sight. The mother fainted in despair, and when her sons were able to revive her, she begged her eldest son to go to the east in search of her brocade, as she announced that it meant more to her than her life (Cole 541). The eldest son set out at once, alone, into the wilderness, again a quintessential requirement for a hero, where after a month of searching, he came upon an old woman who lived in a stone house deep in the forest, which signaled that he would be tested by yet another wise old woman of the forest. Next to the old woman was a stone horse. The woman stopped the eldest son and asked him the purpose of his quest, and upon telling her, the old woman told him that she knew exactly where his mother's brocade was; in fact, she said that it was carried away by the "fairies of the Sun Mountain because it was so beautifully made," and they wanted to copy it (Cole 541). Hearing this, the eldest son was determined to continue his quest, but the old woman told him his journey would be very difficult. As many old women in folktales do upon the quests of males, she instructed the eldest son how to be successful. She told him that he would have to knock out his two front teeth and stick them in the mouth of her stone horse; then, the horse would be able to eat the fruit that hung from the tree in her yard. Once the horse ate this fruit, it would take the eldest son to Sun Mountain, but the old woman warned the boy that he must not ever utter a complaint as he approached the sun, or he would be burned to ashes. Once past the sun, the old woman also warned the eldest son that he must not shiver while crossing the icy sea, or he would immediately fall into the water and drown. The old woman then looked closely at the reaction of the boy, who paled in fear. She laughed at him and stated that she could tell that he would never complete the quest successfully, so she told him to go home with a gift of gold from her and live out his life contentedly. Hearing this, the boy readily took the gold and fled, but he did not go home, as he did not wish to share his newfound wealth with his family.

The mother waited for months and grew quite ill as she longed for her brocade. She begged her second son to go on the same quest toward the east to get her brocade back. At this point, it becomes clear, through the format of the tale's plot, that the mother was orchestrating the quests to test her sons' worthiness, as often mothers in folktales and fairy tales, whether they are alive or dead, initiate or urge their children upon quests to help them fulfill the rite of passage from youth to maturity. Therefore, the second son, to appease his mother, left at once and traced the route of his older brother. But, again, the same events came to pass, and when the old woman offered the gold to the second son, he also took it and left forever.

Finally, the youngest son was asked by his mother to partake on the same quest his brothers failed. The youngest son traced the journey his brothers took, but this time when the old woman told him about the quest requirements to get to Sun Mountain, the youngest son immediately knocked out his two front teeth without a second thought, put them into the mouth of the stone horse, and took off on the transformed horse toward Sun Mountain. After a treacherous journey, that indeed involved all the tasks the old woman promised, the youngest son proved that he had what it took to make it successfully there. The quest tenets thus far certainly meet the requirements of the heroic quest, as the youngest son had to leave his known life for otherworldly realms that held a helper in the form of the archetypical old wise woman. The risk of death upon his journey to get to Sun Mountain also signaled his meeting the requirement of the underworld stage of his quest. Once at Sun Mountain, the youngest son saw a palace surrounded by splendid nature. He immediately knocked on the door of the palace and was greeted by the fairies, who stated that they were quite in love with his mother's brocade, so they were attempting to copy it, but needed one more night to finish. The youngest son agreed to wait until they were done, and as he waited, he was treated according to the customs of the otherworld, as discussed in Chapter 3 of this book, as the fairies gave him all the food and drink he desired. When the fairies finished their copy of the brocade, they were saddened to see that they could not perfectly replicate the beauty of the widow's brocade, so one of the fairies decided to weave herself into the brocade, so that she could always experience "that beautiful human world" (Cole 543). At this, the youngest son took his mother's brocade and rode the magic horse back to the old woman.

The old woman congratulated the youngest son, took her horse back and transformed it again into stone, and then gave the young man a pair of deerskin shoes to help him finish his quest. The young man put on the shoes and found that they too were magic, as they carried him quickly home. Once home, the youngest son gave the brocade to his mother, who was instantly healed of her illness. Showing the mother as healed by her son at the end of his quest signals that he attained apotheosis, as he learned the lesson that his mother intended for him. Mother and son then stepped outside with the brocade and unrolled it, and as they unrolled it, the son saw that it began to spread out, until it covered their surroundings: "Suddenly the silken threads trembled and the picture burst into life. Scarlet flowers waved in the soft wind.... Golden birds darted ... about the grand white house.... It was all exactly as the mother had woven it, except that now there was a beautiful girl in red standing by the fishpond. It was the fairy who had embroidered herself into the brocade" (Cole 544). Thus, the youngest son married the fairy maiden, and the mother invited all of their poor neighbors to live on the renewed land and farm the fertile fields that now existed to benefit everyone.

This folktale shows that the landscape, at the start of the tale, was in a state of barrenness, but because of the vision and mystical effort of the mother, she was able to create a renewed environment, much like a goddess of Chinese mythology would be able to do. Thus, the mother of this tale is shown to be goddess-like in her ability to transform the land and interact with fairies, but instead of just focusing upon the divine skills of the mother, the true intent of the tale is to show the mother as the initiator of quests meant to challenge all of her three sons. The youngest son, the only one to complete his mother's quest, was thus able to reap the benefits of his goddess-like mother, living in an otherworldly environment full of resources with a fairy bride.

There are also many folktales and fairy tales from around the world that portray mothers who serve to guide their heroine daughters upon their quests. Mothers in folktales and fairy tales are particularly adept at showing their daughters how to remain strong, wise, and formidable upon their heroic quests, as well as in their lives after their quests, because they are implicitly portrayed as having already undertaken quests of their own. Furthermore, mothers in folktales and fairy tales often teach daughters lessons connected to the traditional goddess worship of many cultures, such as the three primary elements discussed in Chapter 6 of this book: the reverence of nature, the ability to perform mystical acts, and the secrets of life, death, and rebirth.

For example, many folktales and fairy tales involving mothers and daughters show the mother as educating the daughter about wisdom connected to nature. Sometimes, the mother is portrayed as the heroine's actual mother, and sometimes she is presented as a natural element. For instance, many folktales and fairy tales portray a mother who has been transformed or reincarnated into a natural element that still guides her daughter upon her quest. Also, many tales present nature in general as serving in a maternal role to guide a heroine, as animals or other natural elements are often portrayed as maternal nurturers and/or guides to folkloric and fairy tale heroines. For instance, the Salish of the Pacific Northwest embrace a tale about a young girl who became lost from her mother in the wilderness but was rescued by a kind woman who came across the child's path. Trusting the woman, the young girl followed her home. However, the child found that the woman's home was a cave, and within the cave was a mother bear with her cubs. The child then realized that the woman was in actuality the mother bear. The young girl, though, had come to trust the bear woman, so she lived with her bear family in what became her quest to learn the wisdom of the bears. In adulthood, the heroine of the tale went back to her people and passed on the wisdom of her quest to them, so that they adopted the bear as their sacred totem.

Additionally, mothers who aid heroines in folktales and fairy tales often "possess ... superhuman traits" (Birkhäuser-Oeri 13) and impart this mystical knowledge to their daughters upon their quests. Folktale and fairy tale mothers often are capable of accomplishing mystical tasks themselves, such as transforming the environment or seeing into the future. Thus, these supernatural mothers pass down these mystical skills in quests they design for their daughters.

Finally, mothers often aid daughters upon quests to discover the most spiritual of tenets embraced by many goddess religions—the promise of life, death, and rebirth. Sometimes the mother teaches this lesson through helping her daughter accomplish an underworld journey, and other times the mother teaches it through her own death and rebirth.

Therefore, because mothers often serve as guides to their daughters upon their heroic quests, the mothers meet one of the most important requirements of the heroine's quest—the passing on of the goddess-oriented wisdom they once learned upon their own quests to others. The heroine then, after reaching apotheosis, must act like her mother, and one day move on to become an educator to her own daughter, or other young maidens in her community, about the goddess-oriented wisdom she obtained upon her heroic quest. Thus, the heroine who obtains apotheosis upon her quest gains a goddess-oriented wisdom that was embraced by her mother, grandmother, and great grandmother. In this way, the heroine becomes a symbol of a very old concept within many cultures—that of the united Goddess.

Many world mythologies, such as that of the Greeks, Romans, Egyptians, Indians, Celts, American Indians, etc., envisioned concepts of a universal mother—the Great Mother/Mother Goddess, who was conceived of as encapsulating all goddesses within her. For example, in Roman religion, the concept of the Mater Magna was portrayed in Apuleius's *Golden Ass*: "'I am Nature, the universal Mother, mistress of all elements ... sovereign of all things spiritual, queen of the dead, queen also of the immortals, the single manifestation of all gods and goddesses that are.... Though I am worshipped in many aspects, known by countless names ... yet the whole round earth venerates me'" (Apuleius, 197–8). Similarly, in India, "all the [Hindu] goddesses are considered aspects of one great female deity" (Phillips, Kerrigan, & Gould 93); "This goddess has many names, but her most common designation is simply Devi (goddess).... Mahadevi (great goddess)" or Shakti (Kinsley 132). Cultures that mythically portray goddesses as tripartite figures, like the Celtic the Morrígan, also convey the concept that individualized goddesses were united within a broader concept of a unified Goddess. Likewise, many cultures displayed goddesses as triple figures of youth, motherhood, and old age, such as the Greek goddesses Persephone, Demeter, and Hecate; though these goddesses were separate figures, it was understood that they were connected in a concept of divine unity. This unification of goddesses, despite age, time, or identity, is extended in the realm of folktales and fairy tales to show female characters, such as mothers and daughters, who are similarly united in an effort to preserve the wisdom of a time when goddesses thrived and powerful women served as their representatives. Therefore, quest tales of heroines that portray mothers, or female characters who serve in the role of mother/guide/teacher, should be looked at closely to see the goddess-oriented messages the tales are imparting.

For instance, a folktale from Mexico (Gerson 28–33) portrays a Zapotec princess named Kesne who partakes on a heroine's quest that is largely orchestrated by her mother. Kesne's father, Great Jaguar, proclaimed that Kesne should marry the son of his rival, so he could expand his rule by joining the two kingdoms, but Kesne outright refused her father's demand, and in punishment, her father ordered his sorcerers to transform Kesne into a green bird. This transformation from human to animal form initiated Kesne's heroic quest, signaled by her taking on a new name—Green Bird.

Green Bird defiantly left her father's kingdom, but she was portrayed at the start of her quest as still under his authority, as she struggled to move beyond who she was under the care of her father. For example, when

Green Bird tried to live as a bird, she only felt ashamed and embarrassed of her animal state. She was also terrified within the otherworldly depths of the forest, as every sound she heard filled her with dread. However, Green Bird's mother, Serpent Goddess, whose title shows that she will serve to teach her daughter wisdom connected to goddesses, intervened to help her daughter upon her heroic quest. It is significant that Green Bird's mother is portrayed as living separately from Green Bird's father, as it signals a sense of independence on the part of the mother, an independence that Green Bird will have to fully learn. It is also significant that Serpent Goddess appeared to Green Bird when she entered the forest, as opposed to the patriarchal kingdom of her father, as the tale indicates that Serpent Goddess is connected to the natural environment and will therefore impart its lessons to Green Bird.

While in nature, Serpent Goddess told her daughter that the two of them would have to embark on a further quest together to find the agents that would change Green Bird back to her human form. Mother and daughter journeyed together to find: "thirteen jars filled with freshly cried tears; a rug woven of feathers of every color of the rainbow ... and then, thirteen more jars with nectar from every flower in the forest," so that they could present these items to the divine Heart of the Sky, who held the power to transform Green Bird back to her human shape (Gerson 31). Green Bird found that while she was with her mother, the animals of the forest came to help her upon her quest, bringing her the precise gifts she needed. Turtledoves came and wept into their jars; vibrant birds plucked out their own feathers, so that a rug could be woven; and hummingbirds filled the remaining jars with nectar from every flower. Green Bird began to see, while venturing out far into nature with her mother that instead of being a place to fear, the environment fully embraced her. In receiving such aid from the elements of nature, Green Bird began to realize that she, just like her goddess mother, was able to supernaturally harness the elements of nature to aid her upon her quest. With their journey near completion, mother and daughter next went to the divine Heart of the Sky and asked to have Green Bird transformed back into her human form. Upon seeing that Green Bird finished her quest and learned that she indeed was united with her divine mother, Heart of the Sky transformed Green Bird back into a human woman, as Princess Kesne once more. This transformation signals Kesne's heroic apotheosis.

Showing Kesne as connected to her goddess mother at the tale's resolution sends a message to audiences that the heroine's quest often reveals the heroine as goddess-like herself. This message is reiterated by the fact that at the end of the tale, Kesne is portrayed as now fit to lead her people as queen, since the tale shows that Kesne's father, the king, died while she was on her quest. Therefore, Kesne, as a goddess-like heroine, will move her land beyond the patriarchal restrictions of her father's old kingdom and usher in a new era that embraces and imparts the goddess-oriented concepts she learned upon her heroic quest.

A folktale from Fiji (Ragan 294–5) also shows a courageous young girl named Kumaku who similarly embarked on a quest that was orchestrated by her mother. In this tale, Kumaku's mother is shown as needing some sea water to cook dinner, so she requested that her young daughter journey out to get it, warning her to "'Keep away from the spiders' webs'" (Ragan 294)! Immediately, the tale suggests that this journey for water will become Kumaku's heroic quest, and it is orchestrated to be such by Kumaku's mother in order for her to grow from childhood into womanhood. Kumaku knew that her mother's warning of "spiders' webs" alluded to the giants who lived nearby who caught people in massive spider webs before eating them. But, instead of being afraid, when Kumaku partook on her quest, she instead called the giants to her by singing a song that would alert them that she was near. This partaking on a dangerous task, where she must face elements that could easily kill her, marks the quintessential tenets of the heroic quest of leaving the known for the unknown and entering into otherworldly, even underworld, realms. Just as Kumaku expected, two giants came and took her away with them. But, as the giants were about to eat her, Kumaku simply smiled at her adversaries, as she was in full command of what happened next. Kumaku again sang to the giants: "'Blow, winds from Fiji,/ Blow up the black sand of the sea,/ Fill the giants' eyes/ So that they cannot see./ Blow, winds from Tonga,/ Blow up the white sea sand,/ Dazzle their eyes/ While I fly to the land'" (Ragan 295). It is this mystical song that shows Kumaku's ability to harness, supernaturally, the natural elements around her, as the elements of her environment listened to her song and complied with her request, blinding the giants forever, thus making them harmless to the community. The fact that Kumaku, like Kesne, is able to show her reverence for nature, as well as supernaturally harness its resources, as was seen in the heroines' quests of Chapter 6, shows that Kumaku has passed her heroic quest placed upon her by her mother. The tale suggests that Kumaku's mother took part in the very same quest Kumaku just passed repeatedly throughout her life, as obtaining the needed element of water for her family, which seems symbolic of serving as the source of spiritual wisdom and protection for her family, is an essential task needed for survival. In handing over this responsibility to Kumaku, the mother is thus shaping her daughter into a goddess-like maturity that mimics her own, so that Kumaku can one day move on to spiritually guide and protect her own family.

A folktale from Cape Town, South Africa entitled "Tsélané and the

Marimo" (Tatar 28–9) also tells of a young heroine who was aided upon her heroine's quest by her mother. The tale states that Tsélané's family was moving to find suitable pastures for their flocks, but Tsélané refused to go with them, proclaiming her own independence. In order to test her daughter, Tsélané's mother pretended to scold her daughter, warning her about the Marimos, who were a tribe of cannibals. But, Tsélané passed her mother's initial test and remained undeterred, staying behind to fend for herself as her family left her. Tsélané's mother, still testing her daughter, as she was now upon a quest to prove her own worth, would come to visit Tsélané periodically, asking if she had enough, but Tsélané remained resolute. However, one day a voice called for Tsélané, and it was not the voice of her mother, as this voice was too harsh. Showing wisdom instead of fear upon her quest, Tsélané called out to the voice, saying that she knew it was not her mother's voice, but the voice of a Marimo. Tsélané was right, and her bravery and wit made the Marimo go away, but the Marimo was still intent on tricking Tsélané. So, the Marimo started a fire and stuck a burning hot iron in his mouth to clear his voice and make it sound even more like Tsélané's mother. The Marimo cried out to Tsélané again; however, Tsélané once more did not fall for the trick and told the Marimo to leave her alone. However, the Marimo tried the deceptive trick again, and this time, he was able to get his voice so clear that it did sound just like the voice of Tsélané's mother, and Tsélané fell for the deception, which led to her abduction by the Marimo.

The Marimo put Tsélané in a sack and carried her far from her home, but what the Marimo did not know was that he carried her right to the village where her family was. When the Marimo set down his sack and went to search for a drink at the nearby village, the girls of the village opened his sack, found Tsélané bound within it, and ran to tell Tsélané's mother. Tsélané's mother, like other mothers of folktales and fairy tales who serve as educators to their heroine daughters, showed that she possessed superior wisdom in dealing with supernatural agents. Tsélané's mother retrieved her daughter from the sack, and in her place filled the sack with "a dog, scorpions, vipers, bits of broken pots, and stones" (Tatar 29). When the Marimo came back to his sack, ready to cook and eat Tsélané, he was immediately bitten by the dog, snakes, and scorpions, and was further wounded by the stones and pieces of broken pottery. To alleviate his pain, he threw himself into the mud where his body transformed into a tree, and from that day forward, "Bees made honey in its bark, and in the springtime young girls came and gathered the honey for honey-cakes" (Tatar 29). The tale ends here, which reveals further meaning in line with the role that the mother and the daughter play within its plot.

The fact that Tsélané was portrayed as a defiant, but brave girl is important, as it shows that she, as a heroic daughter, was ready to break away from the sole care of her mother. Her mother eased her into this process, as she asked Tsélané repeatedly if she was ready, and she often came to check on Tsélané when she was living alone. The fact that a Marimo indeed came, just as the mother said he would, suggests that the mother orchestrated the event to test her daughter upon her quest for autonomy. Tsélané was shown to pass the tests of her heroine's quest as she lived alone in the wilderness, thus shedding former definitions of selfhood as a dependent child. She then faced otherworld and underworld components when she met a Marimo, who both showed supernatural qualities and represented the potential death of Tsélané. The Marimo's test of Tsélané as mimicking the voice of her mother is also significant, as it suggests that Tsélané had to know within herself the qualities of her mother. The required intimate knowledge of her mother's voice is symbolic of Tsélané being able to recognize within herself the qualities of her mother. Tsélané succeeded twice in trusting her own recognition of her mother's qualities, but she failed upon her third test. Tsélané's failure, which was only presented in the tale as a stage of her quest, is shown by the fact that the Marimo, again seemingly set up by the mother, brought Tsélané precisely back to the supervision of her mother, revealing that Tsélané simply had more to learn before she could truly become like her powerful mother. Tsélané's mother then was shown within the tale to reveal her full skill set as a goddess-like woman when she knew precisely how to deal with the Marimo using supernatural wisdom. The precise objects that she used against the adversary worked perfectly, as if by magic, to save Tsélané, and thus teach her important lessons that would eventually build her into a traditional goddess representative like her mother. It is further significant that when the Marimo was no longer needed by the mother to test Tsélané, he was transformed into a tree where the young girls of the community gathered. This last element of the folktale suggests further traditional connections of goddess worship with the mother, as the mother possessed the ability to initiate metamorphoses, a skill often tied to goddesses within African mythology. The transformation of the Marimo into a tree where maidens gather also sends a message that the young girls of the community will one day undergo the same initiation to learn the goddess-oriented wisdom that Tsélané was taught by her mother.

A similar fairy tale by the Grimm brothers entitled "The Three Ravens" (J. Grimm & W. Grimm 83–5) shows another heroine who is guided upon her quest to learn supernatural elements connected to goddess-worship by her mother. In this tale, a mother got angry because her "godless" three sons played cards instead of accompanying her to church, so the mother did an act that is more in line with paganism than

Christianity—she transformed her three sons into ravens. The ability of the mother to transform her sons into an animal state identifies her, as it has with many other folktale and fairy tale female characters, with pagan goddesses. Thus, this scene again shows the conflict of differing belief systems that is a part of many tales, as Celtic and/or Germanic pagan features are fused into the character of the mother in this tale who is identified as Christian.

The three sons, as ravens, are then shown in this fairy tale to leave their mother behind to fend for themselves in the wilderness. The brothers' younger sister felt bad for them, so she vowed to care for them, which initiated her to partake on her heroic quest. Because of the mother's role in the course of events, the narrative strongly suggests that the whole ordeal was orchestrated by the mother to teach her daughter the same supernatural, goddess-like, abilities that she possessed. The sister searched for her raven brothers in the wilderness, and at the start of the fairy tale, like many other heroines who must learn to embrace elements of goddess worship, she was identified as not being familiar with the natural environment, as she soon became quite hungry and was unable to find anything in nature to sustain her. But, as the sister journeyed on, her knowledge of nature grew. In fact, the sister showed that she could indeed survive alone in the wilderness for a very long time, as she ventured so far for so long in search of her animalistic brothers, that she finally encountered "the end of the world" (J. Grimm & W. Grimm 84) where she went to the sun and found that it was too hot and ate "small children" (J. Grimm & W. Grimm 84). After this, the sister went to the moon, but there she found that it was too cold, and the moon also ate children. So, the sister went to the stars, who gave her advice that helped her upon her quest, stating that when she got to a gate at the top of a glass mountain, she must sacrifice something to open it. The fact that the sister in this tale traveled so far that she visited celestial elements shows her in a supernatural role connected to divinity. This searching of the boundaries of the earth, also shows the sister as arriving at the underworld stage of her quest, as the sun and moon are identified as capable of killing her. The raven state of the sister's brothers also seems to symbolize death for the maiden, as Celtic and Germanic representations of ravens often displayed them as harbingers of death. Therefore, portraying the sister as seeking her raven brothers also forces her to contend with the fact of mortality.

The sister finally arrived at the mystical glass mountain in which she had to use her ingenuity to find a way up. Once she got to the top, she came to a gate where she again used her own resources to open it by taking the shocking initiative to cut off her own pinky and put it in the lock, which successfully opened the supernatural gate. The fact that the sister is willing to sacrifice a part of herself in order to open the gate to reach her brothers shows that she has understood the lesson about mortality that is imperative to heroic quests during the underworld stage, as she must personally experience loss in order to accomplish her mission. When the gate opened, allowing the sister to transgress what remained off limits to most, the sister's apotheosis was revealed, as she finally found her raven brothers and proceeded to transform them back to human form from their symbolic embodiment of death as ravens. Thus, as with other tales of heroine's journeys, the heroine of this tale proves that she has attained apotheosis by her newfound ability to perform the supernatural acts of many mythic goddesses, such as that of metamorphosis and resurrection. Furthermore, the goddess-like abilities the heroine gained upon her quest are, in fact, the exact powers her mother possessed at the start of her quest, which strongly suggests, again, that the heroine's quest in this tale was also orchestrated by a mother to a daughter, and would one day be passed down from the heroine of this tale to her own daughters.

A folktale from Korea (Barcher 125–6) shows another heroine who was guided upon a quest by her mother. The tale starts with a widowed mother who was near death and had almost nothing to leave her three children. The mother, on her deathbed, gave her children what she thought would help them the most. She gave an axe to her eldest son, a cooking pot to her youngest son, and a walking stick and bowl made from a gourd to her only daughter. Before she died, the mother instructed her children to set out alone upon their own quests to try and discover a better life for themselves. As the folktale continues, it becomes clear that the focus of the tale is upon the daughter's quest. It is further revealed that the mother, after she died, still guided the daughter upon her quest.

First, the daughter set off into the wilderness, which is, as stated many times, a quintessential stage in many heroine's quests, as heroines must learn of the complexity of nature in order to tap into their connection with goddess tenets. The daughter was shown to decide to sleep in a cave; the symbolism of such a choice is important, since, as discussed, caves appear in many myths as the entrance of the underworld, and as the womb of the Earth Mother, serving as a place of both death and regeneration. This symbolism is carried through in the folktale when the daughter, while almost asleep within the cave, was presented with a supernatural meeting. The daughter met a goblin, who asked if she would like to accompany him upon an adventure; however, before she would be permitted to go, she had to prove to the goblin that she was indeed dead. When the goblin asked to feel her skull as proof, she handed him her mother's bowl made from a gourd. When the goblin asked to feel her arm to see if it was only bone, the daughter gave him her mother's walking stick to touch. The fact that the items left to the daughter by her mother are precisely the items needed to prove to the goblin that she is dead, and thus worthy of accompanying him on his supernatural journey, presents the mother in a goddess-like role as one proficient in the ways of the supernatural. The additional fact that the goblin must see evidence that the daughter is dead before she can accompany him to the underworld shows the cave experience of the daughter to be her necessary heroic stage of facing mortality. This folktale, more than the others just discussed, focuses upon the heroic stage of the underworld in a heightened fashion, presumably because the mother herself is dead, which suggests that the wisdom the daughter will gain upon this quest is more spirituality transformative.

The goblin, thus satisfied that the maiden was indeed dead, led her into a heightened experience of death, when she physically journeyed into the underworld. Facing the full weight of mortality, the daughter took in the sights and sounds of death that were a part of the underworld. Once acclimated, the daughter learned that the goblin, again seemingly a direct agent of the mother, took her to the underworld in order to test her. The goblin told her that she must return to the land of the living in order to replace the soul of the future ruler. He then gave the container holding the prince's soul to her. The daughter left the underworld and was signaled as achieving apotheosis upon her symbolic resurrection when, the next day, the daughter went to her people's kingdom and found that they were indeed in mourning at the death of their prince. The apotheotic daughter then told the king and queen that she held the ability to bring the prince back to life. The daughter next revealed the power of her heightened spiritual apotheosis when she was able to accomplish the ultimate supernatural skill of the goddess—resurrection. Again, showing a heroine as descending into the underworld, where she learned that it was a place of death as well as rebirth, connects the heroine to goddess worship, as this is the precise message of many goddesses within mythic narratives around the world. For instance, another Korean myth of the goddess Paritegi presents her as a maiden who journeyed to the underworld and thus learned the ability of resurrecting the dead, which she performed upon her dead father and mother. Because of her mastery of resurrection, based on her experience within the underworld, Paritegi became a goddess within Korean mythology who served as an underworld guide for souls journeying from life, to death, to rebirth. Because of her ability to transcend between realms, the goddess Paritegi is still revered by Korean shamans even today. Thus, this Korean folktale ends in a similar fashion with the prince resurrecting from death at the hands of the now shamanistic heroine, and in gratitude, the prince married her, so that both would go on to rule in the coming years as king and queen. The fact that the heroine first resurrected the prince, before he married her, foreshadows a marriage of mutual rulership, as the prince is assured to always know of his wife's power. This is further illustrated when the queen's brothers appear briefly again at the close of the tale, and as they were both living in poverty, the queen saved them by permitting them to live in her domain.

It is significant that the dead mother in this Korean folktale lives on in the education of her daughter. And, given the importance of shamanism in Korean culture, that still to this day reveres women who hold this role, it seems that the mother orchestrated a shamanistic journey for her daughter that required her to meet all the tenets of the heroine's journey, especially that of the underworld. As discussed in Chapter 2 with shamanistic old wise women, shamans are often portrayed as being able to accomplish supernatural acts because of the wisdom they learned in their own similar quests to the underworld. It was, thus, the intimate knowledge the daughter obtained from her underworld experience that allowed her to see that her mother's death was but momentary when viewed in terms of nature's cycles. This is especially proven when the daughter left the underworld and could herself initiate the supernatural act done by many mythic goddesses and shamans alike—that of resurrection. Therefore, the daughter learned that the mother lived on in the apotheotic wisdom of the goddess that the daughter now held within herself, and would impart to her people as queen.

Wicked Stepmothers

Out of the long history, within many cultures, of contention for goddesses as patriarchal civilizations gained dominance, as discussed in many sections of this book, the presentation of women within mythology, as well as in folktales and fairy tales, often became demoted and even demonized. One historical method for presenting the demotion of divine women in order to promote the elevation of male gods was to portray the desecration or eradication of the power of a mythic mother. For example, the Mesopotamian Marduk killed his supremely powerful mother Tiamet in order to gain supremacy over the pantheon. The Greek Zeus likewise raped his mother Rhea in order to ensure that he superseded her authority. Sered states that "many male-dominated religions recognize that motherhood gives women power" (Sered 72), as motherhood was "believed to bestow upon women deep spiritual insights" (Sered 73). Therefore, many world mythological/religious narratives were created to supersede the power of the mother, such as demoting a divine mother to a human mother, as occurred to many former Greek goddesses who became mortal women impregnated by Zeus or to the Virgin Mary who evolved from mythic goddesses to the mortal mother of Christ. Many divinities were also shown as being created without a mother to showcase them as agents of patriarchal agendas, like the Greek goddess Athena, who was said to be birthed directly from the body of Zeus to ensure that she became a spokesperson for the new patriarchal religion that would replace the old religion of supreme goddess worship within Greece.

This mythic, as well as folktale and fairy tale, attempt to portray formerly divine women in negative terms was seen in Chapter 4 of this book in the presentation of women as monstrous. Oftentimes, cultures, as discussed, displayed male heroes as needing to eradicate monstrous women, who held components of traditional goddess ideology, in order to convert their communities toward new patriarchal belief systems. However, the presentation of former goddesses as monstrous women proved complex, as, again discussed in Chapter 4, sometimes myths, folktales, and fairy tales presented male heroes who instead of just eradicating female monsters, actually ended up learning from them, as the monstrous women still served as preserved remnants of goddess ideology in disguise. The same is true for folktales and fairy tales that display the heroine's quest. Monstrous or evil women often appear within the journeys of heroines, and one of the most common examples of a monstrous folktale or fairy tale woman who either impedes, or seems to impede, the heroine's journey is the wicked stepmother.

Just as in some patriarchal myths, folktales, and fairy tales that present male heroes as becoming more heroic for simply eradicating a monstrous woman, the wicked stepmother in some folktales and fairy tales only serves as a patriarchal device to demonize the power of the mother. Whereas mothers serve as guides for their daughters upon their quests to discover the wisdom held by their mothers, which was presumably passed down to them from their own mothers, stepmothers in folktales and fairy tales are often portrayed as impeding the daughter from learning the wisdom of her mother, which is again the wisdom of goddess-oriented belief systems. Stepmothers in folktales and fairy tales are thus often presented as false mothers, who appear as evil, serving to deter the heroine from her path.

However, in the majority of folktales and fairy tales, the stepmother often appears as wicked, but like many monstrous women who ended up actually serving to guide male heroes toward apotheosis, it is often the stepmother's intervention in the life of a burgeoning heroine that compels the heroine to gain control over her own life. For example, the folktale or fairy tale stepmother often helps the heroine weed out the false elements within herself, like vanity, jealousy, societal expectations, that hold her back from apotheosis. Many folktale and fairy tale heroines are often initially portrayed as weak, as they are dominated by their stepmothers, who are often trapped themselves within households of heightened concern for materialism, intense vanity, fierce jealousy, etc. Furthermore, the folktales and fairy tales that present the quests of heroines often show that the stepmother "cannot be escaped"; in fact, the stepmother often "hunts the heroine down to her death. This symbolic death is the condition of rebirth, in psychological terms of coming to consciousness" (Birkhäuser-Oeri 30). Therefore, in order for the heroine to move past her societal definitions of selfhood, presented often through the example of the seemingly wicked stepmother, who is the false mother, the heroine must be psychologically and often spiritually reborn, so that she may discover her true mother, which is the goddess within herself. True mothers in folktales and fairy tales, as shown in this chapter, are deeply connected with nature and its cycles; therefore, their place is not trapped within materialism, but outside in the wilderness. True mothers age with comfort because they conceive of life as cyclical, and they are not jealous of others because they are complete within themselves—this is the goddess-oriented apotheosis the folktale and fairy tale heroine strives toward, and often the stepmother who appears wicked actually serves to help guide the heroine toward this realization.

Perhaps there is no better tale to display the effect of the wicked stepmother on a heroine's journey than that of "Cinderella." Tales displaying heroines similar to "Cinderella" have appeared in many cultures since ancient times, such as "Yeh-Hsien in China, Cendrillon in Italy, Ashenputtel in Germany, and Catskin in England" (Tatar xiii). In looking at the Grimm brothers' first edition of "Cinderella" (J. Grimm & W. Grimm 69–77), Cinderella's mother is portrayed as having died; her father thus remarried a woman who became Cinderella's wicked stepmother, who along with her two despicable daughters served to oppress Cinderella. The stepmother treated Cinderella like a servant, forcing her to live a life only filled with domestic affairs, similar to the life of many housewives within patriarchal communities that forced this lifestyle upon women by offering few other options to them. The fact that Cinderella at the start of her tale is portrayed as a meek maiden who was willing to endure the lifestyle of a servant, locked within her father's household, immediately portrays Cinderella as a weak and passive product of a patriarchal culture. However, one day the announcement came that a great ball, lasting three nights, would enable the kingdom's prince to choose his bride. The two stepsisters immediately began to prepare for the ball, but they stopped Cinderella from going by forcing her to complete tasks that immediately suggest the start of Cinderella's heroic quest. Instead of joining the festivities,

Cinderella had to complete the seemingly impossible task of sorting lentils and peas through a pile of ashes each of the three nights of the ball; this task, that is reminiscent of the Roman Apuleius's tale of "Cupid and Psyche," solidifies the demand of this task as a requirement placed upon Cinderella to initiate her growth, as it did with Psyche when ordered by the goddess Venus. This challenge placed upon Cinderella by the stepsisters, the offspring of the central stepmother who condones this treatment of her stepdaughter, is then put in place to test Cinderella's connection to the natural world. Many heroines already portrayed in this book attained mystical abilities in connection with nature when achieving apotheosis; thus, a test such as this seems coordinated to see if Cinderella possesses the knowledge and skill of the self-actualized, goddess-like heroine. However, Cinderella initially failed this first test upon her heroine's quest, as she was portrayed at the start of her tale as only a product of her patriarchal environment, seemingly because, according to the tale, she had no mother to guide her. Therefore, Cinderella only despaired at the injustice of her stepmother's and stepsisters' demands, thinking the tasks to be impossible. Yet, as in many folktales and fairy tales, Cinderella soon learned of her crucial, but seemingly forgotten, connection to nature. Forlorn, Cinderella began to try to sort the piles of lentils and peas, when two pigeons landed and asked Cinderella if she would like their help. Happily agreeing, Cinderella was amazed to see that the pigeons easily accomplished the task. The pigeons also told Cinderella that all she needed to do was seek the help of a hazel tree that grew on her mother's grave in order to go the ball, as she was told by the birds to shake the tree, and beautiful clothes would appear. Cinderella followed the advice of her animal helpers, which serves as a quintessential sign that Cinderella was evolving on her quest toward an education of goddess-oriented beliefs. Cinderella thus went to the hazel tree that grew on her mother's grave. The tree responded to Cinderella just as a mother would in a folktale or fairy tale that presented the mother as a guide to her daughter by readily giving Cinderella the items she needed to go to the ball.

It is highly significant that Cinderella's deceased mother is portrayed in this tale as the one who guides Cinderella, even after her death. Showing the mother as a reincarnated tree connects her to portrayals of many mythic goddesses who easily metamorphose shape, even after their deaths, such as the American Indian Corn Mothers who die and reincarnate as corn. The form of a tree to display the reincarnation of Cinderella's mother especially serves as a symbolic image for Cinderella, and the audience of the fairy tale, about the cycles of life, as trees explicitly show that life is renewed each spring after a period of dormancy. Therefore, the explicit proof Cinderella receives from her mother, in the form of a tree, about the cycles of life within nature, as she herself did not fully die but only reincarnated, immediately allowed Cinderella to gain the spiritual wisdom she needed to attain her goddess-like apotheosis. The dazzling attire Cinderella obtained from her tree mother is similar to the jewels that were presented to the Kenyan Marwe after she symbolically resurrected from the underworld; therefore, Cinderella's new look is meant to present her as having attained apotheosis. Further suggesting Cinderella's apotheosis is the fact that she finally decided to defy her stepmother's wishes and go alone to the ball, where nobody recognized her, suggesting that she was a changed woman.

Thus, the stepmother, with the aid of her daughters, pushed Cinderella into transforming herself and her life. Their collective focus on the ball brought the whole affair to Cinderella's attention, and thus initiated Cinderella to begin the process of revising herself. This pressure by the false mother, portrayed as Cinderella's stepmother, allowed Cinderella to finally see that her true mother was with her all along. This true mother, who could die and yet live on as a part of nature, immediately thrust Cinderella into the position of an enlightened heroine, who showing her apotheosis to all in her beautiful attire went independently to the ball and chose her own husband, thus elevating her life to a position of power. As the future queen, Cinderella is assured a platform to impart her goddess-like wisdom to her people, as so many successful heroines are shown to do after accomplishing their quests.

In China, the folktale of "Yeh-hsien" (Tatar 146–8), narrated around 850 CE but believed to be quite older as even the tale states that it dates further back than the Qin (221–206 BCE) and Han (206 BCE–220 CE) dynasties (Tatar 146), outlines similar themes found in later fairy tale renditions of "Cinderella." In this Chinese folktale, the heroine Yeh-hsien lost her mother and father at a young age. Her father was said to be a "cave-master" to the indigenous people living around the "Wu cave" (Tatar 146); this inclusion also dates the story as originating most certainly as an ancient myth, which would suggest a sacred element being imparted by the story's plot. Yeh-hsien's stepmother is presented in the tale as quite cruel to Yeh-hsien; in fact, she regularly forced Yeh-hsien to do household chores that endangered her safety. One day, as Yeh-hsien was collecting water from the deep pools rarely visited by her people because they were so dangerous, Yeh-hsien met a small, but beautiful fish that she took home and cared for until it grew too large for the small bowl she owned. Unable to care for the fish anymore, Yeh-hsien took the fish back to the deep pools and visited it daily; however, the stepmother found out about this and decided to dress up, go to the water, trick the fish with her disguise, and then kill Yeh-hsien's beloved fish. When Yeh-hsien found out what happened, she cried out in anguish. A celestial man from the sky realm heard her cries and came to help her. The celestial man told Yeh-hsien to take the discarded fish's bones back to her home, hide them, and then use them to pray for anything she desired. Thus far in the tale, Yeh-hsien's quest includes classic quest archetypes for the heroine, such as going alone into the isolated wilderness and passing the initial test of revering nature, which Yeh-hsien does by cherishing the small fish. It is also significant that Yeh-hsien is able to seemingly conjure a mystical character, the sky man, into coming to earth to help her. All of these elements portray Yeh-hsien as upon a quest to connect her to traditional goddess worship.

The tale continues to show Yeh-hsien doing as instructed by the celestial man when she took the bones of the fish with her and prayed to them. When she did this, she, like Cinderella and Marwe, gained jewels and magnificent clothing, such as a cloak "spun from kingfisher feathers and shoes of gold" (Tatar 147), which again signified Yeh-hsien's apotheotic understanding that she was connected to the traditional goddesses of her culture. Like the tale of "Cinderella," it is telling that Yeh-hsien achieves apotheotic wisdom only after she experiences an element connected to death. The fact that Yeh-hsien takes the bones of her beloved fish and prays to them suggests ancient ideology that imparts an element of ancestor worship, as the dead fish lives on in its ability to still be able to help Yeh-hsien, similar to Cinderella gaining confirmation that her mother lived on after death in the form of a tree. Thus, the reverence explicitly connected to the natural representation of the fish's bones makes it clear that Yeh-hsien has understood that she must revere nature and its ceaseless cycles.

The tale continues on to show that the cave-festival arrived, and Yeh-hsien's stepmother and stepsister attended, leaving Yeh-hsien to tend to the family's fruit trees. However, as with other similar tales to "Cinderella," Yeh-hsien did not stay home, but decided to take her own life into her hands by going to the festival, wearing the garments she obtained through the help of nature and mysticism. The king of a nearby island saw Yeh-hsien's gold shoe, which she lost, like Cinderella did in her own tale soon after the ball, so the king requested a search to find the owner. When it was discovered that Yeh-hsien was the owner of the shoe, the king asked her if she would become his wife. Again, because the stepmother of the tale forced Yeh-hsien to begin her journey to the natural, and also mystical deep pools reserved seemingly for only the worthy among her people, Yeh-hsien attained knowledge of her true selfhood, the mother/goddess within herself, and thus ended the tale again in a position of authority that will presumably allow her to go on to instruct the people of her community about what she has learned.

In another Chinese tale entitled "Lin Lan" (Tatar 171–5), that holds similar themes as those found in "Cinderella," there is a girl named Beauty who was mistreated by a wicked stepmother, who only loved her biological daughter, Pock Face, identified as such because she had scars upon her face. In this tale, Beauty's mother died at a young age, but the story states that her mother reincarnated as a yellow cow that stayed with Beauty's family. Beauty, like Cinderella, turned to this cow mother whenever she was mistreated by her stepmother and stepsister. Also, like the tale of "Cinderella," this folktale shows the similar theme of making Beauty accomplish seemingly impossible agricultural tasks, like straightening stacks of hemp and separating sesame seeds from piles of beans. And again, it was the mother cow who was responsible for aiding Beauty.

The story continues to show the stepmother eventually finding out that Beauty was able to accomplish her tasks because of the help of her cow mother, so the stepmother killed and ate the cow. Beauty was said to then take the bones of her cow mother and hide them in a pot in her room, cherishing them. The fact that Beauty took the bones of her mother, instead of trusting that the process of nature would allow her mother to reincarnate from a cow into another natural being, shows that she has not yet attained the wisdom to become an apotheotic heroine.

However, proving that she was changing from the meek maiden she was at the start of the tale, Beauty one night grew angry that her stepmother and stepsister yet again left her to go to the theater, so she smashed the pot holding her cow mother's bones. When Beauty did this, a beautiful gown and shoes appeared, signaling, as with Cinderella and Yeh-hsien, that Beauty had attained apotheosis when she was symbolically able to let the bones of her mother go, confirming her understanding of the cycles of life. Beauty then adorned herself in her beautiful attire and left her home, where she eventually met a handsome scholar, who impassioned by her beauty, asked her to be his wife, and she agreed. When Beauty relayed the information of her marriage to her stepmother and stepsister, Pock Face reacted by pushing Beauty into a well when she had a moment alone with her, thus killing her. The stepmother then lied to Beauty's husband, stating that Beauty had fallen ill while visiting her, so Beauty would stay with them until she was well. After some time, the stepmother and stepsister devised a plan to send the stepsister to the husband in place of Beauty, stating that Beauty's illness had been smallpox, and that the illness had thus transformed her face. Upon seeing the stepsister in the place of his wife, the scholar felt that something was wrong, but he did not want to offend his bride who might be Beauty, so he said nothing.

In the meantime, Beauty, confirming her apotheosis, reincarnated after death, just like she learned from her mother, into a sparrow, that came often to visit her husband. The husband eventually found a way to communicate with the sparrow and discovered that it was indeed his wife Beauty. However, Pock Face found out about the connection between the scholar and the sparrow, so she killed the bird, just like her mother had killed Beauty's cow mother. Next, the story states that Beauty, again confirming her apotheosis, reincarnated into bamboo. When Pock Face discovered this, she cut down all the bamboo, used it to make a bed, and then discarded the bed.

The tale continues to show the archetypal figure of an old woman discovering the outcast bed made of bamboo. The old woman found out that when she brought this bed into her home, someone began cooking meals for her while she was away. The old woman decided to wait and see who was doing this and discovered a shadow in the shape of a woman. The old woman, showing her own wisdom as an archetypal wise old woman, was able to communicate with this shadow and discovered that it was Beauty. Beauty, in this shadow form, asked the old woman to gather a "rice pot," "stick," "dish cloth," and "fire hooks" (Tatar 174) and put them together in the form of a woman. The old woman did as she was asked, and Beauty returned to her human form, further securing Beauty's goddess-like apotheosis. The old woman then went to Beauty's husband and told him all that happened since she obtained the bed. Beauty's husband at once declared that Beauty should come home again as his wife, but Pock Face demanded that Beauty and herself undergo a series of tests to see who was the real Beauty. Beauty easily passed the series of tests that required her to walk on eggs, climb a "ladder made of knives," and "jump into a cauldron of hot oil" (Tatar 174–5), which showed her husband that she was his true wife, but more importantly showed herself that she had fully aligned with the wisdom of her mother by being able to master supernatural goddess-like abilities. Her stepsister only destroyed the eggs, cut her feet to the bones on the knives, and died in the boiling oil. For Beauty's final act in the tale, she sent her stepsister's boiled flesh to her stepmother, who died upon the sight, symbolically showing that Beauty dispelled all notions of her previous selfhood that allowed her to succumb to the oppression of her stepmother. Therefore, because Beauty's stepmother served as the crucial catalyst in Beauty's apotheotic quest, Beauty went on to impart her goddess-like abilities and wisdom to the next generations.

The fairy tale of "Snow White," like "Cinderella," may also have ancient connections; for example, a Jewish-Egyptian version of the tale "has the heroine going through quite obviously Snow White–type adventures under the name Pomegranate" (Anderson 44), which might have potential connections to Persephone from Greek mythology, who eats the seeds of a pomegranate, which enables her to experience a symbolic death and rebirth annually. Many cultures have created similar tales throughout the centuries as well, such as a Spanish version that shows the evil stepmother wanting a bottle of the heroine's blood, corked with her big toe, after she was killed, and an Italian version that shows the wicked stepmother as wanting the child's intestines (Tatar 85).

The second and subsequent editions of the Grimm brothers' "Little Snow White" portrays her stepmother as the antagonist of the story, though in the first edition (J. Grimm & W. Grimm 170–7), it is her mother. It is significant that the first edition makes Snow White's own mother the seemingly wicked catalyst that drives Snow White to better herself, as it shows that the goal of the work, and other tales like it, is not transformed with the mother shifting to the stepmother, as both mothers and stepmothers within folktales and fairy tales, even if they appear wicked, can drive heroines to embark on quests to seek apotheosis. Both the first and second editions of the Grimms' "Little Snow White" presents Snow White's mother as possessing mystical abilities, as both versions state that when she was sewing, she pricked her finger, saw the blood, and wished for a child with lips as "red as blood," skin as "white as snow," and black hair as "black as the window frame" (J. Grimm & W. Grimm 170). And mystically, a child just as the queen envisioned was born. This scene, that shows Snow White's mother as holding mystical abilities in connection to fertility, suggests that she is linked to portrayals of goddesses who also possess such powers in mythic narratives. However, the second edition shifts to show that Snow White's mother died after giving birth to Snow White, leaving her with a wicked stepmother to raise her once her father remarried. Therefore, the second edition of the tale makes it appear that Snow White's mother was pure, nurturing, and potentially sacred for her goddess-like attributes, but Snow White's stepmother, who possesses similar mystical abilities as those of the mother, was evil. When the tale shifts to a stepmother leading the apparently evil acts of trying to harm Snow White, which the Grimm brothers did to make the tale more palatable to audiences, it makes the fairy tale women fit stereotypical, patriarchal models of women as either angelic and motherly or evil and jealous, thus eradicating the true message of the tale, which is the education of Snow White toward goddess-like apotheosis. Therefore, remembering that in the first edition of the tale, Snow White's mother accomplished all positive and seemingly negative acts within the narrative, and only became portrayed as separate characters of mother and stepmother in later editions, is essential toward understanding the goddess-oriented message of the tale.

The first and second editions of the fairy tale show that once Snow White enters maidenhood, her seemingly vain mother/stepmother becomes jealous of her young and beautiful daughter/stepdaughter and grows to believe that Snow White, who was beloved by her father, is her competition for the king's love. To show the overemphasized focus on the mother's/stepmother's vanity, she is shown in the tale to obsessively look in a mirror each day to assess her worth according to her own false standards. When a folktale or fairy tale mother/stepmother views her stepchildren/children as competition for her husband's love, the tale highlights women who demean themselves in an effort to gain male approval. Often, folktale and fairy tale stepmothers/mothers become obsessed with their own fear that a male character, who is mostly absent from the plot, will no longer find them attractive if competition is nearby. The purpose of these types of stories is often to show how many women felt that male approval was integral to their survival in patriarchal cultures. However, tales like "Snow White" point out the destruction that is caused when women overemphasize their own value based on their notion of what men perceive about them. In addition to the mother's/stepmother's obsession with vanity serving as an agent within the story to show her heightened worry of male acceptance, her magic mirror also serves as a projection of mortality. Thus, the mother's/stepmother's seeming obsession that she must remain the most beautiful woman in all the land showcases her apparent fear of aging and death. Tatar concurs, "the image that looks back at us [within a mirror] is subject to change. It is ephemeral and marked by mortality. Beauty may appear to mask death, but its image also has a sinister side, reminding us that everything is subject to decay and must die" (Tatar 87–8).

However, it is again important to remember that it was Snow White's mother, who was only later identified as her stepmother, who mystically created Snow White to be as precisely beautiful as she was; therefore, she arguably was not actually overcome with jealousy by the appearance she herself created for Snow White; instead it seems that the mother, and in later editions the stepmother, feigned jealousy to create a quest for Snow White that would teach her to embrace goddess ideology. To further support the presentation of the mother/stepmother as a goddess representative meant to educate Snow White to move beyond the elements, such as vanity and the fear of aging and death, that commonly hold women back from reaching their full goddess-like potential, there is an undeniable aspect in this tale, and others like it, that the mother/stepmother, as the female villain, is far more interesting, active, and powerful than the meek Snow White. For instance, Gilbert and Gubar view the mother/stepmother as the most admirable character in the tale; for them, she is a "plotter, a plot-maker, a schemer, a witch, an artist, and impersonator, a woman of almost infinite creative energy" (Gilbert and Gubar 389–90). Furthermore, villainous females within folktales and fairy tales, like the mother/stepmother of Snow White, usually possess mystical knowledge and supernatural skills that explicitly connect them to traditional goddesses displayed in mythic narratives. When viewed under this lens, the tale strongly suggests that the mother/stepmother indeed serves as an agent to transform Snow White past the passive, weak, and typically patriarchal female she is presented as being throughout the majority of the fairy tale. Tatar concurs stating that the tale of "Snow White" reflects "two possible developmental trajectories [for women], one passive, docile, and compliant with patriarchal norms, the other nomadic, creative, and socially subversive" (Tatar 87). Therefore, this interpretation heightens the story's focus upon Snow White as a maiden who must partake on a quest to ensure that she does not become the woman her mother/stepmother projects to her, which does not mean that the persona the mother/stepmother projects is who she really is.

In the fairy tale, the mother/stepmother was said to so loathe Snow White's beauty that she ordered a huntsman to kill her daughter/stepdaughter by cutting out her lungs and liver and bringing them back to her, so she could eat them. But the huntsman defied his queen and instead killed a boar, so the mother/stepmother ate its lungs and liver instead, believing them to be Snow White's. The boar was a well-known figure of the Germanic goddess Freya (Norse Freyja), so boars were often sacrificed to her and her brother Freyr. In a broader sense, mother goddesses within many cultures, and certainly within Germanic religion, were portrayed as the givers and takers of life, so this imagery in this German fairy tale seems intentional to connect the mother/stepmother to images of traditional goddesses, showing that perhaps the killing and eating of the boar in this tale is intended as a symbolic sacrifice to initiate Snow White's ritualistic quest toward apotheosis as orchestrated by her mother/stepmother.

Like other quests of the heroine, Snow White must first go into the wilderness by herself, away from the life she led as a child, in order to be tested. First, Snow White must overcome her fear of the wilderness, as she originally thought that the animals of the forest would devour her; this signals that Snow White had much to learn about nature before she could become an apotheotic heroine. Snow White also encountered helpers within the forest upon her journey, who appeared as both animals and mystical dwarves. Snow White chose to live with the mystical dwarves as part of her quest, connecting Snow White to the critical heroine quest tenet of learning to become familiar with the otherworld and the mystical elements within it. Again, in Germanic and Norse mythology, dwarves were believed to reside within the interior of the earth, so they held an intimate knowledge of that which was associated with the underworld; mythic "Dwarves generally live in caves, in the earth, and are spirits which are closely connected with Mother Earth" (Birkhäuser-Oeri 98). Thus, the dwarves within "Little Snow White" may serve as symbolic experts of the underworld, as their job in the tale was to mine the interior of the earth, which again brings the theme of mortality back into the tale and signals that Snow White's interaction with the dwarves will help her learn about the lessons of the underworld.

As heroines must face underworld tenets to fully learn the lessons of mythic goddesses, a critical part of Snow White's quest is her facing the elements of mortality. Because of the intervention of her mother/stepmother, Snow White learned intimately about death four times within the tale. The first came when the mother/stepmother ordered the huntsman to kill Snow White. The next three brushes with death occurred when the mother/stepmother learned that Snow White still lived, so she disguised herself as an old woman in order to accomplish the task her huntsman would not. The fact that the mother/stepmother disguised herself as an old woman makes clear a common mythic symbol which portrays the goddess in three forms: the maiden, the mother, and the crone. This presentation of youth, leading to maturity, and then a precursor to death, is, as discussed, a common symbol of nature's cyclical aspect in many myths, folktales, and fairy tales. Therefore, when this fairy tale makes use of the same concept in a story that focuses intensely on the assumed fear of aging, a message connected to goddess symbolism begins to explicitly emerge. As an old woman, the mother/stepmother sought out Snow White in the home of the dwarves. The mother/stepmother first enticed Snow White to take from her colorful laces for her corset, but when she volunteered to tie them for Snow White, she tied them so tight that Snow White could not breathe, and fell over, apparently dead. But, the dwarves found Snow White and, as experts of the underworld, resurrected her by cutting the laces, so she could breathe again. The mother/stepmother, still disguised as an old woman, came back and this time enticed Snow White to take a beautiful comb for her hair, and again once the mother/stepmother put the comb in Snow White's hair, she appeared to die, as the mother/stepmother tainted the comb with poison. Again, the mystical dwarves resurrected Snow White by pulling the poisoned comb from her hair. It is significant that Snow White was enticed to accept gifts—laces for her corset and a comb for her hair—from the mother/stepmother, who is labeled as evil because of her obsession with her appearance, when Snow White herself twice falls victim to the mother's/stepmother's trickery because of her own vanity. Because Snow White falls, not once but twice, for the mother's/ stepmother's challenge, shows that the mother/stepmother is testing Snow White on the very tenet that she herself projected as centrally important to her. This suggests, again, that the whole quest has been orchestrated by the mother/stepmother to teach Snow White about the senselessness of being concerned with what patriarchal societies state women should be concerned with—beauty and aging, so that the mother/stepmother can really push her daughter/stepdaughter into fully facing the reality of mortality. She does this by coming back again, as an old woman, to force Snow White into the true underworld stage of the heroine's quest.

The final time Snow White experienced a symbolic death occurs when she again fell prey to the enticement of the disguised mother/stepmother when she ate an apple that looked impossibly red. The eating of the apple is closely connected with myths of underworld goddesses, like the Greek Persephone who ate the seeds of a pomegranate and thus gained experience of both life and death, again a myth that may be connected to older versions of "Snow White," or the eating of the apple could also be tied to the Christian Eve being enticed to eat from the Tree of Knowledge, thus unleashing death to humankind, but allowing her to gain wisdom. When Snow White ate the apple, she was described as dying in the tale for the third time, but this time the experience lasted much longer than the first two. This time, the dwarves mourned Snow White when they realized they could not resurrect her as they had done the other two times. This extended death of Snow White suggests that she must do more than physically resurrect, as she did twice in the tale, if she is to gain the apotheosis of the goddess. The tale shows that the dwarves placed the body of Snow White in a glass coffin for all to see her beauty in a state of stasis, as the coffin ensured that her body would not age or decay. And it is in this state that a handsome prince happened to come by one day, and instantly fell in love with the visual of the dead Snow White. The reverence paid by the prince to the silent form of Snow White suggests an image of one worshipping an idol of a goddess, similar to the prince in "Sleeping Beauty of the Wood." The prince as a devout worshipper of Snow White's image transformed his life to serve only her, as he could do little else but look at her form, again as if she was a goddess. The prince begged the dwarves to carry Snow White's coffin to his castle, which they agreed to do, but when the coffin was moved, the poisoned piece of apple that was lodged in her throat became dislodged, and Snow White resurrected for a third time. In Snow White's third death and resurrection, a number often associated with goddess worship, Snow White finally learned the goddess's message of mortality, which enabled her apotheosis.

Snow White's apotheosis is confirmed when she is portrayed as finally becoming an active character, instead of the passive and mostly stagnant character she remained throughout most of the tale. Her goddess-like selfhood is made apparent when she unleashes revenge upon her mother/stepmother. The unique form of revenge Snow White chose was to have the dwarves, again those who hold knowledge of death, put scolding hot iron shoes upon her mother/stepmother, so that she danced herself to death. This ending shows that Snow White's mother/stepmother represented to Snow White her own internal concepts associated with patriarchal expectations for women; therefore, when Snow White killed her mother/stepmother, she proved herself an apotheotic heroine who no longer cared about elements connected to vanity and the fear of ageing and death. In addition, the fact that the mother/stepmother is portrayed as dancing toward her death, rather than writhing and moaning on the floor for example, is striking. The mother's/stepmother's dance at her death conjures images of the Hindu Shiva's dance of the Nataraja to symbolize the cyclicality of life and death, or of his consort, the goddess Kali, who dances upon the dead and whose dance can initiate the destruction of earth, which is necessary to initiate the earth's rebirth. Therefore, the dance of the mother/stepmother at her time of death finally and fully shows her to be a goddess representative who knows full well nature's promise of cyclical life. Snow White's active involvement in this scene explicitly proves her apotheotic transformation as a newly initiated goddess representative who will one day carry on the lessons her mother/stepmother taught her.

Snow White's quest taught her the tenets required upon the heroine's journey, as she learned to embrace nature as a part of herself, harness mystical agents in her time among the dwarves, and master the secrets of life, death, and rebirth. And it was the mother/stepmother, despite appearing as evil, who served throughout the whole tale as the educator of Snow White upon her quest. As seen with many generational tales between mothers or stepmothers and daughters or stepdaughters, Snow White's mother/stepmother prepares her to live in the world the way it is, using the full attributes she has as a woman, which if she follows the example of her mother/stepmother, are quite dynamic and formidable. Had her mother/stepmother not intervened to educate Snow White, then the tale suggests that she would have simply faded away as a puppet in the scheme of patriarchy with a princely husband. But, the mother/stepmother helped Snow White move beyond psychological maidenhood where all she cared about was vanity, which equates to only caring about how men defined her worth, to the life of a mature goddess-like woman, so that when Snow White becomes queen, which is again promised at the close of this fairy tale, she will serve as an example to the women in her kingdom of how to live with power and wisdom instead of with only docility.

Folktales and fairy tales that display kind mothers, and even wicked stepmothers, show that a generational attempt to convey messages from perhaps ancient times might have been preserved, at least in part, through the repeated telling of tales that show a young maiden upon a quest being guided by an older generation of women. This imparting of goddess-oriented wisdom from a mother or stepmother to a daughter or stepdaughter also allows the mother or stepmother to meet the final requirement of her own heroine's quest, which entails passing on traditional goddess ideology to the next generation of heroines. Tales, such as the ones discussed in this chapter that display kind mothers, as well as seemingly wicked stepmothers, aiding heroines upon their quests resemble the folktales and fairy tales of heroines who are guided upon quests by female characters who most resemble the goddesses of old—witches.

8

Witches

Out of all the female characters presented in this book, the witches of folktales and fairy tales, also often identified as sorceresses or enchantresses, are most connected to the traditional goddesses of many mythic narratives. Zipes concurs, stating that the witches of folktales and fairy tales directly "owe their existence to pagan goddesses" (Zipes 58). The complex portrayal of witches within folktales and fairy tales allowed centuries of beliefs regarding goddess worship to remain strong in the mindset of the people, as audiences around the world often revered the stories of the witch most of all; "Of the many figures who make their presence felt in a [folktale or] fairy tale, the witch is the most compelling. She is the ... dominant character.... The witch has the ability to place people in death-like trances—and just as easily bring them back to life. Conjurer of spells and concocter of deadly potions, she has the power to alter people's lives. Few figures in [folktales and] fairy tales are as powerful and commanding as the witch" (Cashdan 30). This depiction of witches as being connected to goddesses has a long history.

As discussed, many belief systems around the world eventually adopted patriarchal concepts that in time altered, demoted, or eradicated existing beliefs surrounding goddess worship. Sometimes these concepts were adopted naturally, as cultures moved from primary hunter/gatherer and agricultural subsistence to more technologically advanced civilizations, and sometimes cultures revised existing beliefs due to the introduction of new beliefs from conquest, diffusion, etc. Whatever the cause, many goddesses, and their religious representatives, such as shamanesses, priestesses, healers, midwives, etc., became demoted, and in many cases demonized. For example, many European goddesses "became associated with names of witches throughout Europe in the early and late Middle Ages" (Zipes 58). Likewise, the Christian church often identified women who were connected to goddesses as "diabolical" (Zipes 56). In Scandinavia, for instance, the introduction of Christianity labeled sacred völvas as evil, as "in the Middle Ages, the Danish word for seeress ... meant witch"

("Seeresses"). Similarly, there were many female cults throughout Europe, such as the benandanti in Italy, that worshipped goddesses in the thirteenth and fourteenth centuries CE; "They were the *bonnes dames, bona gens*, good people, and good neighbors ... in such countries as France, Ireland, Scotland, Spain, and Italy" (Zipes, *Irresistible Fairy Tale*, 75). The benandanti stated that they would fly to Sabbath gatherings and enter trance-like states where they would leave their bodies and be "carried to the good goddess in the world of the dead," where she would bestow "prosperity, wealth, and knowledge that the benandanti could carry with them back to the villages, where they were regenerated" (Zipes, *Irresistible Fairy Tale*, 74). However, in 1570, the benandanti were subjected to the Friulian Inquisition that identified their practices as evil. It was this labeling of pagan goddesses and their representatives as evil, such as occurred to the benandanti, that led to the European witch hunts, which was one of the darkest periods of history in regards to patriarchal attacks against women (Zipes 56). During the European Middle Ages and into the Renaissance (c. 1300–1699), thousands of women accused of witchcraft were tortured and murdered based largely on Jakob Sprenger's and Heinrich Kramer's *Malleus Maleifcarum* (1486), which was a "Church-commissioned guide for eradicating witches" (Shlain 366). Thus, the portrayal of an evil witch within a culture's folklore provided a good outlet to house once powerful goddesses and sacred women of bygone religious beliefs in an effort to enforce patriarchal ideology.

Just like folktales and fairy tales that demoted and demonized monstrous women who often held remnants of traditional goddesses, as discussed in Chapter 4 of this book, so too were witches often classified as monstrous in folktales and fairy tales. For example, in African folklore, illness and even death were often believed to be brought about by witchcraft, as witches were believed to "consume the spiritual strength of their victims" (Allan, Fleming, & Philips 58). Also, folkloric witches were often identified as demanding sacrifices, and even as eating the flesh of their victims, "sucking human blood, feeding on it, drinking it, exulting in it, and demanding it as a sacrifice" (A. Ulanov & B. Ulanov 26). This tenet, and many others like it that were meant to convey the witch as evil, was likely connected to components meant to degrade once sacred practices in association with traditional goddesses. For instance, the perceived demands of earth goddesses who required sacrifice for continued life, such as with the myths of Neolithic male consorts, certainly seem to be distorted in such tales that display witches as demanding sacrifices. In addition, often a clear folktale or fairy tale indication that a witch was identified as evil was to present her as an "old, ugly hag" (Zipes 62). This common presentation of a witch as an old woman preys upon the archetypal folktale and fairy tale presentation of old wise women who carry with them tenets associated with traditional goddess worship. In portraying the revered old wise woman in a revised, tainted form that condemns her age and individuality, the folktale or fairy tale transforms the sacred guide characteristics of the old wise woman into untrustworthy characteristics of a witch.

Thus, many folktales and fairy tales present witches who are solely evil; these witches are often quickly eradicated, mostly by male heroes. These portrayals of fully evil witches seem only represented to perpetuate stereotypical views of women within patriarchal cultures, similar to how many former goddesses were recast as evil monsters, and thus destroyed by male heroes within myths in order to portray belief systems associated with goddess reverence as in need of reform. However, many folktales and fairy tales, as this book has conveyed, often preserved bygone pagan belief systems alongside new patriarchal elements. Therefore, many depictions of folktale and fairy tale witches portray them as much more than mere monsters, showing that the culture that created, embellished, and passed on the folktale or fairy tale included elements in the portrayal of their witches that date back to the reverence they once held for goddesses. For example, in Russia "witches are usually ... in the guise of old women and thought to be immortal. The word *ved'ma* (witch) comes from the word 'to know' .... The old women of the community performed the function of priestesses by assuming the persona of the divine mistress of the universe. Like her, witches were said to control the weather. They could devour the moon and the sun and bring disease, crop failure, and death" (Hubbs 40). Thus, this Russian portrayal of the witch closely aligns her with portrayals of goddesses and the holy women who often served them. In fact, many folktales and fairy tales present witches, again sometimes identified as sorceresses or enchantresses, as beneficent women who carry similar abilities as those of traditional goddesses and who are openly revered by their communities. These beneficent witches were considered:

> powerful helpers ... who had a command of some kind of magic and were praised for the qualities that they were assumed to possess. They could bring about any kind of extraordinary transformation, guide young girls and boys through initiation rituals, protect people from calamities, change infertile couples so they could reproduce, provide propitious conditions for hunting and farming, grant wishes, predict the future, make prophecies, and determine the destinies of newly born children. They knew the sources of the fountain of youth and immortality, [and] could guide people to the land of the dead [Zipes 57].

One such example of a beneficent folkloric witch can be found in Italy's embrace of La Befana. La Befana, who is still a part of many celebrations in Italy, is believed to ride a broom throughout the skies of Italy, leaving gifts for good children on the night before Epiphany. La Befana is believed to have pre–Christian roots that may even date as far back as the Neolithic period (Greene); thus, she has been connected to many pagan goddesses in Italy. For instance, the "Romans thought that on the Twelfth Night after Natali Sol Invictus, a woman flew over the cultivated fields to give fertility for the future harvest. For some, this flying woman was identified with Diaba because of the link to vegetation; for others she was Satia or Abundia" (Greene); these goddesses are often linked to the folkloric La Befana. Other scholars think that La Befana was once the Roman goddess Strenua/Strenia, who purified the new year (Greene).

Another beneficent witch can be found in a folktale from Mexico (Mutén 45–50). The witch named La Bruha is described in the folktale as a "beautiful old crone whose magic was known far and wide" (Mutén 45). La Bruha, like many witches of folktales and fairy tales, had command of the natural environment, as she could "make the corn grow high for the farmers when there was no rain. She could tell the miners where to find silver and gold in the mountains. And she knew where the fish could be caught in the sea" (Mutén 45). La Bruha could also foresee the future, and could shapeshift, appearing as a young, beautiful maiden, though she was quite old. Because of her magical qualities, everyone in La Bruha's village knew she was a witch, but they knew that she was a kind witch who only used her abilities for good. However, one day La Bruha was arrested by the police of Córdoba and sentenced to appear before a judge, who declared that she must die for being a witch. Nevertheless, every time the judge looked into the eyes of La Bruha, he felt mesmerized by her beauty. To ward off any magic he felt she must be using against him, he had her locked deep underground in a cellar for her to await her execution.

La Bruha, despite her situation, remained calm. While she was alone in her cellar, she began to draw a picture upon the wall with a piece of charcoal from her fire. After many days passed, the judge came down to the cellar to get La Bruha's confession for being a witch, but he saw instead that she had drawn a massive black crow upon the wall, and upon the crow's back was a giant empty basket. The crow looked so real that the judge grew very afraid. As the judge stepped back, he felt a rush of wind enter the cell. He was horrified to see that the crow appeared to come alive, and what was more, he saw La Bruha impossibly step into the basket upon the crow's back. Suddenly, utterly stupefied, the judge watched as La Bruha and the crow flew away forever.

The fact that this tale shows La Bruha in a positive light, even though she was clearly identified by the patriarchal agents of her community as sinister for being a witch, is important. The tale suggests that the common people, in creating and revering this folktale, chose to maintain a belief in their sacred women instead of solely adopting new patriarchal standards that defined such women as evil. Many traditional Mexican villages revered Wise Woman, who excelled in mystical abilities that preserved the well-being of their communities. The Mexican people of these villages, just as the people portrayed in this folktale, knew the extraordinary power of these witchlike Wise Women and did not define their skills in negative terms, as they were often viewed as needed to protect the community. Thus, this folktale presents the social leaders of the community, who identify La Bruha as evil, as decidedly wrong and unjust; therefore, the tale preserves the people's true feelings for their beloved village witches.

Another example of a beneficent witch comes from an English folktale (Anderson 16) that presents the story of a witch who acts like the divine beings of many ancient myths who test protagonists to see if they are worthy of divine aid, such as the Greek Hera did to Jason by masking herself as an old woman in need of help. This testing by a divine being is also apparent in many religious texts still adopted today, such as the biblical story of Sodom and Gomorrah that shows God sending two angels to test the citizens of Sodom and Gomorrah to see if they are righteous. When it is revealed that the inhabitants of the two cities are deemed sinful by God, he sends fire and brimstone to destroy them, killing all inhabitants, except for a single righteous family. Similarly, many folktales and fairy tales also portray women in the role of goddess-like judge to the mortal characters within a tale, such as was discussed in the Earth Mother tales of the Scottish Cailleach Beira and the German Frau Holle in Chapter 1 and the tales of Chapter 2 that portrayed old wise women guiding characters upon heroic quests. Likewise, in this English folktale, a Quaker woman lived in a house far away from the village church, as the tale explicitly points out. The folktale also shows a witch traveling from house to house within the community looking for hospitality. However, the tale states that the witch was refused entry and not offered any sustenance by any member of the community, who were said to all live close to the village church. It was only when the witch arrived at the house of the Quaker woman, in the wilderness far from town, that she was treated with kindness. The Quaker woman fed and offered shelter to the witch, and similar to many mythic/religious texts, the witch rewarded the Quaker woman by warning her about an impending flood that would come and destroy the village and drown its inhabitants. The folktale further elaborates to explicitly state that the witch then caused the flood to occur (Anderson 16).

It is interesting that the format used to show divine beings from mythic/religious texts testing a subject for righteousness is also used by a witch in this folktale to test the Quaker woman. It is evident that the witch holds the judgmental power of a divine being, as she checks if the subjects who live within the community are virtuous. However, the tale merges Christian and pagan elements by presenting a witch who can use magic to control nature, which immediately signals a pagan past of goddess worship, as the one checking to see if the people of the community are devout according to their own standards of Christian ideology, as showing kindness to strangers is often identified as a Christian virtue. The fact that the witch is portrayed as a worthwhile judge of virtue connects the tale to an older ideology than Christianity, showing her to be connected to belief systems that revered goddesses who could also alter the land and judge the virtue of its inhabitants. The fact that the tale readily identifies the witch as a witch, and presents her with positive, even goddess-like, attributes explicitly reveals this folkloric witch, and perhaps many more like her, as intentionally connected to the goddesses of old.

The witches of many folktales and fairy tales often hold characteristics of all the female archetypes presented in this book; for example, witches can appear as animalistic females, maidens, mothers, stepmothers, monsters, or ghosts. However, the guise witches choose most in folktales and fairy tales is that of the old wise woman, who maintains a flair for the macabre.

Witches, like many mythic goddesses, are also connected deeply with the natural environment. It is often the witches of folktales and fairy tales who live alone in the deep recesses of the wilderness. They are also oftentimes surrounded by natural elements and protectors. In addition, they often are presented as easily able to harness the power of nature, such as changing the weather, transforming humans to animals, and healing the physically or mentally challenged using natural remedies. This connection of the witch to nature has preserved elements connected to goddess worship throughout centuries, as myriad practices involving the worship of nature as sacred, which later were often defined as evil within many cultures, were commonly transferred in folktales and fairy tales as the biddings of a witch.

Witches are also portrayed as possessing extraordinary mystical and spiritual power. For example, witches are often shown to easily be able to shapeshift; they also are often shown to command supernatural elements and creatures. In addition, witches are presented as intimately knowing ritualistic activities that involve elements associated with death and rebirth. This mystical and spiritual wisdom witches often are portrayed as possessing might come from the legacy in many world cultures of women serving as especially connected to their respective cultures' revered goddesses. As repeatedly stated in this book, many cultures embraced high-standing women in religious roles, as they believed that shamanesses, priestesses, oracles, etc., held a direct connection to myriad goddesses. For example, cultures within Iraq, China, Greece, Scandinavia, etc., revered powerful women who held central religious and social roles. Interestingly, even the garments of many high-standing religious women in myriad cultures often reflected the costuming associated with witches. Davis-Kimball discusses how in Kazakhstan, for instance, Saka priestesses were referenced as the "Saka with the pointed hat" in documents from the Achaemenid Empire (Davis-Kimball 77). In Anatolia, "priestesses, and goddesses depicted in religious reliefs and stele, wore a brimless high square headdress called a *polos*," and in western China, priestesses wore "a high, pointed affair with a brim" (Davis-Kimball 77). Davis-Kimball therefore concludes that there is "no coincidence" that the high, pointed headdress worn by the priestesses of many cultures became "the hallmark of the witch centuries later" (Davis-Kimball 77).

Witches are also often portrayed in folktales and fairy tales as intensely individualistic. The "hag-like" appearance of witches is important, as it connotes a woman who does not attempt to meet male standards of beauty. Though many folktale and fairy tale witches prove that they can shapeshift from youth to old age, they most often are portrayed as choosing to appear as an old woman; this presentation of the witch as old, again connects them to the old wise women of many folktales and fairy tales who were often valued by their communities for their plethora of wisdom that came from years of experience. Also choosing to appear as an old woman, when witches could just as easily appear as young and beautiful maidens, or even as men, sends a defiant social message that is contrary to patriarchal tales that promote male heroism and portray stereotypical versions of women as only valuable when they are young and beautiful. In addition, witches are also often portrayed as women who choose to live alone outside of the confines of the known community, within the deep wilderness. Therefore, witches are portrayed as defiantly escaping the confines of patriarchal societies, as they obey no man, and no kingly or religious ideology. In fact, the witch's "solitary existence" is considered essential by A. Ulanov and B. Ulanov, as they state that this allows the witch to attain her wisdom (A. Ulanov & B. Ulanov 33). The solitary existence of witches might also connect them to traditional religious representatives who served goddesses within many cultures, as they too often lived apart from the community in order to maintain their elite spiritual connections (Davis-Kimball 84).

Furthermore, in many folktales and fairy tales, witches are portrayed as knowing the wisdom that heroes and heroines strive toward upon their quests, as again witches fully embrace nature, can easily accomplish mystical feats, and are quite familiar with the processes of life, death, and rebirth. Therefore, in their sheer embrace of a life in resistance to patriarchy, the witch is often presented in folktales and fairy tales as a "wise woman hidden beneath the hag [who] possesses fearsome powers to lay things open [and] ... present truths for others to examine and receive. She plunges further and further, to unearth, to unveil, to exhibit. From this inward place, she instructs, she counsels, she summons. Her power stands ready to flow into the human community" (A. Ulanov & B. Ulanov 74). Thus, many a folktale and fairy tale hero and heroine has to cross the path of a witch before successfully completing their quest. But in particular, witches serve as the ultimate guides upon quests involving heroines because they possess wisdom and skills that are almost identical to the goddesses of mythology.

Baba Yaga

Perhaps the best example of a folkloric witch that closely resembles a pagan goddess is the Slavic Baba Yaga. Baba Yaga "has appeared in hundreds if not thousands of folktales in Russia, Ukraine, and Belarus since the eighteenth century, if not earlier" (Zipes vii). Many scholars believe that Baba Yaga is connected to various Slavic goddesses. Zipes explains that Baba Yaga "is not just a dangerous witch but also a maternal benefactress, probably related to a pagan goddess.... Though it is difficult to trace the historical evolution of this mysterious figure with exactitude, it is apparent that Baba Yaga was created by many voices ... from the pre–Christian era in Russia up through the eighteenth century when she finally became 'fleshed out' ... in the abundant Russian and other Slavic tales collected in the nineteenth century" (Zipes vii). Hubbs states that Baba Yaga is connected to extremely ancient concepts of a Slavic Earth Mother who was revered as the "mistress of the herds and herders ... and as the deity of the farmers. Her persona unites all aspects of fertility.... She is the mistress of the soil and its productions" (Hubbs 42). Cashdan concurs, stating that Baba Yaga "is more than just an evil witch who feeds on defenseless victims. She is a great Earth Mother who holds dominion over the universe" (Casdan 120). This conception of Baba Yaga as a pagan Earth Mother makes sense, as the folkloric Baba Yaga was thought to be associated with corn fields, where she was said to look for children to capture and eat; in fact, in Slavic regions, "the last sheaf of the harvest was often offered" to Baba Yaga to appease her (Phillips & Kerrigan 105). Forrester connects Baba Yaga specifically to the East Slavic goddess Mokosh, Moist Mother Earth, who like Baba Yaga, was revered as "a queen of ... the harvest but also of death, guarding the mysteries of winter and old age.... As Moist Mother Earth 'eats' the bodies of the dead, so Baba Yaga eats human beings" (Forrester xxxiii). Zipes also contends that Baba Yaga may be connected to the "ancient Germanic Perchta, who gave rise to the.... Frau Holle of the Brothers Grimm's and northern German tales," as both figures appear in the late Middle Ages in Europe as not only a "malevolent/benevolent figure that harked back to a great pagan mother goddess and initiation rituals but [also] a majestic, dangerous figure of resistance to Christianity" (Zipes 70).

The folkloric Baba Yaga is said to live alone, deep in the secluded wilderness, which, as stated, is a quality of many folktale and fairy tale witches. The connection of Baba Yaga, like other folktale and fairy tale witches, to nature is also clear, as she explicitly holds dominion over the many aspects of her environment within her tales. In fact, Zipes states that Baba Yaga can be seen as a "protector of the forest as a Mother Earth figure" (Zipes 62). The animals of her forest home surround her and are connected to her. For example, Baba Yaga's home rests on chicken legs. If anyone comes near her, the animals of the forest alert her. She also often uses animals as a test for any transgressors into her forest. In addition, Baba Yaga can command the elements of nature. She can alter the weather to meet her desires. Baba Yaga can also mystically metamorphose into natural forms; for instance, she often abducts her victims in natural guises, like that of a whirlwind. Also, Baba Yaga holds mastery over life, death, and rebirth. Many of her tales shows her either enriching the lives of those who cross her path, or directly causing the death of those who fail her tests. For those who fail, she displays their skulls on the fence outside of her home. In her tales, Baba Yaga can be represented in myriad ways. She appears different in each of the hundreds of tales that she appears in. Baba Yaga can also be killed in one folktale and return again alive and well in other tales. Thus, because of these aspects of the presentation of Baba Yaga, she is clearly one of the best-preserved examples of a mythic goddess.

Like other folktale and fairy tale witches, Baba Yaga also willingly lives outside of the confines of society, showing her as a figure exempt from the expectations of societal, political, cultural, and religious influence. This resistance to dominant social expectations is also displayed in the presentation of Baba Yaga's appearance. Baba Yaga is often presented with quintessential "hag-like" qualities befitting many witches within folktales and fairy tales, such as sharp teeth, pendulous breasts, and a long nose, but she carries these aspects with pride and even flaunts them. Baba Yaga also "opposes Judeo-Christian and Muslim deities and beliefs. She is her own woman" (Zipes 62). In fact, Zipes states that "Baba Yaga is inscrutable and so powerful that she does not owe allegiance to the Devil or God" (Zipes viii).

In many of her tales, Baba Yaga serves to help young men and women transform into heroes and heroines by completing a quest that she has designed for them. Zipes believes that the tales of the hero's and heroine's journey to face Baba Yaga serve as a remnant to "pagan initiation rituals" (Zipes, *Irresistible Fairy Tale*, 70). Russian folktales "often formed pools of stories … that had been part of initiation rituals in pagan times, and as the world changed, so did the sacred initiation tales that became myths and later 'degenerated' into secular wonder tales" (Zipes 68). Baba Yaga tales therefore "had their origins in … [these] initiation ceremonies by which youths passed into … [adult]hood in pre–Christian times. These rituals, which acted out the process of death and rebirth, were carried out in remote cabins at some distances from villages. Baba Yaga's house, with its fowl's legs and grisly garden fence, certainly suggests an entrance to another world beyond our own" (Phillips & Kerrigan 104). And, indeed many Baba Yaga tales show characters undergoing initiations or rites of passage toward heroism, as Baba Yaga often "shows the hero [or heroine] the path" and serves to "test the hero or heroine" (Propp, *Russian Folktale* 202–3). Zipes concurs, stating that Baba Yaga "is the ultimate tester and judge, the desacralized omnipotent goddess, who defends deep-rooted Russian pagan values and wisdom, and demands that young women and men demonstrate that they deserve her help" (Zipes 63). To test the hero or heroine, Baba Yaga demands what many goddess representations in the folktales and fairy tales discussed in this book require; she tests characters to make sure they respect nature; she challenges them to make sure they respect her and what she stands for as a goddess remnant, and she forces characters to meet the requirements of the heroic quest, reaching its culmination with her forcing the initiate to face mortality. Forrester states that "like the Indian goddess Kali, Baba Yaga is terrifying because of her relationship to death. She mediates the boundary of death so that living human beings may cross it and return, alive but in possession of new wisdom, or 'reborn' into a new status" (Forrester xxxiv). Therefore, the characters who pass the tests of Baba Yaga, most of whom are presented in folktales and fairy tales as female, end up reaching the apotheosis of the goddess.

Because Baba Yaga is so closely tied to mythic goddesses, she especially proves an adept guide for heroines upon their quests. Hubbs concurs, stating that Baba Yaga is "the fulfillment of the cycle of life associated with women. She has known all things: virginity (she has no consort), motherhood (her children in plant and animal form are legion), and old age (she gathers all things into her abode to die). In her the cycles of feminine life are brought to completion, and yet she continues them all" (Hubbs, *Mother Russia*, 27). Thus, the heroines who pass the quests designed by Baba Yaga end up realizing their own connection to traditional goddesses and become apotheotic heroines, who like Baba Yaga did for them, pass on the goddess-oriented lessons they learned to those around them.

One of the most famous of the Baba Yaga tales involving a female heroine is "Vasilisa the Beautiful" (Afanasev 439–47). In this tale, Vasilisa's mother died when she was only eight years old. Before she died, Vasilisa's mother gave her a doll and told her to seek its aid anytime she should need help throughout her life. Vasilisa's father, again like many other tales, married a woman who mistreated Vasilisa. Vasilisa's stepmother and her daughters tormented Vasilisa, making her live the life of a servant. However, Vasilisa, with the help of her doll, was always able to complete all the tasks assigned to her by her stepmother and managed to do so while growing into a maiden of astounding beauty. In time, Vasilisa was of marriageable age, and all the eligible men of the community wanted to marry her, while they ignored her stepsisters. In anger, Vasilisa's stepmother began demanding that Vasilisa venture on errands further and further into the wilderness, with the intent of getting her to go close to the house of Baba Yaga. However, Vasilisa's doll always helped her stay far away from Baba Yaga. That is, until one time when the stepsisters demanded that Vasilisa go directly to Baba Yaga's home to get fire for them. Distraught, Vasilisa asked for help from her doll and journeyed into the woods to seek out the witch Baba Yaga.

Meeting the first requirement of the heroine's journey, Vasilisa ventured away from home into the unknown regions of the forest in an area where few ever ventured. In time, Vasilisa encountered a horseman dressed all in white upon a white steed, but she only continued on determined to fulfill her quest. Vasilisa finally arrived at a house that stood upon chicken legs, had a fence made of human bones and skulls, and a mouth filled with teeth for a door lock (Forrester 174–5), so she knew at once that she had found the home of Baba Yaga. As Vasilisa stood trembling by Baba Yaga's house, she saw a horseman dressed in black upon a black steed approach the house and seemingly disappear. Seeing this, Vasilisa wanted to turn back home, but just when she thought about fleeing, she saw that the forest began to make a terrifying noise, and suddenly Baba Yaga appeared riding in her most common form of transportation—a mortar and pestle. Baba Yaga suddenly stopped and asked who was near her home, and though she was mortally terrified, Vasilisa walked straight up to Baba Yaga and said "'I'm here, granny! The stepmother's daughters sent me to get fire from you'" (Forrester 175).

Baba Yaga, seeing the bravery of Vasilisa, allowed Vasilisa to live with her as long as she served her. Baba Yaga demanded that Vasilisa do tasks that resembled the tasks she was forced to do in her stepmother's household, such as cleaning and cooking, and if Vasilisa could not do the assigned projects, then Baba Yaga stated that she would eat Vasilisa. And just like at her stepmother's home, Vasilisa easily completed her tasks with the help of the doll her mother gave her. It is significant that the tale presents Vasilisa as in danger of reentering the same life of servitude she left behind with her stepmother, which would stunt the heroic quest she began and show that she had not matured into her own autonomous identity if she stayed in this role. However, this is not the case, as while Vasilisa worked for Baba Yaga day in and day out, she began to notice that the horseman dressed in black, who she saw at the start of her journey, arrived each night, just as a horseman dressed in white came at the start of each morning, as if they were the cause for the transition in the times of the day. In time, when Baba Yaga saw that Vasilisa always completed all of the tasks she assigned her, she added a more difficult project to Vasilisa's daily requirements, which was clearing the dirt off of each piece of grain in her granary. And again, Vasilisa did the seemingly impossible task with the help of her doll. Accomplishing seemingly impossible agricultural tasks, such as cleaning the dirt from thousands of pieces of grain, is reminiscent of Venus's challenge to the Roman Psyche as well as Cinderella's challenge from her stepmother; such a task signals connections to a distant past when agricultural earth goddesses dominated. Thus, Baba Yaga is apparently teaching Vasilisa here to develop her goddess-like ability to use mysticism, which she already partially possesses from her mother's magic doll, yet Vasilisa at this point in the tale does not seem to know how to properly use her power, as she keeps submitting herself to live in positions of servitude. The fact that Baba Yaga first tested Vasilisa using the tasks that Vasilisa used to do in her old life of servitude, mundane tasks that were traditionally assigned to women, but moved on to assign a more difficult task to her, which involved mysticism surrounding agriculture, shows that Baba Yaga is teaching Vasilisa how to move beyond the patriarchal requirements for women of her culture and era.

The tale continues to show that once Vasilisa proved that she could successfully complete the initial tasks assigned to her, Baba Yaga allowed Vasilisa to become further educated by her, as she stated one day that Vasilisa could gain wisdom by asking her any question she liked. Vasilisa chose to ask about the horsemen who came each day, and she learned that they were at the command of Baba Yaga, and that their arrival indeed initiated the transition of time each day. This knowledge that Vasilisa gained from Baba Yaga shows her that Baba Yaga is more than just an ordinary woman, as her ability to control the transition of day to night, and night to day, undeniably presents her as similar to mythic goddesses who control such events. Once Vasilisa received this understanding of the true nature of Baba Yaga as a goddess representative, then she was ready to go home with the gift of fire for her stepsisters that she sought at the start of her quest, thus having passed the first stage of Baba Yaga's tests; however, before Vasilisa was allowed to go home, Baba Yaga threatened her with death if she proved unworthy of her teaching. This threat from Baba Yaga signals that Vasilisa, though going home, has not yet achieved apotheosis, as Vasilisa must fully recognize that what Baba Yaga represents as a goddess representative is also a part of herself.

The tale shows Vasilisa arriving home with Baba Yaga's gift of fire inside a human skull—a gift that carries much symbolic meaning, as the gift of fire is a part of many world myths that present culture heroes gifting the sacred element of fire to people in need; likewise, fire within a human skull also portrays imagery associated with the obtainment of new wisdom or enlightenment. Once at home, Vasilisa found that her gift was in fact greatly needed by her stepmother and stepsisters, as without Vasilisa serving as their servant, they were unable to start their own fire or even keep a fire going after they got coals from their neighbors; this ineptitude on the part of the stepmother and stepsisters shows that they do not possess the wisdom earned by Vasilisa upon her quest. This is reinforced when Vasilisa held the skull filled with fire up for them to see, and they all burned to ashes. It is this moment that Vasilisa fully encounters the heroic quest tenet of facing her own death in the symbolic underworld, as the stepmother and stepsisters are revealed to be former aspects of Vasilisa herself. When these false aspects of Vasilisa's selfhood, connected to societal expectations for the proper role of women that oppressed her before her quest, burn away, Vasilisa is finally portrayed as achieving apotheosis into the maturity of a goddess representative herself. Vasilisa thus becomes, not what her stepmother and stepsisters were, but what her mother was, and what Baba Yaga is, a woman who values nature, can use mysticism to her advantage, and fully understands the necessity of the cycles of life, death, and rebirth.

The tale ends showing Vasilisa as adopting a life of self-sufficiency by rooming with an old woman and weaving the best cloth in the region in order to make a living; again, the folkloric tenet of weaving further signals Vasilisa's apotheosis, as it directly connects her to many mythic goddesses. When the tsar saw Vasilisa's weaving, he wished at once to meet her, and in doing so, he instantly fell in love with her. The tsar and Vasilisa were married, suggesting as in other folktales and fairy tales of the heroine's quest, that Vasilisa will educate the tsar in her newfound spiritual maturity, but will also influence her people in her newfound role of power as tsarina, thus showing that Vasilisa became an embodiment of her teacher—the witch Baba Yaga.

Other Goddess-like Witches

The fairy tale of "Hansel and Gretel" also displays a witch who guides a maiden toward heroism. In the first edition of the Grimm brothers' tale of "Hansel and Gretel" (J. Grimm & W. Grimm 43–9), the children's biological mother told her husband that because the whole family was near starvation, he must take the children into the deep forest and leave them there, but like other later versions of many Grimm brothers' tales, such as "Little Snow White," the biological mother was switched to the children's cruel stepmother to appease audiences who could not believe a mother would do such a thing. However, if the intent of the work is to show the heroism of the children in successfully completing their quest, then the mother, and later the stepmother, appears not as a villain but as an educator who grants the lessons of the witch to her children/stepchildren.

The fairy tale declares that the children were given back to nature to try and survive, which sets the stage for the tale to articulate a very old ritual recoding the rite of passage from childhood into adulthood, or dependency toward self-sufficiency and self-actualization. In this light, the mother/stepmother thrusts the story into its fateful result, which is the prosperity of her children in what is spelled out within the tale as difficult times. Again, meeting the requirements of the heroic journey, the children go deep into the unknown woods, where mortals seldom go, in order to move past former notions of selfhood that might be hindering them from prosperity. The forest plays a key role in guiding the children to the home where they will face the worst thing they can imagine, which appears in the form of a witch who wishes to consume them. Therefore, their worst fear, of an elder eating them, which comes directly from their dreadful circumstance of starvation at home, is realized with the materialization of the witch. Thus, this psychological episode forces the children, or more aptly Gretel, to move toward self-actualization, as arguably Gretel attains apotheosis through her encounter with the witch, but Hansel does not quite get there.

The witch within "Hansel and Gretel" meets the requirements of a fairy tale witch, and thus of many mythic goddesses. She is old and lives alone in the deep wilderness, and she is terrifying, as she holds the power to destroy and consume that which she destroys. Hansel and Gretel initially greatly feared the witch when she revealed her true self to them, but it was Gretel who eventually pushed past her fear and learned how to defeat the witch. Hansel spends most of his quest being fattened up by the witch as he is trapped in a cage, until he is rescued by his sister; therefore, he mostly remains a static character. However, the fairy tale presents Gretel as being allowed to roam the witch's abode, as she maintained the cooking and cleaning of the witch's home, similar to the role Vasil-isa initially played for Baba Yaga, signaling Gretel as likewise in a position of servitude to societal expectations for women. However, it is this role that, in time, gives Gretel power. Living alongside the witch reveals information about the witch to Gretel, which enables her to eventually move away from a life of servitude that is under the authority of others, into a life of self-reliance and self-actualization, that resembles the life the witch lives. In living with the witch, Gretel saw that the witch lived like a goddess, as she was fully capable of maintaining her independence within the deep wilderness, when everyone else in her life experience was vastly incapable of survival, as her family and community were literally starving to death. Gretel saw that the witch was the only one within her life who possessed the knowledge and ability to cultivate her own food in excess, as her house was literary made of food, suggesting the goddess-like abilities of the witch. To further promote the idea that the witch is connected to mythic portrayals of goddesses, the tale shows that while others could not even survive, the witch's house was filled not only with food, but with priceless jewels. The representation of wealth and abundance within the home of the witch explicitly shows her divine power, just as was found in many folktales and fairy tales that presented characters who were shown as achieving the skills of a goddess by their obtainment of precious jewels, such as the Kenyan Marwe, German Cinderella, or Chinese Yeh-hsien. When Gretel finally pushed the witch into her own oven, thus killing her, the wealth, and more importantly the goddess-like knowledge and abilities of the witch, were symbolically transferred to Gretel, as often in folktales and fairy tales, killing the witch, like Snow White did with her mother/stepmother, signifies the heroine's obtainment of the witch's power within herself, and thus her apotheosis. However, as with tales of Baba Yaga, it is clear that the witch, though seemingly killed by Gretel, is not really dead, as she appears again in innumerable other tales ready to pass on her wisdom to the next worthwhile heroine. Thus, when a witch is killed by a maiden, it merely represents a blip in a never-ending cycle of birth, death, and rebirth, since the newly apotheotic maiden will carry on the lessons of how to live like a witch to the next generation.

The tale closes with Hansel and Gretel going back home to their father, as their mother/stepmother died while they were away, with the witch's jewels, again symbolic of Gretel's newly attained goddess-like wisdom, as she learned how to thrive in nature, master mysticism, and respect the cycles of life and death. The fact that the mother/stepmother died before the apotheotic Gretel returned home suggests that Gretel matured beyond the confines of what her mother/stepmother represented, which was a woman who was incapable of being self-sufficient, though of course in the bigger picture, the mother/stepmother seems to have been connected to the witch as the initiator of Gretel's heroic quest. The tale ends thus promising that Gretel, instead of her father or her brother as expected according to patriarchal norms, will serve as the future provider and instructor of her family and community.

The fairy tale "Rapunzel" also appears in Grimms' *Fairy Tales* (J. Grimm & W. Grimm 37–42), but as with many other folktales and fairy tales, variations of it appear around the world and again date back to ancient times (Anderson 121). The Grimm brothers' tale of "Rapunzel" portrays a witch/sorceress as the "mistress of the garden and forest" near the royal compound of Rapunzel's parents (Zipes, *Irresistible Fairy Tale*, 78). Rapunzel's mother, the queen, was portrayed as initially unable to have children, until she spied the rapunzel growing in the witch's garden outside her window; after this, she mysteriously longed for the plant and demanded that her husband risk his life to attain it. The husband did as his wife asked, stealing the rapunzel from the witch's garden, and when the queen ate the rapunzel, she became pregnant. Thus, this introduction of the tale, with its mystical components, suggests that again the events of the story were orchestrated by a combination of Rapunzel's mother and the witch, both of whom, as with many tales, serve as a united effort to educate the maiden Rapunzel about the ways of mythic goddesses.

Because of the transgression of stealing from the witch's garden, once the queen gave birth to Rapunzel, the witch took her to live deep in the secluded forest. It is significant that the witch brings Rapunzel into the wilderness, as like Gretel, this experience will give her a chance to learn her sacred tie to the environment, a connection the witch assuredly holds, as again the tale identifies the witch as the "mistress of the garden and forest" (Zipes, *Irresistible Fairy Tale*, 78). To even a greater extent than the witch in "Hansel and Gretel," the witch in this tale educated Rapunzel about living life as a witch in the years that Rapunzel interacted with her as her only companion. While the witch watched over Rapunzel, one of her main priorities was to protect Rapunzel from "'male' intrusion" (Zipes, *Irresistible Fairy Tale*, 78). Though many folktales and fairy tales that portray witches and maidens subtlety display this tenet, the witch in "Rapunzel" is portrayed as holding dominion over Rapunzel's maidenhood in a way that is more explicit than many other tales. For example, Vasilisa must contend with Baba Yaga before she can mature and be ready for marriage, and similarly Gretel can only move from childhood into adulthood after having faced the witch. Tales such as these show witches watching over a girl's maidenhood, which represents more than simply virginity, until she is ready to take command of it herself and not just bestow ownership of it to a man. Taking command of one's own maidenhood within folktales and fairy tales directly connects a maiden to her goddess-like power of regeneration; it also represents the transition from childhood to adulthood, where a maiden must shed her belief that she is dependent upon others and instead embrace her own autonomy. Often folktales and fairy tales show a father as declaring dominion over his daughter's maidenhood by choosing who his daughter marries, so that that symbolic ownership of the maiden transfers from the father to the husband and thus protects patriarchal structures. However, when a witch intervenes into the life of a maiden, the witch can successfully guide the maiden from childhood and dependency into the life of a powerful and independent woman. Again, this tenet of a witch's connection to a heroine's maidenhood is heightened in the tale of "Rapunzel," as the witch keeps Rapunzel from having any contact with males by putting her within a tower that places Rapunzel in a goddess-like vantage to any male suitor who should someday see her, as she literally towers above them. The symbolism of the witch putting Rapunzel in a tower that forces any male who spies her to look up at her, as if worshipping her, connects her to maidens like Snow White and Sleeping Beauty who were also portrayed in states that induced the worship of male suitors. Thus, it appears that the witch purposefully orchestrated this scenario to teach Rapunzel about her own goddess-like worth before maturing into a woman. And indeed, a prince eventually discovered Rapunzel in her high tower and immediately fell in love with her when he gazed up at her visage in the clouds.

The prince eventually learned how to gain entrance into Rapunzel's tower by spying on the witch's method for climbing it, which was to command Rapunzel to unleash her long hair, a symbol of her youth and vitality, so that she could climb up, again explicitly showing the witch's command over Rapunzel's maidenhood. Therefore, when the prince tricked Rapunzel into unleashing her hair and proceeded to climb up into her tower, he was portrayed as taking Rapunzel's maidenhood, again symbolic of her sacred feminine power, through deception. And indeed, Rapunzel was portrayed as not yet being an apotheotic heroine, as she proved herself in jeopardy of handing over her autonomy to this new stranger when she instantly agreed to marry him and have sex with him in her tower, thus merely transferring her maidenhood from the witch to the prince. However, as witches in folktales and fairy tales serve to teach maidens how to properly mature into formidable heroines, the tale shows the witch as intervening once more to further educate Rapunzel.

As an intervention, the witch after learning of Rapunzel's meetings with the prince cut off her long hair and forced her to leave the tower and live by her own devices within the secluded wilderness. The tale proceeds to show that Rapunzel, like other heroines at the start of their quests, was initially terrified of nature, but as time went on, Rapunzel learned that she possessed the strength and knowledge to live within her new natural environment. In fact, Rapunzel eventually gave birth to twins while she was alone in the woods and successfully raised them alone within nature for years. Rapunzel's time in the wilderness certainly allowed her to meet the requirements of the heroine's quest, as she had to learn to utilize the natural resources around her to survive and raise her children, just as she had to face death in her struggle to survive. Like Gretel, it seems that Rapunzel's time living with the witch made her knowledgeable about the skills the witch possessed, and thus served to help her upon her journey.

When the witch encountered the prince in the tale, he became a mere victim of her, much like Hansel in "Hansel and Gretel," as when the prince climbed the tower and saw the face of the witch instead of Rapunzel, he proved that he could not confront what the witch represented, which was an autonomous and powerful woman, so he thrust himself from the tower and landed on thorn bushes, making him blind and securing his uselessness in the tale. The prince thus wandered the wilderness for years, not thriving like Rapunzel, but floundering as he ate "nothing but grass and roots" (Zipes, *Irresistible Fairy Tale*, 78), until Rapunzel found him. Rapunzel, who had grown into an autonomous heroine with two children during her solitary quest in nature, showed that she had attained apotheosis when she saw the deplorable state of the prince and used her own tears to heal him of his blindness. This act of healing, that is similar to the acts of resurrection performed by many folktale and fairy tale apotheotic heroines, shows that Rapunzel attained the abilities of mythic goddesses, as she learned to respect the environment, use mysticism at will, and take part in the processes of birth, death, and resurrection. Therefore, again, it is clear in this fairy tale that the witch served as the educator of the maiden, guiding her to realize her own potential as a goddess representative, until she was ready to stand autonomous in this position, which was signaled in the tale when Rapunzel finally married the prince and left to enter her new life as queen, so that she, like many apotheotic heroines, could carry on the lessons she learned to her people.

A Slavic folktale entitled "Ivanushka and Alionushka" (Phillips & Kerrigan 122–3) also presents a heroine who attains goddess-like apotheosis because of her encounter with a witch. The tale relates that Prince Ivanushka was turned into a goat after heedlessly drinking from a sacred well, suggesting his disrespect for nature and its representatives. His sister, Alionushka, still cared for him in his animalistic state, even after she herself married a king, showing her to be a character who, unlike her brother, valued nature. The tale unfolds to show that one day a witch discovered Queen Alionushka and her transformed brother, and wishing to test the queen, like so many witches do to heroines, the witch cast a drought upon the land, showing her power as a witch, as well as a goddess representative. This act of inducing the land to become sterile is again a common component of many myths, folktales, and fairy tales that may connect back to ancient Slavic concepts of aligning the fertility of the land with a worthwhile goddess representative, showing that if Queen Alionushka passes the witch's test, she will attain the same abilities as the witch and will thus restore the land. The witch also tied a stone around Alionushka's neck and threw her identity, but not her body, into the sea. Alionushka was shown to thus be separated from selfhood, as her real identity was presented as living within the sea, but her false self was living her old life, as the witch took over her body. This is also a common plot devise of many folktales and fairy tales, and when it is used, it often serves to show a heroine as needing to find selfhood, through the obtainment of wisdom upon a quest, in order to reunite back into her true form.

The king of this folktale is presented as foolish, as he could not tell at all that his wife's identity had been replaced with that of a witch, which signals to audiences that the true characters of worth are the females within the narrative, such as was the case in "Hansel and Gretel" and "Rapunzel." The witch within Alionushka's body demanded one day that the king slaughter Ivanushka, who was still in goat form; the foolish king only found it slightly odd that his "wife" decreed that her own brother, in goat form, should be slaughtered, but the king still obeyed the queen's wishes and took the goat brother out for one last drink. However, at the water's edge, the goat brother called out to his sister who answered him beneath the sea and told him that she was trapped.

The time Alionushka lived within the sea served as the education of the natural world that is required of heroines upon their quests. Also, Alionushka's facing of her own death, as well as her ability to live on in the sea, taught her the necessary elements of death and rebirth that the witch often teaches heroines during their journeys to find self-actualization. Thus, Alionushka proved that she had reached apotheosis when she no longer accepted the fate of entrapment that the witch seemingly forced upon her, as she finally freed herself by completing the quintessential task in mythology, folktales, and fairy tales that signals that heroines have become a representation of a goddess—she resurrected herself. Alionushka burst forth from the water and immediately returned home with her goat brother. The fact that Alionushka only had to realize that she possessed the ability to save herself is telling, as it especially shows that her ordeal was designed by the witch to teach her of her own strength as a goddess representative. This is reiterated in the tale when the drought-ridden land surrounding Alionushka's castle vibrantly came back to life when in the presence of Alionushka. The resurrection of not only herself but of nature signals that Alionushka finally obtained the same wisdom that the witch possessed.

The folktale ends, like so many other tales of witches, with the witch being put to death by the maiden's decree. In this tale, the witch was killed in the manner that many women accused of witchcraft were, as she was burned at the stake, but again, the witch's demise does not necessarily display her as an agent of evil within the tale. The fact that Alionushka easily freed herself once she learned who she really was, and the witch merely allowed it to happen and simply fell by the wayside, shows that the witch served to guide Alionushka toward becoming like her. Similar to Vasilisa, Gretel, and Rapunzel who all lived alongside a witch for a time, Alionushka was presented with the unique experience of having a powerful witch live within her, so that she intimately was able to learn the ways of the witch. Thus, like tales of wicked stepmothers who were often killed by self-actualized stepdaughters, or like Gretel who had to kill the witch, Alionushka also had to symbolically kill the witch within her to signal that she was no longer the pupil, but had become another teacher of the full power of witches and mythic goddesses.

Hans Christian Andersen's "The Snow Queen" (1844) displays another maiden, named Gerda, who was educated by a sorceress/witch. The tale begins with Kai's grandmother telling Gerda and Kai a story about the Snow Queen, who is portrayed as a sorceress described in goddess-like imagery, as she is closely linked with nature in her ability to initiate the coming of winter. Norse culture envisioned goddesses as initiating the change of seasons, such as the goddess Skadi's ability to transform nature into a state of winter. In this fairy tale, Kai, in typical male heroic fashion, blurted out that if he could catch the Snow Queen, he would melt her by putting her in a stove. With seeming knowledge that the story she recited to the children was meant to test Gerda and not Kai, thus making the grandmother connected to the Snow Queen, the grandmother only patted Kai's head and continued on with her storytelling. In line with the grandmother orchestrating a plan to teach Gerda the ways of the goddess, right after hearing the story, Kai looked out of the window and was shocked to see the Snow Queen herself, who magically appeared as a woman who grew from a single snowflake. The fact that the Snow Queen was able to metamorphose from a snowflake into a woman again presents her as connected to traditional Norse goddesses.

The Snow Queen, showing herself to be a powerful witch, immediately abducted Kai and froze him into a death-like state, so that his skin became almost black with cold, and his memory and identity were wiped away. Kai, like Hansel, therefore becomes a mere prisoner of the witch within the tale and so remains a static character who does not partake on a heroic quest. Kai's entrapment by his state of winter-like dormancy does however initiate Gerda to begin her heroine's quest to find the Snow Queen's remote castle and thus save Kai. At the start of her quest Gerda was portrayed as respecting nature, as right when she left behind her home to enter the wilderness, she was portrayed as comfortable within the natural environment, as she was shown to openly converse with the elements of nature, such as animals, the sunshine, a river, and vegetation, in order to gain assistance upon her quest. The fact that Gerda could communicate with the elements of the environment shows her to be an ideal initiate for a witch/goddess representative to guide her upon a quest to obtain powerful wisdom.

Gerda was eventually directed, by her natural helpers, to the home of an old witch who lived alone in the wilderness. Often when there are multiple witches within one tale, the myriad witches are presented as connected to one another to serve the same purpose of teaching the heroine upon her quest. This witch, like the Snow Queen, was also portrayed as able to control the elements of nature, as she lived in an environment of perpetual summer. This alignment of both witches serving as the ones in command of the changing of the seasons shows that they undoubtedly hold connections with traditional goddesses, like the Scottish goddesses Beira and Bride who similarly transitioned the earth between winter and spring; this connection also makes it clear that both witches are connected to one another in Gerda's quest. The summer witch wanted to keep Gerda at her home, so she put Gerda into a state of psychological stasis, where she quickly forgot the goal of her journey. However, in time, Gerda again turned to nature for guidance by speaking with the flowers in the witch's garden. The flowers told Gerda stories about spiritually powerful females, such as tales about Indian women who performed sati or maidens who danced though they were dead. The tales Gerda heard from the flowers served as a turning point for her, as she moved from being a young girl without selfhood, because the summer witch took it from her in order to entrap her, similar to the captive Gretel, Rapunzel, and Alionushka, into a woman who gained control of her own abilities. Once Gerda realized who she was and what she was capable of, she like Alionushka, freed herself from the witch, in an abundantly easy way—by simply shaking the witch's gate until the lock came loose. Like the tale of Alionushka, the ease of Gerda releasing herself from the witch's captivity shows that the summer witch was not evil, but simply served to educate Gerda along her journey. Because of her time with the summer witch, Gerda learned that the witch's perpetual summer, reminiscent of mythic otherworlds that hold perpetual abundance, was a place that was unnatural. Gerda learned in freeing herself from the witch's perpetual summer that a state of winter, with its dormancy, suffering, and death, was also necessary. Therefore, when Gerda left the summer witch, she learned what she needed to in order to rescue Kai, who resided in perpetual winter, because she now understood that nature must have times of both dormancy and decay, as well as verdant growth.

As Gerda journeyed to the Snow Queen's castle, she crossed the path of more female characters who helped to educate her, such a princess who, though she had many suitors, would only marry one who respected her autonomy. This section of the tale reiterates a dominant theme within the narrative—that female characters in the work are strong and independent all on their own. To carry this message further, Gerda was next abducted by a band of robbers, but was then saved by a robber maiden who also had a mind of her own. The robber maiden was portrayed as physically and mentally strong, as she clearly controlled all the male robbers of her band. When the robber maiden heard the plight of Gerda, she secured for her a talking reindeer that whisked Gerda away to Finland to find Kai. Once there, Gerda again encountered two female characters, the Lapland woman and the Finland woman, who also served as helpers upon her quest. Again, these women were described in the tale as strong and independent, and they additionally possessed mystical qualities. When the talking reindeer asked these women to give Gerda magical powers to protect her from the Snow Queen, the Finland woman simply stated of Gerda "'I can give her no more power than what she has already. Don't you see how great it is? Don't you see how men and animals are forced to serve her'" (Andersen)? This declaration by the Finland woman reveals that Gerda is close in the narrative to attaining her position as a goddess representative, as she has repeatedly proven in the tale that she is capable of being in command of both mysticism and nature and is thus equal to the witches she encounters. The tale supports this by immediately propelling Gerda to finally face the Snow Queen.

In order for Gerda to attain apotheosis though, she still had to experience the underworld stage of her heroine's quest. When Gerda finally arrived at the Snow Queen's castle, she was indeed portrayed as facing death. The Snow Queen appeared to Gerda not as an old ugly hag, like many witches of folktales and fairy tales are often portrayed, but as a beautiful, mature woman who was in full command of her natural and supernatural power. The Snow Queen, like many witches and mythic goddesses, was also shown to be in command of the processes of life, death, and rebirth, as she kept Kai captive in his death-like state of dormancy. Therefore, Gerda was certainly in mortal danger by challenging the powerful Snow Queen. Gerda also faced a symbolic underworld when she saw what death in nature looked like within the Snow Queen's winter palace. In many ancient myths, the underworld was connected to the season of winter, such as in the Akkadian myth of Ishtar and the Greek myth of Persephone that both showed winter as coming about because of the descension of the respective goddesses into the underworld. These myths thus taught that winter was a necessary time of death and decay, so that new life could emerge again, with the ascent of the goddesses, in the spring. Similarly, when Gerda entered the Snow Queen's castle to retrieve Kai, she saw the environment all around her, and her playmate, in what looked like a state of death. However, Gerda showed that she had reached the final stage of her heroic quest, with her attainment of apotheosis, when she saw that what looked like death all around her, both in nature and in Kai, was not death at all, but dormancy. This realization on the part of Gerda reveals her to be a goddess representative because she is portrayed as learning the ultimate lesson witches and mythic goddesses teach—the promise of cyclical life. Showing Gerda's understanding that winter, like death, are but momentary stages in nature's cycles, Gerda herself, as a goddess would, then initiated nature's cycle to continue by easily, so easy that it suggested a natural state, melting away the ice in Kai's heart, restoring him to a spring-like state of life and vibrancy. Again, like the tale of Alionushka, the fact that the Snow Queen simply allowed this to happen portrays her not as evil, but as an educator to Gerda, who wished all along for Gerda to become like her.

The symbolism of Kai's rebirth is further supported by the story's ending, as Kai and Gerda returned home in the full splendor of spring to Kai's grandmother, where the young couple now held hands, acknowledging that they had moved from childhood into adulthood. Andersen suggests by this ending that both Gerda and Kai will now enter a new stage of their relationship, adding the element of their promised fertility to the productive season of spring that Gerda initiated when she renewed Kai from his winter dormancy, signaling Gerda again as a goddess representative for her participation in the cycles of life. Furthermore, the fact that Gerda and Kai return at the end of the tale back to the grandmother, who began the tale with her storytelling of the Snow Queen, greatly suggests that the entire scenario was instigated by her, and that furthermore, she holds connections with all of the women presented in the tale: the summer witch, the female flowers, the independent princess, the robber maiden, the Finland and Lapland women, and the Snow Queen. Thus, the myriad female characters in this tale all united to educate Gerda on the unending unification of women who hold connections with divine goddesses, a connection that Gerda now possesses and will assuredly pass on to the next generation.

Another of Hans Christian Andersen's fairy tales, "The Little Mermaid" (1836), also presents a maiden who is educated on ways connected to mythic goddesses because of her quest with a witch, in this case a sea witch. The little mermaid is portrayed as not being fully content in her otherworldly life beneath the sea, as she fell in love with a human prince and longed to live with him on land. This tale is similar to many other myths, folktales, and fairy tales that portray characters falling in love with otherworldly beings who reside in the sea, such as the Japanese folktale of Urashima; however, in most of these tales the story is reversed, showing male characters as having to go to the otherworld in order to be spiritually transformed by the otherworldly women who live there. Thus, this tale shows that the little mermaid's dream of going to the ordinary realm of humans serves as a demotion for her. The little mermaid's inability to understand this shows that she does not initially recognize her own exceptional abilities as a goddess-like agent of the otherworld.

In order to live amongst humans, the little mermaid sought the help of a sea witch. The portrayal of the sea witch in this tale resembles other folktale and fairy tale portrayals of witches, as her home is made out of the bones of men who died in shipwrecks, much like Baba Yaga's fence made of skeletons, and she is shown as eating a toad, while snakes slithered all over her body and guarded her compound. Though terrified of the sea witch, the little mermaid managed to stammer out her request; therefore, the sea witch granted her what she believed she wanted—human legs—so that she could enter the realm of humans and find love. However, the sea witch placed conditions upon the little mermaid's request, showing her as orchestrating a more worthwhile heroine's quest that would not simply grant the little mermaid the love of a man, making her dependent upon patriarchal standards, but would allow her to realize her own powerful potential as a goddess representative. The sea witch therefore declared to the little mermaid that to possess legs, and be human, she would have to experience suffering, as when she went on land, the pain of walking on false legs would be excruciating. In addition, the little mermaid would also have to remain voiceless, an element that again suggests that her quest for the love of a man she does not know will only leave her void of selfhood. Finally, the sea witch stated, foreshadowing the underworld requirement of the little mermaid's quest, that she would die by turning to sea foam if she failed to secure the prince's love. Thus, the stipulations the sea witch place upon the little mermaid's quest shows that she has designed a heroine's journey for the little mermaid that has nothing to do with securing the love of a prince. The tale confirms this, as the little mermaid is shown to pine away for the prince once she metamorphosed into human form and lived on land for a period of time, but the prince only ended up marrying another woman. The little mermaid's human form then melted away from existence, becoming sea foam, just as the sea witch prophesized.

However, this fairy tale presents the little mermaid as achieving more than she envisioned upon her initial quest to find love, which makes her transformation at the end of the tale into sea foam a sign that she actually achieved apotheosis at the conclusion of her heroic quest. When the little mermaid left her sea environment to enter the realm of humans, she also left behind her adolescence, defined in the narrative as one that was free of worry as she lived in opulence in her father's royal household. The pain of walking on false legs and the ordeals that came with not being able to speak allowed the little mermaid to begin to know herself and her own abilities. Again, on her quest, she attempted to achieve her goal of attaining the love of a stranger, but she ultimately lost this naïve and youthful goal, as she watched the prince she thought she loved marry another woman, which because of the sea witch's decree, spelled the demise of the little mermaid and required her to face the underworld stage of her quest. However, as with many tales of heroines, the underworld experience did not end with the death of the little mermaid, as she did not entirely die but only metamorphosed into sea foam and then, as the text states, one of the "daughters of the air," who could bring cool breezes, spread forth scents of flowers upon the wind, and heal the sick (Andersen). This ending signals that the little mermaid achieved apotheosis after facing death by finally embracing her connection to the natural environment. The fact that the little mermaid initially denied her connection with her natural environment of the sea and viewed her home, as well as the sea witch who commanded this environment, with abhorrence shows that she did not fully understand the lessons of mythic goddesses. However, when the little mermaid merged with nature at the end of her quest, by becoming a mystical "daughter of the air," whose abilities matched those of the sea witch, as well as mythic goddesses, she finally gained apotheosis. This fairy tale, thus, makes it clear that the sea witch, by setting up all the events of the little mermaid's quest with her seemingly harsh stipulations, actually helped empower the little mermaid to become what she always was—an otherworldly goddess representative who could serve to inspire others.

In an Irish folktale entitled "The Horned Women" (Jacobs), witches also help a heroine, who is portrayed not as a maiden but as a mother, reach her potential as a goddess representative. This folktale begins with a mother who was up late at night preparing wool while her family slept. The mother heard a knock at the door, and when she opened it, she was startled to find an old woman with a horn protruding from her head standing there. The old woman helped herself inside and took over the work of the mother, carding her wool with precision. After a moment, the old woman proclaimed that her sisters would be coming soon. At that, there was another knock at the door, and a second old woman appeared, this time with two horns coming out of her head. The second old woman brought a spinning wheel, and after setting it up in the woman's house, she began spinning wool. This same pattern repeated itself, until the mother's house was filled with twelve women who called themselves witches and had the same number of horns protruding out of their heads as the order of their appearance at the mother's home. The mother initially felt quite afraid of these witches and what they might do to her and her family, so she could only sit there and watch as the twelve old witches worked busily to card, spin, and weave the woman's wool. As the witches worked, they sang an "ancient" song (Jacobs).

The supernatural appearance of the witches in this folktale, with horns sticking out of their heads, much like the Celtic horned god Cernunnos, and the fact that the witches convene together and sing "ancient" songs explicitly connects them to representations of Celtic divinities. Additionally, the connection of the witches to the act of spinning and weaving, as has been seen in many folktales involving women and supernatural agents, further aligns them with mythic goddesses. In a similar presentation to this folktale, German and Austrian tales also showcase folkloric figures of former goddesses, such as Perchta/Berchta or Frau Holle, using spinning as a means to check on the worth of women, rewarding or punishing them if they fail to meet the standards of these once divine figures. For instance, as discussed in Chapter 1 of this book, folktales of Perchta, who is believed to have Germanic origins as a former Earth Mother, show her on Perchtentag coming into the homes of women to see if they were properly spinning their flax or wool. If the women proved lazy or unworthy by the goddess representative, she would slit their bellies open and stuff them with straw. Many interpretations exist to the meaning of the folkloric Perchta judging a woman's ability to spin flax or wool, and brutally punishing the woman if she does not meet her standards. By looking at this Irish folktale perhaps it might explain Perchta's behavior, as it so closely resembles the actions of the witches toward the mother of this tale. The witches ambush the mother's home, like Perchta does on Perchtentag, to judge the mother in accordance to spinning, but the folktale will reveal that what the witches are really judging, like so many tales of witches convey, is the worth of the woman to become a goddess representative. The ancient act of spinning shows the witches' former role as divinities, as again Greek, Celtic, Germanic, Scandinavian, etc., goddesses were often connected to spinning in ways that bound them to the fate of mortals or served as evidence of their reign over all elements of the environment. Likewise, portraying women as connected to spinning within folktales and fairy tales reveals their ability to master mystical skills associated with goddesses, such as was discussed with "Rumpelstiltskin" and "Whuppity Stoorie" in Chapter 6 of this book. Therefore, when the witches enter the mother's home in this tale, they appear to judge her process of spinning wool, that she had only just begun as she was merely preparing the wool for spinning before the witches interjected themselves into her home; however, what the witches will really assess is the worth of the mother to serve as a goddess representative. The witches' test begins when they demand a seemingly impossible task from the mother, which thrusts her upon her heroine's quest.

The witches, like all of the witches thus far presented in this chapter, designed a quest for the mother of this tale by demanding that she retrieve water from her well out of a sieve and then use the water to bake them a cake. The mother left her house at once to try and complete the seemingly impossible task. She grabbed a sieve and went to her well where she appealed to the spirit within the well to help her accomplish the goal. The fact that the heroine mother appeals to a water spirit for help shows her respect of nature as sacred; it also shows a lasting connection of her culture to a belief in goddess worship, as Celtic belief systems maintained that goddesses often guarded over sources of water, such as the Celtic goddess Brigid. Thus, in knowing the sacrality of the element of water, the heroine mother passed her first test put forth by the witches. As a reward, the water spirit indeed helped the heroine mother upon her quest and instructed her to put "clay and moss in the sieve," so that it could hold water (Jacobs). This easy solution, using natural elements, helped the heroine mother understand the "secrets" of nature, known by witches and goddesses alike, allowing her to further her education to become a goddess representative herself.

The heroine mother also learned from the water spirit that the witches had made a cake that contained blood from each member of her family, so that they may control them. This point of the narrative propels the heroine mother into her underworld stage of her quest, as she must face the possibility that the powerful witches may harm the ones she holds most dear. The water spirit told the heroine mother that to complete her quest, she must get rid of the witches from her life once and for all. As Gretel and Alionushka had to do in their respective tales, the heroine mother of this folktale must learn to dispel the witches' power over her before she can prove that she has attained a mastery of the same abilities they hold. To show the heroine mother's mastery of supernatural abilities, the tale shows her thrusting water that she used to wash her children's feet upon the path leading to her home, a symbolic act that shows the heroine as claiming her own divine power as a creator of life to protect her family and their domain. Then the heroine mother found the witches' cake, that contained the blood of her off-spring, so again showing her mastery of the same supernatural skills the witches possessed, she broke the cake into pieces and placed a portion in the mouth of each one of her family members to save them from being controlled by the witches. Then the heroine mother gathered the cloth that was woven by the witches—the product of their divine spinning and thus symbolic of their divine power—and, instead of destroying it, she contained it in a chest to signal that she had finally fully attained the same power that the witches held. And, indeed, the tale ends with the witches leaving the newly apotheotic heroine mother and her family alone forever. The fact that the heroine of this tale is a mother is important, as it solidifies that she, like many other heroines in this book, will pass on her sacred teaching of the goddess to her children, thus preserving it.

Finally, a Japanese folktale entitled "The Witch of the Mountain" (Reider 403–27) features the famous Japanese witch—Yamamba, sometimes Yamauba. This tale relates how an old woman, instead of a maiden or a mother, undergoes a heroine's quest to obtain apotheosis, proving that no woman is too old to learn the lessons of the witch. The tale begins with a group of villagers who lived at the base of Tefukuyama Mountain. All of the villagers feared Yamamba, the witch of the mountain, telling terrifying stories about her ferocious ways. For instance, Yamamba was said to have eyes that "were sunk deep into her head but still her eyeballs protruded. She had a big mouth, and the fangs from her lower jaw almost touched the edges of her nose. That nose resembled a bird's beak, and her forehead was wrinkled up; her hair looked as though she had recently worn a bowl on her head.... On her skull were fourteen or fifteen small horn-like bumps" (Reider 414). Yamamba was also known for eating her victims.

One day Yamamba came down from her mountain and confronted the people of the small village. She stated that she had just given birth, but that she had run out of food and thus needed the assistance of the villagers. Yamamba threatened the people that if they did not bring rice cakes to her mountain home, so that she may feed her infant son, she would eat them instead and destroy the land. Yamamba's demand of the people's sacrifice to maintain favor resembles the demand of a fertility goddess who requires sacrifice to maintain favorable environmental conditions. And indeed, Yamamba is thought to be a remnant of the Japanese fertility goddess Jūni-sama, a fertility goddess who continually gave birth to divine children who initiated the seasons of rain and growth in Japan (Reider 415). Therefore, Yamamba's request in this folktale for food from the villagers to feed her infant son certainly seems reminiscent of Jūni-sama's children requiring veneration so they may provide abundance in the seasons of growth.

The folktale continues to show the villagers quickly gathering rice cakes from each household to give to Yamamba. The villagers also designated their beloved male hero, Kmayasu Gonroku, to go to Yamamba's mountain home and deliver the rice cakes to her, as he was believed to be the bravest among them. However, Kmayasu Gonroku stated that he did not know the way to Yamamba's home, so the heroine of the tale emerges in an old woman who stepped forward and stated that she knew the way and would thus lead Kmayasu Gonroku to Yamamba. The fact that the old woman in the tale knows the way to Yamamba's home immediately signals her as a prime candidate for a heroine's journey, as she already possesses mystical knowledge that could be further harnessed by her interactions with the witch Yamamba. Thus, Kmayasu Gonroku and the old woman set forth upon their quest up the mountain.

As required of all heroic quests, the pair faced the harsh qualities of the wilderness, until they finally arrived at the home of the witch, which was a deep, dark cave. When the fearsome Yamamba emerged from her cave, Kmayasu Gonroku proved that he was no hero at all, as "the brave young man trembled like a leaf on the wind at the sound of her voice. Then crying in fear, he fled down the side of the mountain" ("The Witch"), thus ending his heroic quest in failure. Kmayasu Gomroku's departure left the old woman to face Yamamba alone. However, the old woman remained as calm as she could and entered Yamamba's cave. The imagery of the terrifying Yamamba living within a cave immediately signals that the old woman has stepped into the underworld stage of her heroic quest. However, upon entering Yamamba's cave, the old woman, like many other heroines, found that the witch did not intend to kill her, but instead wished for her help. Yamamba presented the old woman with many tasks to aid her in her housework and in the raising of her son, and the old woman showed that she respected Yamamba by doing any task asked of her all through the autumn and winter, until spring began to come forth once more. Like Vasilisa, Gretel, and Rapunzel, living with the witch taught the old heroine vital skills that connected her to the witch's wisdom, which was of course wisdom connected to traditional goddess worship. In living through the seasons of dormancy alongside the witch, and doing any task asked of her that was intended to educate her, the old woman was deemed by the witch to pass her tests. There are many Japanese folktales that feature the witch Yamamba serving to educate female heroines by testing them in similar household duties. For instance, in the folktales "Komebuku and Awabuku" and "Ubakawa (Old Woman's Skin)" (Reider 403–27), maidens must live with Yamamba, performing various tasks for her as she tests to see if they are worthy of her education. If the heroines succeed, they are rewarded with riches, but if they fail, as one maiden does in "Komebuku and Awabuku," they are punished with death.

In this folktale, upon the arrival of spring, Yamamba declared that the old woman should go back home to live amongst her people once more. To signal that the old woman passed Yamamba's test, the witch gave her a package, that she told the old woman not to open until home. Yamamba then performed a supernatural act reminiscent of a goddess when she waved her hand and produced a warm, "mountain breeze" that carried the old woman "safely to her village" ("The Witch") and initiated the coming of spring for the villagers. The fact that the old woman arrived to her village upon a warm breeze that brought forth the season of spring signals that she attained apotheosis because of her instruction from the witch Yamamba. The villagers believed that the old woman had been consumed by the ferocious witch, but the old woman revealed her newfound apotheotic wisdom to the villagers by stating, "'She is not a wicked witch of Tefukuyama Mountain, nor is she scary'" ("The Witch"). This revelation to the villagers from the old woman heroine of the tale portrays a prime example of the reason for the heroine's quest as designed by myriad folktale and fairy tale witches. In stating that the witch is nothing to fear, the old heroine passes on her apotheotic wisdom to her people in order to educate them about the true nature of the witch—not as a fearsome monster, but as a traditional goddess figure who, when embraced, can reveal transformative wisdom that can benefit the people. This lesson is further reiterated in the folktale when the old heroine ends the tale opening the package the witch gave her in front of the villagers, revealing a miraculous piece of cloth that would never run out no matter how many items were sewn from it by the villagers. This supernatural gift of never-ending cloth for the people connects Yamamba again to goddess figures associated with spinning and weaving, such as the witches of the previous folktale, but it also serves as a symbolic promise of the never-ending abundance of nature's cycles that can be promised by one's embrace of the lessons of the goddess. In addition, the tale's final scene that shows the old heroine sewing dresses for her granddaughters, again promises that the wisdom obtained from this heroine's quest will be passed on to the next generation, so that it, like the never-ending cloth, will never be lost. The old woman of this tale thus serves as an exemplary heroine who shows that all women, no matter how old, can always undergo the challenge of the witch's quest, and if successfully completed, gain wisdom that, though it has been demoted and often hidden behind folkloric and fairy tale figures, such as witches, will never be fully eradicated as long as heroines continue to pass it on.

Again, the witches of folktales and fairy tales present the best examples of the preservation of divine women, as they are wise, independent, closely aligned with nature, and they possess mystical abilities that serve to transform the lives of the people around them. Thus, the witches of many tales, though they are presented as often scary or hideous, still manage to come out of their stories as the true models for women to strive toward in lives that otherwise might leave them unfulfilled. The witches of countless tales around the world teach women that it is sometimes better to choose a life on the outskirts of society than under the command of a patriarchal system. They teach women that a life in nature, fully attuned with one's abilities while in solitude, can be an empowering life. It is the witches of folktales and fairy tales who teach women that there are no boundaries between what they can and cannot do. They teach women to strive for whatever their hearts' desire. They teach women that seemingly magic acts can be possible and within their grasp. Witches teach women that there is no separation from life and death within nature, and that death can be overcome with natural rebirth. Most importantly, witches teach women that they are firmly connected to a rich history when women once reigned supreme as divine beings, and it is this past that witches invite all women to remember, even to tap into, if they are brave enough to become witches themselves.

Conclusion

Throughout the years, many folktales and fairy tales that have been captured for publication or revised into versions for film, television, theater, etc., have been "regularly subverted…, promoting … stories that showed women as weak or witless or, at the very best, waiting prettily and with infinite patience to be rescued" (Yolene xvii). However, it seems like the current trend of contemporary times reveals an effort to capture a revised portrayal of formidable female leads in folktale and fairy tale adaptations. For instance, *Mulan* (1998; 2020), *Brave* (2012), *Moana* (2016) *Gretel and Hansel* (2020), *Raya and the Last Dragon* (2021), etc., are all recent films that have adapted folktales and fairy tales to show strong female leads. Furthermore, many modern and contemporary films, books, television shows, cartoons, etc., also carry on the folktale and fairy tale female archetypes that were discussed in this book, such as the archetype of women possessing the mystical ability to shapeshift from natural elements to human form, which can be found in the films *Cat People* (1942) and *Ladyhawke* (1985), and in Louise Erdrich's novel *Antelope Woman* (2016) and Stephenie Meyer's *Twilight* series (2005–2020). In addition, wise old women can be found in the modern and contemporary characters of Mademoiselle Reisz in Kate Chopin's *Awakening* (1899), Baby Suggs in Tony Morrison's *Beloved* (1987), and Professor Minerva McGonagall in J.K. Rowling's Harry Potter series (1997–2007). Also, modern and contemporary formidable maidens who teach males important lessons about life appear in Tanizaki Jun'ichirô's "The Tattooer" (1910) and as Marla in Chuck Palahniuk's novel *Fight Club* (1996). Monstrous women appear in films such as *Sea-Creature* (1956), *Attack of the 50 Foot Woman* (1958), the *Alien* films (1979–1997), and *Lethal Attraction* (1987); they also still haunt countless contemporary urban legends today. Defiant women and women warriors abound in modern and contemporary sources as well, such as in the films *Thelma and Louise* (1991), *Erin Brokovich* (2000), *Wonder Woman* (2017), *Halloween* (2018), etc. In addition, many modern and contemporary sources focus intently upon the journey of the heroine, such as Leslie Marmon Silko's "Yellow Woman" (1993), Cheryl Strayed's *Wild* (2012), and the film *Whale Rider* (2003). Mothers and stepmothers are also shown to impact the modern and contemporary quests of women in Maxine Hong Kingston's *Woman Warrior* (1976), Amy Tan's *Joy Luck Club* (1989), and Lisa See's *The Island of Sea Women* (2019) and in the films *Freaky Friday* (1976; 2003), *Mommie Dearest* (1981), *Terms of Endearment* (1983), *Stepmom* (1998), and the musical *Mamma Mia* (1999). Finally, witches, or characters who appear as witches, still interact with heroines in L. Frank Baum's *Wizard of Oz* (1900) and in Salman Rushdie's *Midnight Children* (1981), as well as in the films *Misery* (1990), *Brave* (2012), *Maleficent* (2014), *The Witch* (2015), *Gretel and Hansel* (2020), *Fear Street* (2021), etc.

However, in all of these examples of female characters who show autonomy and strength, and who often teach others to better themselves, arguably there is still not a sizable effort to portray women characters as related to the terms that once portrayed folktale and fairy tale heroines as connected to goddesses. As stated, many modern and contemporary works display female characters who meet some of the attributes that connect them to tenets of goddess representations, like being wise old women or formidable maidens, but all too often, female characters within modern and contemporary works still end up perpetuating the journeys of male characters, or only partially gaining self-actualization. Therefore, often these female characters of modern and contemporary works lack the heightened spiritual abilities that many folktale and fairy tale women discovered within themselves in order to reach goddess-like apotheosis.

This book has strived to portray how the female characters of folktales and fairy tales hold many important similarities with the most powerful imaginings of femininity that cultures around the world once envisioned—the goddesses of mythology. Countless folktale and fairy tale women received educations within their mythic narratives that taught them that they belonged to a long line of feminine strength that was connected to the belief that the highest forms of power, wisdom, ferocity, and compassion were conceived in the form of a woman. Contrary to this, in many religions that strove to eradicate or demote goddesses, many of which are still practiced today, men were made in the image of God, and women were made from men; thus, patriarchal belief systems often proclaimed that men should serve as social and religious authorities over women. To counter this and preserve at least part of the reverence of goddesses, as well as the memory of the powerful religious and social roles women once held as representatives of goddesses, thousands of folktales and fairy tales were created, told, and retold, often by women storytellers, with the intent of educating audiences of men and women about the true potential for all women.

Recognizing the strength of women within folktales and fairy tales encouraged the women of bygones eras, as well as today, to be brave while in maidenhood. The tales also reminded, and continue to remind, women to learn from the older women in their lives, especially the ones who live alone in isolated, natural locations. The tales also reminded, and still remind, women to listen to their mothers and stepmothers, even the ones who teach harsh lessons. They encouraged, and still encourage, women to learn from the women in their lives who appear monstrous. They also told, and still tell, women that they should be teachers to the men in their lives, reminding them of the true value of women. They taught, and continue to teach, women to embrace their own identity in the highest forms they can imagine. They instructed, and continue to instruct, women to revere nature, develop their own seemingly mystical skills, and embrace all the cycles of life—thus becoming goddess-like. Once having achieved apotheosis, the tales reminded women, and continue to remind us today, that it is our duty to pass on to our daughters and granddaughters the wisdom that is imparted in the myths, folktales, and fairy tales of bygone days, as well as in their many renditions today, so that we can preserve the connection that all women hold with the highest envisioning of feminine power, wisdom, and spirituality—that of the Goddess.

Bibliography

Afanas'ev, Alexander. *Russian Fairy Tales* (1945). Trans. Norbert Guterman. New York: Pantheon, 1973.

Alexander, Hartley Burr. *Mythology of All Races, Vol. XI—Latin America* (1920). Web. Retrieved April 19, 2022.

Allan, Tony, and Charles Phillips. *Chinese Myth: Land of the Dragon.* London: Duncan Baird, 1999, 44–45.

Allan, Tony, Charles Phillips, and Michael Kerrigan. *Persian Myth: Wise Lord of the Sky.* London, Duncan Baird, 1999, 122–23.

Allan, Tony, Clifford Bishop, and Charles Phillips. *Medieval Myth: Legends of Chivalry.* London: Duncan Baird, 2000, 66–67.

Allan, Tony, Fergus Fleming, and Charles Phillips. *African Myth: Voices of the Ancestors.* London: Duncan Baird, 1999.

Allan, Tony, Fergus Fleming, and Michael Kerrigan. *Oceanian Myth: Journeys through Dreamtime.* London: Duncan Barid, 1999.

Allan, Tony, Michael Kerrigan, and Charles Phillips. *Japanese Myth: Realm of the Rising Sun.* London: Duncan Baird, 2000.

Anderson, Graham. *Fairytale in the Ancient World.* London: Routledge, 2000.

Aoki, Michiko Y. "Women in Ancient Japan." *Women's Roles in Ancient Civilizations.* Edited by Bella Vivante. Westwood, CT: Greenwood Press, 1999, 63–84.

Apuleius. *Golden Ass.* Trans. Jack Lindsay. Bloomington: Indiana UP, 2005.

The Arabian Nights: Tales from a Thousand and One Nights. Trans. by Richard Burton. New York: Modern Library Classics, 2004.

Armstrong, Karen. "Introduction." *Daughters of Abraham: Feminist Thought in Judaism, Christianity and Islam.* Gainesville: UP of Florida, 2001, vii–xiii.

Asbjørnsen, Peter Christen, and Jørgen Moe. "East of the Sun and West of the Moon." https://www.pitt.edu/~dash/norway034.html. Accessed on May 13, 2019.

Auerbach, Loren, and Jacqueline Simpson. *Sagas of the Norsemen: Viking and German Myth.* London: Duncan Baird, 1997.

Bain, R. Nisbet. *Russian Fairy Tales* (3rd ed.). London: A. H. Bullen, 1901. Web. Retrieved May 20, 2019.

Barchers, Suzanne I. *Wise Women: Folk and Fairy Tales from around the World.* Englewood, CO: Libraries Unlimited, 1990.

Baring, Anne, and Jules Cashford. *The Myth of the Goddess: Evolution of an Image.* London: Penguin, 1993.

Bierhorst, John. *Mythology of South America.* New York: William Morrow, 1988, 71–72.

Birkhäuser-Oeri, Sibylle. *The Mother: Archetypal Image in Fairy Tales.* Edited by Marie-Louise Von Franz. Trans. Michael Mitchell. Toronto: Inner City Books, 1988.

Bruchac, Joseph. *Native American Animal Stories.* Golden, CO: Fulcrum, 1992.

Bruhns, Karen Olsen, and Karen E. Stothert. *Women in Ancient America.* Norman: U of Oklahoma P, 1999.

Caldecott, Moyra. *Women in Celtic Myth: Tales of Extraordinary Women from the Ancient Celtic Tradition.* Rochester, VT: Destiny Books, 1988.

Campbell, Joseph. *Goddesses: Mysteries of the Feminine Divine.* Edited by Safron Rossi. Novato, CA: New World Library, 2013.

_____. *Hero with a Thousand Faces* (3rd ed.). Novato, CA: New World Library, 2008.

Carter, Angela, editor. *Old Wives' Fairy Tale Book.* New York: Pantheon Books, 1990.

Cashdan, Sheldon. *The Witch Must Die: How Fairy Tales Shape Our Lives.* New York: Basic Books, 1999.

Christ, Carol P. *Womanspirit Rising: A Feminist Reader in Religion.* Edited by Carol P. Christ and Judith Plaskow. San Francisco: Harper and Row, 1976.

Chu, Nan. "Goddess Chang E Ascends to the Moon." *Women in Chinese Folklore.* Beijing: China Publications Centre, 1983, 61–68.

Cole, Joanna, editor. *Best Loved Folktales from Around the World.* New York: Anchor Books, 1982.

Cross, Robin, and Rosalind Miles. *Warrior Women: 3000 Years of Courage and Heroism.* New York: Metro Books, 2011.

Darnton, Robert. "Peasants Tell Tales." *The Classic Fairy Tales* (2nd ed.). Edited by Maria Tatar. New York: Norton, 2017, 363–74.

Dashú, Max. "Woman Shamanism: the Suppressed History." *The Cuyamungue Institute.* Web. Retrieved May 10, 2022.

Datta, Saurav Ranjan. "Remembering Brave Indian Queens: 10 Powerhouses History has Forgotten." *Ancient Origins.* April 16, 2020. Web. Retrieved February 23, 2021.

Davis-Kimball, Jeannine. *Warrior Women: An Archeologist's Search for History's Hidden Heroines.* New York: Warner Books, 2002.

Don, Lari. *Girls and Goddesses: Stories from Around the World.* Minneapolis: Darbycreek Publishers, 2016.

Estés, Clarissa Pinkola. *Women Who Run with Wolves: Myths and Stories of the Wild Woman Archetype.* New York: Random House, 1992.

Fernyhough, Timothy, and Anna Fwernyhough. "Women, Gender History, and Imperial Ethiopia." *Women and the Colonial Gaze.* Edited by Tamara L. Hunt and Micheline R. Lessard. New York: New York UP, 2002, 188–201.

Forrester, Sibelan. *Baba Yaga: The Wild Witch of the East in Russian Fairy Tales.* Jackson: UP of Mississippi, 2013.

Frankel, Valerie Estelle. *From Girl to Goddess: The Heroine's Journey through Myth and Legend.* Jefferson, NC: McFarland, 2010.

Gerson, Mary-Joan. *Fiesta Femenina: Celebrating Women in Mexican Folklore.* New York: Barefoot Books, 2001

Gilbert, Sandra M., and Susan Gubar. "Snow White and Her Wicked Stepmother." *The Classic Fairy Tales* (2nd ed.). Edited by Maria Tatar. New York: Norton, 2017, 387–93.

"Gluscabi and the Wind Eagle." Angel Fire Stories. Web. Retrieved May 6, 2016.

Greene, Heather. "La Befana Turns Winter into a Season for the Witch." *The Wild Hunt.* January 10, 2016. Web. Retrieved February 7, 2022.

Grimm, Jacob, and Wilhelm Grimm. *The Complete First Edition: The Original Folk and Fairy Tales of the Brothers Grimm.* Translated and edited by Jack Zipes. Princeton: Princeton UP, 2014.

Grumet, Robert Steven. "Sunksquaws, Shamans, and Tradeswomen: Middle Atlantic Coastal Algonkian Women During the 17th and 18th Centuries." *Women and Colonization: Anthropological Perspectives.* Edited by Mona Etienne and Eleanor Leacock. New York: Bergin & Garvey, 1980, p. 43–62.

Guiley, Rosemary Ellen. *The Encyclopedia of Ghosts and Spirits.* New York: Facts on File, 1992.

Gupto, Arun. *Goddesses of Kathmandu Valley: Grace, Rage, and Knowledge.* New York: Routledge, 2016.

"Haida Mother Bear Story." First People—The Legends. Web. Retrieved April 19, 2022.

Hays-Gilpin, Kelley A. *Ambiguous Images: Gender and Rock Art.* Lanham, MD: Altamira Press, 2004.

Heiner, Heidi Anne, collector and editor. *Beauty and the Beast Tales from Around the World*. Garden City, NY: SurLaLune Press, 2013.

Hubbs, Joanna. *Mother Russia: The Feminine Myth in Russian Culture*. Bloomington: Indiana UP, 1988.

Jackson, Guida M. *Women Who Ruled*. Oxford: Clio Press, 1990.

Jacobs, Joseph. *Celtic Fairy Tales* (1892). Retrieved June 23, 2019, from sacred-texts.com.

Jiao, Tianlong. "Gender Studies in Chinese Neolithic Archeology." *Gender and the Archeology of Death*. Edited by Bettina Arnold and Nancy L. Wicker. Lanham, MD: Altamira Press, 2001, 51–62.

Johnson, Buffie. *Lady of the Beasts: The Goddess and Her Sacred Animals*. Rochester, VT: Inner Traditions International, 1994.

Keller, Mara Lynn. "Violence against Women and Children in Religious Scriptures and in the Home." *The Rule of Mars: Readings and Origins, History and Impact of Patriarchy*. Manchester, CT: Knowledge, Ideas, and Trends Publishers, 2005, 225–40.

Kerrigan, Michael, Charles Bishop, and Fergus Fleming. *Tibetan and Mongolian Myth: The Diamond Path*. London: Duncan Baird, 1998.

Kidwai, M.H. *Woman Under Different Social and Religious Laws (Buddhism, Judaism, Christianity and Islam)*. Delhi: Seema Publications, 1976.

Kinney, Anne Behnke. "Women in Ancient China." *Women's Roles in Ancient Civilizations*. Edited by Bella Vivante. Westwood, CT: Greenwood Press, 1999, 3–34.

Kinsley, David. *Hindu Goddesses: Visions of the Divine Feminine in the Hindu Religious Tradition*. Berkeley: U of California P, 1988.

Kobayashi, Fumihiko. *Japanese Animal Wife Tales: Narrating Gender Reality in Japanese Folklore Tradition*. New York: Peter Lang, 2015.

Lang, Andrew. "The Wounded Lion." *The Pink Fairy Book* (1889). Retrieved July 18, 2019, from sacred-texts.com.

Lankford, George E. *Native American Legends*. Little Rock: August House Publishers, 1987, 213–15.

Larrington, Carolyne. *The Feminist Companion to Mythology*. London: Pandora Press, 1992, 156.

Leavy, Barbara Fass. *In Search of the Swan Maiden: A Narrative on Folklore and Gender*. New York: New York UP, 1994.

LePrince de Beaumont, Jeanne-Marie. "Beauty and the Beast" (1756). *Project Gutenberg*. Web. Retrieved May 3, 2022.

Lerner, Gerda. *The Creation of Patriarchy*. New York: Oxford UP, 1986.

Lubell, Winifred Milius. *The Metamorphosis of Baubo: Myths of Woman's Sexual Energy*. Nashville: Vanderbilt UP, 1994.

Mackenzie, Donald Alexander. "Beira: Queen of Winter." *Wonder Tales from Scottish Myths and Legends*. New York: Frederick A Stokes Co., 1917, 22–32.

Martín, Paula. *Pachamama Tales: Folklore from Argentina, Bolivia, Peru, Paraguay, and Uruguay*. Santa Barbara, CA: Libraries Unlimited, 2014.

Mayor, Adrienne. *The Amazons: Lives and Legends of Warrior Women Across the Ancient World*. Princeton: Princeton UP, 2014.

McCoppin, Rachel. *Ecological Heroes of Amerindian Mythology*. Dubuque, IA: Kendall Hunt, 2019.

_____. *Goddess Lost: How the Downfall of Female Deities Degrades Women's Status in World Cultures*. Jefferson, NC: McFarland, 2022.

_____. *The Hero's Quest and the Cycles of Nature: An Ecological Interpretation of World Mythology*. Jefferson, NC: McFarland, 2016.

_____. *The Lessons of Nature in Mythology*. Jefferson, NC: McFarland, 2015.

Murdock, Maureen. *The Heroine's Journey*. Boston: Shambhala Publications, 1990.

Mutén, Burleigh. *Grandmother Stories: Wise Women Tales from Many Cultures*. New York: Barefoot Books, 1999.

Nauwald, Nana. *Flying with Shamans in Fairy Tales and Myths*. Havelte, Holland: Binkey Kok, 2004.

Nelson, Sarah Milledge. *Ancient Queens: Archeological Explorations.* New York: Altamira Press, 2003.

Ogunleye, Tolagbe. "Women in Ancient West Africa." *Women's Roles in Ancient Civilizations.* Edited by Bella Vivante. Westwood, CT: Greenwood Press, 1999, 189–218.

Paradiž, Valerie. *Clever Maids: The 2.*

Perrault, Charles. *The Complete Fairy Tales.* Trans. Christopher Betts. Oxford: Oxford Publishing, 2009.

Phelps, Ethel Johnston. *Sea Girl: Feminist Folktales from Around the World.* New York: Feminist Press, 2017.

_____. *Tatterhood and Other Tales.* New York: Feminist Press, 1978.

Phillips, Charles, and Michael Kerrigan. *Forests of the Vampire: Slavic Myth.* London: Duncan Baird, 1999.

Phillips, Charles, Michael Kerrigan, and David Gould. *The Eternal Cycle: Indian Myth.* London: Duncan Baird, 1998.

Pijoan, Teresa. *White Wolf Woman and Other Native American Transformation Myths.* Little Rock: August House Publishers, 1992, 59–62.

Propp, Vladimir. "From Morphology of the Folktale." *The Classic Fairy Tales* (2nd ed.). Edited by Maria Tatar. New York: Norton, 2017, 502–07.

Ragan, Kathleen, editor. *Fearless Girls, Wise Women, and Beloved Sisters: Heroines in Folktales from Around the World.* New York: W.W. Norton, 1998.

Reaves, William P. *Odin's Wife: Mother Earth in Germanic Mythology.* Coppell, TX: William P. Reaves Publishing, 2018.

Reider, Noriko. "Yamauba and Oni-Women: Devouring and Helping Yamauba are Two Sides of the Same Coin." *Asian Ethnology* 78.2, 2019, 403–427.

Rose, Carol. *Giants, Monsters, and Dragons: An Encyclopedia of Folklore, Legend, and Myth.* New York: W.W. Norton, 2000.

Sax, Boria. *The Serpent and the Swan: The Animal Bride in Folklore and Literature.* Blacksburg, VA: McDonald & Woodward, 1998.

"Seeresses of the Viking Period." *National Museum of Denmark.* Retrieved December 3, 2020. Web.

Sered, Susan Starr. *Priestess, Mother, Sacred Sister: Religions Dominated by Women.* Oxford: Oxford University Press, 1994.

Shafer, Edward H. *The Divine Woman: Dragon Ladies and Rain Maidens.* San Francisco: North Point Press, 1980.

Shlain, Leonard. *The Goddess versus the Alphabet.* New York: Penguin, 1998.

Stone, Merlin. *Ancient Mirrors of Womanhood: A Treasury of Goddess and Heroine Lore from around the World.* Boston: Beacon Press, 1990.

Straparola, Giovanni Francesco. "The Pig King" (1550–1555). *Genius.* Web. Retrieved May 3, 2022.

Stuckey, Johanna H. *Women's Spirituality: Contemporary Feminist Approaches to Judaism, Christianity, Islam and Goddess Worship.* Toronto: Inanna Publications, 2010.

Swanton, John R. *Tlingit Myths and Legends* (1909). Brighton, MI: Native American Book Publishers, 1990, 33–36.

Tatar, Maria, editor. *The Classic Fairy Tales* (2nd ed.). New York: Norton, 2017.

Tedlock, Barbara. *The Woman in a Shaman's Body.* New York: Bantam, 2005.

Uchida, Yoshiko, translator. "The Wise Old Woman." Web. Retrieved June 6, 2022.

Ulanov, Ann, and Barry Ulanov. *The Witch and the Clown: Two Archetypes of Human Sexuality.* Wilmette, IL: Chiron Publications, 1987.

Van Deusen, Kira. *The Flying Tiger: Women Shamans and Storytellers of the Amur.* Montreal: McGill Queen's UP, 2001.

Vivante, Bella. "Women in Ancient Greece." *Women's Roles in Ancient Civilizations.* Edited by Bella Vivante. Westwood, CT: Greenwood Press, 1999, 219–56.

Vycinas, Vincent. *The Great Goddess of the Aistian Mythical World.* New York: Peter Lang, 1990.

Warner, Marina. "From The Old Wives' Tale." *The Classic Fairy Tales* (2nd ed.). Edited by Maria Tatar. New York: W.W. Norton, 2017, 405–14.

"The Witch of the Mountain." *Zeluna: Fairies and Fairy tales.* Web. Retrieved February 9, 2022.

Yolene, Jane. "Forward: The Female Hero and the Women Who Wait." *Fearless Girls, Wise Women, and Beloved Sisters: Heroines in Folktales from Around the World.* Edited by Kathleen Ragan. New York: W.W, 1998, xvii–xviii.

Young, Serenity. *Women Who Fly: Goddesses, Witches, Mystics, and Other Airborne Females.* New York: Oxford UP, 2018, 173–78.

Yusa, Michiko. "Japanese Buddhism and Women: The Lotus, Amida, and Awakening." The Dao Companion to Japanese Buddhist Philosophy. June 2019. 83–133.

Zipes, Jack. "Foreword." *Baba Yaga: The Wild Witch of the East in Russian Fairy Tales.* Jackson: UP of Mississippi, 2013.

_____. "Introduction." Grimm, Jacob and Wilhelm Grimm. *The Complete First Edition: The Original Folk and Fairy Tales of the Brothers Grimm.* Tranlsated and edited by Jack Zipes. Princeton: Princeton UP, 2014.

_____. *The Irresistible Fairy Tale.* Princeton: Princeton UP, 2012.

Index

Abuk 87
Abundia 214
Achilles 144–5, 183
African 11, 23, 39, 52–3, 69–70, 87–8, 99,
    111–3, 175–7, 190–2, 212, 225
Aicha Kandisha 102
Akka 29
Akkadian 97, 174, 233
Ala 12
Amaterasu 28, 149–50
Amazons 127–30, 143–6
Amerindian 11–2, 20, 23, 26, 39, 60–1, 99,
    159–60, 168, 187–8, 199
Andersen, Hans Christian 124, 230–5
Andraste 151
Angus 13
animal brides 8–9, 18–31, 38, 97, 103, 113,
    157
animal grooms 33–7, 159–60, 165–6
Antiope 144
Anu 12
Aphrodite 3, 69, 80, 99, 127, 129, 162, 183
Apsara 98
Arabic 56
Argentinian 51–2
Ariadne 71–2, 74
Artemis 19, 31t, 129–30, 145
Artio 19
Asian 23, 39, 69, 98–9, 105
Atalanta 78, 128–30, 135
Athena 19, 60, 100, 110, 143, 197
Australian 99, 105, 107–8
Austrian 16, 236
Aztec 69, 97, 123

Baba Yaga 64, 218–23, 225–6, 234
Baduhenna 152
Banshee 121
Basile, Giambattista 5
Bavarian 16
"Beauty and the Beast" 34–5
La Befana 213–4
Berchta 14, 16–8, 236
"Bluebeard" 140–2
Bodrima 122

Bona Dea 81
Boudica 151–2
Brahma 114, 142
Bran 92–3, 95
"Briar Rose" 80–3
Bride 13, 231
Brìghde 13
Brigid 94, 237
Bronze Age 42–3, 45, 106, 109
La Bruha 214–5
Buddhism 25–6, 28, 98–9, 116, 174
Bunyip 107–8

Cailleach Beira 12–6, 215, 231
Cailleach Bheur 13–7
Calisto 19
Cambodian 19
Campbell, Joseph 7, 59, 82, 156–7
Cathubodua 151
Celtic 4, 11, 13–4, 19, 48–51, 58, 60, 63, 66–7,
    73–5, 77, 80–1, 89–95, 98, 121, 143, 151,
    168–9, 171, 173, 183, 188, 193, 236–7
Ceridwen 48, 61–2, 86
Cernunnos 236
Chang'e 94
Charybdis 100, 111
Chilean 51–2
Chinese 11, 19, 24–6, 28, 35–6, 42–6, 54, 76,
    77, 94–5, 99, 103, 105–7, 113–4, 120, 130–2,
    147–9, 174, 183–6, 198, 217, 225
"The Chinese Princess" 113–4
Christianity 4, 12, 14, 16–8, 23, 41, 43, 48–51,
    53, 57–8, 63, 75, 99, 101, 105–6, 112–3, 116,
    139, 152, 180–2, 193, 197, 200–3, 208, 211,
    214–6, 218–20
Churels 122
"Cinderella" 198–203, 222, 225
Circe 32, 60
Civacoatlv 123
Clíodhna 121
colonization 4, 23, 99, 109, 112–3
Columbian 12
Confucianism 25–6, 28, 43–6, 99, 106, 116,
    130, 148
Corn Mother 199

"Cupid and Psyche" 160–2
Cybele 19, 31

Dakinis 103
Dana 12
Danu 12
Defiant women 9, 126–42
Demeter 3, 174, 188
Devi 188
"The Devil and his Grandmother" 56–8
Diaba 214
Divoká Šárka 152
Dragon 106–7, 114, 130–1
Draupadi 78
Dumuzi 70, 109, 137
Durga 142, 150

Earth goddess 19, 21, 23, 26, 29, 31, 38, 70, 93, 95, 101, 111–2, 212, 222
Earth Mother 11–8, 21, 31, 40, 69, 87, 97, 100, 194, 215, 218, 236
"East of the Sun and West of the Moon" 165–7
Egyptian 19, 69, 85, 87, 104–5, 138, 143, 171, 177, 183, 188, 203
Eostre 4
Ereshkigal 97, 174
Ernmas 12
Ertha 14
Europa 100
European 23, 39, 43, 58, 69–70, 77, 80–1, 98, 105, 109
Eurydice 83–4, 168
Eurynome 105
Eve 106, 140–2, 208

Fairies 48–9, 80, 98, 171–3, 184–6
"The Fairy Serpent" 35–6
Fates 80, 97, 169
fauna 81
Fijian 190
Finnish 29–31
Fire Mother 26
"Fitcher's Bird" 141–2
Flora 69
"The Forest Bride" 29–31
"Frau Gauden" 17–8
Frau Holda 14
Frau Holle 8, 14–5, 17–8, 215, 219, 236
French 37, 49–50
Frey 2
Freya 14, 17, 21, 206
Freyja 4, 14 , 17, 21, 69, 103, 139–40, 143, 152, 206
Frigg 4, 14, 17, 98, 140
Frija 14, 17
"Frog King" 36–7
Furies 97, 101

Gaia 12, 37, 86–7, 100, 105
Ganash 183

Gawain 58–9, 62–3
Gerda 230–3
German 37, 75–8, 80–2, 103–4, 141–2, 158–9, 162–4, 169–71, 192–4, 198, 203–9, 215, 219, 224–8, 236
Germanic 14–8, 21, 54, 75, 77, 152, 193, 206, 219
Ghost Women 9, 97, 120–5, 216
Gilgamesh 32, 83, 86, 117–9
Gimbutas, Marija 2
Glooscap 60
Gorgon 110–111
Grandmother Sun 40–1, 45, 65
Grandmother Woodchuck 60
grandmothers 3, 10, 40–1, 45, 56–60, 65, 67, 124,157–8, 163–4, 179–82, 230, 233
Gray Ladies 123
Great Mother 11, 25–6, 69, 111, 188
Greek 3, 11–2, 19, 31, 34, 37, 54, 60, 69–71, 78, 80–1, 97, 99–101, 105, 110–11, 117–8, 126–30, 141, 143–6, 168–9, 174, 183, 188, 196–7, 203, 208, 215, 217, 233, 236
Grimm Brothers 5, 15–6, 17–8, 36–7, 56–8, 75–8, 80–3, 141–2, 158–9, 162–4, 169–71, 192–4, 198, 203–9, 219, 224–8
Guan Yin 76, 77, 174
Guinevere 58

Hades 84, 99, 110, 174
Haida 159–60
"Hans My Hedgehog" 37–8
"Hansel and Gretel" 224–6, 228–30, 239
Harpies 100–1, 111
Hathor 19
Havfrue 104
Hecate 34, 85, 101, 188
Hel 97
Hera 3, 60, 98–100, 111, 117–8, 128, 143, 215
Heracles 111, 117–9, 127–8, 143–5
Heroines and nature 159–69
Heroines and supernatural wisdom 169–73
Heroines and the underworld 173–82
Heroine's quest 9, 59, 69, 125, 131–42, 143–82, 186–241, 243
Hero's quest 7–8, 20–31, 33–8, 59–96, 109–120, 155–9, 177–8, 183–6, 197, 213, 217–8, 220
"Hervor and the Cursed Sword" 152–3
Hinduism 97, 113–5, 134–5, 142, 188, 209
Hine-nui-te-Po 118–9
Hippolyta 127–8, 143–4
"The Horned Women" 235–8
Horus 138, 183
"The Hunter and His Magic Flute" 111–3

Inanna 70–1, 80, 137
Inari 115
Indian 11–2, 37, 70, 97–8, 105, 109, 114, 122, 134–5, 142, 150–1, 183, 188, 220
Indo-European 3, 21, 23, 98–9, 101, 109, 114, 127

Inuit 37, 40–1, 76, 119–20
Io 100
Irish 12–5, 37, 48–9, 67, 92–4, 104, 120–1, 212, 235–8
Ishtar 32, 69, 80, 83, 86, 97, 117, 137, 174, 233
Isis 69, 85, 87, 138, 171, 177, 183
Islam 4, 53, 99, 113–5, 136, 219
Italian 38, 198, 204, 212–4
"Ivanushka and Alionushka" 228–31
Izanami 37, 97

"Jack and the Beanstalk" 6, 65–6
"Janet and Tam Lin" 172–3
Japanese 27–9, 37, 45–6, 54–6, 95–7, 99, 102–4, 115–6, 121–2, 131–4, 149–50, 175, 234, 238–40
Jason 34, 60, 85–7, 111, 127, 215
Jingū 150
Judaism 99, 136, 141, 203, 219
Jūni-sama 238

Kali 97, 150, 209, 220
Kashmiri 113–4
Kaya-no-hime 28
Kesne 188–90
Khutulun 146–7
Korean 37, 99, 150, 164–5, 194–6
Krampus 17
Kumaku 190
Kumba 52–3
Kunapipi 108
Kyrgyz 147

"Lady of the Fountain" 93–4
Lady of the Lake 58
Lakshmi 115
Lamia 100
Leto 100
Li Chi 130–5
Libyan 100
"Lin Lan" 201–3
"The Little Match Girl" 124
"The Little Mermaid" 233–5
"Little Red Cap" 162–4
"Little Red Riding Hood" 162
La Llorona 123–4
Louhi 29
Lūwat-uwadjīgï-cānak 61

Macha 60
Madame White 25–6
"The Magic Brocade" 183–6
Mahadevi 188
Maichak 20–2
Maiden, Mother, Crone 49, 124, 188, 207
"The Maiden Tsar" 63–6
"The Maiden Without Hands" 75–8
maidens 8–9, 69–96, 109, 113, 116, 155–235, 239, 243–4; and death 83–92; as prizes 8, 71, 78–83

male consort 70, 79–80, 82–3, 94, 109, 117, 157, 212
Manasa 114
Marduk 50, 110, 196
Maruisa 179–82
Marwe 176–7, 182, 200, 225
Maui 118–9
"Mbango and the Whirlpool" 175–6
Medb 60, 151
Medea 34, 85–7
Medusa 110–111
Melanesian 23–4, 26
mermaids 104
Mesopotamian 32, 50, 69, 83, 105, 109–10, 117, 171, 196
Mexican 123–4, 188–90, 214–5
Mictēcacihuātl 97
Middle Eastern 23, 69–70, 98, 105, 109, 114, 135–7
Milapukala 108
Minerva 143
minotaur 71–2
Mistresses of Animals 8, 31–8, 51
Mokosh 218
Mongol 146–7
monstrous females 8–9, 99–120, 157, 197, 212, 216, 243, 245
Mór Muman 12
Morgan le Fay 58, 62–3
Moroccan 102
Morrígan 19, 50, 63, 91, 143, 151, 188
Mother Goddess 69–70, 101, 188, 206, 219
"Mother Holle" 15–6
Mother Nature 8, 11–8, 63, 219
Mother Toman 26
mothers 9, 158, 179, 182–96, 216, 235–8, 244–5
Mu Guiying 148–9
Mulan 148

Nagas 114
Neolithic 19, 24, 31, 42, 69–72, 79–80, 86, 98, 106, 109–11, 114, 117, 212, 214
Nerthus 14
Nišan shaman 44–5
Nixies 104
Norns 80, 97, 169
Norse 17, 21–3, 54, 69, 80, 97–8, 103, 138–9, 152–3, 169, 206, 230
Norwegian 137–40, 165–7
Nu Wä 19, 24–5, 105–6

Odin 17, 21, 54, 98
Odysseus 32, 60, 100, 111
Ogetsuno 47
"The Old Woman, the Merchant, and the King" 56
Omosi-mama 45
Oracles 54–9, 169, 216–7
Orithyia 144
Orpheus 83–5, 87, 96, 110, 168

Osiris 85, 177
Ostara 4
otherworldly women 9, 69–71, 92–8, 185–6, 234
Owain 93–4, 96

Pachamama 4
Paleolithic 11, 18–9, 39, 69
Pandora 140–2, 162
Paritegi 195
Parvati 115, 135, 183
Penthesilea 144–5
Perchta 14, 16–8, 219, 236
Perrault, Charles 5, 140–2, 162
Persephone 69–70, 81, 84, 174, 188, 203, 208, 233
Perseus 110–11
Persian 37, 122
Perun 101
Phrygian 19, 31
"The Pig King" 38
Polish 37
Poludnitsa 101
Polynesian 118–9
priestess 8, 32, 34, 80, 137, 211, 213, 216–7
"The Prince and the Three Fates" 87–8
"Princess Sivatra" 134–5
Propp, Vladimir 6
Proserpine 161–2
Psyche 160–2, 165–6, 199, 222
"The Pumpkin Child" 37
Pythia 50

Queen Mother of the West 103

Ra 171
Rainbow Serpent 105
"Rapunzel" 226–30, 239
Rhea 183, 196
Rhiannon 80, 183
Rhipsunt, Bear Mother 159–60, 162
"River God's Wife" 43
Roman 11–2, 33, 54, 69, 80–1, 107, 143, 151, 183, 188, 199, 214, 222
Romi Kumu 12
"Rumpelstiltskin" 169–71, 237
Rusalki 101–2
Russian 36, 63–5, 101–2, 146, 213, 218–23, 218

Sacred Marriage 70, 86, 137
Saikal 147
Saka 146–7, 217
Salish 187
Sandraudiga 152
Saraswati 115
Satia 214
Scandinavian 14, 17, 21–4, 39, 54, 104, 152–3, 211, 217, 236
Scáthach 60, 143, 151
Scheherazade 135–7

Scottish 12–4, 37, 73–4, 89–92, 102, 104, 120–1, 143, 169–73, 212, 215, 231
Scylla 100, 111
Scythian 146–7
"The Sea Maiden" 89–92
Sedna 37, 41, 76
Sekhmet 143
Selkies 104
Semele 100
Serpent 35–6, 50, 85, 87–8, 97, 105–6, 110–1, 113–4, 117
Serpent Goddess 188–90
"The Seven Mermaids" 104–5
Shakti 188
Shaman 8, 20, 26, 28–9, 39–54, 61, 65, 97, 107, 169, 195–6, 211, 216–7
Shamhat 32
Shinto 28, 56
Shiva 114, 135, 142, 209
Shuka Dei 151
Siberian 26, 39, 41–2, 45
Sicilian 31–4
"Sir Gawain and the Green Knight" 62–3
Sirens 100–1, 105
Sirona 51
Skadi 230
"The Skeleton Woman" 119–20
Slavic 4, 11, 64, 101–2, 152, 179–82, 218–23, 228–30
"The Sleeping Beauty in the Wood" 78–83, 98, 208, 227
"The Snake Who Bore Witness for a Maiden" 32–3
"The Snotty Goat" 36
"The Snow Child" 37
"The Snow Queen" 230–3
"Snow White" 203–9, 224, 227
South African 190–2
South American 51–2, 54
Spanish 33–4, 37, 51, 167–8, 204, 212
spinning 14–5, 34, 48, 80, 166, 169–72, 236–7, 240
stepmothers 158, 176, 182, 196–210, 216, 221–5, 230, 244–5
Strenua 214
Succubus 102
Sudanese 87–8
Sumerian 70, 80
"Sun, Moon, and Talia" 79–80, 82
"Swan Maiden" 21–2
swan maidens 21–4, 26
Swiss 16
Sybil 50

"The Tale of the Oki Islands" 131–4
Tangkalsingh 26
"Tatterhood" 137–40
Theseus 71–2, 74, 144
Thetis 183
Thor 21
"The Three Ravens" 192–4

Tiamet 50, 105, 110, 196
Tibetan 103
"The Tiger's Whisker" 164–5
Tokoyo 131–5
"Tom Tit Tot" 169
Tomoe Gozen 149–50
Totem 18–21, 24, 26, 28–9, 31, 33, 37, 187
Trieu Au 149
Tru'ung sisters 149
"Tsélané and the Marimo" 190–2
Tsukuyomi 175

Ukemochi 175
"Urashima the Fisherman" 95–6, 234

Valkyries 22, 97, 140, 152
Vampire 181
"Vasilisa the Beautiful" 221–3, 226, 230, 239
Veikko 30–1
Veles 101
Venus 161–2, 183, 199, 222
Vietnamese 149
Virgin Mary 4, 197
Vishnu 114, 142
Völva 39, 50, 211

Wadjet 87, 105
Warrior Women 9, 126, 128, 140, 142–54, 243
"The Water of Life" 167–8
"The Wedding of Sir Gawain and Dame
    Ragnelle" 58–9

Welsh 12, 61–2
were-animals 103–4
werewolf 103–4
West African 12, 52–3, 111–3, 175–6
White Buffalo Calf Woman 80
White Ladies 121
"Whuppity Stoorie" 169–71, 237
Wild Hunt 17–8, 140
"The Wise Old Woman" 54–5
wise old women 8–9, 38–68, 97, 109, 113, 116,
    157, 164, 166, 169, 175–6, 179, 184–5, 196,
    203, 207–8, 213, 215–7, 243–4
Witch 9, 43, 64, 104, 158, 166, 205, 210–241,
    244
"The Witch of the Mountain" 238–40
Woden 17
"The Wounded Lion" 33–5

Xochiquetzal 69
Xüxan 24–6

Yama 134–5
Yamamba 238–40
"Yeh-hsien" 200–2, 225
Yoruba 111–3
Yuki-onna 102–3
Yun Ok 164–5

Zeus 3, 98–100, 110, 117, 141, 183, 196–7
Zipes, Jack 6–7, 73, 80–1, 211, 218–20

www.ingramcontent.com/pod-product-compliance
Lightning Source LLC
Chambersburg PA
CBHW031124270326
41929CB00011B/1489